150 LEADING CASES

Equity and Trusts

THIRD EDITION

ELIZABETH CASSELL
MA (Cantab), LLM, Solicitor

OLD BAILEY PRESS

OLD BAILEY PRESS
at Holborn College, Woolwich Road,
Charlton, London, SE7 8LN

First published 1999
Third edition 2004

ISBN 1 85836 534 1

British Library Cataloguing-in-Publication

A catalogue record for this book is available from the British
Library.

Printed and bound in Great Britain

Contents

Acknowledgements

The publishers and author would like to thank the Incorporated Council of Law Reporting for England and Wales for their kind permission to reproduce extracts from the Weekly Law Reports, Butterworths for their kind permission to reproduce extracts from the All England Law Reports and Sweet & Maxwell for their kind permission to reproduce extracts from the Commercial Law Cases.

Preface

Old Bailey Press 150 Leading Cases are intended as companion volumes to the Textbooks but they are also invaluable reference tools in themselves. Their aim is to supplement and enhance a student's understanding and interpretation of a particular area of law and provide essential background reading. Companion Revision WorkBooks and Cracknell's Statutes are also published.

The emphasis of the '150 Leading Cases' series is on recent developments and these have come thick and fast in Equity and Trusts law. They include: *Twinsectra Ltd* v *Yardley and Others* (2002) (constructive trust and *Quistclose* trust); *Pennington and Another* v *Waine and Others* (2002) (imperfect gift); *Abacus Trust (Isle of Man) and Another* v *Barr and Others* (2003) (mistake as to settlor's intentions); *Jennings* v *Rice* (2003) (proprietary estoppel); *Schmidt* v *Rosewood Trust Ltd* (2003) (disclosure of trust documents); *Russell-Cooke Trust Co* v *Prentis and Others* (2003) (tracing into a mixed fund); *National Westminster Bank plc* v *Somer International (UK) Ltd* (2003) (estoppel by representation); and the House of Lords' decision in *Dubai Aluminium Co Ltd* v *Salaam and Others* (2003) (dishonest assistance).

Recent developments up to 1 March 2004 have been taken into account.

Table of Cases

Cases in bold type are the leading cases. Page numbers in bold indicate the main references to them.

1 The Three Certainties

Adams and the Kensington Vestry, Re (1884) 27 Ch D 394 Court of Appeal (Baggallay, Cotton and Lindley LJJ)

- *Certainty of intention – precatory words*

Facts
The testator left his property 'unto and to the absolute use of my wife … in full confidence that she will do what is right as to the disposal thereof between my children, either in her lifetime or by will after her decease'.

Held
The words were precatory words – words expressing a desire – they did not impose a trust and the wife took the property absolutely.

Cotton LJ:

'The question before us is whether, upon the true construction of the will of George Smith, he imposed upon his wife Harriet a trust. Now just let us look at it, in the first instance, alone, and see what we can spell out of it, and see what was expressed by the will. Reading that will … it seems to me perfectly clear what the testator intended. He leaves his wife, his property absolutely, but what was in his mind was this: "I am the head of the family, and it is laid upon me to provide properly for the members of my family – my children: my widow will succeed me when I die, and I wish to put her in the position I occupied as the person who is to provide for my children." Not that he entails upon her any trust so as to bind her, but he simply says, in giving her this, I express to her, and call to her attention the moral obligation which I myself had and which I feel that she is going to discharge. The motive of the gift is, in my opinion, not a trust imposed on her by the gift in the will. He leaves the property to her; he knows that she will do what is right and carry out the moral obligation which he thought lay on him, and on her, if she survived him, to provide for the children.

… I have no hesitation in saying myself that I think some of the older authorities went a great deal too far in holding that some particular words appearing in a will were sufficient to create a trust. Undoubtedly, confidence, if the rest of the context shows that a trust is intended, may make a trust, but what we have to look at is the whole of the will which we have to construe, and if the confidence is that she will do what is right as regards the disposal of the property, I cannot say that that is, on the true construction of the will, a trust imposed upon her. Having regard to the later decisions, we must not extend the old cases in any way, or rely upon the mere use of any particular words, but, considering all the words which are used, we have to see what is their true effect, and what was the intention of the testator as expressed in his will. In my opinion here he has expressed his will in such a way as not to shew an intention of imposing a trust on the wife but on the contrary in my opinion, he has shewn an intention to leave the property, as he says he does, to her absolutely …'

Comment
This case marked a change in the approach of the Court to precatory words – the intention of the testator to create a trust had to be shown with much greater certainty.

Barlow's Will Trusts, Re [1979] 1 WLR 278 Chancery Division (Browne-Wilkinson J)

• *Certainty of objects – construction of 'any friends of mine'*

Facts

The will contained a provision, after making specific bequests, that the remainder of the testatrix's paintings be sold, but that 'any members of my family and any friends of mine who wish to do so' be permitted to purchase any of the paintings at their catalogue price or at probate value, whichever was the lower.

Held

The direction to allow 'friends' to purchase the paintings did not require all the members of the class to be ascertained because any uncertainty as to some of the beneficiaries did not affect the quantum of the gift to those who qualified. In the absence of issue, the prima facie meaning of 'family' means 'relations', ie blood relatives of the testatrix.

Browne-Wilkinson J:

'In my judgment, it is clear that Lord Upjohn in *Re Gulbenkian* was considering only cases where it was necessary to establish all the members of the class. He made it clear that the reason for the rule is that in a gift which requires one to establish all the members of the class, (eg 'a gift to all my friends in equal shares') you cannot hold the gift good in part, since the quantum of each friend's share depends on how many friends there are. So all persons intended to benefit by the donor must be ascertained if any effect is to be given to the gift. In my judgment, the adoption of Lord Upjohn's test by the House of Lords in *McPhail* v *Doulton* is based on the same reasoning, even though in that case the House of Lords held that it was only necessary to be able to survey the class of objects of a power of appointment and not to establish who all the members were. But such reasoning has no application to a case where there is a condition or description attached to one or more individual gifts; in such cases, uncertainty as to some other persons who may have been intended to take does not in any way affect the quantum of the gift to persons who undoubtedly possess the qualification.

The effect ... is to confer on friends of the testatrix a series of options to purchase. Although it is obviously desirable as a practical matter that steps should be taken to inform those entitled to the options of their rights, it is common ground that there is no legal necessity to do so. Therefore, each person coming forward to exercise the option has to prove that he is a friend; it is not legally necessary, in my judgment, to discover who all the friends are. In order to decide whether an individual is entitled to purchase, all that is required is that the executors should be able to say of that individual whether he has proved that he is a friend. The word "friend", therefore, is a description or qualification of the option holder.'

Comment

In this case, the wishes of the testatrix could be fulfilled without the necessity for the whole class to be ascertained – there was no question of a division of the subject matter of the gift.

Don King Productions Inc v *Warren and Others* [1999] 2 All ER 218 Court of Appeal (Morritt, Aldous and Hutchison LJJ)

• *Certainty of subject matter – whether benefit of contracts was capable of being the subject matter of a trust*

Facts

Don King was the leading boxing promoter in the United States and Frank Warren was the leading boxing promoter in the United Kingdom. King's company and Warren entered into two successive partnership agreements. In the first agreement Warren assigned all his existing management contracts to the new partnership even though some of the contracts contained an express provision against assignment. The second agreement provided that the new partnership should hold all agreements relating to the business of the partnership for the benefit of the partnership absolutely. Subsequently Warren entered into a multi-fight agreement for his own benefit. Don King Productions brought proceedings to wind up the partnership in which the judge at first instance held that the benefit of the promotion and management agreements entered into by the partners personally during the duration of the new partnership was held on trust by the partner for the benefit of the new partnership, and that Warren was in breach of his partnership duties by entering into the multi-fight agreement for his own benefit. Warren appealed.

Held

Appeal dismissed. On the true construction of the agreement, each partner held the entire benefit of any management or promotion agreement entered into by him on trust for the partnership. The benefit to which the partnership was entitled did not terminate on or by reason of the dissolution of the partnership but continued until such time as the agreement expired or was properly disposed of by the winding up of the partnership.

Morritt LJ:

'The trial of those preliminary issues came before Lightman J ... His declarations ... included a declaration:

"Each of DKP Mr King Mr Warren ... holds on trust for the Partnership the entire benefit of (a) Any Management Agreement with a European Registered Boxer to which DKP Mr King or Mr Warren ... was or now is a party and which was in force at a Relevant Time (c) Any Management Agreement or Promotional Agreement with a European Registered Boxer to which DKP Mr King Mr Warren ... was or now is or hereafter

at any time before the Termination date [defined as the completion of the winding up of the affairs of the partnership] becomes a party and which was or now is or at any time hereafter becomes in force entered into by way of variation renewal or replacement of any such Management Agreement or Promotional Agreement as is mentioned in the foregoing sub-paragraphs (a) and (b) (d) Any agreement which was or now is or hereafter at any time before the Termination Date comes into force (1) entered into by way of exploitation (including for the avoidance of doubt the release) of any of the rights conferred by any such Management or Promotional Agreement as is mentioned in the foregoing sub-paragraphs (a) to (c) or (2) for the purposes of exploitation of any of those rights ... PROVIDED THAT nothing in the foregoing declarations shall prevent any party to this action from contending ... (7) in relation to any particular agreement or agreements entered into by way of renewal of a Management or Promotional Agreement which was in force at a Relevant Time that the benefit of such renewal agreement does not fall within the principle of *Keech* v *Sandford* and is accordingly not held on trust for the Partnership."

Mr Warren contends that the judge was wrong in law to make such a declaration on two grounds. First, though he accepts that the assets of the partnership include "the proceeds obtained from" any management or promotion agreement in force between 16 September 1994 and the date of dissolution, "the benefit of" such agreements are not assets of the partnership. Second, he submits, that the rights of the partnership, whatever they were, ceased on the date of dissolution so that thereafter neither the benefit nor the proceeds obtained from the exploitation of any management or promotion agreement nor any renewal thereof could be assets of the partnership.

It is not disputed that the resolution of these issues depends, in part, on the proper construction of the first, and, more importantly, the second agreement. It is also accepted that the test adopted by the judge was the correct one. Such test was formulated by the judge in these terms:

> "The essential task in construction is to deduce, if this is possible, from the two agreements construed as a whole against their commercial background the commercial purpose which the businessmen and entities who were parties to them must as a matter of business common sense have intended to achieve by entering into them; and if such intent can fairly be deduced and if this is necessary to effectuate that intent, the court may have to require what may appear to be errors or inadequacies in the choice of language to yield to that intention and be understood as saying what (in the light of that purpose) that language must reasonably be understood to have been intended to mean."

Lightman J applied that principle to the construction of both the first and the second agreements. With regard to the first issue which arises on this appeal, described … above, his conclusions appear from the following passage from his judgment:

> "The only clear message from all the provisions of the first agreement is that all [management and promotion] agreements held at the date of the first agreement by Mr Warren should be assigned to the partnership as part of its capital and that DKP should pay a sum of equivalent value into the partnership as its contribution of capital. It seems to me equally clear for the reasons set out in part II(b) above that any new [management and promotion] agreements secured during the life of the partnership whether by the efforts of Mr Warren or DKP should likewise be vested in and belong to the partnership. The partners, and most particularly Mr Warren, were to use their best efforts to promote the business of the partnership, to secure such agreements, in whoever's name secured, were to belong to the partnership.
>
> 2. *Second Agreement* The second agreement proceeds on the basis that: (1) the partnership business has been in existence continuously since the date of the first agreement; and (2) (as set out in cl

10(1) and schedule 2) Mr Warren has assigned to the partnership in satisfaction of his obligations to provide by way of capital the sum of $US525,236.13 all the [management and promotion] agreements referred to in cl 6 of the first agreement. As I have already pointed out in part II (d) above, this state of affairs is confirmed and reinforced by cl 7(2). This provision is apt to bite both on agreements which should in the past have been, but for any reason have not been, assigned, and on agreements arising in the future. The intention that all [management and promotion] agreements obtained in the future by the partnership, the partners or Mr Warren shall likewise be assigned to or at least belong to the partnership is further manifested in other clauses of the second agreement. This is the rationale for cl 7.3 (providing for the partnership to pay the cost of the acquisition or maintenance of any promotional or management agreement); and it is plainly intended as well as the legally inevitable consequence of the fiduciary duties of the partners and the non-compete covenant of the partners and to be procured from Mr Warren."

Having thereby ascertained the intention of the parties to be that

> "all the [management and promotion] agreements relating to European registered boxers held at any time during the subsistence of the partnership by the partnership or either partner (and accordingly held by Mr Warren) should be assigned to or be held for the benefit of the partnership absolutely …"

Lightman J then considered whether the effect could be given to such intention given that, as he held and is common ground, the benefit of such contracts could not be assigned so as, at law, to vest them in the partners jointly. He noted that the parties agreed that some effect might be given in equity to such intention but differed as to what that effect could be. Mr Warren contended that such effect was limited to creating a trust of the receipts in the hands of the would be assignor. DKP submitted that a trust of the contract and the rights under it could be and had been created.

Lightman J considered at length the principles to be applied and the authorities bearing on them. His conclusion was:

"Accordingly in principle I can see no objection to a party to contracts involving skill and confidence or containing non-assignment provisions from becoming trustee of the benefit of being the contracting party as well as the benefit of the right conferred. I can see no reason why the law should limit the parties' freedom of contract to creating trusts for the fruits of such contracts received by the assignor or to creating an accounting relationship between the parties in respect of the fruits. The broader approach which I favour appears to be in accord with the authorities, so far as they go,. The leading authority is *Re Turcan*. The Vice-Chancellor of the County Palatine of Lancaster (Bristowe V-C) in that case held that an agreement to assign a non-assignable policy constituted the assignor a trustee of the policy for the assignee. The Court of Appeal dismissed the appeal. At the date of the hearing the proceeds of the policy were represented by certain assets and the Court of Appeal upheld the validity of the trusteeship of these assets, and Lord Browne-Wilkinson in *Linden Gardens Trust Ltd* v *Lenesta Sludge Disposals Ltd* ... referred to *Re Turcan* as authority for the proposition that a party to a contract may agree with a third party to account for him for the fruits he receives from the other contracting party. No doubt was cast by the Court of Appeal in *Re Turcan* or by the House of Lords in the *Linden Gardens* case on the decision of Bristowe V-C. As Lord Browne Wilkinson said in the *Linden Gardens* case ... the House of Lords only had to consider the validity of the restriction of an assignment which would have the effect of bringing the assignee into direct contractual relations with the other party to the contract ..."

With respect to the second issue on this appeal to which I have referred ... the judge concluded that the interest of the partnership in the management and promotion agreements did not terminate on dissolution. He said:

"It is plain that both under the first and second agreements the partnerships thereby constituted were intended to be absolute owners of the [management and promotion] agreements. The purchase of the [management and promotion] agreements from Mr Warren was paid 'out and out' for \$US525,236.13. The obligation under cl 7.2 is that the [management and promotion] agreements shall be held to the benefit of the partnership 'absolutely'. Under ordinary partnership principles, a partnership acquires an absolute interest in assets purchased or acquired or held by a partner or other fiduciary for its benefit. There is no hint, still less any clear manifestation of intention, in the second agreement that the interest of the partnership is determinable, or that there is any right of reverter in favour of Mr Warren, on dissolution."

The consequence of the findings to which I have referred was, as recognised by Lightman J:

"The agreements have accordingly at all times been held by the partners as trustees for the partnership. Accordingly the ordinary equitable principles apply (including the rule in *Keech* v *Sandford*) and the partnership assets include all renewal and replacement agreements obtained by any partner during the partnership and over the period between dissolution and the completion of winding up."

Morritt LJ rejected counsel's contention that the benefit of the agreements was not 'property' and that, if an item could not be sold, it could not be an asset of the partnership and continued:

'Of course, if one partner seeks to avoid the agreement he has made with his partners then questions may arise as to how the interests of the other partners are to be protected. But there are many ways in which that may be done without the need to interfere in the performance of the contract. I agree with the judge that *Re Turcan* ... shows clearly that the court will protect the interests of those contractually entitled to have the benefit of an inalienable asset before the fruits of the asset have been realised. In that case, as the

House of Lords considered in *Linden Gardens Trust Ltd* v *Lenesta Sludge Disposals Ltd* ... the court gave effect to the intention of the parties by means of a declaration of trust. But, it is objected, the existence of such a trust would enable one partner to interfere in the management of the personal contract made by a third party with the other partner. I do not agree. The other partner cannot insist on rendering vicarious performance of the personal obligations arising under the contract. Rules and procedures designed to enable a beneficiary to sue in respect of a contract held in trust for him would not be applied so as to jeopardise the trust property. As Lord Browne-Wilkinson observed in *Target Holdings Ltd* v *Redferns (A Firm)*,

> "... In my judgment it is in any event wrong to lift wholesale the detailed rules developed in the context of traditional trusts and then seek to apply them to trusts of quite a different kind. In the modern world the trust has become a valuable device in commercial and financial dealings. The fundamental principles of equity apply as much to such trusts as they do to the traditional trusts in relation to which those principles were originally formulated. But in my judgment it is important, if the trust is not to be rendered commercially useless, to distinguish between the basic principles of trust law and those specialist rules developed in relation to traditional trusts which are applicable only to such trusts and the rationale of which has no application to trusts of quite a different kind." '

Comment

The Court of Appeal adopted Lightman J's judgment at first instance on the point of subject matter of the trust and added very little. Note, once more, the reluctance of the court to interfere with the intention of businessmen entering into an agreement 'as a matter of business common sense'. Note also the dicta of Lord Browne-Wilkinson in *Target Holdings Ltd* v *Redferns (A Firm)* on the role of the trust in commercial and financial dealings.

Golay, Re [1965] 1 WLR 1969
Chancery Division (Ungoed-Thomas J)

- *Certainty of subject matter*

Facts

The testator directed his executors to let his daughter enjoy one of his flats during her lifetime 'and to receive a reasonable income from my other properties ...'. The court had to decide whether the direction to let the daughter enjoy a reasonable income was void for uncertainty.

Held

A 'reasonable income' could be determined by the court in order to give effect to the testator's intention.

Ungoed-Thomas J:

> '... the yardstick indicated by the testator is not what he or any other specified person subjectively considers to be reasonable but what he identifies objectively as "reasonable income". The court is constantly involved in making such objective assessments of what is reasonable and it is not to be deterred from doing so because subjective influences can never be wholly excluded. In my view, the testator intended by 'reasonable income' the yardstick which the court could and would apply in quantifying the amount so that the direction in the will is not in my view defeated by uncertainty.'

Comment

A test of reasonableness is one which the court is well used to applying.

Hunter v *Moss* [1994] 3 All ER 215
Court of Appeal (Dillon, Mann and Hirst LJJ)

- *Certainty of subject matter*

Facts

The defendant held 950 shares in a company with an issued share capital of 1,000 shares. He promised the plaintiff a 5 per cent holding in the company. It was held at first instance that the defendant held 50 of his 950 shares on trust for the plaintiff. The defendant applied to have the judgment set aside on the ground that his own failure to appropriate the relevant shares gave rise to uncertainty of subject matter.

Held

The test for certainty did not require segregation or appropriation of the subject matter of the trust. All the shares were of the same category and, for the trust property to be ascertainable, all that was necessary was quantification of the number of shares held on trust.

Dillon LJ:

'I pass then to the second point of uncertainty. It is well established that for the creation of a trust there must be the three certainties referred to by Lord Langdale in his judgment in *Knight* v *Knight*. One of those is, of course, that there must be certainty of subject matter. All these shares were identical in one class: 5 per cent was 50 shares and Mr Moss held personally more than 50 shares. It is well known that a trust of personalty can be created orally ...

In the present case there was no question of an imperfect transfer. What is relied on is an oral declaration of trust. Again, it would not be good enough for a settlor to say "I declare that I hold fifty of my shares on trust for B" without indicating the company he had in mind of the obvious various companies in which he held shares. There would be no sufficient certainty as to the subject matter of the trust. But here the discussion is solely about the shares of one class in the one company.

It is plain that a bequest by Mr Moss to Mr Hunter of 50 of his ordinary shares in MEL would be a valid bequest on Mr Moss's death which his executors or administrators would be bound to carry into effect...

Mr Hartman, however, relied on two authorities in particular. One is a decision of Oliver J in the case of *Re London Wine Co (Shippers) Ltd* which was decided in 1975. That was a case in which the business of the company was that of dealers in wine and over a period it had acquired stocks of wine which were deposited in various warehouses in England. Quantities were then sold to customers (but in many instances the wine remained at the warehouse) by the company. There was no appropriation – on the ground, as it were – from bulk, of any wine, to answer particular contracts. But the customer received from the company a certificate of title for wine for which he had paid which described him as the sole and beneficial owner of such-and-such wine of such-and-such a vintage. The customer was charged for storage and insurance, but specific cases were not segregated or identified.

Subsequently, at a stage when large stocks of wine were held in various warehouses to the order of the company and its customers, a receiver was appointed by a debenture holder. The question that arose was whether the customers who had received these certificates of title had a good title to the quantity of wine referred to in the certificate as against the receiver appointed under a floating charge. The judge held that it could not be said that the legal title to the wine had passed to individual customers and the description of the wine did not adequately link it with any given consignment or warehouse. And, furthermore, it appeared that there was a lack of comparison at the time the certificates were issued in that, in some cases, the certificates were issued before the wine which had been ordered by the company had actually been received by the company. It seems to me that that case is a long way from the present. It is concerned with the appropriation of chattels and when the property in chattels passes. We are concerned with a declaration of trust, accepting that the legal titled remained in Mr Moss and was not intended, at the time the trust was declared, to pass immediately to Mr Hunter. Mr Moss was to retain the shares as trustee for Mr Hunter.'

Comment

It would clearly be inequitable if the defendant could rely on his own omission – not allocating the 50 shares – to avoid his trust obligation.

Kayford Ltd, Re [1975] 1 WLR 279
Chancery Division (Megarry J)

• *Certainty of intention*

Facts

Fearing insolvency and acting on professional advice, a mail order company set up a separate bank account called Customers' Trust Deposit Account into which all monies received from customers were paid pending delivery of their goods so that, if the company went into liquidation, the money could be returned to customers. Subsequently the company went into liquidation and the question arose whether the monies in the account were held on trust for the customers or formed part of the general assets of the company.

Held

A trust for the customers had been created. All the requirements for a valid trust of personalty were present and the company had shown a clear intention to create a trust in its efforts to ensure that the monies sent remained in the beneficial ownership of those who had sent them.

Megarry J:

'The property concerned is pure personalty, and writing, though desirable, is not an essential. There is no doubt about the so-called three certainties of a trust. The subject-matter to be held on trust is clear and so are the beneficial interests therein, as well as the beneficiaries. As for the requisite certainty of words, it is well settled that a trust can be created without using the words "trust" or "confidence" or the like: the question is whether in substance a sufficient intention to create a trust has been manifested.'

Comment

At a time of high inflation and much insolvency, this was a useful device for protecting customers by ensuring that the money advanced never became part of the assets of the insolvent company.

Knight v *Knight* (1840) 3 Beav 148
Rolls Court (Lord Langdale MR)

• *The three certainties*

Facts

The testator left all his estates, real and personal, to his brother, Thomas Andrew Knight and, failing him, to his nephew, Thomas Andrew Knight the younger. The will stated:

'I do hereby constitute and appoint the person who shall inherit my said estates under this my will my sole executor and trustee, to carry the same and everything contained therein duly into execution; confiding in the approved honour and integrity of my family, to take no advantage of any technical inaccuracies, but to admit all the comparatively small reservations which I make out of so large a property …'

The will stated that the testator's intention was that the estates should be settled on the next descendant in the direct male line of the testator's grandfather. On the testator's death, his brother succeeded to the estates. In 1827, Thomas Andrew Knight the younger died, childless and intestate. The testator's brother settled the estates on persons who were not the next descendants in the direct male line of the testator's grandfather. The court had to decide whether the testator had imposed a binding trust on his brother.

Held

The words used by the testator in his will were not sufficiently imperative to create a trust which was binding.

Lord Langdale MR:

'… it is not every wish or expectation a testator may express nor every act which he may wish his successors in title to do that can or ought to be executed or enforced as a trust in this Court; and in the infinite variety of expressions which are employed, and of the cases which thereupon arise, there is often the greatest difficulty in determining whether the act desired or recommended is an act which the testator intended to be executed as a trust, or which the Court ought to deem fit to be, or capable of being enforced as such …

As a general rule, it has been laid down that, when property is given absolutely to any person, and the same person is, by the giver who has power to command, recommended or entreated, or wished, to dispose of that property in favour of another, the recommendation, entreaty or wish shall be held to create a trust.

First, if the words were so used, that upon the whole, they ought to be construed as imperative;

Secondly, if the subject of the recommendation or wish be certain; and

Thirdly, if the objects or persons intended to have the benefit of the recommendation or wish be also certain.

In simple cases there is no difficulty in the application of the rule thus stated. …

On the other hand, if the giver accompanies his expression of wish or request by other words from which it is to be collected that he did not intend the wish to be imperative; or it if appears from the context that the first taker was intended to have a discretionary power to withdraw any part of the subject from the object of the wish or request; or if the objects are not such as may be ascertained with sufficient certainty, it has been held that no trust is created.'

Comment

This is the case from which the three certainties are derived.

McPhail v *Doulton* [1971] AC 424
House of Lords (Viscount Dilhorne, Lords Reid, Hodson, Guest and Wilberforce)

• *Certainty of objects – discretionary trusts and powers*

Facts

Under a trust deed dated 17 July 1941, Bertram Baden established a fund for the benefit of the staff of Matthew Hall & Co Ltd. In 1960 he died and the executors of his estate claimed that the trust deed was invalid for uncertainty of objects. Clause 9(a) of the trust deed provided as follows:

'The Trustees shall apply the net income of the Fund in making at their absolute discretion to or for the benefit of any of the officers and employees or ex-officers or ex-employees of the company or to any relatives or dependants of any such persons in such amounts at such times and on such condition (if any) as they think fit and any such grant may at their discretion be made by payment to the beneficiary or to any institution or person to be applied for his or her benefit and in the latter case, the Trustees shall be under no obligation to see to the application of the money.'

The executors of the estate claimed that cl 9(a) constituted a trust and not a power and that, following the decision of the Court of Appeal in *IRC* v *Broadway Cottages Trust*, the trust was not valid because it was not possible to draw up a complete list of all the possible beneficiaries. The trustees of the fund contended that *IRC* v *Broadway Cottages Trust* should be overruled and a new test of certainty of objects laid down.

Held

1. Clause 9(a) was a trust power and took effect as a trust. The language used in the deed was mandatory: the word 'shall' combined with a power of selection created a trust for the distribution of income.

2. The test of certainty of objects to be applied was similar to that applied to powers. If it can be said with certainty that any given postulant is or is not a member of the class, then the trust will not fail merely because it is impossible to ascertain every member of the class.

Lord Wilberforce:

'Before dealing with these two questions some general observations, or reflections may be permissible. It is striking how narrow and in a sense artificial is the distinction, in cases such as the present, between trusts or as the particular type of trust is called, trust powers. It is only necessary to read the learned judgments in the Court of Appeal to see that what to one mind may appear as a power of distribution coupled with a trust to dispose of the undistributed surplus, by accumulation or otherwise, may to another appear as a trust for distribution coupled with a power to withhold a portion and accumulate or otherwise dispose of it. A layman, and I suspect also a logician, would find it hard to understand what difference there is.

It does not seem satisfactory that the entire validity of a disposition should depend on such delicate shading. And if one considers how in practice reasonable and competent trustees would act, and ought to act, in the two cases, surely a matter very relevant to the question of validity, the distinction appears even less significant. To say that there is no obligation to exercise a mere power and that no court will intervene to compel it, whereas a trust is mandatory and its execution may be compelled, may be legally correct enough but the proposition does not contain an exhaustive comparison of the duties of persons who are trustees in the two cases. A trustee of an employees' benefit fund, whether given a power or a trust power, is still a trustee and he would surely consider in either case that he has a fiduciary duty; he is most likely to have been selected as a suitable person to administer it from his knowledge and experience, and would consider he has a responsibility to do so according to its purpose. It would be a complete misdescription of his position to say that, if what he has is a power unaccompanied by an imperative trust to distribute, he cannot be controlled by the court unless he exercised it capriciously, or outside the field permitted by the trust … Any trustee would surely make it his duty to know what is the permissible area of selection and then consider responsibly, in individual cases, whether a contemplated beneficiary was within the power and whether, in relation to other possible claimants, a particular grant was appropriate.

Correspondingly a trustee with a duty to distribute, particularly among a potentially very large class, would surely never require the preparation of a complete list of names, which anyhow would tell him little that he needs to know. He would examine the field by class and category; might indeed make diligent and careful inquiries, depending on how much money he had to give away and the means at his disposal, as to the composition and needs of particular categories and of individuals within them; decide upon certain priorities or proportions, and then select individuals according to their needs or qualifications. If he acts in this manner, can it really be said that he is not carrying out the trust?

Differences there certainly are between trust (trust powers) and powers, but as regards validity, should they be so great as that in one case, complete, or practically complete ascertainment is needed, but not in the other? Such distinction as there is would seem to lie in the extent of the survey which the trustee is required to carry out: if he has to distribute the whole of a fund's income, he must necessarily make a wider and more systematic survey than if his duty is expressed in terms of a power to make grants. But just as, in the case of a power, it is possible to underestimate the fiduciary obligation of the trustee to whom it is given, so in the case of a trust (trust power) the danger lies in overstating what the trustee requires to know or to inquire into before he can properly execute his trust. The difference may be one of degree rather than of principle: ... trusts are often blended, and the mixture may vary in its ingredients.

With this background I now consider whether the provisions of cl 9(a) constitute a trust or a power ... Naturally read, the intention of the deed seems to me clear: cl 9(a), whose language is mandatory ("shall"), creates, together with a power of selection, a trust for distribution on the income, the strictness of which is qualified by cl 9(b) ... I therefore agree with Russell LJ and would to that extent allow the appeal, declare that the provisions of cl 9(a) constitute a trust and remit the case to the Chancery Division for determination whether on this basis cl 9 is ... valid or void for uncertainty.

This makes it necessary to consider whether, in so doing, the court should proceed on the basis that the relevant test is that laid down in *Inland Revenue Commissioners* v *Broadway Cottages Trust* or some other test.

That decision gave the authority of the Court of Appeal to the distinction between cases where trustees are given a power of selection and those where they are bound by a trust for selection. In the former case the position as decided by this House is that the power is valid if it can be said with certainty whether any given individual is or is not a member of the class and does not fail simply because it is impossible to ascertain every member of the class (*In re Gulbenkian's Settlements*). But in the latter case it is said to be necessary, for the trust to be valid, that the whole range of objects ... should be ascertained or capable of ascertainment.

The respondents invited your Lordships to assimilate the validity test for trusts to that which applies to powers. Alternatively they contended that in any event the test laid down in the *Broadway Cottages* case was too rigid and that a trust should be upheld if there is sufficient practical certainty in its definition for it to be carried out, if necessary with the administrative assistance of the court, according to the expressed intention of the settlor. I would agree with this, but this does not dispense from examination of the wider argument. The basis for the

Broadway Cottages principle is stated to be that a trust cannot be valid unless, if need be, it can be executed by the court, and ... that the court can only execute it by ordering an equal distribution in which every beneficiary shares... Assuming ... that the test of validity is whether the trust can be executed by the court, it does not follow that execution is impossible unless there can be equal division .

As a matter of reason, to hold that a principle of equal division applies to trusts such as the present is certainly paradoxical. Equal division is surely the last thing the settlor ever intended: equal division among all may, probably would, produce a result beneficial to none. Why suppose that the court would lend itself to a whimsical execution? ... I do not find that the nature of the trust, and of the court's powers over trusts, calls for any such rigid rule. Equal division may be sensible and has been decreed, in cases of family trusts, for a limited class; here there is life in the maxim "equality is equity", but the cases provide numerous examples where this has not been so, and a different type of execution has been ordered appropriate in the circumstances. ...

... The conclusion which I would reach, implicit in the previous discussion, is that the wide distinction between the validity test for powers and that for trust powers in unfortunate and wrong, that the rule recently fastened upon the courts by *Inland Revenue Commissioners* v *Broadway Cottages Trust* ought to be discarded, and that the test for the validity of trust powers ought to be similar to that accepted by this House in *In re Gulbenkian's Settlements* for powers, namely that the trust is valid if it can be said with certainty that any given individual is or is not a member of the class ...

... Assimilation of the validity test does not involve the complete assimilation of trust powers with powers. As to powers ... although the trustees may, and normally will, be under a fiduciary duty to consider whether or in what way they should exercise their power, the court will not normally compel its exercise. It will intervene if the trustees exceed their powers, and possibly if they are proved to have exercised it capriciously. But in the case of a trust power, if the trustees do not exercise it, the court will … in the manner best calculated to give effect to the settlor's or testator's intentions … Then as to the trustees' duty of inquiry or ascertainment, in each case the trustees ought to make such a survey of the range of objects or possible beneficiaries as will enable them to carry out their fiduciary duty. A wider and more comprehensive range of inquiry is called for in the case of trust powers than in the case of powers.

Two final points: first, as to the question of certainty. I desire to emphasise the distinction … between linguistic or semantic uncertainty which, if unresolved by the court, renders the gift void, and the difficulty of ascertaining the existence or whereabouts of members of the class, a matter with which the court can appropriately deal on an application for directions. There may be a third case where the meaning of the words used is clear but the definition of beneficiaries is so hopeless wide as not to form "anything like a class" so that the trust is administratively unworkable or … one that cannot be executed (*Morice* v *Bishop of Durham*). I hesitate to give examples for they may prejudice future cases, but perhaps "all the residents of Greater London" will serve. I do not think a discretionary trust for "relatives" even of a living person falls within this category. I would allow the appeal.'

Comment

This case was then sent back to the High Court and subsequently the Court of Appeal for these tests of certainty of objects to be applied: *Re Baden's Deed Trusts (No 2)*.

The example of a gift to 'all the residents of Greater London', given obiter in *McPhail* v *Doulton,* was later applied in *R* v *District Auditor, ex parte West Yorkshire Metropolitan County Council*.

Stapylton Fletcher Ltd, Re; Ellis, Son & Vidler Ltd, Re [1994] 1 WLR 1181
Chancery Division (Paul Baker J)

- *Certainty of subject matter*

Facts

ESV Ltd and S Ltd were independent wine merchant companies, control of which was acquired by the same person. Administrative receivers were subsequently appointed for both companies and a question arose as to the ownership of stocks of wine held for customers in bonded warehouses or duty paid warehouses. ESV Ltd recorded ownership of the wine on a card system but did not segregate the stocks held for each individual customer, but when the company was acquired the new owner moved the wine to his private residence and lost many of the index cards. All stocks of wine held by S Ltd in their duty paid warehouse had been sufficiently allocated and these wines were released to the customers by the receivers. But in S Ltd's bonded warehouse none of the wines had been allocated to individual customers or to allocate the wines between the company and its customers generally. The receivers sought directions as to whether the wines were sufficiently 'ascertained' for property to have passed to the customers in accordance with ss16–18 of the Sale of Goods Act 1979.

Held

The wines were sufficiently ascertained for the purposes of the Sale of Goods Act 1979 but these contracts did not per se create an equitable interest in the stocks held in favour of the customers.

Paul Baker J:

'Many of the sales of wine to be considered here are sales of goods forming part of a bulk. The claimants approach this problem with two separate lines of argument. First, they seek to show that the provision has been satisfied by ascertainment of the goods claimed. Secondly, they seek to show that the seller has become a trustee or fiduciary of some description, thus circumventing the section.

Both lines were pursued unsuccessfully in *In re London Wine Co (Shippers) Ltd*. The company had substantial stocks of wine in a number of warehouses. Large quantities were sold but in many instances remained warehoused with the company. There was no appropriation from the bulk of any wine to answer particular contracts but the customer received from the company a "certificate of title" describing the wine for which he had paid. He was charged storage and insurance periodically. When receivers were appointed, there weere sufficient stocks to satisfy all claims.

They considered three types of transaction: (a) a single purchaser of the total stock of a particular wine; (b) a number of purchasers whose combined purchases exhausted the total stock of a particular wine; (c) a number of purchasers whose combined purchases did not exhaust the relevant stock. Oliver J held that legal title had not passed in that case. There was no ascertainment. Orders could have been fulfilled from any source, not necessarily existing stocks. There was no undivided interest. There might be an estoppel resulting from the representations in the "certificate of title" but that did not give a proprietary interest good against the debenture holder, but would merely preclude a defence to an action for damages.

There was no trust for there was no certainty of subject matter. No proprietary right arose from the payment of purchase money. The existence of a right to specific performance does not necessarily imply a proprietary interest in the subject matter. The carrying out of the order would bring a out the ascertainment of the goods, but there would not necessarily be any pre-existing equitable right. Hence the claims wholly failed …

I do not regard that decision as inevitably governing the case before me. One obvious difference in the present case is the segregation of the wine purchased by the customers in a separate part of the warehouse and the careful maintenance of records within the company. Further as the London Wine Co was free to sell its stock and satisfy the customers from other available source, there was no ascertainable bulk in that case.'

The judge then reviewed the cases argued before him by counsel (including United States cases) and continued:

'The reference to English law as rejecting the solution of undivided shares is a reminder that in the United States of America that solution has been adopted. As will be seen, English law does not reject the possibility of a tenancy in common in relation to goods in all circumstances. Mustill J was considering the case where, in order to perform a number of individual contracts for sale, a bulk has to be divided. He was not considering a case where there was an intention to segregate and retain goods in bulk. In all the cases so far considered, other than *In re London Wine Co (Shippers) Ltd*) there was simply a contract for the sale of goods to be delivered in the normal course of business. The transactions with which I am concerned present the following features.

From the point of view of ESV; the reserve stocks were completely segregated from the trading stock, and the documentation was in good order. The company did not regard the wine as still belonging to them even to the extent of refraining from borrowing it. This can be contrasted with the situation revealed as existing at the London Wine Co.

The customers were looking to have their wine properly stored and not unduly disturbed. Further, the nature of the commodity is such that it would be pointless for them to inspect the cases or bottles, and impracticable to inspect their contents. One case of wine of a particular type and vintage is in practice to be regarded as identical with every other case of the same wine, breakages and missing bottles apart. From this two consequences follow. First, it is of secondary importance that the customer's name should be attached to any particular case. Secondly, the customer's assent to any appropriation of specific cases without consultation can be safely inferred. Accordingly, it must seem strange to those not acquainted with the Sale of Goods Act 1979 that a customer's entitlement should differ according to whether a stack of identical cases is allocated to a single customer or is to be shared between two or more.

Having regard to those considerations, the proper legal analysis must begin by recognising that we are not here dealing only with a contract for the sale of goods, but with two separate, if related, contracts, the second with its own consideration being a contract to store wines indefinitely.

Let us assume that each buyer of duty paid wine went to Cliffe [the warehouse], took delivery of his wine from Unit 13, then handed it back to Mr Steedman to be added to a stack in Unit 12, knowing that the stack already contained wine belonging to others and that he would not necessarily get the identical cases or bottles back for very good reasons connected with the proper care of his and the other owners' wine. The proper inference there, in my judgment, is that he agreed to become a tenant in common of the entire stack in the proportion that his cases bears to the total number of the cases in the stack for the time being, that total being liable to increase by addition and decrease by removals, where the tenancy in common is determined pro tanto by partition. That such a tenancy in common in goods can exist is not open to doubt …

… In summary, on the facts here, I conclude that if a number of cases or bottles of identical wine are held, not mingled with the trading stock, in store for a group of customers, those cases or bottles will be ascertained for the purposes of s16 of the Sale of Goods Act 1979 even though they are not immediately apportioned to each individual customer. Property will pass by common intention and not pursuant to s18 (rule 5). They will take as tenants in common.

At this point I can conveniently return to the transfer of assets in June 1986 from the former ESV to the present company. According to my analysis, the property in the goods then in the customers' reserve at Cliffe would have already passed to the customers. The present ESV simply took over the storage contracts and became bailees. The customers accepted this by continuing to pay the storage charges to the new company. Had anyone objected, he could have removed his wine. …

I have to reject the claim of Mr Jamieson to any proprietary interest. The wine that he had ordered had not left France when the receivers were appointed. It remained part of the generic stock of the vineyards, but subject to a contract for its sale to ESV. It plainly had not been ascertained under the contract between ESV and Mr Jamieson. It is true that Mr Jamieson had paid in full in advance. However there can be no question of any trust of the purchase money as was found in *Re Kayford*. The money was used and intended to be used to finance the purchase of the wine in France. There was no question of segregating it in a separate trust account to await the import of the wine into this country.'

Comment

This approach is affirmed by the Court of Appeal in *Hunter* v *Moss* (see above).

2 Formal Requirements for Creating a Trust

Grey v Inland Revenue Commissioners [1960] AC 1 House of Lords (Viscount Simmonds, Lords Radcliffe, Cohen, Keith and Reid)

• *Formal requirements – s53(1)(c) Law of Property Act 1925*

Facts
The Stamp Act 1891, s54, imposes stamp duty on instruments 'whereby any property, or any estate or interest in any property, upon the sale thereof is transferred to or vested in a purchaser, or any other person on his behalf or by his direction'. Stamp duty is imposed on the documents and not on the transfer made thereby and the amount of duty payable is related to the value of the beneficial interest transferred. In order to avoid paying stamp duty, settlors often made transfers of beneficial interests without using a document.

In this case the settlor, Mr Hunter, transferred property to trustees on trust for his grandchildren in 1949. In 1955 he transferred 18,000 £1 shares to the same trustees to hold as nominees for himself on six bare settlements he had previously created. Subsequently, he orally directed the trustees to hold the shares in the six settlements for his grandchildren so that there was no transfer document which would attract stamp duty.

Later, the trustees executed deeds declaring that they held the shares on trust for the grandchildren and the settlor also executed them to confirm his oral transfer. The Inland Revenue claimed that stamp duty was payable on the deed because s53(1)(c) required the disposition of an equitable interest to be in writing and there had been no effective disposition of the settlor's interest in the shares until the deeds had been executed.

Held
The settlor's oral instructions to the trustees were a 'disposition' to the trustees of his equitable interest in the shares. However, since they were not in writing they were ineffective. This defect had been rectified by the subsequent deed and stamp duty was therefore payable. The ordinary meaning of 'Disposition' in s53(1)(c) was sufficiently wide to cover every method by which a beneficial interest was transferred.

Lord Radcliffe:

'My Lords, if there is nothing more in this appeal than the short question whether the oral direction that Mr Hunter gave to his trustees on 18 February 1955 amounted in any ordinary sense of the words to a "disposition of an equitable interest or trust subsisting at the time of disposition", I do not feel any doubt as to my answer. I think that it did. Whether we describe what happened in technical or in more general terms, the full equitable interest in the 18,000 shares concerned , which at the time was his, was ... diverted by his direction from his ownership into the beneficial ownership of the various equitable owners, present and future, entitled under his six existing settlements. But that is not the question which has led to difference of opinion in the courts below. Where opinions have differed is on the point whether his direction was a "disposition" within the meaning of s53(1)(c) of the Law of Property Act, 1925, the argument for giving a more restricted meaning in that context being that s53 is to be construed as no more than a consolidation of three sections of the Statute of Frauds …

In my opinion, it is a very nice question whether a parol declaration of trust of this kind was or was not within the mischief of s9 of the Statute of Frauds. The point has never, I believe, been decided and perhaps it never will be. Certainly it was long established as law that, while a declaration of trust respecting land or any interest therein required writing to be effective, a declaration of trust respecting personalty did not. Moreover, there is warrant for saying that a direction to his trustee by the equitable owner of trust property prescribing new trusts of that property was a declaration of trust. But it does not necessarily follow from that that such a direction, if the effect of it was to determine completely or pro tanto the subsisting equitable interest of the maker of the direction, was not also a grant or assignment for the purposes of s9 and, therefore, required writing for its validity. Something had to happen to that equitable interest in order to displace it in favour of the new interests being created by the direction; and it would be at any rate logical to treat the direction as being an assignment of the subsisting interest to the new beneficiary or beneficiaries or, in other cases, a release or surrender of it to the trustee.'

Comment

The Court of Appeal applied the primary rule of statutory interpretation and gave 'disposition' its literal meaning.

Holt's Settlement Trusts, Re

See Chapter 13.

Neville and Another v *Wilson and Another* [1996] 3 WLR 460 Court of Appeal (Nourse, Rose and Aldous LJJ)

- *Formal requirements – s53(2) Law of Property Act 1925*

Facts

JEN Ltd was a small private company which owned a beneficial interest in shares of UEC Ltd. It was held be the Court of Appeal that the shareholders of JEN Ltd had entered into a formal agreement to wind up JEN Ltd and distribute its assets. However, the company was never formally wound up. After the agreement most of the assets were distributed to the shareholders and the company was struck off the Register of Companies. Nothing was done about JEN Ltd's interest in UEC Ltd. In a dispute between the shareholders of JEN Ltd, the Court of Appeal had to decide the status of the beneficial interest in UEC Ltd and whether the informal agreement had the effect of disposing of the shares between the shareholders in accordance with s53(1)(c) LPA 1925.

Held

Following the agreement, it was an undisputed fact that JEN Ltd was treated by all concerned as being defunct. The effect of such an agreement was that each shareholder had agreed to assign his interest in the other shareholders' equitable interests in exchange for the assignment by the other shareholders of their interests in his own share. The effect of each individual agreement was to constitute the shareholder an implied or constructive trustee for the other shareholders so that the requirement of writing in s53(1)(c) was dispensed with by s53(2) Law of Property Act 1925 which provided that s53(1)(c) did not affect the creation or operation of constructive trusts.

Nourse LJ:

'The effect of the agreement, more closely analysed, was that each shareholder agreed to assign his interest in the other shares of JEN's equitable interest in exchange for the assignment by the other shareholders of their interests in his own aliquot share. Each individual agreement having been a disposition of a subsisting equitable interest not made in writing, there then arises the question whether it was rendered ineffectual by s53 of the Law of Property Act 1925.

Those provisions have been considered in a number of authoritative decisions starting with *Grey* v *IRC* and *Oughtred* v *IRC* and *Vandervell* v *IRC*. In the *Vandervell* cases the facts were materially different and neither is of assistance here. The question depends on the correct view of a point left open in *Oughtred* v *IRC*.

The simple view of the present case is that the effect of each individual agreement was to constitute the shareholder an implied or constructive trustee for the other shareholders, so that the requirement for writing contained in subsection 1(c) of s53 was dispensed with by subsection 2. That was the view taken by Upjohn J [1958] Ch 383 at first instance and by Lord Radcliffe in the House of Lords in *Oughtred* v *Inland Revenue Commissioners*. ...

We do not think that there is anything in the speeches in the House of Lords which prevents us from holding that the effect of each individual agreement was to constitute the shareholder an implied or constructive trustee for the other shareholders. In this respect we are of the opinion that the analysis of Lord Radcliffe, based on the proposition that a specifically enforceable agreement to assign an interest in property creates an equitable interest in the assignee, was unquestionably correct ... A greater difficulty is caused by Lord Denning's outright rejection of the application of s53(2) with which Lord Cohen appears to have agreed.

So far as it is material to the present case, what subsection (2) says is that subsection (1)(c) does not affect the creation or operation of implied or constructive trusts. Just as in *Oughtred* v *IRC* the son's oral agreement created a constructive trust in favour of the mother, so here each shareholder's oral or implied agreement created an implied or constructive trust in favour of the other shareholders. Why then should subsection (2) not apply? No convincing reason was suggested in argument and none has occurred to us since. Moreover, to deny its application in this case would be to restrict the effect of general words when no restriction is called for, and to lay the ground for fine distinctions in the future. With all the respect which is due to those who have thought to the contrary, we hold that subsection 2 applies to an agreement such as we have in this case.

For these reasons we have come to conclusion that the agreement entered into by the shareholders of JEN in or about April 1969 was not rendered ineffectual by s53 of the Act of 1925.'

Comment
Pointing out that no reasons were given for the majority decision of the House of Lords in *Oughtred*, the Court of Appeal were able to follow the dissenting judgment of Lord Radcliffe and apply the literal meaning of s53(2).

Vandervell v *Inland Revenue Commissioners* [1967] AC 291
House of Lords (Lords Reid, Pearce, Upjohn, Donovan and Wilberforce)

• *Formal requirements*

Facts
Mr Vandervell wished to donate £150,000 to found a Chair in Pharmacology. He orally directed his bank who held shares on trust for him to transfer them to the Royal College of Surgeons so that they could receive dividends of £145,000. Not wishing the College to have control of the shares, which were in a family company, he gave trustees of a family trust an option to purchase the shares from the College for £5,000 after the dividends had been paid to fund the donation. He did not say which trust fund was to have the benefit of the option. The IRC claimed that surtax was due from Mr Vandervell on the dividends. The Court had to decide whether Mr Vandervell had divested himself of all his interest in the shares and whether s53(1)(c) applied to the transfer of Mr Vandervell's equitable interest.

Held
1. (By a majority of 3:2) Mr Vandervell had retained an equitable interest in the shares

by way of resulting trust because he had retained control over the exercise of the option.

2. Section 53(1)(c) did not apply when, as here, the legal interest and the equitable interest remained under the control of the equitable owner.

Lord Upjohn:

'The object of the section, as was the object of the old Statute of Frauds, is to prevent hidden oral transactions in equitable interests in fraud of those truly entitled, and making it difficult, if not impossible, for the trustees to ascertain who are in truth the beneficiaries. When the beneficial owner, however, owns the whole beneficial estate and is in a position to give directions to his bare trustee with regard to the legal as well as the equitable estate, there can be no possible ground for invoking the section where the beneficial owner wants to deal with the legal estate as well as the equitable estate.'

Lord Donovan:

'If owning the entire estate, legal and beneficial, in a piece of property, and desiring to transfer that entire estate to another, I do so by means of a disposition which ex facie deals only with the legal estate, it would be ridiculous to argue that s53(1)(c) has not been complied with, and that therefore the legal estate alone had passed. The present case, it is true, is different in its facts in that the legal and equitable estates in the shares were in separate ownership; but when the taxpayer, being competent to do so, instructed the bank to transfer the shares to the College, and made it abundantly clear that he wanted to pass, by means of that transfer, his own beneficial or equitable interest, plus the bank's legal interest, he achieved the same result as if there had been no separation of interests. The transfer thus made pursuant to his intention and instructions was a disposition, not of the equitable interest alone, but of the entire estate in the shares. In such a case, I see no room for the operation of s53(1)(c).'

Comment

Mr Vandervell successfully avoided the error in the scheme in *Grey* v *IRC* (above) by retaining control over both the legal and the beneficial interest in the shares. However, this scheme was defeated because he retained control over the exercise of the option. The saga continued in the following case.

Vandervell's Trusts (No 2), Re
[1974] Ch 269 Court of Appeal (Lord Denning MR, Lawton and Stephenson LJJ)

• *Formal requirements*

Facts

In 1961 Mr Vandervell directed the trustees to exercise the option. They paid £5,000 to the Royal College of Surgeons out of the children's settlement. The trustees' solicitors wrote to the Inland Revenue informing them that the shares were now held for the children's settlement. Mr Vandervell made no provision for the children under the terms of his will believing that they would benefit from the settlement. The Inland Revenue continued to pursue their claim that Mr Vandervell had not divested himself of all interest in the shares. So, in 1965, he executed a deed transferring all right, title and interest in the option to the trustees for the benefit of the children's settlement. Mr Vandervell died in 1967. His executors brought an action against the trustees claiming all the dividends paid on the shares between 1961 and 1965, on the ground that Mr Vandervell had not disposed of his beneficial interest in writing in accordance with s53(1)(c) of the Law of Property Act 1925.

Held

The executors' claim failed. Between 1961 and 1965 the shares were held for the children's settlement.

Lord Denning MR:

'Whereas previously the trustee company

had only a chose in action of one kind – an option – it now had a chose in action of a different kind – the actual shares. This trust property was not held by the trustee company beneficially. It was held by the company on trust. On this occasion a valid trust was created at the time of the transfer. It was manifested in clear and unmistakable fashion. It was precisely defined. The shares were to be held on the trusts of the children's settlement. The evidence of intention is indisputable: (1) the trustee company used the children's money – £5,000 – with which to acquire the shares; this would be a breach of trust unless they intended the shares to be an addition to the children's settlement; (2) the trustee company wrote to the Revenue authorities the letter of 2 November 1961, declaring expressly that the shares "will henceforth be held by them upon the trusts of the children's settlement"; (3) thenceforward all the dividends received by the trustee company were paid by it to the children's settlement and treated as part of the funds of the settlement. This was all done with the full assent of Mr Vandervell. Such being the intention, clear and manifest, at the time when the shares were conveyed to the trustee company, it is sufficient to create a trust.

Counsel for the executors admitted that the intention of Mr Vandervell and the trustee company was that the shares should be held on trust for the children's settlement. But he said that this intention was of no avail. He said that during the first period Mr Vandervell had an equitable interest in the property, namely, a resulting trust; that he never disposed of this equitable interest (because he never knew he had it); and that in any case it was the disposition of an equitable interest which, under s53 of the Law of Property Act 1925, had to be in writing, signed by him or his agent, lawfully authorised by him in writing (and there was no such writing produced). He cited *Grey* v *IRC* and *Oughtred* v *IRC*.

There is a complete fallacy in that argument. A resulting trust for the settlor is born and dies without any writing at all. It comes into existence wherever there is a gap in the beneficial ownership. It ceases to exist whenever that gap is filled by someone becoming beneficially entitled. As soon as the gap is filled by the creation or declaration of a valid trust, the resulting trust comes to an end. In this case, before the option was exercised, there was a gap in the beneficial ownership. So there was a resulting trust for Mr Vandervell. But, as soon as the option was exercised and the shares registered in the trustees' name, there was created a valid trust of the shares in favour of the children's settlement. Not being a trust of land, it could be created without any writing. A trust of personalty can be created without writing. Both Mr Vandervell and the trustee company had done everything which needed to be done to make the settlement of these shares binding on them. So there was a valid trust: see *Milroy* v *Lord* per Turner LJ ...

Even if counsel for the executors were right in saying that Mr Vandervell retained an equitable interest in the shares, after the exercise of the option, the question arises whether Mr Vandervell can in the circumstances be heard to assert the claim against his children. Just see what happened. He himself arranged for the option to be exercised. He himself agreed to the shares being transferred to the trustee company. He himself procured his products company to declare dividends on the shares and to pay them to the trustee company for the benefit of the children. Thenceforward the trustee company invested the money and treated it as part of the children's settlement. If he himself had lived, and not died, he could not have claimed it back. He could not be heard to say that he did not intend the children's trust to have it. Even a court of equity would not allow him to do anything so inequitable and unjust. Now that he has died, his executors are in no better position. If authority were needed, it is to be found in *Milroy* v *Lord*. In that case, Thomas Medley assigned to Samuel Lord 50 shares in the Bank of Louisiana on trust for his niece, but the shares were not formally transferred into the name of Samuel Lord. The bank, however, paid the dividends to Samuel Lord. He paid them to the niece, and then, at Thomas

Medley's suggestion, the niece used those dividends to buy shares in a fire insurance company – taking them in the name of Thomas Medley. After Thomas Medley's death, his executors claimed that the bank shares belonged to them as representing him, and also the fire insurance shares. Knight-Bruce and Turner LJJ held that the executors were entitled to the bank shares, because "there is no equity in this court to perfect an imperfect gift". But the executors were not entitled to the fire insurance shares. Turner LJ said:

> "… the settlor made a perfect gift to [the niece] of the dividends upon these shares, so far as they were handed over or treated by him as belonging to her, and these insurance shares were purchased with dividends which were so handed over or treated."

So here Mr Vandervell made a perfect gift to the trustee company of the dividends on the shares, so far as they were handed over or treated by him as belonging to the trustee company for the benefit of the children. Alternatively, there was an equitable estoppel. His strict rights (under a resulting trust) having regard to the dealings which had taken place between the parties …

I would allow the appeal and dismiss the claim of the executors.'

Comment

To say this is a much criticised judgment is an understatement.

3 Completely and Incompletely Constituted Trusts

Cannon v *Hartley* [1949] Ch 213 Chancery Division (Romer J)

- *Covenant to settle – covenantee a volunteer*

Facts
A deed of separation was executed between a husband and wife to which their daughter was a party. The husband covenanted to settle his after-acquired property on certain trusts under which the daughter was the ultimate beneficiary. The husband failed to settle his property according to the terms of the covenant and the daughter sued him for damages for breach of covenant.

Held
The daughter, though a volunteer, could sue in her own name as a direct covenantor and claim damages. Since the contract was made under seal, the daughter's failure to provide consideration was immaterial. However, specific performance would not be granted to her in equity for settlement of the actual property specified in the covenant, because she was a volunteer.

Romer J:

'In the present case, the plaintiff, although a volunteer, is not only a party to the deed of separation but is also a direct covenantee under the very covenant upon which she is suing. She does not require the assistance of the court to enforce the covenant for she has a legal right to enforce it. She is not asking for equitable relief but for damages at common law for breach of covenant.

For my part, I am quite unable to regard *In re Pryce,* which was a different case dealing with totally different circumstances, or anything which Eve J said therein, as amounting to an authority negativing the plaintiff's right to sue in the present case. I think that what Eve J was pointing out in *In re Pryce* was that the next of kin who were seeking to get an indirect benefit had no right to come to a court of equity because they were not parties to the deed and were not within the consideration of the deed and, similarly they would have no right to proceed at common law by an action for damages, as the court of common law would not entertain a suit at the instance of volunteers who were not parties to the deed which was sought to be enforced, any more than the court of equity would entertain such a suit.'

Comment
The question of marriage consideration does not arise here because the deed was not entered into in contemplation of marriage.

Cole, Re [1964] Ch 175 Court of Appeal (Harman and Pearson LJJ, Pennycuick J)

- *Incompletely constituted trust – imperfect gift*

Facts
A husband bought a house in London in 1945 and furnished it for his family who lived elsewhere at the time. The wife came up to London and the husband showed her the house and said: 'It's all yours.' When the husband was declared bankrupt in 1962 the wife claimed as against his trustee in bankruptcy that the house and its contents belonged to her.

Held

A gift of chattels cannot be perfected merely by showing them to the donee and speaking words of gift. The donee must prove some unequivocal act of delivery or change in possession.

Pearson LJ:

'... an act to constitute delivery must be one which in itself shows an intention of the donor to transfer the chattel to the donee. If the act in itself is equivocal – consistent equally with an intention of the husband to transfer the chattels to his wife or with an intention on his part to retain possession but give to her the use and enjoyment of the chattels as his wife – the act does not constitute delivery.

In the present case the intended gift was from husband to wife. Be it assumed that he spoke words of gift – words expressing an intention of transferring the chattels to her and not merely an intention to give her the use and enjoyment of them as his wife – and that in the circumstances the chattels intended to be given were sufficiently identified by the words of gift. There was no pre-existing possession of the donee in this case. The husband was the owner of the chattels and therefore considered in law to be in possession of them. No act of delivery has been proved, because the acts relied upon are in themselves equivocal – consistent equally with an intention of the husband to transfer the chattels to his wife or with an intention on his part to retain possession but give to her the use and enjoyment of them as his wife.

Mr Megarry's main proposition was that there is a perfect gift where the intending donor shows the chattel to the donee and utters words of present gift in the presence of the donee and the chattel. He also relied upon several special features of this case as adding strength to his main proposition. The special features mentioned were (a) that the husband brought the wife to the chattels; (b) that some of the chattels were bulky, so that handing over would not be a natural mode of transfer; (c) that the chattels were in a place where they would be under the wife's physical control, and she could touch and move them; and (d) the wife handled some of the chattels in the husband's presence.

The argument was clearly and cogently presented, but in the end the answer to it is simply that it fails to show any delivery of the chattels ...'

Comment

Would this case be decided in the same way today when, following *Williams & Glyn's Bank* v *Boland*, the wife's rights in property are not longer considered to be a shadow of her husband's?

Cook's Settlement Trusts, Re
[1965] Ch 902 Chancery Division (Buckley J)

• *Covenant to settle – consideration*

Facts

In 1934 a settlement of family property was made between Sir Herbert Cook, his son Sir Francis and the trustees of the settlement. Certain paintings became the son's absolutely but the son covenanted for valuable consideration that should any of the paintings be sold during his lifetime, the proceeds of sale should be paid to the trustees of the settlement for the benefit of the son's children. The son gave his wife a Rembrandt painting in 1962. The wife wished to sell it. The question arose whether on the sale of the Rembrandt the trustees would not be obliged to enforce the covenant.

Held

As the covenant was not made in consideration of marriage, the children could not have it enforced by this means. Therefore, the children were mere volunteers and the court would make a declaration that the trustees would be obliged to enforce the covenant.

Buckley J:

'Mr Goff, appearing for Sir Francis, has submitted first that, as a matter of law, the covenant contained in cl 6 of the settlement is not enforceable against him by the trustees of the settlement … [He] submits that the covenant was a voluntary and executory contract to make a settlement in a future event and was not a settlement of a covenant to pay a sum of money to the trustees. He further submits that as regards the covenant, all the beneficiaries under the settlement are volunteers, with the consequence that not only should the court not direct the trustees to take proceedings on the covenant but it should positively direct them not to take proceedings. He relies upon *Re Pryce* and *Re Kay's Settlement*. Counsel for the second and third defendants have contended that on the true view of the facts there was an immediate settlement of the obligation created by the covenant, and not merely a covenant to settle something in the future. It was said … that by the agreement Sir Herbert bought the rights arising under the covenant for the benefit of the cestui que trust under the settlement and that, the covenant being made in favour of the trustees, these rights became assets of the trust … I am not able to accept that argument. The covenant with which I am concerned did not, in my opinion, create a debt enforceable at law, that is to say, a property right, which, although to bear fruit only in the future and upon a contingency, was capable of being made the subject of an immediate trust, as was held in the case of *Fletcher* v *Fletcher*. Nor is this covenant associated with property which was the subject of an immediate trust as in *Williams* v *Codrington*. Nor did the covenant relate to property which then belonged to the covenantor, as in *Re Cavendish-Browne's Settlement Trusts*. In contrast to all these cases, this covenant upon its true construction is, in my opinion, an executory contract to settle a particular fund or particular funds of money which at the date of the covenant did not exist and which might never come into existence. It is analogous to a covenant to settle an expectation or to settle after-acquired property. The case in my judgment, involves the law of contract, not the law of trusts.'

Comment
Even though the trustees were parties to the original agreement, the court did not permit them to take action on behalf of the beneficiaries who were volunteers.

Gonin, Re [1979] Ch 16 Chancery Division (Walton J)

• *Imperfect gift not perfected under* Strong v Bird – *no continuing intention*

Facts
The plaintiff was born out of wedlock but her parents subsequently married. In 1944 the plaintiff's parents asked her to give up her job at the Air Ministry to return home to look after them. The plaintiff agreed and in return the parents promised to give her the house and its contents. The plaintiff's father died in 1957 and the plaintiff's mother died intestate in 1968. Prior to her death, the mother believed that she could not make a valid will in favour of the plaintiff because she was illegitimate. However, the mother sold off several building plots from the grounds of the house and offered the plaintiff the money she received which the plaintiff refused to take. In addition, the mother made gifts of several items of furniture to the plaintiff. As administratrix of her mother's estate, the plaintiff claimed that the house and its contents should be vested in her as beneficial owner under the rule in *Strong* v *Bird*.

Held
The rule in *Strong* v *Bird* did not apply to the house because there was no continuing intention on the part of the mother to make a gift of it. The manner in which she had sold off plots of land and offered the plaintiff the proceeds of sale, not as owner but as recompense for her hard work without remuneration, pointed against any continuing intention. So far as the furniture and contents were concerned, there was a continuing intention and the subsequent gifts of items of furniture by

the mother to the plaintiff were merely affir-
mation of her intention.

Walton J criticised the decision in *Re
James* where Farwell J held that *Strong* v *Bird*
applied to cases where the gift was perfected
through the donee being appointed an administrator. He said:

'I start from the simple proposition that if
the defendant in *Strong* v *Bird* itself had
been an administrator instead of an executor the case would have been decided the
other way, since it distinctly proceeded on
the basis that at law the appointment of the
person as an executor effected a release of
any debt due from the executor to the testator, a doctrine which was never applied to an
administrator ...

One can see why this should be so: by
appointing the executor the testator has by
his own act made it impossible for the
debtor to sue himself. And, indeed, so far
has the rule been taken, that although it will
no longer apply if the person appointed
executor has renounced probate, yet it will
apply if power to prove has been reserved
to him ...

The appointment of an administrator, on
the other hand, is not the act of the deceased
but of the law. It is often a matter of pure
chance which of many persons equally entitled to a grant of letters of administration
finally takes them out. Why, then should
any special tenderness be shown to a person
so selected by law and not the will of the testator, and often indifferently selected among
many with an equal claim?

It would seem an astonishing doctrine of
equity that if the person who wishes to take
the benefit of the rule in *Strong* v *Bird*
manages to be the person to obtain a grant
then he will be able to do so, but if a person
equally entitled manages to obtain a prior
grant, then he will not be able to do so. This
appears to me to treat what ought to be a
simple rule of equity, namely that if the
legal title to a gift is perfected by the
appointment by the intending donor of the
intended donee as his executor ... as something in the nature of a lottery.'

Comment
The deceased does not choose his/her administrators and does not necessarily know that
the legal title in the property will pass to the
individual appointed and, on this ground, the
judge refused to extend the rule in *Strong* v
Bird.

Milroy v *Lord* (1862) 4 De GF & J 264 Court of Appeal in Chancery (Knight, Bruce and Turner LJJ)

• *Completely and incompletely constituted trusts*

Facts
A settlor purported to assign 50 shares in the
Louisiana Bank to Lord upon trust for the
benefit of the plaintiffs. The settlor gave the
share certificates to Lord who held a power of
attorney which authorised him to transfer the
shares and directed him to effect the transfer.
Lord never exercised the power but during the
settlor's lifetime he paid the dividends to the
plaintiffs. On the settlor's death Lord gave the
shares to the settlor's executor. The plaintiffs
claimed that the shares were held on trust for
them by Lord and succeeded at first instance.
The executor appealed, claiming that the
shares could only be transferred by entry of
the name of the new owner into the books of
the bank. Since this was never carried out, the
trust was imperfect and therefore ineffectual.

Held
There was no trust of the shares in favour of
the plaintiffs, they were never legally vested in
Lord as trustee for them. If Lord held the
shares as trustee at all, it was for the settlor by
virtue of the fact that he held the power of
attorney as agent of the settlor. Further, it
could not be maintained that the settlor
himself held the shares on trust for the plaintiffs because it was never his intention to constitute himself a trustee of the settlement but
rather that the trust should be vested in Lord.

Turner J:

'I take the law of this court to be well settled that, in order to render a voluntary settlement valid and effectual, the settlor must have done everything which according to the nature of the property comprised in the settlement, was necessary to be done in order to transfer the property and render the settlement binding upon him. He may, of course, do this by actually transferring the property to the persons for whom he intends to provide and the provision will then be effectual, and it will be equally effectual if he transfers the property to a trustee for the purposes of the settlement, or declares that he himself holds it in trust for those purposes; and if the property be personal, the trust may, as I apprehend, be declared either in writing or by parol; but in order to render the settlement binding, one or other of these modes must, as I understand the law of this court, be resorted to, for there is no equity in this court to perfect an imperfect gift. The cases, I think, go further to this extent: that if the settlement is intended to be effectual by one of the modes to which I have referred, the court will not give effect to it by applying another of these modes. If it is intended to take effect by transfer, the court will not hold the intended transfer to operate as a declaration of trust, for then every imperfect instrument would be made effectual by being converted into a perfect trust. These are the principles by which as I conceive, this case must be tried.'

Comment

This case sets out very clearly the criteria for constituting a trust – but see *Re Rose* below.

Paul v *Constance* [1977] 1 WLR 527 Court of Appeal (Cairns, Scarman and Bridge LJJ)

• *Completely constituted trust – declaration of self as trustee*

Facts

Mr Constance lived with Mrs Paul. They had a joint bank account into which Mr Constance paid £950 paid which he received as damages for personal injuries. Later they added their bingo winnings. Both Mr Constance and Mrs Paul drew on the account and on many occasions, both prior to the money being deposited and subsequently, Mr Constance told Mrs Paul that the money was as much hers as his. From time to time, further sums of money were withdrawn and shared between Mr Constance and Mrs Paul. Mr Constance died intestate in 1974 and his wife took out letters of administration to his estate. At Mr Constance's death the original £950 was still in the bank account. His wife closed the account. Mrs Paul claimed the money, contending that Mr Constance had declared a trust of it for himself and her.

Held

The words used by Mr Constance on many occasions that the money was as much Mrs Paul's as his were sufficient to constitute a declaration of trust. There was a clear intention to create a trust; Mrs Paul was entitled to the £950 accordingly.

Scarman LJ:

'In this court the issue becomes: was there sufficient evidence to justify the judge reaching that conclusion of fact? [That is, that there had been a declaration of trust.] In submitting that there was, counsel for the plaintiff draws attention first and foremost to the words used. When one bears in mind the unsophisticated character of Mr Constance and his relationship with the plaintiff during the last few years of his life, counsel for the plaintiff submits that the words that he did use on more than one occasion namely: "This money is as much yours as mine" convey clearly a present declaration that the existing fund was as much the plaintiff's as his own. The judge accepted that conclusion. I think he was well justified in doing so and, indeed, I think he was right to do so.'

Comment

This case demonstrates that no set form of words is necessary for a valid declaration of trust. However, Scarman LJ points out that the court only heard argument on the question of whether this was a valid express trust. No argument on the question of a constructive trust, for example, was offered. Would it be more appropriate to consider whether this arrangement gave rise to a constructive trust?

Pennington and Another v *Waine and Others* [2002] 1 WLR 2075
Court of Appeal (Schiemann, Clarke and Arden LJJ)

- *Imperfect gift – valid equitable assignment*

Facts

C (Ada) informed P, a partner in the company's auditors, that she wished to tranfer with immediate effect 400 shares in a company of which she was a director to her nephew, H. P prepared the necessary stock transfer form and C signed it and returned it to him, but it was kept on file and nothing further was done to effect the transfer. C also informed H that she intended him to have the shares since he needed at least one share in order to qualify to be a director of the company. P sent H a form of consent to be a director which both H and C signed, but H was informed by P that no further action was required on his part.

Subsequently, C made a will which included specific bequests of her other shares in the company but which made no mention of the 400 shares which she believed were now registered in H's name. Proceedings were brought to establish whether the 400 shares were part of the estate or whether they were held on trust for H. The judge held that C had transferred the whole beneficial interest to H and that C and her executors were bare trustees of the legal title to the shares. C's executors appealed to the Court of Appeal on the ground that the gift was incomplete because the share transfer form had not been delivered to either H or to the company.

Held

The appeal was dismissed. C intended to make an immediate gift of the shares to H. He could not have become a director of the company had she failed to do so. Further, it would have been unconscionable for C herself to have recalled the gift and delivery of the stock transfer form was not required in order to perfect the gift.

Arden LJ:

'According to counsel's researches, the situation in the present case has not arisen in any reported cases before. I note that in her recent work, *Personal Property Law: Text and Materials* (2000) p241, Dr Worthington takes it as axiomatic that –

"… notwithstanding any demonstrable intention to make a gift, there will be no effective gift in equity if the donor simply places matters (such as completed transfer forms accompanied by the relevant share certificates) in the hand of the donor's agents. In those circumstances the donor remains at liberty to recall the gift simply by revoking the instructions previously given to the agent. The donor has not done all that is necessary, and the donee is not in a position to control completion of the transfer. It follows that the intended gift will not be regarded as complete either at law or in equity."

Secondly, equity has tempered the wind (of the principle that equity will not assist a volunteer) to the shorn lamb (the donee) by utilising the constructive trust. This does not constitute a declaration of trust and thus does not fall foul of the principle (see *Milroy* v *Lord* and *Jones* v *Lock*) that an imperfectly constituted gift is not saved by being treated as a declaration of trust. Thus, for example, in *T Choithram International SA* v *Pagarani* the Privy Council held that the assets which the donor gave to the foundation of which he was one of the trustees were held upon trust to vest the same in all the trustees of the foundation on the terms of the trusts of the foundation. This particular trust obligation was not a term of the express trust constituting the foundation but a constructive trust adjunct to it. So, too, in *Re Rose*, *Rose* v *IRC*, the Court of Appeal held that the beneficial interest in the shares passed when the share transfers were delivered to the transferee, and that consequently the transferor was a trustee of the legal estate in the shares from that date. At one stage in his judgment Evershed MR went further and held that an equitable interest passed when the document declaring a gift was executed. Evershed MR said:

> "If a man executes a document transferring all his equitable interest, say, in shares, that document, operating and intended to operate, as a transfer, will give rise to and take effect as a trust, for the assignor will then be a trustee of the legal estate in the shares for the person in whose favour he has made an assignment of his beneficial interest. For my part, I do not think that *Milroy* v *Lord* is an authority which compels this court to hold that in this case, where in the terms of the judgment of Turner LJ, the settlor did everything which, according to the nature of the property comprised in the settlement, was necessary to be done by him in order to transfer the property, the result necessarily negatives the conclusion that, pending registration, the settlor was a trustee of the legal interest for the transferee."

I will need to return to this point below.

Thirdly, equity has tempered the wind to the shorn lamb by applying a benevolent construction to words of gift. ... An imperfect gift is not saved by being treated as a declaration of trust. But where a court of equity is satisfied that the donor had an intention to make an immediate gift, the court will construe the words which the donor used as words effecting a gift or declaring a trust if they can fairly bear that meaning and otherwise the gift will fail. This point can also be illustrated by reference to the *Choithram* case. In that case the donor signed the trust deed setting up the

foundation and then simply made an oral declaration of gift of all wealth to the foundation. The Privy Council held that the gift to "the foundation" could only properly be construed as a gift to the purposes declared by the trust deed and administered by the trustees. Lord Browne-Wilkinson giving the judgment of the Privy Council referred to the arguments that the courts below had accepted, namely that –

> "... the court will not give a benevolent construction so as to treat ineffective words of outright gift as taking effect as if the donor had declared himself a trustee for the donee (see *Milroy* v *Lord*). So, it is said, in this case TCP [the donor] used words of gift to the foundation (nor words declaring himself a trustee); unless he transferred the shares and deposits so as to vest title in all the trustees, he had not done all that he could in order to effect the gift. It therefore fails. Further it is said that it is not possible to treat TCP's words of gift as a declaration of trust because they make no reference to trusts. Therefore the case does not fall within either of the possible methods by which a complete gift can be made and the gift fails." ...

Lord Browne-Wilkinson disagreed with this conclusion:

> "*Although equity will not aid a volunteer, it will not strive officiously to defeat a gift* (my emphasis). This case falls between the two common-form situations mentioned above. Although the words used by TCP are those normally appropriate to an outright gift – 'I give to X' – in the present context there is no breach of the principle in *Milroy* v *Lord* if the words of TCP's Gift (ie to the foundation) are given their only possible meaning in this context. The foundation has no legal existence apart from the trust declared by the foundation trust deed. Therefore the words 'I give to the foundation' can only mean 'I give to the trustees of the foundation trust deed to be held by them on the trusts of the foundation trust deed.' Although the words are apparently words of outright gift, they are essentially words of gift on trust.

But, it is said, TCP vested the properties not in all the trustees of the foundation but only in one, ie TCP. Since equity will not aid a volunteer, how can a court order be obtained vesting the gifted property in the whole body of trustees on the trusts of the foundation? ...

... In their Lordships' view there should be no question. TCP has, in the most solemn circumstances, declared that he is giving (and later that he has given) property to a trust which he himself has established and of which he had appointed himself to be a trustee. All this occurs at one composite transaction taking place on 17th February. There can in principle be no distinction between the case where the donor declares himself to be sole trustee for a donee or a purpose and the case where he declares himself to be one of the trustees for that donee or purpose. In both cases his conscience is affected and it would be unconscionable and contrary to the principles of equity to allow such a donor to resile from his gift."

Accordingly the principle that, where a gift is imperfectly constituted, the court will not hold it to operate as a declaration of trust, does not prevent the court from construing it to be a trust if that interpretation is permissible as a matter of construction, which may be a benevolent construction. The same must apply to words of gift. An equity to perfect a gift would not be invoked by giving a benevolent construction to words of gift or, it follows, words which the donor used to communicate or give effect to his gift.

The cases to which counsel have referred us do not reveal any, or any consistent single policy consideration policy behind the rule that the court will not perfect an imperfect gift. The objectives of the rule obviously include ensuring that donors do not by acting voluntarily act unwisely in a way that they may subsequently regret. This objective is furthered by permitting donors to change their minds at any time before it becomes completely constituted. This is a paternalistic objective, which can outweigh the respect to be given to the donor's original intention as gifts are often held by the courts to be incompletely constituted despite the clearest intention of the donor to make the gift. Another valid objective would be to safeguard the position of the donor: suppose, for instance, that (contrary to the fact) it had been discovered after Ada's death that her estate was insolvent, the court would be concerned to ensure that the gift did not defeat the rights of creditors. But, while this may well be a relevant consideration, for my own part I do not consider that this need concern the court to the exclusion of other considerations as in the event of insolvency there are other potent remedies available to creditors where insolvents have made gifts to defeat their claims ... There must also be, in the interests of legal certainty, a clearly ascertainable point in time at which it can be said that the gift was completed, and this point in time must be arrived at on a principled basis.

There are countervailing policy considerations which would militate in favour of holding a gift to be completely constituted. These would include effectuating, rather than frustrating, the clear and continuing intention of the donor, and preventing the donor from acting in a manner which is unconscionable. As Mr McGhee points out, both these policy considerations are evident in the *Choithram* case. It does not seem to me that this consideration is inconsistent with what Jenkins LJ said in *Re McArdle (decd), McArdle v McArdle*. His point is that there is nothing unconscionable in simply (without more) changing your mind. That is also the point which Dr Worthington makes in the passage I have cited above.

If one proceeds on the basis that a principle which animates the answer to the question whether an apparently incomplete gift is to be treated as completely constituted is that a donor will not be permitted to change his or her mind if it would be unconscionable, in the eyes of equity, vis-à-vis the donee to do so, what is the position here? There can be no comprehensive list of factors which makes it unconscionable for the donor to change his or her mind: it must depend on the court's evaluation of all the considerations. What then are the relevant facts here? Ada made the gift of her own free will: there is no finding that she was not competent to do this. She not only told Harold about the gift and signed a form of transfer which she delivered to Mr Pennington for him to secure registration: her agent also told Harold that he need take no action. In addition Harold agreed to become a director of the Company without limit of time, which he could not do without shares being transferred to him. If Ada had changed her mind on (say) 10 November 1998, in my judgment the court could properly have concluded that it was too late for her to do this as by that date Harold had signed the form 288A, the last of the events identified above to occur.

There is next the pure question of law: was it necessary for Ada to deliver the form of transfer to Harold? I have referred above to the difference of view between Evershed MR and Jenkins LJ. In *Re Rose, Rose* v *IRC* the issue was whether the gift was perfected by 10 April 1943, by which date the donor had executed the declaration of gift and delivered the share transfers to reflect the gifts to the transferees. Argument was not therefore directed to the question whether a beneficial interest in the shares passed on the dates of the declarations of trust or on the date on which the share transfers were handed over. For my own part I do not consider that it was necessary to the conclusions of Evershed MR that the gift should have taken effect before the transfers were delivered to the transferees. Indeed for him so to hold would not in my view be consistent with the second sentence cited from the relevant part of his judgment or with the fact that he went on to approve as a correct statement of the law the decision of Jenkins J in *Re Rose*, *Midland Bank* v *Rose* (where the share transfers having been delivered to the donee, the gift was held to be perfect because there was nothing else the donor could do) or with the fact that Morris LJ agreed with both judgments. Moreover if this were the view of Evershed MR it seems to me that it would not in my view be possible to reconcile it with *Milroy* v *Lord* and

in particular with the principle that the court will not convert an imperfect gift into a declaration of trust. There could not be a constructive trust until the gift was perfected. The conclusion of Jenkins LJ was predicated on the basis that delivery of the transfer to the donee was necessary and had occurred. Likewise the decision of this court in *Mascall* v *Mascall* and of the Privy Council in *Trustee of the Property of Pehrsson (A Bankrupt)* v *von Greyerz* (16 June 1999, unreported) were predicated on the same basis. I have summarised those cases earlier in this judgment. Accordingly the ratio of *Re Rose, Rose* v *IRC* was as I read it that the gifts of shares in that case were completely constituted when the donor executed share transfers and delivered them to the transferees even though they were not registered in the register of members of the company until a later date.

However, that conclusion as to the ratio in *Re Rose, Rose* v *IRC* does not mean that this appeal must be decided in the appellants' favour. Even if I am correct in my view that the Court of Appeal took the view in *Re Rose, Rose* v *IRC* that delivery of the share transfers was there required, it does not follow that delivery cannot in some circumstances be dispensed with. Here, there was a clear finding that Ada intended to make an immediate gift. Harold was informed of it. Moreover I have already expressed the view that a stage was reached when it would have been unconscionable for Ada to recall the gift. It follows that it would also have been unconscionable for her personal representatives to refuse to hand over the share transfer to Harold after her death. In those circumstances, in my judgment, delivery of the share transfer before her death was unnecessary so far as perfection of the gift was concerned.

It is not necessary to decide the case simply on that basis. After the share transfers were executed, Mr Pennington wrote to Harold on Ada's instructions informing him of the gift and stating that there was no action that he needed to take. I would also decide this appeal in favour of Harold on this further basis. If I am wrong in the view that delivery of the share transfers to the Company or the donee is required but is dispensed with by reason of the fact that it would be unconscionable for Ada's personal representatives to refuse to hand the transfers over to Harold, the words used by Mr Pennington should be construed as meaning that Ada and, through her, Mr Pennington became agents for Harold for the purpose of submitting the share transfer to the Company. This is an application of the principle of benevolent construction to give effect to Ada's clear wishes. Only in that way could the result "this requires no action on your part" and an effective gift be achieved. Harold did not question the assurance and must be taken to have proceeded to act on the basis that it would be honoured.

Accordingly, in my judgment the judge was right in the conclusion that he reached.'

Comment

Arden LJ held that the point at which the trust is constituted is that at which the donor's conscience is caught – at this point the need to register the share transfer form can be dispensed with.

Pullan v *Koe* [1912] 1 Ch 9
Chancery Division (Swinfen Eady J)

• *Marriage settlement – constitution of the trust – covenant to settle*

Facts

By a marriage settlement made in 1859, a wife covenanted to settle after-acquired property of £100 and over. In 1879 she received a gift of £285 from her mother. The money was paid into her husband's bank account on which she had power to draw and later invested in securities which remained at the bank On the husband's death in 1909 the trustees of the marriage settlement claimed the securities from the husband's executor. The executor pleaded the Statute of Limitations in defence.

Held

The property was not part of the husband's estate. When received by the wife it was immediately bound by the covenant and subject to the trusts in favour of the children as persons within the marriage consideration. The trustees' claim at law for damages for breach of contract arising in 1879 was statute-barred by lapse of time but a claim in equity for the property itself, still unsettled, could be maintained.

Swinfen Eady J:

'It was contended that the bonds never in fact became trust property as both the wife and husband were only liable in damages for breach of covenant, and that the case was different from cases where property which has once admittedly become subject to the trusts of an instrument has been improperly dealt with, and is sought to be recovered. In my opinion as soon as the £285 was paid to the wife it became in equity bound by and subject to the trusts of the settlement. The trustees could have claimed that particular sum, could have obtained at once the appointment of a receiver of it, if they could have shown a case of jeopardy, and, if it has been invested and the investment could be traced, could have followed the money and claimed the investment.

The point was dealt with by Jessel MR in *Smith* v *Lucas* where he said:

"What is the effect of such a covenant in equity? It has been said that the effect in equity of the covenant of the wife, as far as she is concerned, is that it does not affect her personally, but that it binds the property: that is to say, it binds the property under the doctrine of equity that that is to be considered as done that which ought to be done. That is the nature of specific performance of the contract no doubt. If, therefore, this is a covenant to settle the future-acquired property of the wife, and nothing more is done by her, the covenant will bind the property."

Again, in *Collyer* v *Isaacs,* Jessel MR said:

"A man can contract to assign property which is to come into existence in the future, and when it has come into existence, equity, treating as done that which ought to be done, fastens upon that property, and the contract to assign thus becomes a complete assignment. If a person contracts for value, eg in his marriage settlement, to settle all such real estate as his father shall leave him by will, or purports actually to convey by the deed such real estate, the effect is the same. It is a contract for value which will bind the property if the father leaves any property to his son."

The property being thus bound, these bonds became trust property, and can be followed by the trustees and claimed from a volunteer.

Again trustees are entitled to come into a Court of Equity to enforce a contract to create a trust, contained in a marriage settlement, for the benefit of the wife and the issue of the marriage, all of whom are within the marriage consideration. The husband covenanted that he and his heirs, executors, and administrators should, as soon as circumstances would admit, convey, assign, and surrender to the trustees the real or personal property to which his wife should become beneficially entitled. The trustees are entitled to have that covenant specifically enforced by a Court of Equity. In *In re D'Angibau* and in *In re Plumptre's Marriage Settlement* it was held that the Court would not interfere in favour of volunteers not within the marriage consideration, but here the plaintiffs are the contracting parties and the object of the proceeding is to benefit the wife and issue of the marriage.'

Comment

The judge gives a clear explanation of the marriage consideration. Although the common law contractual claim was statute-barred a claim in rem was permitted in equity.

Ralli's Will Trusts, Re [1964] Ch 288 Chancery Division (Buckley J)

• *Covenant to settle perfected under* Strong v Bird

Facts
By his will of 1892 a testator left the residue of his estate on trust for his wife for life with remainder to his two daughters, Helen and Irene, absolutely. By her marriage settlement of 1924 Helen covenanted to settle all her existing and after-acquired property on certain trusts which failed and ultimately for the children of Irene. Irene's husband was appointed as trustee of the marriage settlement and in 1946 he was also appointed a trustee of the testator's will of 1892. Helen died in 1956 and the testator's widow died in 1961. At the latter date Irene's husband held the residue of the testator's estate as trustee of the will. The case was defended by the personal representatives of Helen who claimed her half-share of the residue.

Held
The covenant to settle after-acquired property had been satisfied, the rule in *Strong v Bird* applied and it was irrelevant how the trustee had become the legal owner.

Buckley J:

'In my judgment, the circumstance that the plaintiff holds the fund because he was appointed a trustee of the will is irrelevant. He is, at law, the owner of the fund, and the means by which he became so have no effect upon the quality of his legal ownership. The question is: For whom, if anyone, does he hold the fund in equity? In other words, who can successfully assert an equity against him disentitling to stand upon his legal right? It seems to me to be indisputable that Helen, if she were alive, could not do so, for she has solemnly covenanted under seal to assign the fund to the plaintiff, and the defendants can stand in no better position ... It is also true that, if it were necessary to enforce the performance of the covenant, equity would not assist the beneficiaries under the settlement, because they are mere volunteers ... As matters stand, however, there is no occasion to invoke the assistance of equity to enforce the performance of the covenant.

It is for the defendants to invoke the assistance of equity to make good their claim to the fund. To do so, they must show that the plaintiff cannot conscientiously withhold it from them. When they seek to do this, he can point to the covenant which, in my judgment, relieves him from any fiduciary obligation he would otherwise owe to the defendants as Helen's representatives. In doing so, the plaintiff is not seeking to enforce an equitable remedy against the defendants on behalf of persons who could not enforce such a remedy themselves: he is relying upon the combined effect of his legal ownership of the fund and his rights under the covenant ...'

Comment
The case seems to rest on the conscionability of an order of the court that the executor should deal with the property in breach of his duty as trustee of the earlier trust.

Richards v *Delbridge* (1874) LR 18 Eq 11 Court of Chancery (Sir George Jessel MR)

• *Completely and incompletely consti-tuted trusts*

Facts
A grandfather who had leasehold business premises endorsed and signed the back of the lease in the following terms: 'This deed and all thereto belonging I give to [my grandson] EB Richards from this time forth, with all my stock in trade.' The lease was delivered to EB Richards' mother for safe custody as he was an infant. On the grandfather's death there was no mention of the business premises in his will. A claim was made that the endorsement and delivery of the lease to EB Richards' mother on his behalf created a valid trust. The principle laid down in *Milroy* v *Lord* that there was no equity to perfect an imperfect gift was distinguishable, it was argued, in that it did not apply to cases where there was a clear intention to create a trust even though this was in an informal document.

Held
Although the grandfather had made an assignment of the lease, it was ineffectual as it was not under seal as required by law. The court would not construe this ineffectual transfer as a declaration of trust even if it was clear that there was an intention to create a trust.

Sir George Jessel MR:

'The principle is a very simple one. A man may transfer his property without valuable consideration in one of two ways: he may either do such acts as amount in law to a conveyance or assignment of the property, and thus completely divest himself of the legal ownership, in which case the person who by those acts acquires the property takes it beneficially, or on trust, as the case may be; or the legal owner of the property may, by one or other of the modes recognised as amounting to a valid declaration of trust, constitute himself a trustee and, without an actual transfer of the legal title, may so deal with the property as to deprive himself of its beneficial ownership, and declare that he will hold it from that time forward on trust for the other person. It is true he need not use the words "I declare myself a trustee", but he must do something which is equivalent to it, and use expressions which have that meaning; for however anxious the court may be to carry out a man's intention, it is not at liberty to construe words otherwise than according to their proper meaning.

The cases in which the question has arisen (ie whether an intention to create a trust in an informal instrument which fails to transfer property from a donor to a donee constitutes a declaration of trust) are nearly all cases in which a man, by documents insufficient to pass a legal interest, has said: "I give or grant certain property to AB". Thus, in *Morgan* v *Malleson* the words were "I hereby give and make over to Dr Morris an India bond", and in *Richardson* v *Richardson* the words were: "grant, convey and assign". In both cases the judges held that the words were ineffectual declarations of trust. In the former case, Lord Romilly considered that the words were the same as these: "I undertake to hold the bond for you" which would undoubtedly have amounted to a declaration of trust.

The true distinction appears to me to be plain and beyond dispute: for a man to make himself a trustee there must be an expression of intention to become a trustee, whereas words of present gift show an intention to give over property to another, and not to retain it in the donor's hands for any purpose, fiduciary or otherwise.

In *Milroy* v *Lord*, Turner LJ after referring to the two modes of making a voluntary settlement valid and effectual, adds these words: "The cases, I think, go further to this extent, that if the settlement is intended to be effectual by one of the modes to which I have referred, the court will not give effect to it by applying another of those modes. If it is intended to take effect by transfer, the court will not hold the intended transfer to operate as a declaration of trust, for then every imperfect instrument would be made effectual by being converted into a perfect trust."

It appears to me that that sentence contains the whole law on the subject. If the decisions of Lord Romilly (in *Morgan* v *Malleson*) and of Vice-Chancellor Wood (in *Richardson* v *Richardson*) were right, there never could be a case where an expression of a present gift would not amount to an effectual declaration of trust, which would be carrying the doctrine on that subject too far ...'

Comment

The grandfather had not complied with the formalities for a transfer of an interest in land and, in any case, as an infant, the grandson could not hold legal title to land. The words used are words of gift, not a declaration of trust, so the gift failed.

Rose, Re [1952] Ch 499 Court of Appeal (Sir Raymond Evershed MR, Jenkins and Morris LJJ)

• *Completely and incompletely constituted trusts – transfer to trustees*

Facts

The settlor transferred two blocks of shares in a property company to trustees to be held on certain trusts in March 1943. The transfer was made in a form which corresponded exactly with the requirements of the company's regulations. The transfer was registered in June 1943 by the company. The settlor died more than five years after he had made the transfer of the shares but less than five years after the transfer had been registered with the company. Under the Finance Act 1894, a voluntary disposition of property made more than five years before a person's death was exempt from estate duty. The question therefore arose as to whether the shares were exempt and this depended on the date of transfer of the shares.

Held

The settlor had done all in his power to transfer the shares to the trustees and the transfer was accordingly completed in March 1943. There was no duty payable.

Sir Raymond Evershed:

'... but if a document is apt and proper to transfer the property – is, in truth, the appropriate way in which the property must be transferred – then it does not seem to me to follow from the statement of Turner LJ that, as a result, either during some limited period or otherwise, a trust may not arise, for the purpose of giving effect to the transfer. The simplest case will, perhaps, provide an illustration. If a man executes a document transferring his equitable interest, say, in shares, that document, operating and intended to operate, as a transfer, will give rise to and take effect as a trust, for the assignor will then be a trustee of the legal estate in the shares for the person in whose favour he has made an assignment of his beneficial interest. As for my part, I do not think that *Milroy* v *Lord* is an authority which compels this court to hold that in this case, where, in terms of Turner LJ's judgment, the settlor did everything which, according to the nature of the property comprised in the settlement, was necessary to be done by him in order to transfer the property, the result necessarily negatives the conclusion that, pending registration, the settlor was a trustee of the legal interest for the transferee.

The view of the limitations of *Milroy* v *Lord* which I have tried to express was much better expressed by Jenkins J in the recent case which also bears the name of *Re Rose* (though that is a coincidence). It is true that the main point, the essential question to be determined, was whether there had been a transfer eo nomine of certain shares within the meaning of a will. The testator in that case, Rose, by his will had given a number of shares to one Hook, but the gift was subject to this qualification: "If such ... shares have not been transferred to him previously to my death." The question was: Had the shares been transferred to him in these circumstances? He had executed (as had this Mr Rose) a transfer in appropriate form, and handed the transfer and the certificate to Hook, but at the time of his death, the transfer had not been registered. It was said, therefore, that there had been no transfer, and (following the argument of counsel for the Crown) there had been no passing to Hook of any interest, legal or beneficial, whatever, by the time the testator died. If that view were right, then, of course Hook would be entitled to the shares under the will. But Jenkins J went a little more closely into the matter because it was obvious that on one view of it, if it were held that there was a "transfer" within the terms of the will, though the transfer was inoperative in the eye of the law and not capable of being completed after the death, then Mr Hook suffered the misfortune of getting the shares neither by gift inter vivos nor by testamentary benefaction. Therefore Jenkins J considered *Milroy* v *Lord* and in regard to it he used this language:

"I was referred on that to the well-known case of *Milroy* v *Lord* and also to the recent case of *Re Fry*. Those cases, as I understand them, turn on the fact that the deceased donor had not done all in his power, according to the nature of the property given, to vest the legal interest in the property in the donee. In such circumstances, it is, of course, well settled that there is no equity to complete the gift at the date of the donor's death; the court will not compel his personal representatives to do that act and the gift remains incomplete and fails. In *Milroy* v *Lord* the imperfection was due to the fact that the wrong form of transfer was used for the purpose of transferring certain bank shares. The document was not the appropriate document to pass any interest in the property at all."

Then he referred to *Re Fry* which is another illustration, and continued:

"In this case, as I understand it, the testator had done everything in his power to divest himself of the shares in question to Mr Hook. He had executed the transfer. It is not suggested that the transfer was not in accordance with the company's regulations. He had handed that transfer together with the certificate to Mr Hook. There was nothing else the testator could do."

I venture respectfully to adopt the whole of the passage I have read which, in my judgment, is a correct statement of the law. If that be so, then it seems to me that it cannot be asserted on the authority of *Milroy* v *Lord*, and I venture to think it also cannot be asserted as a matter of logic and good sense or principle, that because, by the regulations of the company, there had to be a gap before Mrs Rose could, as between herself and the company claim the rights which the shares gave her vis-à-vis the company. Mr Rose was not in the meantime a trustee for her of all his rights and benefits in the shares. That he intended to pass all those rights, as I have said, seems to me too plain for argument.'

Comment
The judge was able to distinguish *Milroy v Lord* on the grounds that Mr Rose *had* done everything in his power to dispose of his interest in the shares.

Sen v *Headley* [1991] Ch 425 Court of Appeal (Purchas, Nourse and Leggatt LJJ)

• *Whether land can be the subject matter of a donatio mortis causa*

Facts
The deceased gave a friend the key to a steel box in which, he told her, the deeds to his house were to be found, and he indicated that, knowing that he was dying, he wished her to have the house on his death. He died intestate, and the friend claimed a valid donatio mortis causa in respect of the house. This claim was dismissed at first instance by Mummery J and the friend then appealed to the Court of Appeal.

Held
A valid donatio mortis causa had been constituted and the appeal was allowed.

Nourse LJ outlined the three general requirements which must be satisfied for a valid donatio mortis causa to arise:

'First, the gift had to be made in contemplation, although not necessarily in expectation, of impending death. Second, the gift had to be made upon the condition that it was to be absolute and perfected only on the donor's death, being revocable until that event and ineffective otherwise. Third, there had to be a delivery of the subject matter of the gift, or the essential *indicia* of title thereto, which amounted to a parting with dominion and not mere physical possession over the subject matter.'

At first instance, Mummery J, while accepting that the first two of these requirements had been fulfilled, took the view that the deceased had not effectively parted with dominion over the house in that he retained until his death the whole of the legal and equitable interest in it.

In the Court of Appeal, Nourse LJ, while accepting the need for a parting of dominion took the view that this condition had been fulfilled by parting with dominion over 'the essential *indicia* of title' – ie the title deeds to the house. Although the view expressed obiter by Lord Eldon in *Duffield* v *Elwes* to the effect that the subject matter of a donatio mortis causa had hitherto generally been accepted, the point was never, in fact, actually decided by the Court.

Nourse LJ:

'*Donationes mortis causa* may be said to have been an anomaly in our law; both for their immunity to the Statute of Frauds and the Wills Act and as exceptions to the rule that there is no equity to perfect an imperfect gift. But both Lord Hardwicke and Lord Eldon, while making to regret the doctrine, established extensions of it beyond a simple gift of a chattel by its delivery; the former to a gift of money secured by a bond, by delivery of the bond; the latter to a gift of money secured by a mortgage of land, by delivery of the mortgage deed. Later decisions have included gifts of other choses in action by delivery of the essential *indicia* of title. What has never before been directly decided in England is whether the doctrine applies to a gift of land by delivery of the title deeds. Lord Eldon undoubtedly thought that it did not, a view which has generally been assumed to be correct. Now, Mummery J, at first instance, has given a decision in line with that assumption and we have to say whether we agree with him or not.

It cannot be doubted that title deeds are the essential *indicia* of title to unregistered land. Moreover, on the facts found by the judge there was here a constructive delivery of the title deeds of 56 Gordon Road equivalent to an actual handing of them by Mr Hewett to Mrs Sen. And it could not be suggested that Mr Hewett did not part with dominion over the deeds. The two questions which remain to be decided are first, whether Mr Hewett parted with dominion over the house; secondly, if he did, whether land is capable of passing by way of a *donatio mortis causa*. We have traced the need for there to be a parting with dominion over the subject matter of the gift, that is, with the ability to control it, to the judgment of Lord Kenyon CJ in *Hawkins* v *Blewitt*, where he said:

> "In the case of a *donatio mortis causa*, possession must be immediately given. That has been done here; a delivery has taken place; but it is also necessary that by parting with the possession, the deceased should also part with the dominion over it. That has not been done here."

A similar view was taken in *Reddell* v *Dobree* and in *Re Johnson*. In each of those three cases the alleged donor delivered a locked box to the alleged donee and either retained or took back the key to it; in *Reddell* v *Dobree* he also reserved and exercised a right to take back the box. In each of them it was held that the alleged donor had retained dominion over the box and that there had been no *donatio mortis causa*.

It appears therefore that the need for there to be a parting with dominion was first identified in cases where the subject matter of the gift was a locked box and its contents. In *Birch* v *Treasury Solicitor*, as we have seen, a similar need was recognised where the subject matter of the gift was a chose in action. Without in any way questioning that need, we think it appropriate to observe that a parting with dominion over an intangible thing such as a chose in action is necessarily different from a parting with dominion over a tangible thing such as a locked box and its contents. We think that in the former case a parting with dominion over the essential *indicia* of title will *ex hypothesi* usually be enough. Mummery J found great difficulty in seeing how the delivery of the title deeds could ever amount to a parting with dominion over the land to the extent that the donor "has put is out of his power to alter the subject matter of the gift between the date of the gift and the date of his death". We respectfully think that that test, which

was taken from the judgment of Farwell J in *Re Craven's Estate* was misunderstood by the judge. Having pointed out that Mr Hewett retained until his death the entire legal and equitable interest in the house, he continued:

> "Without taking any action against Mrs Sen to recover the title deeds from her, he was fully empowered as absolute owner to make a declaration of trust in respect of the house in favour of another person for the sale of the house. The beneficiary under such a declaration of trust and the purchaser under such a contract would be entitled to an equitable interest in the house which would take priority over an claim that Mrs Sen would have by way of donatio mortis causa on Mr Hewett's death."

To that it must be answered that the same objection could be taken in the case of a chose in action. A donor of money secured by a bond or a mortgage who had delivered the bond or the mortgage deed to the donee could in like manner constitute himself a trustee of the benefit of his security for some third party or he could assign it for value. But it has never been suggested that the donor's continuing ability to take either of those steps amounts to a retention of dominion over the chose in action. We therefore respectfully disagree with the judge's view, if such it was, that a delivery of title deeds can never amount to a parting with dominion over the land. As appears from *Birch* v *Treasury Solicitor* the question is one to be decided on the facts of the individual case.

We do not suggest that there might never be a state of facts where there was a parting with dominion over the essential *indicia* of title to a chose in action but nevertheless a retention of dominion over the chose itself. And it is just possible to conceive of someone, who, in contemplation of impending death, had parted with dominion over the title deeds of his house to an alleged donee, nevertheless granting a tenancy of it to a third party; for which purpose proof of the title to the freehold by production of the deeds is not usually necessary. On facts such as those there might be a case for saying that the alleged donor had not parted with dominion over the house. But nothing comparable happened here. It is true that in the eyes of the law Mr Hewett, by keeping his own set of keys to the house, retained possession of it. But the benefits which thereby accrued to him were wholly theoretical. He uttered the words of gift, without reservation, two days after his readmission to hospital, when he knew that he did not have long to live and when there could have been no practical possibility of his ever returning home. He had parted with dominion over the titled deeds. Mrs Sen had her own set of keys to the house and was in effective control of it. In all the circumstances of the case, we do not believe that the law requires us to hold that Mr Hewett did not part with dominion over the house. We hold that he did.

Having now decided that the third of the general requirements for a *donatio mortis causa* was satisfied in this case, we come to the more general question whether land is capable of passing by way of such a gift. For this purpose we must return to *Duffield* v *Elwes*. While that decision was supported by pronouncements from both Lord Hardwicke and Lord Mansfield, we believe that it was, for its times, creative, if not quite revolutionary.

Let it be agreed that the doctrine is anomalous. Anomalies do not justify anomalous exceptions. If due account is taken of the present state of the law in regard to mortgages and choses in action, it is apparent that to make a distinction in the case of land would be to make just such an exception. A *donatio mortis causa* of land is neither more nor less anomalous than any other. Every such gift is a circumvention of the Wills Act 1837. Why should the additional statutory formalities (such as the requirements of s53(1)(b) of the Law of Property Act 1925 and s2 of the Law of Property (Miscellaneous Provisions) Act 1989 for the creation and transmission of interests in land be regarded as some larger obstacle. The only step which has to be taken is to extend the application of the implied or constructive trust arising on the donor's death from the conditional to the absolute estate. Admittedly, that is a step which the House of Lords would not have taken in *Duffield* v *Elwes*, and, if the point had been a subject of decision, we would have loyally followed it in this court. But we cannot decide a case in 1991 as the House of Lords would have decided it, but did not decide it, in 1827. We must decide it according to the law as it stands today. Has any sound reason been advanced for not making the necessary extension? Having carefully considered the reasons put forward by Mummery J as elaborated in the argument of Mr Leeming for the defendant, we do not think that there has. While we fully understand the judge's view that there was a special need for judicial caution at his level of decision, it is notable that the two previous authorities in this court, *Re Dillon* and *Birch* v *Treasury Solicitor*, have extended rather than restricted the application of the doctrine. Indeed, we think that the latter decision may have put others of the earlier authorities on choses in action in some doubt. Moreover, certainty of precedent, while in general most desirable, is not of as great an importance in relation to a doctrine which is infrequently invoked as this. Finally, while we certainly agree that the policy of the law in regard to the formalities for the creation and transmission of interests in land should be upheld, we have to acknowledge that that policy has been substantially modified by the development to which we have referred ...'

We hold that land is capable of passing by way of *donatio mortis causa* and that the three general requirements for such a gift were satisfied in this case. We therefore allow Mrs Sen's appeal.'

Comment

Parting with dominion is not the same as parting with ownership since the gift only takes effect from the donor's death and the property remains in the donor's ownership if the donor survives.

T Choithram International SA and Others v *Pagarini and Others* [2001] 2 All ER 492 Privy Council (Lords Browne-Wilkinson, Jauncey of Tullichettle, Clyde, Hobhouse of Woodborough and Millett)

• *Trust or imperfect gift – rule in* Strong v Bird – *whether property properly vested when property transferred to one trustee*

Facts

The testator (TCP) was a businessman and philanthropist who made provision for his first wife, Lalibai, and their family during his lifetime and wished to leave most of his remaining assets to a charitable foundation when he died. Some considerable time after he first declared this intention, he executed a trust deed in order to establish the T Choithram Foundation (which in statements given in evidence was also referred to as 'the trust') and he was also named as one of the trustees. The deed setting up the trust was only executed, in an elaborate ceremony, after it was discovered that TCP was suffering from cancer. After executing the trust deed TCP said words to the effect that 'I now give all my wealth to the trust' or 'I'm handing all my gift, all my wealth, all my shares, to the trust'. TCP then said that his accountant, Mr Param, knew what to do He instructed Mr Param to 'transfer all my wealth with the companies to the trust'. Minutes of board meetings of TCP's holding companies recorded that, having been elected chairman, TCP reported that the trust had been established and all his wealth transferred to it.

Solicitors other than those setting up the trust had been instructed to prepare TCP's will which provided for the whole of his estate except for his property in India to go to the foundation. At the time the will was drafted the foundation was not constituted. The solicitor preparing the will therefore advised TCP to bequeath the estate for general charitable purposes and the property could then be transferred to the foundation after his death. TCP instructed the solicitor to revise the will accordingly and said that he would begin the transfer of the property to the foundation. Although a declaration of trust and a memorandum of addition were drawn up, they were not signed by TCP, who had an aversion to signing such documents and he had been advised that the documents were not necessary. At the same time he repeatedly said that he had done his bit, that he had given all his wealth to the foundation and that there was nothing further for him to do. TCP told his daughter 'I have given up everything and I feel very happy now'. At the same time, the accountant deleted TCP's name as a creditor of the company and substituted the foundation. However, the record in one of the companies remained unaltered and, at the time of TCP's death, TCP had not signed the forms necessary to transfer the shares in the companies into the names of the trustees. It was only after TCP's death that the share transfer formalities were completed. When TCP died, his son Lekhraj obtained a grant of letters of administration under which he obtained legal title to the property which was claimed by the foundation. Lekhraj was one of those named as trustees of the foundation. TCP's first wife and her children began proceedings in the British Virgin Islands in which they claimed that there was neither a perfect gift of the property the foundation nor a valid declaration of trust. The judge at first instance and the Court of Appeal of the British Virgin Islands held that there had been an imperfect gift which would not be enforced against TCP's estate. The defendants appealed to the Privy Council.

Held

The appeal was allowed. In the context in which the gift was made, the words used by TCP were essentially words of trust.

Lord Browne-Wilkinson:

'On the main issue the defendants advanced a number of arguments with a view to demonstrating that the gift to the foundation was an immediate perfected gift by TCP of all or some of TCP's wealth. Their primary argument was that TCP, having executed the foundation trust deed under which he was one of the trustees made a gift of all his wealth to "the foundation", thereafter held all his assets (or at least his shares in and deposits with the British Virgin Island companies which are the first four defendants) as trustee on the trusts of the foundation trust deed. The defendants also had a number of alternative arguments. First they argued that the principle in *Strong* v *Bird* entitled them to succeed because a grant of letters of administration to the estate of TCP had been obtained by Lekhraj, one of the trustees of the foundation. Next they argued that, as to the sums deposited with the companies, those companies had attorned to the trustees of the foundations when Mr Param or Mr Tejwani made the changes in the companies' books. Next they submitted that TCP's words and actions amounted to an equitable assignment of the deposits with the companies to the trustees of the foundation, or alternatively constituted a release by TCP to the companies in consideration of the companies' undertaking contractual obligations to pay the trustees of the foundation a similar sum. Finally, the defendants repeated their argument before the judge because of certain provisions in the articles of the company or under s30 of the International Business Companies Ordinance 1984. Their Lordships will deal first with the main argument since, in their view, that is sufficient to dispose of the appeal.

In order to have made an effective gift of his shares and deposit balances to the foundation TCP must have intended to make an immediate gift on 17 February. The judge found, and repeated his finding on a number of occasions throughout the judgment, that on that date, TCP did make, or attempted to make, a present immediate and unconditional gift to the foundation which was intended to be complete. This finding, if it had stood alone, would have been fully sufficient to establish TCP's intention to make an outright gift. However, at a later stage in his judgment the judge made a further

finding. At this stage in the judgment the judge was seeking to answer the second question of fact left to him by counsel for decision (viz did TCP continue his intention of gift down to the date of death?) a question only relevant to the *Strong* v *Bird* argument. The judge reviewed the evidence as to the events occurring after the oral declaration of trust on 17 February and was very impressed by two elements in the evidence: first, that despite Lekraj's promptings TCP refused to sign the further documents put before him and, second, that by the draft will (which he never executed) TCP expressly excluded his Indian property (which had been the home of Lalibai) and also contained a gift of his estate to the foundation. He reached the conclusion that the gift was not intended by the deceased to be irrevocable.

Their Lordships do not feel able to accept the judge's inference that TCP intended the gift to be revocable. ...

Their Lordships consider that, once it is understood that, in any event, the transaction was to be carried through by TCP declaring that he held assets already vested in him as a trustee for the foundation, there is no ground for inferring that the gift was intended by TCP to be revocable or conditional on the transfer of the specific assets.

...

The judge and the Court of Appeal understandably took the view that a perfect gift could only be made in one of two ways, viz. (a) by a transfer of the gifted asset to the donee, accompanied by an intention in the donor to make a gift or (b) by the donor declaring himself to be a trustee of the gifted property for the donee. In case (a), the donor has to have done everything necessary to be done which is within his own power to do in order to transfer the gifted asset to the donee. If the donor has not done so, the gift is incomplete since the donee has no equity to perfect an imperfect gift (see *Milroy* v *Lord*; *Richards* v *Delbridge*; *Re Rose (deceased), Midland Bank Executor and Trustee Co Ltd* v *Rose*; *Re Rose, Rose* v *IRC*). Moreover, the court will not give a benevolent construction so as to treat ineffective words of outright gift as taking effect as if the donor had declared himself a trustee for the donee (see *Milroy* v *Lord*). So, it is said, in this case TCP used words of gift to the foundation (not words declaring himself a trustee): unless he transferred the shares and deposits so as to vest title in all the trustees, he had not done all that he could in order to effect the gift. It therefore fails. Further it is said that it is not possible to treat TCP's words of gift as a declaration of trust because they make no reference to trusts. Therefore the case does not fall within either of the possible methods by which a complete gift can be made and the gift fails.

Though it is understandable that the courts below should have reached the conclusion since the case does not fall squarely within either of the methods normally stated as being the only possible ways of making a gift, their Lordships do not agree with that conclusion. The facts of this case are novel and raise a new point. It is necessary to make an analysis of the rules of equity as to complete gifts. Although equity will not aid a volunteer, it will not strive officiously to defeat a gift. This case falls between the two common-form situations mentioned above. Although the words used by TCP are those normally appropriate to an outright gift – "I give to X" – in the present context there is no breach of the principle in *Milroy* v *Lord* if the words of TCP's gift (ie to the foundation) are given their only possible meaning in this context. The foundation has no legal existence apart from the trust declared by the foundation trust deed. Therefore the words "I give to the foundation" can only mean "I give to the trustees of the foundation trust deed to be held by them on the trusts of the foundation trust deed". Although the words are apparently words of outright gift they are essentially words of gift on trust.

But, it is said, TCP vested the properties not in all the trustees of the foundation but only in one, ie TCP. Since equity will not aid a volunteer, how can a court order to obtained vesting the gifted property in the whole body of trustees on the trusts of the

foundation? Again, this represents an over-simplified view of the rules of equity. Until comparatively recently the great majority of trusts were voluntary settlements under which beneficiaries were volunteers having given no value. Yet beneficiaries under a trust, although volunteers, can enforce the trust against the trustees. Once a trust relationship is established between trustee and beneficiary, the fact that a beneficiary has given no value is irrelevant. It is for this reason that the type of perfect gift referred to in class (b) above is effective since the donor has constituted himself a trustee for the donee who can as a matter of trust law enforce the trust.

What then is the position here where the trust property is vested in one of the body of trust deed, viz TCP? In their Lordships' view there should be no question. TCP has, in the most solemn circumstances, declared that he is giving (and later that he has given) property to a trust which he himself has established and of which he has appointed himself to be a trustee. All this occurs as one composite transaction taking place on 17th February. There can in principle be no distinction between the case where the donor declares himself to be one of the trustees for that donee on purpose. In both cases his conscience is affected and it would be unconscionable and contrary to the principles of equity to allow such a donor to resile from his gift. Say, in the present case, that TCP had survived and tried to change his mind by denying the gift. In their Lordships' judgment in the absence of special factors where one out of a larger body of trustees has the trust property vested in him he is bound by the trust and must give effect to it by transferring the trust property into the name of all the trustees. ...

What then are the gifted assets? It will be recalled that TCP referred to the subject of the gift in a number of different ways: "all my wealth", "everything", "all my wealth, all my shares to the trust", "all his balances ... with the company ... and his shares as well", "all my wealth with the companies". The judge found that TCP made a gift of all his wealth with the companies, ie the deposit balances and the shares in the four defendant companies which together constitute his whole wealth in the British Virgin Islands and are the only assets at issue in these proceedings. It was submitted that the gift of "all my wealth" was void for uncertainty. Their Lordships express no view on that point since there can be no question but that the deposit balances and the shares in the four companies were identified by TCP as being included in the gift and the gift to them is pro tanto valid.

Their Lordships will therefore humbly advise Her Majesty that the appeal ought to be allowed and the action dismissed on the grounds that at TCP's death the deposit balances and the shares in the companies were held on the trusts of the foundation trust deed and the same are now validly vested in the trustees of the foundation.'

Comment

The Privy Council looked at TCP's words of gift in their context and construed them as a declaration. Although he had not completed the formalities to transfer the property, TCP was himself one of a number of trustees of the foundation and, through him, Lekhraj acquired legal title as his administrator. Although legal title was held by only one trustee, the beneficiaries could have enforced the trust against him.

4 Secret Trusts

Adams and the Kensington Vestry, Re

See Chapter 1.

Blackwell v Blackwell [1929] AC 318 House of Lords (Lord Hailsham LC, Viscount Sumner, Lords Buckmaster, Carson and Warrington)

• *Secret trusts*

Facts

By a codicil to his will, a testator gave a legacy of £12,000 to five persons upon trust 'for the purposes indicated by me to them'. The testator informed one of the legatees in detail as to the objects of the trust and informed the other four in outline of the same before the execution of the will.

In fact, the objects were the testator's mistress and illegitimate son. The plaintiffs, who were the testator's wife and child and the residuary legatees under his will, brought an action seeking a declaration that there was no valid trust in favour of the mistress and illegitimate son because parol evidence was inadmissible to establish the purposes communicated by the testator to the legatees. As this was a half-secret and not a fully secret trust, the plaintiffs argued that fraud could not justify the admission of parol evidence contrary to s9 Wills Act 1837.

Held

A valid half-secret trust had been established in favour of the mistress and illegitimate son and it was outside the provisions of s9 and within the law of trusts by virtue of the communication of the purpose to the legatees and the acquiescence on their part.

Viscount Sumner:

'In itself the doctrine of equity, by which parol evidence is admissible to prove what is called "fraud" in connection with secret trusts, and effect is given to such trusts when established, would not seem to conflict with any of the Acts under which from time to time the legislature has regulated the right of testamentary disposition. A court of conscience finds a man in the position of an absolute legal owner of a sum of money, which has been bequeathed to him under a valid will, and it declares that, on proof of certain facts relating to the motives and actions of the testator, it will not allow the legal owner to exercise his legal right to do what he will with his own. This seems to be a perfectly normal exercise of general equitable jurisdiction. The facts commonly, but not necessarily, involve some immoral and selfish conduct on the part of the legal owner. The necessary elements, on which the question turns, are intention, communication and acquiescence. The testator intends his absolute gift to be employed as he and not as the donee desires; he tells the proposed donee of this intention and, either by express promise or by the tacit promise, which is satisfied by acquiescence the proposed donee encourages him to bequeath the money in the faith that his intentions will be carried out. The special circumstance that the gift is by bequest only makes this rule a special case of the exercise of a general jurisdiction, but in its application to a bequest the doctrine must in principle rest on the assumption that the will has first operated according to its terms. It is because there is no one to whom the law can give relief in the premises that relief, if any, must be sought in equity. So far, and in the bare case of a legacy absolute on the face of it, I do not see how the statute-law relating to the form of a valid will is concerned at all, and the expressions, in which the doctrine has been habitually described, seem to bear this out. For the prevention of fraud equity fastens on the conscience of the legatee a trust, that is, which otherwise would be inoperative; in other words it makes him do what the will in itself has nothing to do with; it lets him take what the will gives him and then makes him apply it as the court of conscience directs, and it does so in order to give effect to wishes of the testator which would not otherwise be effectual.

To this two circumstances must be added to bring the present case to the test of the general doctrine, first that the will states on its face that the legacy is given on trust but does not state what the trusts are, and further contains a residuary bequest and, second, that the legatees are acting with perfect honesty, seek no advantage to themselves, and only desire, if the court will permit them, to do what in other circumstances the court would have fastened it on their conscience to perform.

Since the current of decision down to *Re Fleetwood* and *Re Huxtable* has established that the principles of equity apply equally when these circumstances are present as in cases where they are not, the material question is whether and how the Wills Act affects this case. It seems to me that, apart from legislation, the application of the principle of equity which was made in *Fleetwood*'s case and *Huxtable*'s case was logical, and was justified by the same considerations as in the cases on fraud and absolute gifts. Why should equity forbid an honest trustee to give effect to his promise, made to a deceased testator, and compel him to pay another legatee, about whom it is quite certain that the testator did not mean to make him the object of his bounty? In both cases the testator's wishes are incompletely expressed in his will. Why should equity, over a mere matter of words, give effect to them in one case and frustrate them in the other? No doubt the words "in trust" prevent the legatee from taking beneficially, whether they have simply been declared in

conversation or written in the will, but the fraud, when the trustee, so called in the will, is also the residuary legatee, is the same as when he is only declared a trustee by word of mouth accepted by him. I recoil from interfering with decisions of long standing, which reject this anomaly, unless constrained by statute …

I think the conclusion is confirmed, which the frame of s9 of the Wills Act seems to carry on its face, and the legislation did not purport to interfere with the exercise of a general equitable jurisdiction, even in connection with secret dispositions of a testator, except insofar as reinforcement of the formalities required for a valid will might indirectly limit it. The effect, therefore, of a bequest being made in terms on trust without any statement in the will to show what the trust is, remains to be decided by the law as laid down by the courts before and since the act and does not depend on the Act itself.

The limits beyond which the rules as to unspecified trusts must not be carried have often been discussed. A testator cannot reserve to himself a power of making future unwitnessed dispositions by merely naming a trustee and leaving the purposes of the trust to be supplied afterwards, nor can a legatee give testamentary validity to an unexecuted codicil by accepting an indefinite trust, never communicated to him in the testator's lifetime … To hold otherwise would indeed be to enable the testator to "give the go-by" to the requirements of the Wills Act because he did not choose to comply with them. It is communication of the purpose to the legatee, coupled with acquiescence or promise on his part, that removes the matter from the provision of the Wills Act and brings it within the law of trusts, as applied in this instance to trustees, who happen also to be legatees …'

Comment
Communication and acceptance of the half-secret trust must take place on or before the execution of the will.

Cooper (Colin), Re [1939] Ch 811
Court of Appeal (Sir Wilfred Greene MR, Clauson and Goddard LJJ)

• *Fully secret trust – communication to legatee*

Facts

By his will the testator gave a £5,000 legacy jointly to two persons to hold on a secret trust which he had communicated to them before executing the will. The testator executed another will at a later date which purported to cancel the earlier will except for certain bequests and stated: 'The sum of £5,000 bequeathed to my trustees in the will now cancelled is to be increased to £10,000, they knowing my wishes regarding that sum.' The increased bequest was never communicated to the legatees by the testator in his lifetime.

Held

There was a secret trust of the first £5,000 but not the second £5,000.

Sir Wilfred Greene MR:

'In the present case there is no question that when the testator made his will of 10 February 1938 the legacy of £5,000 thereby bequeathed to the two named trustees was effectively given and the giving of it complied with the requirements of a secret trust; the terms had been communicated, the trustees had acquiesced and the testator made his will upon the faith of that acquiescence. But the only trust which was in the picture on that occasion was one which related to a defined and stated sum of £5,000. That was the legacy the intention to bequeath which was communicated to the trustees; that was the legacy in respect of which they gave their acceptance; that was the legacy which the testator, induced by that acceptance, in fact bequeathed. At a later date when, after an unfortunate sudden illness which proved fatal in South Africa, the testator made a will on 27 March 1938, he had no communication with those trustees with regard to the dispositions which he thereby made; there was no acquiescence by the trustees in the dispositions in question: he made that will not induced by any such acquiescence by the trustees although he made it quite clearly in the belief that what he was doing would be effective and that his trustees would carry it out; but none of the necessary elements to constitute a valid secret trust were present on the occasion of the making of that will. The actual form of that will was a cancellation of the will of February 1938, and the reinstatement of an earlier will. He then goes on to say: "The sum of £5,000 bequeathed to my trustees in the will now cancelled is to be increased to £10,000, they knowing my wishes regarding this sum." The learned judge construed the testamentary instructions of the testator by saying that the original gift of £5,000 was not revoked by this will and that in substance the effect of this will was to leave that gift in the earlier will unrevoked and to add to it a further £5,000. Speaking for myself, I do not think that any difference in principle emerges based on a distinction between the revocation of the original legacy and the bequest of the new legacy of a larger amount. It does not seem to me possible to say that anything can turn on so fine a point. The substance of the matter is that, having imposed on the conscience of these two trustees the trust in relation to the legacy of £5,000 and having written that legacy into his will of February 1938, by this will he in effect is giving another legacy of the same amount to be held upon the same trusts. It seems to me that upon the facts of this case it is impossible to say that the acceptance by the trustees of the onus of trusteeship in relation to the first and earlier legacy is something which must be treated as having been repeated in reference to the second legacy or the increased legacy, whichever way one chooses to describe it.

In order that a secret trust might be made effective with regard to that added sum in my opinion precisely the same factors were necessary as were required to validate the original trusts, namely, communication, acceptance or acquiescence, and the making of the will on the faith of such acceptance or acquiescence. None of these elements, as I have said, were present. It is not possible, in my opinion, to treat the figure of £5,000 in relation to which the consent of the trustees was originally obtained as something of no essential importance. I cannot myself see that the arrangement between the testator and the trustees can be construed as though it had meant "£5,000 or whatever sum I may hereafter choose to bequeath". That is not what was said and it was not with regard to any sum other than the £5,000 that the consciences of the trustees (to use a technical phrase) were burdened. It must not be thought from what I have been saying that some trifling excess of the sum actually bequeathed over the figure mentioned in the first bequest to the trustees would necessarily not be caught. Such an addition might come within the rule of de minimis if the facts justified it. Similarly, it must not be thought that if a testator, having declared to his trustees trusts in relation to a specified sum, afterwards in his will inserts a lesser sum, that lesser sum would not be caught by the trusts. In such a case the greater would I apprehend be held to include the less. In the present case neither of these two possible methods of dealing with the difficulty is available, because here we have something to which the rule of de minimis could not possibly apply, for it is an increase and a very substantial increase of the legacy originally bequeathed. There is no ground, in my opinion, which would justify the Court in treating the reference to that specific sum which passed between the testator and the trustees as having a significance of so loose and indeterminate a character that it could be expanded at will.'

Comment

The court will not infer acceptance of a variation of a secret trust from acceptance of the original trust.

Goodchild v *Goodchild* [1997] 3 All ER 63 Court of Appeal (Leggatt, Morritt and Phillips LJJ)

• *Nature of mutual wills*

Facts

In 1988 Dennis and Joan Goodchild executed identical wills. They wanted their son, Gary, to inherit their combined estates. On Joan's death, Dennis married Margot Alison Goodchild and made a new will in her favour. Dennis died four months later. Gary brought an action claiming that the 1988 wills were mutual wills, a contention which the judge at first instance rejected for lack of evidence but he made an award in Gary's favour under the Inheritance (Provision for Family & Dependants) Act 1975. These decisions were challenged in the Court of Appeal.

Held

For mutual wills to exist, there must be a contract and there was no evidence of an express or an implied contract here. Mutual wills rest on the irrevocability of the testators' intention and are binding from the date of the first death. By contrast, the rationale for secret trusts rests on an understanding between the testator and the secret trustee. Joan's understanding was that Gary would benefit from her estate and this imposed on Dennis a moral obligation to provide for Gary. On this basis both decisions of the lower court were upheld.

Leggatt J referred to the line of cases from *Dufour* v *Pereira* ending with *Gray* v *Perpetual Trustee Co Ltd* as approved by Morritt J in *Re Dale*. He referred to dicta of Viscount Haldane in *Gray* v *Perpetual Trustee Co Ltd* and continued, approving dicta of the judge at first instance in the instant case as follows:

'"… if a clear agreement can be found, in the wills or elsewhere, that they are to be mutually binding, whether or not that is expressed in language of revocation, the law will give effect to that intention by way of a 'floating trust' which becomes irrevocable following the death of the first testator and crystallises on the death of the second."

Two wills may be in the same form as each other. Each testator may leave his or her estate to the other with a view to the survivor leaving both estates to their heir. But there is no presumption that a present plan will be immutable in future. A key feature of the concept of mutual wills is the irrevocability of the mutual intentions. Not only must they be binding when made, but the testators must have undertaken, and so must be bound, not to change their intentions after the death of the first testator. The test must always be: suppose that during the lifetime of the surviving testator the intended beneficiary did something which the survivor regarded as unpardonable, would he or she be free not to leave the combined estate to him? The answer must be that the survivor is so entitled unless the testators agreed otherwise when they executed their wills. Hence the need for a clear agreement. Dennis and Joan executed wills in the same terms, save that each left his or her estate to the other. Thus, the survivor was to have both estates. They wanted Gary to inherit the combined estates. But there was no express agreement not to revoke the wills. Nor could any such agreement be implied from the fact that the survivor was in a position to leave both estates to Gary. The fact that each expected that the other would leave them to him is not sufficient to impress the arrangement with a floating trust, binding in equity. A mutual desire that Gary should inherit could not of itself prevent the survivor from resiling from the arrangement. What is required is a mutual intention that both wills should remain unaltered and that the survivor should be bound to leave the combined estates to the son. That is what is missing here. The judge found that Joan regarded the arrangement as irrevocable, but that Dennis did not. No mutual intention was proven that the survivor should be bound to leave the joint estate to Gary. That is what they meant to achieve. It could not happen unless they first left their respective estates to the survivor of

them. But the fact that each was able to leave the combined estate to Gary does not, without more, mean that both were bound to do so.'

Comment

In the absence of clear evidence of the necessary intention on the part of both testators, the Court was not prepared to apply the less stringent tests relating to secret trusts in order to establish that identical wills imposed the trust obligations of mutual wills.

Keen, Re [1937] Ch 236 Court of Appeal (Lord Wright MR, Greene and Romer LJJ)

- *Half-secret trust – communication*

Facts

By cl 5 of his will the testator gave £10,000 to his executors and trustees 'to be held on trust and disposed of by them among such person, persons or charities as may be notified by me to them or either of them during my lifetime'. Before making his will the testator handed one of the executors a sealed envelope containing the name of the intended beneficiary and directed her not to open the envelope until after the testator's death. She was not informed of the contents. On the testator's death the executors sought a declaration as to whether there was a valid secret trust or whether the £10,000 fell into residue because the secret trust was invalid. On appeal:

Held

As the sealed envelope was delivered before the date of the will, it was not a communication consistent with the terms of the will. Consequently there was no effective communication of the terms of the secret trust. Further, on the true construction of the will, the testator had reserved the power to make a future unattested disposition contrary to s9 Wills Act 1837.

Lord Wright MR:

'There are two main questions: first, how far parol evidence is admissible to define the trust under such a clause as this and secondly and in particular, how far such evidence if admissible at all would be excluded on the ground that it would be inconsistent with the true meaning of cl 5. ...

As in my judgment cl 5 should be considered as contemplating future dispositions and as reserving to the testator the power of making such dispositions without a duly attested codicil simply by notifying them during his lifetime, the principles laid down by Lord Sumner [in *McCormick* v *Grogan*] must be fatal to the appellant's claim. Indeed they would be equally fatal even on the construction for which Mr Roxburgh contended, that the clause covered both anterior or contemporaneous notifications as well as future notifications. The clause would be equally invalid, but ... I cannot accept that construction.

But there is still a further objection which in the present case renders the appellant's claim unenforceable; the trusts which it is sought to establish by parol evidence would be inconsistent with the express terms of the will. That such an objection is fatal appears from the cases already cited, such as *In re Huxtable*. In that case an undefined trust of money for charitable purposes was declared in the will as in respect of the whole corpus, and accordingly evidence was held inadmissible that the charitable trust was limited to the legatee's life so that he was free to dispose of the corpus after his death. ...

In the present case, while cl 5 refers solely to a future definition or to future definitions of the trust subsequent to the date of the will, the sealed letter relied on as notifying the trust was communicated (as I find the facts) before the date of the will. That it was communicated to one trustee only and not to both would not, I think, be an objection ... But the objection remains that the notification sought to be put in evidence was anterior to the will and hence not within the language of cl 5, and inadmissible simply on that ground as being inconsistent with what the will prescribes.

It is always with reluctance that a Court refuses to give effect to the proved intention of the testator. In the present case it may be said that the objection is merely a matter of drafting and that the decision in *Blackwell* v *Blackwell* would have been applicable if only cl 5 had been worded as applying to trusts previously indicated by the testator. The sealed letter would then have been admissible, subject to proof of the communication and acceptance of the trust. This may be true, but the Court must deal with the matter as in fact it is. It would be impossible to give effect to the appellant's contention without not merely extending the rule laid down in *Blackwell* v *Blackwell* but actually contravening the limitations which have been placed on that rule as necessarily arising from the Wills Act and, in addition, from the fact that the conditions prescribed by the will cannot be contradicted.'

Comment

For a secret trust to be valid the communication to the trustees must be consistent with the terms of the will and must be communicated to the trust so that the trustee is aware of the obligations imposed.

Ottaway v *Norman* [1972] Ch 698 Chancery Division (Brightman J)

• *Fully secret trust – acceptance by legatee*

Facts

By his will the testator devised his bungalow together with all the furniture, fixtures and fittings to his housekeeper, Mrs Hodges, apparently absolutely. He also gave her a legacy of £1,500 and half the residue. On the occasion of a visit to the testator's home from one of the testator's sons, the testator told his son, in the presence of Mrs Hodges, that it was his intention that Mrs Hodges should have the bungalow for the rest of her life but that she should leave it to him on her death. Mrs Hodges agreed to this. When the testator died, Mrs Hodges immediately made a will leaving the

bungalow to his son. However, in 1967 she
had a disagreement with the son and made a
new will leaving the bungalow to someone
else. On her death in 1968, the son sought a
declaration that the bungalow was held on
trust for him.

Held
There was a secret trust. Clear evidence
showed that the testator had communicated
the secret trust to Mrs Hodges and she had
accepted it.

Brightman J:

'It will be convenient to call the person on
whom such a trust is imposed the "primary
donee" and the beneficiary under the trust
the "secondary donee". The essential elements which must be proved to exist are, (1)
the intention of the testator to subject the
primary donee to an obligation in favour of
the secondary donee; (2) communication of
that intention by the primary donee; and (3)
the acceptance of that obligation by the
primary donee either expressly or by acquiescence. It is immaterial whether these elements precede or succeed the will of the
donor. I am informed that there is no recent
reported case where the obligation imposed
on a primary donee is an obligation to make
a will in favour of the secondary donee as
distinct from some form of inter vivos transfer. But it does not seem to me that that can
really be a distinction which can validly be
drawn on behalf of the defendant in the
present case. The basis of the doctrine of a
secret trust is the obligation imposed on the
conscience of the primary donee and it does
not seem to me that there is any materiality
in the machinery by which the donor intends
that that obligation shall be carried out ...'

Comment
The settlor can stipulate that the transfer of
property from the secret trustee to the beneficiary can be effected by will as an alternative
to a transfer inter vivos.

Pugh's Will Trusts, Re [1967] 1 WLR 1262 Chancery Division (Pennicuick J)

• *Half-secret trusts – disposition of residue*

Facts
By his will the testator appointed his solicitor
executor and trustee and after giving £1,500
legacies to each of his two brothers, he left the
residue to the solicitor 'to dispose of the same
in accordance with any letters or memoranda
I may leave with this my will and otherwise
in such manner as he may in his absolute discretion think fit'. The testator died in 1964
without leaving any letters or memoranda with
his will. The solicitor sought a declaration as
to whether he was entitled to take the residue
beneficially or whether he held it for the testator's next of kin.

Held
The direction to apply the residuary estate in
accordance with letters and memoranda
imposed a fiduciary obligation on the solicitor in the nature of a trust. As this trust had no
defined objects, it was void for uncertainty.

Pennycuick J:

'This direction clearly imposes upon the
trustee, at any rate, some degree of fiduciary
obligation, and it is impossible to construe
the gift as a simple and absolute gift to the
trustee. The nature of the fiduciary obligation is first to dispose of the residuary estate
in accordance with any letters or memoranda which the testator may leave with the
will and secondly otherwise – and that I
think means subject to any such letter or
memorandum – to dispose of the residuary
estate in such manner as the trustee may in
his absolute discretion think fit. I have so
far referred to the duty imposed upon the
trustee as a fiduciary obligation, but one
may as well use the word "trust" because
that fiduciary obligation is in the nature of
a trust. It is impossible to say that a direction
to dispose of the estate in accordance with

letters or memoranda does not constitute the trustee a trustee of the estate to the extent to which there are effective letters or memoranda left with the will. The construction of cl 6 then is, quite free from doubt.

It remains then to consider what, as a matter of law, is the effect of a provision in those terms. At first sight the second limb of the direction looks like a general power, but there is a long train of authority which is, I think, conclusive to the contrary. The effect of the authorities, to which I will refer in a moment, is that where one finds a gift upon trust to apply the subject matter in such manner or for such purposes, or whatever the words may be, as the donee may think fit, then that represents a trust for undefined objects such as the court cannot execute, and the trust is void, always of course in the absence of any further indication of intention ...'

Comment

A more recent application of the principles established in the older cases.

Rees, Re [1950] Ch 204 Court of Appeal (Sir Raymond Evershed MR, Cohen and Asquith LJJ)

• *Half secret trusts – residue*

Facts

By his will the testator appointed a friend and his solicitor to be executors and trustees thereof and devised and bequeathed the whole of his property to 'my trustees absolutely they well knowing my wishes concerning the same'. The testator told the executors and trustees at the time of making the will that he wished them to make certain payments out of the estate and retain the remainder for their own use. After the payments were made there was a substantial surplus. The executors contended that they were entitled to keep the surplus in that there was no secret trust but a gift to them conditional on making certain payments.

Held

That part of the estate which was not required to give effect to the testator's wishes was undisposed of by his will and passed on intestacy. The executors and trustees could not claim it because a fiduciary obligation had been imposed upon them.

Sir Raymond Evershed MR:

'That makes it necessary to consider the second question. As I have already indicated, I agree with the judge that to admit evidence to the effect that the testator informed one of the executors – or, I will assume in Mr Milner Holland's favour, both of the executors – that he intended them to take beneficial interests and that his wishes included that intention, would be to conflict with the terms of the will as I have construed them; for the inevitable result of admitting that evidence and giving effect to it would be that the will would be regarded not as conferring a trust estate only upon the two trustees, but as giving them a conditional gift which on construction is the thing which, if I am right, it does not do. Mr Milner Holland's answer is that, once the "wishes concerning the same", so far as they relate to third parties, are admitted, then there is no inconsistency, since this, after all, is part of the wishes. According to the evidence, I think that not entirely clear, but I assume it in Mr Milner Holland's favour. Still, as I think, that does not get over the difficulty. The admission of this evidence would involve that the trustees took not a trust estate but a conditional gift. The point was thus put by my brother Cohen during the argument: suppose the express wishes were contained in some document, and that the document stated that, subject to the satisfaction of these various gifts, the residue should belong to the two named persons absolutely: what would be the situation then? My first answer would be that that does not happen to be the fact in this case; but if it were so and such a document were referred to in the will, then it seems to me that prima facie that document would have to be included in the probate, and the ques-

tion then would have been one of the construction of the two documents, the will and
the memorandum together …

… The judge in the next sentence
expressed some regret at having come to a
conclusion which probably defeated the
wishes of the testator. I also am not insensi-
ble to that. At the same time my own regrets
are moderated to this extent: in the general
public interest it is not to be forgotten that
Parliament has laid it down that prima facie
a will disposing of the property of a
deceased person must follow certain strict
forms. These courts have also been very
insistent on the importance of the principle
that those who assume the office of trustees
should not, so far as they fairly can prevent
it, allow themselves to be in an position in
which their interests and their duties conflict. This is a case in which the will, as I
have said, was drawn by a solicitor, or by a
member of the solicitor's firm, and the claim
is that that solicitor is entitled, either absolutely or jointly with another, to the whole
beneficial interest. In the general public
interest it seems to me desirable that if a testator wishes his property to go to his solicitor and the solicitor prepares the will, that
intention on the part of the testator should
appear plainly on the will and should not be
arrived at by the more oblique method of
what is sometimes called a secret trust …'

Comment

Another application of the rule that the terms
of the secret trust must be in accordance with
the terms of the will. Note also the public
policy reasons for the decision.

Snowden (deceased), Re [1979] Ch 528 Chancery Division (Megarry V-C)

• *Fully secret trust – legal not moral obligation required – standard of proof*

Facts

A testatrix who could not decide how to divide
her residuary estate among her numerous
nephews and nieces instructed her solicitor to
draft a will leaving all her residue to her
brother. She told the solicitor that her brother
could then distribute the residue 'between her
nephews and nieces equally' and that her
brother 'could then see everybody and look
after the division for her'. Other evidence
showed that the testatrix wanted to be fair to
'everyone' and that her brother 'would know
what to do'. The brother agreed to deal with
everything for the testatrix. The testatrix died
six days after making the will, and the brother
died six days later, leaving all his estate to his
only son. The question arose whether a secret
trust was imposed on the brother.

Held

The standard of proof required to establish a
secret trust was the ordinary civil standard
required to establish an ordinary trust. The testatrix had clearly executed the will on the
basis of some arrangement between herself
and her brother. To see if this arrangement
was a secret trust it was necessary to show that
she intended the sanction of the court to
enforce the arrangement if the brother did not
carry it out. On the evidence there was no such
intention, there was only a moral obligation on
the brother and he accordingly took the
residue free from any trust.

Megarry V-C:

'I cannot say that there is no evidence from
which it could be informed that a secret trust
was created. At the same time, that evidence
is far from being overwhelming. One question that arises is thus whether the standard
of proof required to establish a secret trust is
merely the ordinary civil standard of proof,
or whether it is a higher and more cogent
standard. If it is the latter, I feel no doubt
that the claim that there is a secret trust must
fail. On this question, *Ottaway* v *Norman*
was cited; it was, indeed, the only authority
that was put before me. According to the
headnote, the standard of proof "was not an
exceptionally high one but was analogous to
that required before the court would rectify
a written instrument". When one turns to the

judgment, one finds that what Brightman J said was that Lord Westbury's words in *McCormick* v *Grogan*, a case on secret trusts, did not mean that an exceptionally high standard of proof was needed, but meant more that:

> "If a will contains a gift which is in terms absolute, clear evidence is needed before the court will assume that the testator did not mean what he said. It is perhaps analogous to the standard of proof which this requires before it will rectify a written document, for there again, a party is saying that neither meant what they have written."

On this, I would make four comments. First, the headnote seems to me to be liable to mislead, since it omits the judge's precautionary word "perhaps" which preceded the "analogous" and so gives a firmness to the proposition which the judge avoided.

Second, the standard for rectification is indeed high, and certainly higher than the ordinary standards ...

Third, I feel some doubt about how far rectification is a fair analogy to secret trusts in this respect. Many cases of rectification do, of course, involve a party in saying that neither meant what they have written and requiring that what they have written should be altered. On the other hand, the whole basis of secret trusts, as I understand it, is that they operate outside the will, changing nothing that is written in it, and allowing it to operate according to its tenor, but then fastening a trust on to the property in the hands of the recipient ...

Fourth, I am not sure that it is right to assume that there is a single uniform standard of proof for all secret trusts. The proposition of Lord Westbury in *McCormick* v *Grogan* with which Brightman J was pressed in *Ottaway* v *Norman* was that the jurisdiction in cases of secret trusts was:

> "... founded altogether on personal fraud. It is a jurisdiction by which a Court of Equity, proceeding on the ground of fraud, converts the party who has committed it into a trustee for the party who is injured by that fraud. Nor, being a juris-

diction founded on personal fraud, it is incumbent on the Court to see that a fraud, a malus animus, is proved by the clearest and most indisputable evidence."

Of that it is right to say that the law on the subject has not stood still since 1869, and that it is now clear that secret trusts may be established in cases where there is no possibility of fraud. *McCormick* v *Grogan* has to be read in the light of both earlier cases that were not cited, and also of subsequent cases, in particular, *Blackwell* v *Blackwell*. It seems to me that fraud comes into the matter in two ways. First, it provides an historical explanation of the doctrine of secret trusts: the doctrine was evolved as a means of preventing fraud. That, however, does not mean that fraud is an essential ingredient for the application of the doctrine, the reason for the rule is not part of the rule itself. Second, there are some cases within the doctrine where fraud is indeed involved. There are cases where for the legatee to assert that he is a beneficial owner, free from any trust, would be a fraud on his part.

It is to this latter aspect of fraud that it seems to me that Lord Westbury's words are applicable. If a secret trust can be held to exist in a particular case only by holding the legatee guilty of fraud, then no secret trust can be held to exist in a particular case only by holding the legatee guilty of fraud, then secret trust should be found unless the standard of proof suffices for fraud. On the other hand, if there is no question of fraud, why should so high a standard apply? In such a case, I find it difficult to see why the mere fact that the historical origin of the doctrine lay in the prevention of fraud should impose the high standard of proof for fraud in a case in which no issue of fraud arises. In accordance with the general rule of evidence, the standard of proof should vary with the nature of the issue and its gravity ...

I therefore hold that in order to establish a secret trust where no question of fraud arises, the standard of proof is the ordinary civil standard of proof that is required to establish an ordinary trust ... I cannot therefore dispose of the case summarily on the footing that a high standard of proof has plainly not been achieved, but I must consider the evidence in some detail to see whether the ordinary standard of proof has been satisfied. The initial question, of course, is whether the brother was bound by a secret trust, or whether he was subject to no more than a moral obligation.

In considering this, I have found considerable assistance in two passages in the judgment of the Court of Appeal in Ireland in *McCormick* v *Grogan* delivered by Christian LJ. Speaking of the testator in that case he said:

> "The real question is, what did he intend should be the *sanction*? Was it to be the authority of a Court of Justice, or the conscience of the devisee? In my opinion, expressly and exclusively the latter."

Then later he said that if we could look into the thoughts of the testator as they were when he was writing the will and the letter that he left with it –

> "I am persuaded that what we should find there would be a purpose to this effect – to set up after his decease, not an executor or trustee, but as it were a second self, whom, while he communicates to him confidentially his ideas as to the distribution of his property, he desires to invest with all his own irresponsibility in carrying them into effect.'"

Comment

This is a modern authority for the required standard of proof. A moral obligation does not give rise to sufficient certainty of intention.

5   Implied and Resulting Trusts

***Air Jamaica Ltd and Others v Joy
Charlton and Others*** [1999] 1 WLR
1399 Privy Council (Lords Steyn,
Hope of Craighead, Millett, Sir
Christopher Slade and Sir Andrew
Leggatt)

• *Surplus in pension fund – whether
powers void for perpetuity – whether
surplus was held for beneficiaries under a
resulting trust or went bona vacantia*

Facts
In 1994 the Jamaican government disposed of
its controlling interest in Air Jamaica, following which no further contributions were paid
by the employer into the company pension
trust fund. All but four employees of the
company were made redundant and purported
amendments were made to the pension trust
deed to discontinue the pension plan and to
release the surplus funds so that they could be
applied to purchase annuities for the ex-
employees and employees of the company and
to provide additional benefits for their widows
or designated beneficiaries. Subsequently the
remaining four employees were made redundant. A representative group of ex-employees
challenged these amendments on the ground
that they were void for perpetuity. The
Jamaican judge at first instance held that the
amendments were void for perpetuity and
ordered that the surplus should be paid bona
vacantia to the Crown. The Jamaican Court of
Appeal, by a majority, allowed the plaintiffs'
appeal and ordered that the pension fund
should be dealt with under the terms of the
original trust deed and that the Jamaican government should honour its undertaking to
replenish the pension fund, paying compound

interest on the sum to be repaid. The company,
the pension fund manager and the Attorney
General for Jamaica appealed to the Privy
Council.

Held
1. Pension schemes were subject to the
    common law rule against perpetuities. The
    pension plan was not void for perpetuity
    ab initio. Whenever a new employee
    joined the scheme, a new settlement was
    created of the contributions made in
    respect of that employee. Each employee
    was a life in being applicable to that par-
    ticular settlement. Since the benefits
    payable on death or retirement were fixed
    from the outset, the trusts were valid.
    However, the powers given to widows to
    designate a beneficiary and to change the
    identity of a beneficiary were void for per-
    petuity, as were other provisions under the
    original deed which might take effect
    outside the 21-year perpetuity period.
2. The plan validly conferred on the
    company liberty to discontinue the
    scheme, but the amendments were made
    after discontinuance of the scheme when
    contributions ceased and were invalid
    because they were in breach of the rule
    against perpetuity. Further, the company
    was obliged to exercise the power to
    amend in good faith and could not do so
    in order to confer an interest in the trust
    fund to the company (something which
    was in any event expressly prohibited by
    the trust deed).
3. The surplus in the trust fund did not revert
    bona vacantia to the Crown but was held
    on resulting trust. Under the resulting
    trust, which arose by operation of law
    outside the scheme:

53

a) the company was entitled to receive that part of the surplus which was attributable to its contributions; and

b) since the members had not received all they had bargained for under the plan, that part of the surplus which was attributable to their contributions should go pro rata to the members and to the deceased members in proportion to their contributions without regard to the value of the benefits they had received and the dates when their contributions had been made.

In accordance with its undertaking, the company must repay the sums taken from the pension fund together with compound interest. Compound interest was payable because the government had undertaken to replenish the fund 'to the full extent required'.

Lord Millett:

'*The effect of the rule against perpetuities*
The classic formulation of the rule is stated in *Gray on Perpetuities* 4th edn (1942) p191. Its effect is that no interest is valid unless it must vest, if it vests at all, within a period of a life in being at the date of the gift plus 21 years. The rule is applied remorselessly. A gift is defeated if by any possibility, however remote, it may vest outside the perpetuity period. It is not saved by the fact that, in the event, it vests inside the period. This can create many traps. One well known trap relates to "the unborn widow". A gift to A for life with remainder to his widow for life, where A is a life in being at the date of the settlement, is valid: the gift to the widow must vest, if it vests at all, on A's death. But A's widow cannot be ascertained until A's death. However old A may be, and however young his wife, in theory his wife may die and he may remarry a woman not yet born at the date of the settlement. His widow is not, therefore, a life in being, and she may survive A by more than 21 years. A gift which may not vest until her death is accordingly void for perpetuity.

The rule against perpetuities also applies to the administrative trusts and powers of the trustees. Such powers must not be capable of being exercised outside the perpetuity period, and they may be void even if all the trusts to which they are attached are valid. Where, therefore, there is a trust for A for life with remainder to his widow for life, and the trustees are given a power to sell or lease land comprised in the settlement, the power is void ab initio because it is capable of being exercised at any time during the widow's life, and she may survive A by more than 21 years: see *In re Allott: Hammer* v *Allott*. The same rule applies to a power to alter beneficial interests, such as a power of appointment. Such a power may, however, be saved if its objects are such that, even if it is expressed to be exercisable without limit of time, the power is in fact only capable of being exercised within the perpetuity period.

The original trust deed and pension plan contained no royal lives clause. The trusts of the scheme are therefore of unlimited and indefinite duration. It does not, however, follow that, as the judge held and the Attorney-General and the company both claimed, the whole of the trusts declared by the pension plan are void ab initio.

Their Lordships have considered the analysis of the effect of the rule against perpetuities on pension schemes made by the English Law Commission in its recent Report on the *Rules against Perpetuities and Excessive Accumulations* (1998) (Law Com No 251) at p38 para 3.53. They regard it as correct, at least in relation to a defined benefit scheme like the present. In their Lordships' view such a scheme can properly be regarded as comprising a series of separate settlements. Every time an employee joins the scheme, a new settlement is created. The settlement comprises the contributions made in respect of the employee whether by him or by the company. The rule against perpetuities must be applied separately to each individual settlement, and each employee must be treated as a life in being in relation to his own settlement. On this footing, any benefits, whether payable as a lump sum or by way of an annuity, which are payable on the death or earlier retirement of the employee are valid.

Their Lordships do not accept the appellants' submission that the analysis is inappropriate where the trust fund is a common fund to which all members have contributed. It would fail to save the trusts if it could be said that the contributions made by one member and which were not used to fund his own benefits could be made available to provide benefits to other members who were not lives in being at the date of his settlement. But the essential feature of a defined benefits pension scheme is that the benefits payable in respect of each member are fixed at the outset at an amount which is capable of being funded by the contributions payable in respect of the member without recourse to the contributions of any other member. Of course, in practice some members will receive more than they contribute and others will receive less; but this ought not to render the trusts void for perpetuity. The trust fund is only a security for the payment of benefits and a defined benefits scheme can be regarded for this purpose as a form of mutual insurance. Where each member's contributions are sufficient to fund his own pension by the purchase of an annuity from an insurance company, there is no perpetuity merely because they are in effect employed in the purchase of the pension from the trust fund. Regarded in this light, the pension payable to a member who takes out more than he puts in can be said to derive, not from the funds of settlements made by other members, but from the successful investment of his own settlement funds.

On this analysis, the only provisions of the pension plan which are struck down are the widow's power to designate a beneficiary to receive benefits ... and to change the identity of a designated beneficiary ... and the important trust contained in section 10.3(ii) of the original plan. This trust arises in the event of discontinuance and requires the trustees, after providing for all accrued benefits, to employ any surplus in providing additional benefits to members, their widows and designated beneficiaries. The trust cannot be saved by treating the pension plan as constituting a series of separate settlements made by each of the members. The trust is contingent on the discontinuance of the scheme, which may occur more than 21 years after the death of any particular member. This would not matter if the beneficiaries of the trust were confined to persons who were all lives in being at the date of the particular settlement. But it is a class gift in favour of members (which cannot be read distributively to confine it in each case to the member who made the settlement), their widows and dependants. These are not all lives in being at the date of any individual settlement. ...

The validity of the 1994 amendments
Their Lordships are satisfied that the 1994 amendments are incurably bad. There are several reasons for this. In the first place, as their Lordships have already explained, any power to amend the trusts is void for perpetuity. This does not mean that an amendment is wholly without effect. An employee who joins the plan after an amendment makes settlement upon the trusts of the plan as amended. But an amendment cannot affect existing members. The 1994 amendments, which were made after the plan had been closed to new members, were therefore without effect.

In the second place, and perpetuity apart, the company's power to amend the plan was subject to an obligation to exercise it in good faith: see *Imperial Group Pension Trust Ltd* v *Imperial Tobacco Ltd*. The company was not entitled simply to disregard or override the interests of the members. Once it became likely that the plan would be wound up, the company would have to take this fact into account, and it is difficult to see how the plan could lawfully be amended in any significant respect once it had actually been discontinued. But even if it could, their Lordships are satisfied that it could not be amended in order to confer any interest in the trust fund on the company. This was expressly prohibited by Clause 4 of the trust deed. The 1994 amendment included a purported amendment to the trust deed to remove this limitation, but this was plainly invalid. The trustees could not achieve by two steps what they could not achieve by one.

Destination of the surplus

Prima facie, the surplus is held on a resulting trust for those who provided it. This sometimes creates a problem of some perplexity. In the present case, however, it does not. Contributions were payable by the members with matching contributions by the company. In the absence of any evidence that this is not what happened in practice, the surplus must be treated as provided as to one half by the company and to one half by the members.

The Attorney-General contended that neither the company nor the members can take any part in the surplus, which has reverted to the Crown as bona vacantia. He argued that clause 4 of the trust deed precludes any claim by the company, while the members cannot claim any part of the surplus because they have received all that they are entitled to. There is authority for both propositions. Their Lordships consider that they can be supported neither in principle nor as a matter of construction.

In *In re ABC Television Ltd Pension Scheme*, Foster J held that a clause similar to clause 4 of the present trust deed "negatives the possibility of implying a resulting trust." This is wrong in principle. Like a constructive trust, a resulting trust arises by operation of law, though unlike a constructive trust it gives effect to intention. But it arises whether or not the transferor intended to retain a beneficial interest – he almost always does not – since it responds to the absence of any intention on his part to pass a beneficial interest to the recipient. It may arise even where the transferor positively wishes to part with the beneficial interest, as in *Vandervell* v *Inland Revenue Commissioners*. In that case the retention of a beneficial interest by the transferor destroyed the effectiveness of a tax avoidance scheme which the transferor was seeking to implement. The House of Lords affirmed the principle that a resulting trust is not defeated by

evidence that the transferor intended to part with the beneficial interest if he has not in fact succeeded in doing so. As Plowman J had said in the same case at first instance:

> "As I see it, a man does not cease to own property simply by saying 'I don't want it'. If he tries to give it away, the question must always be has he succeeded in doing so or not."

Lord Upjohn ([1967] AC 291) expressly approved this.

Consequently their Lordships think that clauses of this kind in a pension scheme should generally be construed as forbidding the repayment of contributions under the terms of the scheme, and not as a pre-emptive but misguided attempt to rebut a resulting trust which would arise dehors the scheme. The purpose of such clauses is to preclude any amendment that would allow repayment to the company. Their Lordships thus construe clause 4 of the trust deed as invalidating the 1994 amendments but not as preventing the company from retaining a beneficial interest by way of a resulting trust in so much of the surplus as is attributable to its contributions.

The members' contributions stand on a similar footing. In *Davis* v *Richards & Wallington Industries Ltd* ... Scott J held that the fact that a party has received all that he bargained for is not necessarily a decisive argument against a resulting trust but that in the circumstances of the case before him a resulting trust in favour of the employees was excluded. The circumstances that impressed him were two-fold. He considered that it was impossible to arrive at a workable scheme for apportioning the employees' surplus among the different classes of employees and he declined ... to "impute to them an intention that would lead to an unworkable result." He also considered that he was precluded by statute from "imputing to the employees an intention" that they should receive by means of a resulting trust sums in excess of the maximum permitted by the relevant tax legislation.

These formulations also adopt the

approach to intention that their Lordships have already considered to be erroneous. Their Lordships would observe that, even in the ordinary case of an actuarial surplus, it is not obvious that, when employees are promised certain benefits under a scheme to which they have contributed more than was necessary to fund them, they should not expect to obtain a return of their excess contributions. In the present case, however, the surplus does not arise from overfunding but from the failure of some of the trusts. It is impossible to say that the members "have received all that they bargained for." One of the benefits they bargained for was that the trustees should be obliged to pay them additional benefits in the event of the scheme's discontinuance. It was the invalidity of this trust that gave rise to the surplus. Their Lordships consider that it would be more accurate to say that the members claim such part of the surplus as is attributable to their contributions because they have not received all that they bargain for.

Pension schemes in Jamaica, as in England, need the approval of the Inland Revenue if they are to secure the fiscal advantages that are made available. The tax legislation in both countries places a limit on the amount which can be paid to the individual employee. Allowing the employees to enjoy any part of the surplus by way of resulting trust would probably exceed those limits. This fact is not, however in their Lordships' view a proper ground on which to reject the operation of a resulting trust in favour of the employees. The Inland Revenue had an opportunity to examine the pension plan and to withhold approval on the ground that some of its provisions were void for perpetuity. They failed to so do. There is no call to distort principle in order to meet their requirements. The resulting trust arises by operation of the general law, dehors the pension scheme and the scope of the relevant tax legislation.

Scott J was impressed by the difficulty of arriving at a workable scheme for apportioning the surplus funds among the members and the executors of deceased members. This was because he thought it necessary to value the benefits that each member had received in order to ascertain his share in the surplus. On the separate settlement with mutual insurance analysis which their Lordships have adopted in the present case, however, no such process is required. The members' share of the surplus should be divided pro rata among the members and the estates of the deceased members in proportion to the contributions made by each member without regard to the benefits each has received and irrespective of the dates on which the contributions were made.'

Comment

1. Lord Millett gave a very clear analysis of the common law rule against perpetuity.

2. He approved the principle in the *Imperial Tobacco* case that trustees can only use their powers for the benefit of the beneficiaries (in this case the employees and other beneficiaries of the pension fund).

3. He reviewed Scott J's ruling in *Davis* v *Richards & Wallington Industries* that the surplus related to the employees' contributions should go bona vacantia to the Crown and used the principle 'equality is equity' to resolve the difficulty of ascertaining how much each beneficiary can claim.

Barclays Bank v *Quistclose Investments Ltd* [1970] AC 567
House of Lords (Lords Reid, Morris, Guest, Pearce and Wilberforce)

• *Resulting trust on the failure of a purpose for which money was lent*

Facts

During the closing stages of Rolls Razor Limited's collapse, Quistclose lent money to the company expressly and solely for the purpose of paying a dividend on the company's shares. Before that could be done the company went into liquidation. The money had been paid into an account at the company's bank.

Held

The money having been lent for a primary purpose which had failed, was then held on a secondary trust for the lender. The bank had notice of the purpose and could not use the money to reduce the company's overdraft.

Lord Wilberforce:

'Two questions arise, both of which must be answered favourably to the respondents if they are to recover the money from the appellants. The first is whether, as between the respondents and Rolls Razor Ltd, the terms on which the loan was made were such as to impress on the sum of £209,719 8s 6d a trust in their favour in the event of the dividend not being paid. The second is whether, in that event, the appellants had such notice of the trust or of the circumstances giving rise to it as to make the trust binding on them.

It is not difficult to establish precisely on what terms the money was advanced by the respondents to Rolls Razor Ltd. There is no doubt that the loan was made specifically in order to enable Rolls Razor Ltd to pay the dividend. There is equally, in my opinion, no doubt that the loan was made only so as to enable Rolls Razor Ltd to pay the dividend and for no other purpose. This follows quite clearly from the terms of the letter of Rolls Razor Ltd to the appellants of July 15, 1964, which letter, before transmission to the appellants, was sent to the respondents under open cover in order that the cheque might be (as it was) enclosed in it. The mutual intention of the respondents and of Rolls Razor Ltd and the essence of the bargain, was that the sum advanced should not become part of the assets of Rolls Razor Ltd but should be used exclusively for payment of a particular class of its creditors, namely those entitled to the dividend. A necessary consequence from this, by process simply of interpretation, must be that if, for any reason, the dividend could not be paid, the money was to be returned to the respondents; the word "only" or "exclusively" can have no other meaning or effect.

That arrangements of this character for the payment of a person's creditors by a third person, give rise to a relationship of a fiduciary character or trust, in favour, as a primary trust, of the creditors, and secondarily, if the primary trust fails, of the third person, has been recognised in a series of cases over some 150 years.

Lord Wilberforce reviewed the cases and continued:

'These cases have the support of longevity, authority, consistency and, I would add, good sense. But they are not binding on your lordships and it is necessary to consider such arguments as have been put why they should be departed from or distinguished.

It is said, first, that the line of authorities … stands on its own and is inconsistent with other, more modern, decisions. These are cases in which money had been paid to a company for the purpose of obtaining an allotment of shares … I do not think it necessary to examine these cases in detail, nor to comment on them, for I am satisfied that they do not affect the principle on which this appeal should be decided. They are merely examples which show that, in the absence of some special arrangement creating a trust … payments of this kind are made on the basis that they are to be included in the company's assets. They do not negative the proposition that a trust may exist where the mutual intention is that they should not be included.

The second, and main, argument for the appellants was of a more sophisticated character. The transaction, it was said, between the respondents and Rolls Razor Ltd was one of loan giving rise to a legal action of debt. This necessarily excluded the implication of any trust, enforceable in equity, in the respondents' favour: a transaction may attract one action or the other, it could not admit of both.

My lords, I must say that I find this argument unattractive. Let us see what it involves. It means that the law does not permit an arrangement to be made by which one person agrees to advance money to another, on terms that the money is to be used exclusively to pay debts of the latter, and if, and so far as not so used, rather than becoming a general asset of the latter available to his creditors at large, is to be returned to the lender. The lender is obliged, in such a case, because he is a lender, to accept, whatever the mutual wishes of lender and borrower may be, that the money he was willing to make available for one purpose only shall be freely available for others of the borrower's creditors for whom he has not the slightest desire to provide.

I should be surprised if an argument of this kind- so conceptualist in character – had ever been accepted. In truth it has plainly been rejected by the eminent judges who from 1819 onwards have permitted arrangements of this type to be enforced, and have approved them as being for the benefit of creditors and all concerned. There is surely no difficulty in recognising the co-existence in one transaction of legal and equitable rights and remedies: when the money is advanced, the lender acquires an equitable right to see that it is applied for the primary designated purpose:... When the purpose has been carried out (ie the debt paid) the lender has his remedy against the borrower in debt: if the primary purpose cannot be carried out, the question arises if a secondary purpose (ie repayment to the lender) has been agreed, expressly or by implication: if it has, the remedies of equity may be invoked to give effect to it, if it has not (and the money is intended to fall within the general fund of the debtor's assets) then there is the appropriate remedy for recovery of a loan. I can appreciate no reason why the flexible interplay of law and equity cannot let in these practical arrangements, and other variations if desired: it would be to the discredit of both systems if they could not. In the present case the intention to create a secondary trust for the benefit of the lenders, to arise if the primary trust, to pay the dividend, could not be carried out, is clear and I can find no reason why the law should not give effect to it.'

Comment
Goodhart and Jones ((1980) 4 MLR 489)

comment that this is 'a just and commendable decision. No creditor has been misled into making a further loan by the existence of the separate dividend account; and there was no doubt that the bank knew of the agreement between the parties.' Moffatt (*Trusts Law: Text & Materials* 2nd edn 1994) asks whether *Barclays Bank* v *Quistclose Investments Ltd* and *Carreras Rothmans Ltd* v *Freeman Matthews Treasure Ltd* (below) are examples of a 'new model constructive trust'.

Bull v *Bull* [1955] 1 QB 234 Court of Appeal (Denning, Hodson and Parker LJJ)

• *Co-owners who have contributed unequal shares – tenancy in common and trust for sale*

Facts
In 1949 the plaintiff and his mother, the defendant, together purchased a freehold house, the plaintiff contributing a larger part of the purchase price than the defendant. The conveyance was taken in his name alone. The money contributed by the defendant was not intended to be a gift from her to the plaintiff and the defendant accordingly became entitled to an equitable interest proportionate to her contribution – there was a resulting trust in favour of the defendant. They lived together in the house until April 1953, when the plaintiff married, and it was arranged that the defendant should occupy two rooms and that the plaintiff and his wife should occupy the rest of the house. Differences arose between the parties and the plaintiff brought this action for possession of the rooms occupied by the defendant.

Held
The effect of the purchase of the house in 1949 was that the plaintiff and defendant became beneficial tenants in common of the proceeds of sale of the property which was subjected to a statutory trust for sale. The

defendant had an equitable interest which entitled her to remain in the house as tenant in common with the plaintiff until the house was sold. If they disagreed, the house should be sold and the proceeds divided between them in the proper proportions. The plaintiff could not turn the defendant out at will and his action for possession failed.

Denning LJ:

'The son is, of course, the legal owner of the house, but the mother and son are, I think, equitable tenants in common. Each is entitled in equity to an undivided share in the house, the share of each being in proportion to his or her respective contribution ... Each of them is entitled to possession of the land and to the use and enjoyment of it in a proper manner. Neither can turn out the other; but if one of them should take more than his proper share, the injured party can bring an action for account. If one of them should go so far as to oust the other, he is guilty of trespass ...

... I realise that since 1925 there has been no such thing as a legal tenancy in common. All tenancies in common now are equitable only and they take effect behind a trust for sale ... Nevertheless, until a sale takes place, these equitable tenants in common have the same right to enjoy the land as legal tenants used to have ...

My conclusion therefore, is that when there are two equitable tenants in common, then, until the place is sold, each of them is entitled concurrently with the other to the possession of the land and to the use and enjoyment of it in a proper manner: and that neither of them is entitled to turn out the other.

The question may be asked: "What is to happen when the two fall out, as they have done here?" The answer is that the house must then be sold and the proceeds divided between mother and son in the proper proportions. The son is legal owner and he holds it on the statutory trust for sale. He cannot, at the present moment, sell the house because he cannot give a valid receipt for the proceeds. It needs two trustees to give a receipt. The son could get over this difficulty by appointing another trustee who would agree with him to sell the house. The two trustees would no doubt have to consider the mother's wishes, but as the son appears to have made the greater contribution, he could in theory override her wishes about a sale (Law of Property Act 1925 s26(3)). The difficulty of the two trustees would be a practical difficulty because so long as the mother is there, they could not sell with vacant possession.

... The mother here is in possession and in actual occupation as equitable co-owner and, by virtue of that interest, she could not be turned out by the trustees except with her consent. In this situation, if the trustees wished to sell with vacant possession, the only thing they could do would be to apply to the court under s30 of the Law of Property Act 1925 on the ground that the mother's consent could not be obtained. The court could then make such order as it thought fit and this would include, I think, an order to turn the mother out if it was right and proper for such an order to be made.'

Comment

Lord Denning recognised, however, that the mother's share in the property under the resulting trust would be too small to enable her to defeat an application by two trustees for the sale of the property under s30 of the Law of Property Act 1925 (now re-enacted as s14 of the Trusts of Land and Appointment of Trustees Act 1996).

Burns v *Burns* [1984] Ch 317 Court of Appeal (Waller, Fox and May LJJ)

• *Beneficial interests in property jointly acquired or occupied*

Facts

The plaintiff who was known as Mrs Burns, left home in 1961 and began to live with the defendant when aged 20. She then had a job as a tailor earning £12 per week. This relationship lasted 19 years and the parties were never

married. Initially they lived in rented accommodation and the plaintiff gave birth to a child
in 1962. In 1963 the parties moved to a house
which the defendant purchased in his sole
name for £4,900. The plaintiff had another
child in 1963. Up until 1975 the plaintiff did
not earn, as she had to stay at home to look
after the children. When she did earn she made
no distinction between her own earnings and
the housekeeping money which the defendant
gave her. She used this for fixtures and fittings
for the house, decorations, electrical goods
and furniture. When the plaintiff was forced to
leave the house in 1980 after her relationship
with the defendant broke down, she brought
proceedings, claiming that she was entitled to
a beneficial interest in the house by reason of
her contributions to the household over the 19-
year relationship. At first instance Dillon J
held that the plaintiff was not entitled to any
beneficial interest in the house. The plaintiff
appealed.

Held
The plaintiff's appeal was dismissed. The
powers conferred by the Matrimonial Causes
Act 1973 in relation to the division of property
of married couples on divorce did not apply
to unmarried couples so the court had no
power to make an order on the basis of what
was fair and reasonable. There was no evidence that the plaintiff had made any contribution direct or indirect to the purchase of the
house. Further, there was nothing to impute a
common intention to the parties down to the
date of separation that the plaintiff should
have a beneficial interest in the property, and
the Court would not infer such an intention
from the fact that the relationship had lasted
19 years.

May LJ:

'I think that the approach which the courts
should follow, be the couples married or
unmarried, is now clear. What is difficult
however, is to apply it to the facts and circumstances of any given case. Where the
family home is taken in the joint names,
then unless the facts are very unusual, I

think that both the man and the woman are
entitled to a share in the beneficial interest.
Where the house is bought outright and not
on mortgage, then the extent of their respective shares will depend on a more or less
arithmetical calculation of the extend of
their contributions to the purchase price.
Where, on the other hand, as is more usual
nowadays, the house is bought with the aid
of a mortgage, then the court is only entitled to look at the financial contributions,
or their real or substantial equivalent, to the
acquisition of the house; that the husband
may spend his weekends redecorating or
laying a patio is neither here nor there, nor is
the fact that the woman has spent so much
of her time looking after the house, doing
the cooking and bringing up the family.

The inquiry becomes even more difficult
when the home is taken in only one of the
two names. For the present purpose I will
assume that it is the man, although the same
approach will be followed if it is taken in
the name of the woman. Where a matrimonial or family home is bought in the man's
name alone on mortgage by the mechanism
of deposit and instalments, then if the
woman pays or contributes to the initial
deposit this points to a common intention
that she should have some beneficial interest
in the house. If thereafter she makes direct
contributions to the instalments, then the
case is a fortiori and her rightful share is
likely to be greater. If the woman, having
contributed to the deposit, but although not
making direct contributions to the instalments, nevertheless uses her own money for
other joint household expenses so as to
enable the man the more easily to pay the
mortgage instalments out of his money, then
her position is the same. Where a woman
has made no contribution to the initial
deposit, but makes regular and substantial
contributions to the mortgage instalments,
it may still be reasonable to infer a common
intention that she should share the beneficial
interest from the outset, or infer a fresh
agreement after the original conveyance that
she should acquire such a share. It is only
when there is no evidence on which a court
can reasonably draw an inference about the

extent of the share of the contributing woman that it should fall back on the maximum "equity is equality". Finally, when the house is taken in the man's name alone, if the woman makes no "real" or "substantial" financial contribution towards either the purchase price, deposit or mortgage instalments by means of which the family home was acquired, then she is not entitled to any share in the beneficial interest in that home even though over a very substantial number of years she may have worked just as hard as the man in maintaining the family, in the sense of keeping house, giving birth to and looking after and helping to bring up the children of the union.'

Comment

Nothing less than a direct contribution to the purchase price of the property, by cash contribution or contribution to the mortgage repayments, will establish a beneficial interest in the property.

Carreras Rothmans Ltd v *Freeman Matthews Treasure Ltd* [1984] 3 WLR 1016 Chancery Division (Peter Gibson J)

• Quistclose *trust – resulting or constructive trust*

Facts

Carreras Rothmans Ltd (CR), a cigarette manufacturer, used Freeman Matthews Treasure (FMT), an advertising agency, to do their advertising work. CR paid FMT on a monthly basis and the fee paid by CR to FMT was for FMT's services as well as the costs involved in placing advertisements in the media. In 1983 FMT got into financial difficulties and CR feared that the collapse of FMT could do considerable damage to its business. Consequently, CR made special arrangements with FMT for payment of FMT's monthly invoices. A special bank account was opened into which CR would pay a sum every month

which FMT was to use solely for settling its fees due from CR and the monies owed to media creditors for CR advertising. On 26 July 1983 CR paid £597,128.00 into the special bank account but on 3 August 1983 FMT went into liquidation. The liquidator of FMT would not pay any money out of the special bank account. CR claimed that the money in the account was held on trust for the sole purpose of paying FMT's fees and monies owed to media creditors and sought a declaration accordingly.

Held

Applying *Barclays Bank* v *Quistclose Investments Ltd*, the money in the special bank account was held upon trust.

Peter Gibson J:

'Mr Millett contended that the language of the contract letter was apt to create a trust and that such trust was fully constituted as to the *moneys* in the special account when FMT agreed to the terms of the contract letter and received the moneys from CR. He relied on the line of cases of which *Barclays Bank Ltd* v *Quistclose Ltd* is the highest authority...

... CR was concerned about the adverse effect on it if FMT, which CR knew to have financial problems, ceased trading and third party creditors of FMT were not paid at a time when FMT had been put in funds by CR ... For this purpose a special account was to be set up with a special designation. The moneys payable by CR were to be paid not to FMT beneficially but directly into that account so that FMT was never free to deal as it pleased with the moneys so paid. The moneys were to be used only for the specific purpose of paying third parties and, as the cheque letter indicated, the amount paid matched the specific invoices presented by FMT to CR. The account was intended to be little more than a conduit pipe, but the intention was plain that whilst in the conduit pipe the moneys should be protected. There was even a provision covering the possibility that there might be a balance left after payment and in that event the balance was to be paid to CR and not kept by FMT. It was thus clearly intended that the moneys once paid would never become the property of FMT. That was the last thing CR wanted in view of its concern about FMT's financial position …

… There is, of course ample authority that moneys paid by A to B for a specific purpose which has been made known to B are clothed with a trust. In the *Quistclose* case Lord Wilberforce referred to the recognition, in a series of cases over some 150 years, that arrangements for the payment of a person's creditors by a third person gives rise to a "relationship of a fiduciary character or trust, in favour, as a primary trust, of the creditors, and secondarily, if the primary trust fails, of the third person". Lord Wilberforce, in describing the facts of the *Quistclose* case said a little earlier that the mutual intention of the provider of the moneys and the recipient of the moneys, and the essence of the bargain, was that the moneys should not become part of the assets of the recipient but should be used exclusively for payment of a particular class of its creditors. That description seems to me to be apt in relation to the facts of the present case too …'

Comment
The outcome of the case, however, was that money in the special bank account was awarded to the liquidator. FMT had dealt with the money in accordance with the terms of their contract with CR.

Davis v *Richards and Wallington Industries* [1990] 1 WLR 1511
Chancery Division (Scott J)

• *Whether surplus in pension fund is held on resulting trust for the contributors*

Facts
In 1975 a group of companies set up a pension scheme which replaced an earlier scheme established in 1968. The pension scheme operated under a trust. The fund came from three sources: funds transferred from the earlier scheme; employers' contributions; and employees' contributions. In 1982, having got into financial difficulties, the scheme was terminated. The question was whether the surplus funds of some £3 million were held on resulting trust for the contributors or went bona vacantia to the Crown.

Held
The employers' contributions were held for them on resulting trust. The employees' contributions went bona vacantia to the Crown.

Scott J:

'I am satisfied that it is possible for a disposition of property to be made on terms which make it plain that the transferor affirmatively desires to exclude all possibility of a resulting trust in his favour. The presumption of law is against this and such an expression needs to be clear and unambiguous, more especially as the likely result is that the property concerned, if there is such a failure as would normally give rise to a resulting trust, will pass as bona vacantia and that is a result which should not lightly be imputed to any transferor.

The provision in a trust deed necessary to exclude a resulting trust need not, in my opinion, be express. In the absence of any express provision, it would, I think, often be very difficult for a sufficiently clear intention to exclude a resulting trust to be established. But, in general, any term that can be expressed can also, in suitable circumstances, be implied. If the intention of a contributor that a resulting trust should not apply is the proper conclusion, it would not be right, in my opinion, for the law to contradict that intention. In my judgment, therefore, the fact that a payment to a fund has been made under contract and that the payer has obtained all that he or she bargained for under the contract is not necessarily a decisive argument against resulting trust.

I must apply these principles to the surplus in the present case. The fund was, as I have said, fed from three sources: employees' contributions, transfers from other pension schemes and employers' contributions. The employees' contributions were made under contract. Employees were obliged to contribute 5 per cent of salary. They were entitled, in return, to the specified pension and other benefits. The funds from other pension schemes, too, were transferred under contract. There would have been three parties to all these contracts, namely, the trustees of the transferor scheme, the trustees of the 1975 scheme and the transferring members themselves. Perhaps the employer company would have been a party as well. The transfer would certainly have been made with its consent. Under these contracts, by implication if not expressly, the transferor trustees would have been discharged from liability in respect of the transferred funds, whether liability to the transferring employee members or liability to the employer company.

Finally, there are the employers. They, too, made their contributions under contract; they made them under the contracts of employment between themselves and their employees. But there is a very important difference between the contractual obligation of the employees and that of the employers. The employees' contractual obligation was specific in amount – 5 per cent of salary. The employers' contractual obligation was conceptually certain but the amount was inherently uncertain. The obligation was to pay whatever was necessary to fund the scheme. The terms of rule 3 of Part II of the 1975 rules describe accurately, in my opinion, the contractual obligation of the employers:

> "The employer will pay to the trustees such amounts as may from time to time be necessary to enable the trustees to maintain the benefits ..."

In practice, the amount of the employers' contributions in respect of each employee was actuarially calculated. The calculations were based on assumptions as to the time when the benefits would become payable and as to the amount of the employee's final salary at that time. If the scheme should terminate before that time, the amount paid would be bound to have been more than needed to have been paid in order to fund the employee's benefits as at the date of termination.

Two separate questions seem to me to require to be answered. First, to what extent should the surplus, the £3 million odd, be regarded as derived from each of these three sources? One possible answer is that there should be a calculation of the total amount of employees' contributions, the total amount of funds transferred from other companies' pension schemes and the total amount of employers' contributions, and that the surplus should be regarded as derived from these three sources in the same proportions as the three totals bear to one another. I do not accept that this is right. It ignores the different bases on which these contributions were paid. Since the employers' obligation was to pay whatever was from time to time necessary to fund the various scheme benefits and since the employees' 5 per cent contributions and the amount of the transferred funds constituted the base from which the amount of the employers' contributions would from time to time have to be assessed, it is logical, in my judgment, to treat the scheme benefits as funded first by the employees' contributions and the transferred funds, and only secondarily by the employers' contributions, and, correspondingly, to treat the surplus as provided first by the employers' contributions, and only secondarily by the employees' contributions and the transferred funds.

There are two possible factual situations to be considered. It is possible (although, I think, very unlikely) that the employees' contributions and the funds transferred from the pension schemes of other companies would, without there having been any contribution at all from the employers, have been sufficient to provide in full for all the scheme benefits and, perhaps, still to have left some surplus. If that is the position, it would follow that, with the advantage of hindsight, the employers need not have made any contribution at all in order to have funded the benefits. This situation would, in my judgment, require that that surplus (which would be bound, I think, to be very small) should be regarded as derived from the employees' contributions and the transferred funds and that the balance of the surplus should be regarded as derived from the employers' contributions.

The much more likely situation is that some contribution at least was required from the employers in order to produce assets sufficient to provide all the scheme benefits to which employees became entitled on 31 July 1982. In that event the whole of the surplus, in my judgment, should be regarded as derived from the employers' contributions. This conclusion is, to my mind, in accordance both with logic and with equity. The actuarial calculations on which the employers' actual contributions were based were themselves based upon a series of assumptions. The termination of the scheme invalidated the assumptions. The employers had, in the event, made payments exceeding the amount necessary to discharge their obligation to fund the benefits to which the employees eventually became entitled. There is a well established equity that enables accounts drawn up under a mistake to be reopened ... In cases such as the present, there was no mistake at the time the contributions were assessed and paid. The actuarial calculations were, I am sure impeccable. But subsequent events having invalidated some of the assumptions underlying the calculations, the case is, in my opinion, strongly analogous to that of an account drawn up under a mistake. In my opinion, equity should treat the employers as entitled to claim the surplus, or so much of it as derived from the overpayments.

The second question is whether a resulting trust applies to the surplus, or to so much of the surplus as was derived from each of the three sources to which I have referred. As to the surplus, derived from the employers' contributions, I can see no basis on which the resulting trust can be excluded. The equity to which I referred in the previous paragraph demands, in my judgment, the conclusion that the trustees hold the surplus derived from the employers' contributions, on trust for the employers. There is no express provision excluding a resulting trust and no circumstances from which, in my opinion, an implication to that effect could be drawn. On the other hand, in my judgment, the circumstances of the case seem to me to point firmly and clearly to the conclusion that a resulting trust in favour of the employees is excluded.

The circumstances are these:

(1) Each employee is paid his or her contributions in return for specific financial benefits from the fund. The value of these benefits would be different for each employee, depending on how long he had served, how old he was when he joined and how old he was when he left. Two employees might have paid identical sums in contributions but have become entitled to benefits of a very different value. The point is particularly striking in respect of the employees (and there were several of them) who exercised their option to a refund of contributions. How can a resulting trust work as between the various employees inter se? I do not think it can and I do not see why equity should impute to them an intention that would lead to an unworkable result.

(2) The scheme was established to take advantage of the legislation relevant to an exempt approved scheme and a contracted out scheme. The legislative requirements placed a maximum on the financial return from the fund to which each employee would become entitled. The proposed rules would have preserved the statutory requirements. A resulting trust cannot do so. In my judgment, the relevant legislative requirements prevent imputing to the employees an intention that the surplus of the fund derived from their contributions should be returned to them under a resulting trust. In my judgment, therefore, there is no resulting trust for the employees.

Finally, there are the transferred funds. The intention, in my judgment, appears sufficiently clear from the documents by which the transfers were effected and from the surrounding circumstances that the trustees of the transferred schemes were divesting themselves once and for all of the transferred funds. So far as the employee members of the transfer schemes were concerned, there could not, for the same reasons as those I have already given, be a resulting trust in favour of them. So far as the employer contributors to those funds were concerned, ie the companies whose shares had been taken over, they were not all in the same position vis-à-vis the transferred funds. Some of the transferor schemes expressly excluded any refund of assets to the employer contributors. Those employers could not, therefore, assert any resulting trust. As to the others, it is possible to regard the transferred funds as being subject to some contingent resulting trust. As to the others, it is possible to regard the transferred funds as being subject to some contingent resulting trust of surplus in favour of employer contributors. But, as I understand the evidence, it would be virtually impossible now to identify the part of the £3 million odd surplus that represented the surplus (if there was one) inherent in any of the transferred funds. In my judgment, it is reasonable in the circumstances to regard the employer contributors to the transferred funds, as well as the employee contributors, as intending that the funds should vest in the 1975 scheme trustees to the entire exclusion of any claim under the transferor scheme, whether under the rules thereof or by way of resulting trust. Here again, I do not think equity should impute to the parties an impracticable and unworkable intention.

Accordingly, in my judgment, if any part of the surplus has derived from employees' contributions or from the funds transferred from the pension schemes of other companies, that part of the surplus devolves as bona vacantia. Subject thereto, the surplus is, in my judgment, held upon trust for the employer contributors.'

Comment

The nature of occupational pension schemes is both contract and trust based. Under the terms of the contract between employer and employee any surplus in the fund usually accrues to the employer since the contract provides that the employee receives a percentage of final salary and the employer's obligation is merely to ensure that the pension fund is big enough to meet this liability.

GKN Bolts & Nuts Ltd (Automotive Division), Birmingham Works Sports and Social Club , Re, Leek v Donkersley [1982] 1 WLR 774 Chancery Division (Sir Robert Megarry V-C)

* *Dissolution of unincorporated association*

Facts
GKN's Sports and Social Club had ceased to function – the facilities were unused, no new membership cards were issued and the bar stock had been sold off. The last AGM was held in February 1975 and no accounts were kept after that date. The club ceased to be registered for VAT. On 18 December 1975 it was agreed by the members that the land should be sold but the sale fell through. The sports ground was eventually sold in 1978. The court had to decide whether the club had ceased to exist and if so, from what date were the assets distributable to the members.

Held
1. The club ceased to exist on 18 December 1975, the date of the resolution to sell the sports ground.
2. Distribution of the assets would be on the basis of equality between the members.

Sir Robert Megarry V-C:

'The starting point is to consider whether there was a dissolution of the club on 18 December 1975, the date of the resolution to sell. The rules of the club do not help, for they are all directed to the operation of the club as a going concern. It is plain that there never was an agreement by the entire membership that the club should be dissolved, and of course, there has been no exercise by the court of its inherent jurisdiction to order a dissolution. The question therefore is whether there has been what was called in argument a spontaneous dissolution of the club.

As a matter of principle I would hold that it is perfectly possible for a club to be dissolved spontaneously. I do not think that mere inactivity is enough: a club may do little or nothing for a long period, and yet continue in existence. A cataleptic trance may look like death without being death. But inactivity may be so prolonged or so circumstanced that the only reasonable inference is that the club has become dissolved.

In such cases there may be difficulty in determining the punctum temporis of dissolution: the less activity there is, the greater the difficulty of fastening upon one date rather than another as the moment of dissolution. In such cases the court must do the best it can by picking a reasonable date somewhere between the time when the club could still be said to exist and the time when its existence had clearly come to an end.'

The Vice-Chancellor reviewed the cases and continued:

'Mere inactivity is equivocal: suspended animation may be continued life, not death; and the mere cessation of function that was mentioned in the *Abbatt* case would not, I think, suffice per se. But inactivity coupled with other circumstances may demonstrate that all concerned regard the society as having ceased to have any purpose or function, and so as no longer existing. I think that short inactivity coupled with strong circumstances or long inactivity coupled with weak circumstances may equally suffice. The question is whether, put together, the facts carry sufficient conviction that the society is at an end and not merely dormant. For myself, I would hesitate a little about the use of the phrase "substratum has gone" in this context. It has a beguiling sound, but it has strong overtones of the Companies Court. There, it may form the basis of a winding up order, but it does not by itself initiate or complete that termination of the existence of the company. It therefore seems not altogether appropriate for establishing that there has been a spontaneous dissolu-

tion. I also hesitate to use the term "frustration", with all its contractual overtones. However, this is a mere matter of nomenclature and does not affect the principle. The question is whether on the facts of the present case the society ceased to exist on 18 December 1975. On that date, the position was that the club had ceased to operate as a club for several months. The picture was not one of mere inactivity alone; there were positive acts towards the winding up of the club. The sale of the club's stock of drinks was one instance, and others were the ending of the registration for VAT, and the dismissal of the steward. The cessation of any club activities, the ending of the use of the sports ground and the abandonment of preparing accounts or issuing membership cards were all in one sense examples of inactivity; but I think that there was in all probability some element of deliberation in these matters, and not a mere inertia. In Mr Sher's phrase, there was a systematic dismantling of the club and its activities.

However that may be, the resolution to sell the sports ground seems to me to conclude the matter. Having taken all steps, active or passive, required to terminate the activities of the club, short of passing a formal resolution to wind it up or dissolve it, the general meeting of the club resolved to sell the club's last asset.

The cessation of all club activities, the general knowledge of attempts to get planning permission in order to sell the sports ground, and then the holding of a general meeting to discuss a sale, even with (on this assumption) inadequate notice, seem to me to mark an acceptance by all concerned that the club was a club no more but merely a collection of individuals with expectations of dividing the proceeds of sale of the one remaining asset of the club. Whether it is put in terms of the club ceasing to function, or whether it is expressed as being a case where the substratum has gone or whether it is said that the club had become inactive and the surrounding circumstances sufficiently indicated that those concerned regarded the club as having ceased to have any purpose or function, and so as no longer existing, the answer in each case is the same. The rules of 1974 stated that the objects of the club were "to promote the different games of sport, to provide facilities for recreation and to encourage good fellowship among all members"; and all must have recognised that the club had become incapable of carrying out any of its objects. If the resolution to sell the sports ground is valid, as I think it is, that merely reinforces my conclusion that the club ceased to exist as such on 18 December 1975.

I turn to the question of the shares in which those who were members on 18 December 1975 are to divide the assets of the club.

For the reasons I gave in *Re Sick and Funeral Society of John's Sunday School, Golcar* (a case which was applied in *Re Bucks Constabulary Widows' and Orphans' Fund Friendly Society (No 2)*, I think that where, as here, there is nothing in the rules or anything else to indicate a different basis, the distribution should be on a basis of equality, irrespective of the length of membership or the amount of the subscriptions paid. That seems to me to be particularly appropriate where, as here, the amount of the subscription is so small and the acquisition of the last remaining asset of the club occurred so long ago.'

Comment
In the absence of a formal resolution to wind up the association, the court will decide on the facts of each individual case the date of dissolution.

Goodman v *Gallant* [1986] 2 WLR 236 Court of Appeal (Slade and Purchas LJJ, Sir Robert Cumming-Bruce)

* *Resulting trusts and joint tenants*

Facts
Mrs Goodman owned a house with her husband. They separated and Mr Gallant moved in and acquired Mr Goodman's interest

in the house, whereupon it was conveyed into the names of Mrs Goodman and Mr Gallant as joint tenants which implied that they held the property in equal shares. On the breakdown of their relationship, Mrs Goodman served a notice severing the joint tenancy and claimed three quarters of the proceeds of sale as this was the amount she had contributed to the purchase price.

Held
The declaration of joint tenancy was conclusive of the interests of the parties and the court could not go behind it except for fraud or mistake, neither of which were present.

Slade LJ:

'In a case where the legal estate in property is conveyed to two or more persons as joint tenants, but neither the conveyance or any other written document contains any express declaration of trust concerning the beneficial interests in the property (as would be required for an express declaration of this nature by virtue of s53(1)(b) of the Law of Property Act 1925) the way is open for persons claiming a beneficial interest in it or its proceeds of sale to rely on the doctrine of "resulting, implied or constructive trusts" ... If, however, the relevant conveyance contains an express declaration of trust which comprehensively declares the beneficial interests in the property or its proceeds of sale, there is no room for the application of the doctrine ... unless and until the conveyance is set aside or rectified; until that event the declaration contained in the document speaks for itself.'

Comment
If the parties are unmarried, the declaration of joint tenancy will fix each party with an equal share in the property. For married couples, this share may be varied in divorce or separation proceedings

Lowson v *Coombes* [1999] Ch 373 Court of Appeal (Nourse, Henry and Robert Walker LJJ)

• *Resulting trust of mistress's home – illegality*

Facts

A married man bought a house jointly with his mistress. The house was conveyed into the sole name of the mistress in order to prevent his wife from having a claim over it. When the relationship ended the man claimed a share under a resulting trust.

Held

There was a common intention that the mistress should hold the property on trust for them both in equal shares and the property should therefore be sold and the proceeds divided between them.

Nourse LJ:

'... Before turning to the authorities, I think it necessary to determine exactly what the judge found. Mr Short, for the defendant, submits that he found that, because it was the common intention that each property should be put out of the reach of the plaintiff's wife and because the plaintiff was shrewd and honest, he must have intended that each property should belong beneficially to the defendant alone since that was the only honest intention he could have had. While that was the construction which the judge felt obliged by the authorities to put upon the intention of the parties, it was not his finding as to their actual intention. What he found was that the evidence disclosed a common intention to purchase the original property (and therefore the subsequent properties) in more or less equal shares and that, had it not been for the potential claim by the plaintiff's wife, the properties would have been in joint names throughout. In other words, the judge found that the parties' actual intention was that they should be joint beneficial owners of the properties.

I should add this. The case was not pleaded as one of illegality and, no doubt for that reason, *Tinsley* v *Milligan* was not cited to the judge. Moreover, Mr Short has satisfied me that the judge did not treat it as a case of illegality. However, his finding as to the purpose of putting the properties into the sole name of the defendant has made it one of illegality by reason of section 37 of the Matrimonial Causes Act 1973. Shortly stated, subsection (2)(b) of that section provides that if the court is satisfied that one party to a marriage has, with intention of defeating the other's claim to financial relief, made a reviewable disposition, then, subject to exceptions, it may make an order setting aside the disposition. That power can be exercised however many years beforehand the disposition was made. The disposition is therefore different from one made to protect the property disposed of against the disponor's creditors generally. Notwithstanding Mr Shot's submissions to the contrary, I am satisfied that a disposition, such as the conveyances in the present case, whose purpose is to prevent the other party to the marriage from being able to look to the asset disposed of in any future financial proceedings and, in the process, from seeking an order under section 37(2)(b) of the Act of 1973 is one made with an illegal purpose.

In *Tinker* v *Tinker* a husband brought a garage business in Cornwall and found a house nearby for his family. He decided to buy the house in his wife's name so that, if his garage business was not a success, his creditors would not be able to take it. Shortly after the purchase the marriage broke up and the husband sought to recover the house from the wife. This court held that he was unable to do so. The factual basis on which the registrar had dismissed the wife's claim was stated by Lord Denning MR:

"He found that the husband was an honest business man intending and able to honour his financial commitments; that he intended this house to belong to him beneficially; and accordingly that the wife held the house in trust for her husband absolutely."

Lord Denning MR read from the notes of the husband's evidence:

"I was advised that should the business fail the house would be taken as part of the assets of the business. Recommended therefore house should be put in wife's name. This was explained to my wife by [the solicitor] in his office."

Lord Denning MR expressed his decision:

"Accepting that in the present case the defendant was honest – he acted, he said, on the advice of his solicitor – nevertheless I do not think he can claim that the house belongs to him. The solicitor did not give evidence. But the only proper advice that he could give was: 'in order to avoid the house being taken by your creditors, you can put it into your wife's name: but remember that, if you do, it is your wife's and you cannot go back on it'. But whether the solicitor gave that advice or not, I am quite clear that the husband cannot have it both ways. So he is on the horns of a dilemma. He cannot say that the house is his own and, at one and the same time say that it is his wife's. As against his wife, he wants to say that it belongs to him. As against his creditors, he wants to say that it belongs to her. That simply will not do. Either it was conveyed to her for her own use absolutely: or it was conveyed to her as trustee for her husband. It must be one or the other. The presumption is that it was conveyed to her for her own use; and he does not rebut that presumption by saying that he only did it to defeat his creditors. I think it belongs to her."

Salmon LJ said:

"The burden of displacing the presumption of advancement is therefore on the husband. This burden can in many cases be displaced without much effort. It seems to me, however, that in this case the husband's evidence, far from displacing the presumption, has done much to reinforce it."

Having referred to the husband's evidence as to the advice given by the solicitor and having pointed out that there would have been nothing wrong in the husband's putting the property into his wife's name in order to protect it from his creditors, Salmon LJ continued:

"It seems to me to follow from the registrar's finding that he was an honest man that the husband must have intended that the house should belong to his wife. That is why I say that his evidence strengthens the presumption of advancement. As far as I can see, the only possible alternative to what I have just described would be the husband dishonestly putting the house in his wife's name, with the intention of himself having the beneficial interest in it, and also with the intention, when he failed in business, to go to his creditors and say quite untruthfully and dishonestly: 'I have no interest in this house. You can look at the documents, and they are plain enough to show that I have none.' The registrar negatived that dishonest frame of mind and certainly this court would not interfere with that finding."

Cross LJ agreed with both judgments.

Cantor v *Cox* was, like the present case, a dispute about the beneficial ownership of a house in which an unmarried couple had formerly lived together. It had been purchased in the sole name of the woman. The executrix of the will of the woman claimed possession of the house in which the man was still living. He counterclaimed for a declaration that he was beneficially entitled to it. The brief report records Sir Anthony Plowman V-C's judgment thus:

"Here the legal estate was in the testatrix, and the defendant came to the court seeking equitable relief. The equitable presumption of a resulting trust which arose where the purchase money was provided by someone other than the person taking the legal estate was always rebuttable by evidence of actual intention. The evidence in this case was perfectly plain. The defendant put the house into the name of the testatrix in order to be out of reach of his creditors."

Having referred to the defendant's evidence that he did not intend to give the testatrix the house, the report continues:

"In [Plowman V-C's] judgment, that evidence was enough to rebut the presumption of a resulting trust which might otherwise have arisen in the defendant's favour, assuming, as [his Lordship] did for the moment, that he provided the whole of the purchase money. To apply what Lord Denning said in the analogous case of *Tinker* v *Tinker,* the only way consistent with honesty that the defendant could have ensured that the house would not be available for his creditors was to give it – and that meant give it beneficially – to the testatrix. He could not be heard in court to allege a dishonest motive, for it was axiomatic that he who came to equity must come with clean hands. And, in circumstances such as the present, Lord Eldon once said 'Let the estate lie where it falls' … It followed that the plaintiff was entitled to succeed in this action on the strength of the legal estate."

The reference to Lord Eldon LC's dictum was to what he said in *Muckleston* v *Brown*.

In *Tinsley* v *Milligan* it was held by a majority of the House of Lords that, where, in order to achieve an illegal purpose, property is transferred by one person into the name of another, being persons between whom the presumption of advancement does not apply, the transferor can recover the property on the ground that he is not forced to rely on the illegality but only on the resulting trust that arose in his favour on the transfer. In all material respects the present case is on all fours with that decision. In order to achieve the illegal purpose of putting the properties out of the reach of the plaintiff's wife, they were conveyed into the sole name of the defendant. The plaintiff and the defendant, being an unmarried couple, were persons between whom the presumption of advancement did not apply. Accordingly, if the judge's finding as to the parties' actual intention is put on one side, the defendant held each property on trust to give effect to beneficial interests therein corresponding to the parties' respective contributions to its purchase price, which the judge found were made in equal shares. In other words, the defendant held one half of

the beneficial interest in each property on a resulting trust for the plaintiff.

In *Tinsley* v *Milligan* the leading speech for the majority was given by Lord Browne-Wilkinson. In considering the authorities dealing with the position in equity where A transferred property to B for an illegal purpose, his Lordship … read from Lord Eldon LC's judgment in *Muckleston* v *Brown* ("Let the estate lie where it falls"), the principle being that equity will not aid a plaintiff who has transferred property to another for an illegal purpose. He then continued:

"It is against this background that one has to assess the more recent law. Although in the cases decided during the last 100 years there are frequent references to Lord Eldon's wide principle, with one exception (*Cantor* v *Cox*) none of the English decisions are decided by simply applying that principle. They are all cases where the unsuccessful party was held to be precluded from leading evidence of an illegal situation in order to rebut the presumption of advancement. Lord Eldon's rule would have provided a complete answer whether the transfer was made to a wife or child (where the presumption of advancement would apply) or to a stranger. Yet with one exception none of the cases in this century has been decided on that simple basis. The majority of cases have been those in which the presumption of advancement applied: in those authorities the rule has been stated as being that a plaintiff cannot rely on evidence of his own illegality to rebut the presumption applicable in such cases that the plaintiff intended to make a gift of the property to the transferee."

Lord Browne-Wilkinson then referred to a number of cases in which the presumption of advancement had applied, including *Tinker* v *Tinker*. He said that in each case the rule was stated to be that the plaintiff could not recover because he had to rely on the illegality to rebut the presumption.

In my view, the effect of the authorities, as they now stand, on the present case is a follows. *Tinker* v *Tinker* was recognised by both Lord Denning MR and Salmon LJ as being a case where the presumption of advancement applied. The husband was seeking to rebut the presumption. The essential ground on which it was held that he was unable to do so was that his evidence, so far from rebutting it, reinforced the presumption. However, the facts were very special, in that the house had been put into the wife's name because that course had been recommended by the solicitor as the means of achieving the legal purpose of putting it out of the reach of the husband's creditors. The husband must therefore have intended that the house should belong to the wife. That was not the position here. The parties did not act under legal advice and the purpose was illegal. The judge did not find, and it cannot reasonably be inferred, that the parties knew the purpose was illegal. They must be taken to have intended that they should take joint beneficial interests but that they thought it would be safer if the properties were put into the defendant's sole name. That is not inconsistent either with shrewdness or with honesty. On those grounds *Tinker* v *Tinker* is distinguishable.

The judge's finding as to the actual intention of the parties is of assistance to the plaintiff only in so far as it serves further to distinguish the present case from *Tinker* v *Tinker*. It does not go beyond that because the plaintiff cannot rely on the illegality in order to establish his beneficial interest in the properties. That, however, does not matter because *Tinsley* v *Milligan* enables him to rely on the resulting trust.

In *Cantor* v *Cox* it appears that Sir Anthony Plowman V-C, relying on *Tinker* v *Tinker*, may have attributed an artificial intention to the defendant in order to rebut the presumption of a resulting trust. In so far as the basis of the decision was the principle that he who comes to equity must come with clean hands, I agree with Mr Reade [for the plaintiffs] that the decision cannot stand with *Tinsley* v *Milligan*. Indeed, I am satisfied that Lord Browne-Wilkinson, in the passage I have read, intended to disapprove it on that basis. However, although the Vice-Chancellor's

findings appear to have been unduly influenced by those made in *Tinker* v *Tinker*, it may be possible to justify the decision on its own facts.

In the result, the case being one of illegality, I am of the opinion that the defendant holds one-half of the beneficial interest in 1 Queenswood Road on a resulting trust for the plaintiff. Had there been no illegality, the judge's finding as to the actual intention of the parties would have led to the same result. Either way, the plaintiff would be entitled to the declaration he seeks and I would allow the appeal accordingly.'

Comment
The man was 82 and the woman was 83 at the time of the hearing. Where the lower court were unable to apply *Tinsley* v *Milligan* since it was not pleaded before them, the Court of Appeal applied the newer House of Lords case.

Lloyds Bank plc v *Rosset*
See Chapter 6.

Tinsley v *Milligan* [1994] 1 AC 340 House of Lords (Lords Keith of Kinkel, Goff of Chieveley, Jauncey of Tullichettle, Lowry and Browne-Wilkinson)

• *Defence of illegality*

Facts
T and M were lovers who both contributed to the purchase of a lodging house in T's sole name. The lodging house was run as a business. It was purchased in the sole name of T to enable M to defraud the Department of Social Security. They shared the proceeds of the fraud. M eventually informed the DSS of the fraud. She and T quarrelled and T moved out. T brought a claim for possession of the house, asserting ownership of it. M counterclaimed, contending that T held the house on trust for the parties in equal shares. T claimed

that M was barred ex turpi causa from denying T's ownership <u>because her own ownership was tainted with illegality</u>. The court at first instance and the Court of Appeal dismissed T's claim. She then appealed to the <u>House of Lords.</u>

Held

By a majority of 3:2 (Lords Keith and Goff dissenting): <u>The equitable owner may be able to establish a claim as long as she can do so without relying on the illegality.</u>

Lord Browne-Wilkinson:

'Neither in law nor in equity will the law enforce an illegal contract which has been partially, but not fully, performed. However, it does not follow that all acts done under a partially performed contract are of no effect. In particular it is now clearly established that at law (as opposed to in equity), property in goods or land can pass under, or pursuant to, such a contract. <u>If so, the rights of the owner of the legal title thereby acquired will be enforced</u>, provided that the plaintiff <u>can establish such title without pleading</u> or leading evidence of the illegality. It is said that the property lies where it falls, even though legal title to the property was acquired as a result of the property passing under the illegal contract itself …'

His lordship reviewed the authorities:

'From these authorities the following propositions emerge: (1) <u>property in chattels and land can pass under a contract which</u> is illegal and therefore would have been unenforceable as a contract; (2) a plaintiff can at law enforce property rights so acquired <u>provided that he does not need to rely on the illegal contract for any purpose other than providing the basis of his claim to a property right</u>; (3) it is irrelevant that the illegality of the underlying agreement was either pleaded or emerged in evidence: if the plaintiff has acquired legal title under the illegal contract that is enough.

I have stressed the common law rules as to the impact of illegality on the acquisition and enforcement of property rights because <u>it is the appellant's contention that different principles apply in equity</u>. In particular, it is said that equity will not aid Miss Milligan to assert, establish or enforce an equitable, as opposed to a legal, proprietary interest since <u>she was a party to the fraud on the DSS</u>. The house was put in the name of Miss Tinsley alone (instead of joint names) to facilitate the fraud. <u>Therefore, it is said, Miss Milligan does not come to equity with clean hands</u>: consequently, equity will not aid her. Most authorities to which we were referred deal with enforcing proprietary rights under a trust: I will deal with them in due course. But before turning to them, I must point out that if Miss Tinsley's argument is correct, the results would be far reaching and, I suggest, very surprising. There are many proprietary rights, apart from trusts, which are only enforceable in equity. For example, an agreement for a lease under which the tenant has entered is normally said to be as good as a lease, since under such an agreement equity treats the lease as having been granted and the "lessee" as having a proprietary interest enforceable against the whole world except the bona fide purchaser for value without notice …

In my judgment to draw such distinctions between property rights enforceable at law and those which require the intervention of equity would be surprising. More than 100 years has elapsed since law and equity became fused. The reality of the matter is that, in 1993, English law has one single law of property made up on legal and equitable interests. Although for historical reasons legal estates have differing incidents, the person owning either type of estate has a right of property, a right in rem not merely a right in personam. If the law is that a party is entitled to enforce a property right acquired under an illegal transaction, in my <u>judgment the same rule ought to apply to any property right so acquired, whether such</u> right is legal or equitable.

<u>In the present case, Miss Milligan claims</u> under a resulting or implied trust. The court below have found, and it is not now disputed, that apart from the question of illegality Miss Milligan would have been enti-

tled in equity to a half share in the house in accordance with the principles exemplified in *Gissing* v *Gissing, Grant* v *Edwards* and *Lloyds Bank plc* v *Rosset*. The creation of such an equitable interest does not depend upon a contractual obligation but on a common intention acted upon by the parties to their detriment. It is a development of the old law of resulting trust under which, where two parties have provided the purchase money to buy a property which is conveyed into the name of one or more of them alone, the latter is presumed to hold the property on a resulting trust for both parties in shares proportionate to their contributions to the purchase price. In arguments, no distinction was drawn between strict resulting trusts and a *Gissing* v *Gissing* type of trust.

A presumption of resulting trust also arises in equity when A transfers personalty to B ... Before 1925, there was also a presumption of resulting trust when land was voluntarily transferred by A to B; it is arguable, however, that the position has been altered by the 1925 property legislation ... The presumption of a resulting trust is, in my view, crucial in considering the authorities. On that presumption (and on the contrary presumption of advancement) hinges the answer to the crucial question "does a plaintiff claiming under a resulting trust have to rely on the underlying illegality?" Where the presumption of resulting trust applies, the plaintiff does not have to rely on the illegality. If he proves that the property is vested in the defendant alone but that the plaintiff provided part of the purchase money, or voluntarily transferred the property to the defendant, the plaintiff establishes his claim made under a resulting trust unless either the contrary presumption of advancement displaces the presumption of resulting trust or the defendant leads evidence to rebut the presumption of resulting trust. Therefore, in cases where the presumption of advancement does not apply, a plaintiff can establish his equitable interest in the property without relying in any way on the underlying illegal transaction. In this case, Miss Milligan, as defendant, simply pleaded the common intention that the property should belong to both of them and that she contributed to the purchase price: she claimed that in consequence the property belonged to them equally. To the same effect was her evidence in chief. Therefore, Miss Milligan was not forced to rely on the illegality to prove her equitable interest. Only in the reply and the course of Miss Milligan's cross-examination did such illegality emerge: it was Miss Tinsley who had to rely on that illegality.

Although the presumption of advancement does not directly arise for consideration in this case, it is important when considering the decided cases to understand its operation. On a transfer from a man to his wife, children or others to who he stands in loco parentis, equity presumes an intention to make a gift. Therefore, in such a case, unlike the case where the presumption of resulting trust applies, in order to establish any claim the plaintiff has himself to lead evidence sufficient to rebut the presumption of gift and in so doing will normally have to plead and give evidence of, the underlying illegal purpose.

His lordship reviewed the authorities in which property had been transferred for an illegal purpose, including dicta of Lord Eldon in *Curtis* v *Perry* as follows:

"The moment the purpose to defeat the policy of the law by fraudulently concealing that this was his property is admitted, it is very clear he ought not to be heard in this court to say, that this is his property. In the case of a bill filed to have a reconveyance of a qualification given by the plaintiff to his son to enable him to sit in Parliament, the purpose being answered, the bill was very properly dismissed by Lord Kenyon with costs."

He continued:

'Although in the cases decided during the last 100 years there are frequent references to Lord Eldon's wide principle, with one exception (*Cantor* v *Cox)* none of the English decisions are decided by simply applying the principle. There are all cases where the unsuccessful party was held to be precluded from advancement. Lord Eldon's rule would have provided a complete answer whether the transfer was made to a wife or a child (where the presumption of advancement would apply) or to a stranger. Yet with one exception none of the cases in this century has been decided on that simple basis. The majority of cases have been those in which the presumption of advancement applied: in those authorities the rule had been stated as being that a plaintiff cannot rely on evidence of his own illegality to rebut the presumption applicable in such cases that the plaintiff intended to make a gift of the property to the transferee ... The crucial point was said to be the inability of the plaintiff to lead evidence rebutting the presumption of advancement. In each case, the plaintiff was claiming to recover property voluntarily transferred to, or purchased in the name of a wife or child, for an illegal purpose. Although reference was made to Lord Eldon's principle, none of those cases was decided on the simple ground (if it were good law) that equity would not in any circumstances enforce a resulting trust in such circumstances. On the contrary, in each case, the rule was stated to be that the plaintiff could not recover because he had to rely on the illegality to rebut the presumption of advancement. ...

I therefore reach the conclusion that, although there is no case overruling the whole principle stated by Lord Eldon, as the law has developed the equitable principle has become elided into the common law rule. In my judgment the time has come to decide clearly that the rule is the same whether a plaintiff founds himself on a legal or equitable title: he is entitled to recover if he is not forced to plead or rely on the illegality, even if it emerges that the title on which he relied was acquired in the course of carrying through an illegal transaction.

As applied in the present case, that principle would operate as follows. Miss Milligan established a resulting trust by showing that she had contributed to the purchase price of the house and that there was common understanding between her and Miss Tinsley that they owned the house equally. She had no need to allege or prove why the house was conveyed into the name of Miss Tinsley alone, since that fact was irrelevant to her claim: it was enough to show that the house was in fact vested in Miss Tinsley alone. The illegality only emerged at all because Miss Tinsley sought to raise it. Having proved these facts, Miss Milligan had raised a presumption of resulting trust. There was no evidence to rebut that presumption. Therefore Miss Milligan should succeed ...

Finally, I should mention a further point which was relied on by Miss Tinsley. It is said that once the illegality of the transaction emerges, the court must refuse to enforce the transaction and all claims under it whether pleaded or not ... Therefore, it is said, it does not matter whether a plaintiff relies on or gives evidence of the illegality: the court will not enforce the plaintiff's rights. In my judgment, this submission is plainly ill founded. There are many cases where a plaintiff has succeeded, notwithstanding that the illegality of the transaction under which she acquired the property has emerged ... In my judgment the court is only entitled and bound to dismiss a claim on the basis that it is founded on an illegality in those cases where the illegality is of a kind which would have provided a good defence if raised by the defendant. In a case where the plaintiff is not seeking to enforce an unlawful contract but founds his case on collateral rights acquired under the contract (such as a right of property), the court is neither bound nor entitled to reject the claim unless the illegality of necessity forms part of the plaintiff's case.

I would, therefore, dismiss the appeal.'

Comment

This is a landmark decision where the court tempered its strict rules on illegality. Both parties to the action were implicated in the fraud on the DSS so that equity had to be done between two parties who had acted illegally. By the time the case came to court, all sums due had been repaid to the DSS.

Tribe v *Tribe* [1995] 3 WLR 913
Court of Appeal (Nourse, Millett and Otton LJJ)

• *Presumption of advancement – father transferred property to son for an illegal purpose which was never carried out.*

Facts

The father transferred to his son all his shares in a business which was run by the son. The purpose of the transfer was to deceive the plaintiff's creditors. It was agreed between father and son that the shares were held on trust for the father pending settlement of the creditors' claims. The dispute with the creditors was settled without the need to carry the father's illegal purpose into effect. The son failed to return the shares. The father sought a declaration that he was entitled to the return of the shares which was granted at first instance. The son appealed to the Court of Appeal claiming that the father could not rely on his illegal purpose to rebut the presumption of advancement from father to son.

Held

The appeal was dismissed. In order for the presumption of advancement to be rebutted it was necessary to show

1. That the illegal purpose had not been carried out
2. That there was compelling evidence that he intended to retain a beneficial interest
3. The he concealed his interest from his creditors.

Millett LJ:

'In *Tinsley* v *Milligan* Lord Browne-Wilkinson summarised the common law rules which govern the effect of illegality on the acquisition and enforcement of property rights in three propositions: (1) property in chattels and land can pass under a contract which is illegal and therefore would have been unenforceable as a contract; (2) a plaintiff can, at law, enforce property rights so acquired provided that he does not need to rely on the illegal contract for any purpose other than providing the basis of his claim to a property right; (3) it is irrelevant that the illegality of the underlying agreement was either pleaded or emerged in evidence: if the plaintiff has acquired legal title under the illegal contract that is enough.

The decision of the majority of their lordships in that case was that the same principles applied in equity. It is, therefore, now settled that neither at law nor in equity may a party rely on his own fraud or illegality in order to found a claim or rebut a presumption, but that the common law and equity alike will assist him to protect and enforce his property rights if he can do so without relying on the fraud or illegality. This is the primary rule.

It is, however, also settled both at law and in equity that a person who has transferred property for an illegal purpose can nevertheless recover his property provided that he withdraws from the transaction before the illegal purpose has been wholly or partly performed. This is the doctrine of the locus poenitentiae and it applies in equity as well as at law... The availability of the doctrine in a restitutionary context was expressly confirmed by Lord Browne-Wilkinson in *Tinsley* v *Milligan*.

While both principles are well established, the nature of the relationship between them is unclear. Is the doctrine of the locus poenitentiae co-extensive with and by way of general exception to, the primary rule? The question in the present case is whether a plaintiff who has made a gratuitous transfer of property to a person in whose favour the presumption of advancement arises, can withdraw from the transaction before the illegal purpose has been carried into effect and then recover the property by leading evidence of his illegal purpose in order to rebut the presumption. Closely connected with this question is its converse: is a plaintiff who has made such a transfer in circumstances which give rise to a resulting trust so that he has no need to rely on the illegal purpose, as in *Tinsley* v *Milligan* itself, barred from recovering if the illegal purpose has been carried out? If both questions are answered in the negative, then either the locus poenitentiae is a common law doctrine which has no counterpart in equity or it is a contractual doctrine which has no place in the law of restitution.

It is convenient to consider first the position at common law. It is important to bear in mind that the common law starts from the opposite premise from that on which equity bases the presumption of resulting trust. In an action for money had and received, for example, whatever the relationship between the parties, the burden lies on the plaintiff to prove that the money was not paid by way of gift or pursuant to an enforceable contract. Absence of consideration is not of itself a ground of restitution: it is for the transferor to show that no gift was intended. ...

Prior to *Tinsley* v *Milligan* no transferor had ever succeeded in recovering his property by enforcing a resulting trust where he had transferred the property for an illegal purpose and that purpose had been carried out ...

A resulting trust, like the presumption of advancement, rests on a presumption which is rebuttable by evidence ... The transferor does not need to allege or prove the purpose for which property was transferred into the name of the transferee; in equity he can rely on the presumption that no gift was intended. But the transferee cannot be prevented from rebutting the presumption by leading evidence of the transferor's subsequent conduct to show that it was inconsistent with any intention to retain a beneficial interest. Suppose, for example, that a man transfers property to his nephew in order to conceal it from his creditors, and suppose that he afterwards settles with his creditors on the footing that he has no interest in the property. Is it seriously suggested that he can recover the property? I think not. The transferor's own conduct would be inconsistent with the retention of any beneficial interest in the property. I can see no reason why the nephew should not give evidence of the transferor's dealings with his creditors to rebut the presumption of a resulting trust and show that a gift was intended. He would

not be relying on any illegal arrangement, but implicitly denying it. The transferor would have to give positive evidence of his intention to retain a beneficial interest and dishonestly conceal it from his creditors, evidence which he would not be allowed to give once the illegal purpose had been carried out. ...

In my opinion, the weight of the authorities supports the view that a person who seeks to recover property transferred by him for an illegal purpose can lead evidence of his dishonest intention whenever it is necessary for him to do so provided he has withdrawn from the transaction before the illegal purpose has been carried out. It is not necessary, if he can rely on an express or resulting trust in his favour; but it is necessary (1) if he brings an action at law, and (2) if he brings proceedings in equity and needs to rebut the presumption of advancement ... I would not willingly adopt a rule which differentiated between the rule of the common law and that of equity in a restitutionary context.

It is, of course, true that equity judges are fond of saying that a party "cannot be heard to say" that his purpose was dishonest and that this approach represents a mainspring of equitable jurisprudence. A man who puts himself in a position where his interest conflicts with his duty, for example, "cannot be heard to say" that he acted in accordance with his interest; he is treated as having acted in accordance with his duty ... But this is a substantive rule of equity, not a merely procedural rule, as the primary rule appears to be, and it does not preclude the court from taking cognisance of an uneffectuated intention from which the party in question has resiled.

At heart the question for decision in the present case is one of legal policy. The primary rule which precludes the court from lending its assistance to a man who founds his cause of action on an illegal or immoral act often leads to a denial of justice. The justification for this is that the rule is not a principle of justice but a principle of policy ... The doctrine of the locus poenitentiae is an exception which operates to mitigate the harshness of the primary rule. It enables the court to do justice between the parties even though, in order to do so, it must allow a plaintiff to give evidence of his own dishonest intent. But he must have withdrawn from the transaction while his dishonesty still lay in intention only. The law draws the line once the intention has been wholly or partly carried into effect.'

Comment
One of the issues of public policy here is the deterrent effect of allowing the recovery of the property if the illegal purpose is not carried out.

Twinsectra Ltd v *Yardley and Others*
See Chapter 6.

Re Vandervell's Trusts (No 2) [1974] 1 All ER 47 Chancery Division (Megarry J)

• *Automatic resulting trust*

Facts
See the facts and the Court of Appeal's decision in Chapter 2.

Held
In a decision which was subsequently overturned on other grounds by the Court of Appeal, Megarry J made the following observations:

'It seems to me that the relevant points on resulting trusts may be put in a series of propositions as follows:

(1) If a transaction fails to make an effective disposition of any interest it does nothing. This is so at law and in equity, and has nothing to do with resulting trusts.

(2) Normally the mere existence of some unexpressed intention in the breast of the owner of the property does nothing: there must at least be some expression of that intention before it can effect any result. To yearn is not to transfer.

(3) Before any doctrine of resulting trust can come into play, there must at least be some effective transaction which transfers or creates some interest in property.

(4) Where A effectually transfers to B (or creates in his favour) any interest in any property, whether legal or equitable, a resulting trust for A may arise in two distinct classes of case. For simplicity I shall confine my statement to cases in which the transfer or creation is made without B providing any valuable consideration, and where no presumption of advancement can arise; and I shall state the position for transfers without specific mention of the creation of new interests.

(a) The first class of case is where the transfer to B is not made on any trust. If, of course, it appears from the transfer that B is intended to take beneficially. But in other cases there is a rebuttable presumption that B holds on a resulting trust for A. The question is not one of the automatic consequences of a dispositive failure by A, but one of presumption: the property has been carried to B, and from the absence of consideration and any presumption of advancement B is presumed not only to hold the entire interest on trust, but also to hold the beneficial interest for A absolutely. The presumption thus establishes both that B is to take on trust and also what that trust is. Such resulting trusts may be called "presumed resulting trusts".

(b) The second class of case is where the transfer to B is made on trusts which leave some or all of the beneficial interest undisposed of. Here B automatically holds on a resulting trust for A to the extent that the beneficial interest has not been carried to him or others. The resulting trust here does not depend on any intentions or presumptions but is the automatic consequence of A's failure to dispose of what is vested in him. Since ex hypothesi the transfer is on trust, the resulting trust does not establish the trust but merely carries back to A the beneficial interest that has not been disposed of. Such resulting trusts may be called "automatic resulting trusts".

(5) Where trustees hold property in trust

for A, and it is they who, at A's direction, make the transfer to B, similar principles apply, even though on the face of the transaction the transferor appears to be the trustees and not A. If the transfer to B is on trust, B will hold any beneficial interest that has not been effectually disposed of on an automatic resulting trust for the true transferor, A. If the transfer to B is not on trust, there will be a rebuttable presumption that B holds on a resulting trust for A.'

Comment

This analysis of the trusts in *Vandervell* provided a useful analysis of the automatic resulting trust, now called into question, however, by *Westdeutsche Landesbank Girozentrale* v *Islington London Borough Council* (see Chapter 14).

West Sussex Constabulary Widows, Children and Benevolent (1930) Fund Trusts, Re [1971] Ch 1
Chancery Division (Goff J)

• *Automatic resulting trust fulfilment of purpose*

Facts

A fund was established to provide payments to widows and dependants of deceased members of the West Sussex Constabulary. Receipts to the fund came from members' subscriptions, the proceeds of entertainments, sweepstakes, raffles, collecting-boxes and donations and legacies. The Constabulary was amalgamated with other police forces on 1 January 1968 and there were no longer any persons able to receive those benefits. The question as to the distribution of the fund arose.

Held

The fund should be distributed on the following basis:

1. Where members of the Constabulary had made contributions through subscriptions these had been made on the basis of £1 per member per month and existing members of the Constabulary could not claim these because they had received all they contracted for, either because their widows and dependants had received or were in receipt of prescribed benefits or because they did not have a widow or dependant. Past members of the Constabulary could not claim either because they put their money up on a contractual basis and not on the basis of a trust. Accordingly, such contributions by way of subscription went bona vacantia to the Crown.

2. As to the proceeds of entertainments, raffles and sweepstakes, these went bona vacantia to the Crown being paid under a contract rather than a trust.

3. The proceeds of collecting-boxes by unknown donors went to the Crown as bona vacantia on the assumption that they intended to part out and out absolutely with the money.

4. Larger donations, including legacies if any, were returnable by way of resulting trust.

Goff J:

'Then counsel divided the outside moneys into three categories, first the proceeds of entertainments, raffles and sweepstakes, secondly, the proceeds of collecting boxes; and, thirdly, donations including legacies, if any, and he took particular objections to each.

I agree that there cannot be any resulting trust with respect to the first category. I am not certain whether Harman J in *Re Gillingham Bus Disaster Fund* meant to decide otherwise. In stating the facts at p304 he referred to "street collections and so forth". In the further argument at p309 there is mention of whist drives and concerts but the judge himself did not speak of anything other than gifts. If, however, he did, I must respectfully decline to follow his judgment in that regard, for whatever may be the true position with regard to collecting-boxes, it appears to me to be impossible to apply the doctrine of resulting trust to the proceeds of entertainments and sweepstakes and such-like money-raising operations for two reasons: first, the relationship is one of contract and not of trust; the purchaser of a ticket may have the motive of aiding the cause or he may not; he may purchase a ticket merely because he wishes to attend the particular entertainment or to try for the prize, but whichever it be, he pays his money as the price of what is offered and what he receives; secondly, there is in such cases no direct contribution to the fund at all; it is only the profit, if any, which is ultimately received and there may even be none.

In any event, the first category cannot be any more susceptible to the doctrine than the second to which I now turn. Here one starts with the well-known dictum of P O Lawrence J in *Re Welsh Hospital (Netley) Fund* where he said:

"So far as regards the contributors to entertainments, street collections, etc, I have no hesitation in holding that they must be taken to have parted with their money out-and-out. It is inconceivable that any person paying for a concert ticket or placing a coin in a collecting-box presented to him in the street should have intended that any part of the money so contributed should be returned to him when the immediate object for which the concert was given or the collection made had come to an end. To draw such an inference would be absurd on the face of it."

This was adopted by Upjohn J in *Re Hillier's Trusts*, where the point was actually decided ...

[The analysis of Upjohn J] was approved by Denning LJ in the Court of Appeal although it is true he went on to say that the law makes a presumption of charity. I quote from p714:

"Let me first state the law as I understand it in regard to money collected for a specific charity by means of a church collection, a flag day, a whist drive, a dance or some such activity. When a man gives money on such an occasion, he gives it, I think, beyond recall. He parted with his money out-and-out."

In *Re Ulverston and District New Hospital Building Trusts* Jenkins LJ threw out a suggestion that there might be a distinction in the case of a person who could prove that he puts a specified sum in a collecting box, and in the *Gillingham* case Harman J after noting this, decided that there was a resulting trust with respect to the proceeds of collections. ...

It will be observed that Harman J considered that *Re Welsh Hospital (Netley) Fund*; *Re Hillier's Trusts* and *Re Ulverston and District New Hospital Building Trusts* did not help him greatly because they were charity cases. It is true that they were, and, as will presently appear, that is in my view very significant in relation to the third category, but I do not think it was a valid objection with respect to the second, and for my part I cannot reconcile the decision of Upjohn J in *Re Hillier's Trust* with that of Harman J in the *Gillingham* case. As I see it, therefore, I have to choose between them. On the one hand it may be said that Harman J had the advantage, which Upjohn J had not, of considering the suggestion made by Jenkins LJ. On the other hand, that suggestion, with all respect, seems to me somewhat fanciful and unreal. I agree that all who put their money into collecting-boxes should be taken to have the same intention, but why should they not all be regarded as intending to part with their money out-and-out absolutely in all circumstances? I observe that P O Lawrence J in *Re Welsh Hospital* used very strong words. He said any other view was inconceivable and absurd on the face of it. That commends itself to my humble judgment, and I therefore prefer and follow the judgment of Upjohn J in *Re Hillier's Trusts* ... Therefore, where as in the present case, the object was neither equivocal nor charitable, I can see no justification for infecting the third category with the weaknesses of the first and second, and I cannot distinguish this part of the case from *Re Abbott Fund Trusts.'*

Comment

This is a clear restatement of the rules applying on the distribution of a surplus held by an unincorporated association.

Westdeutsche Landesbank Girozentrale v *Islington London Borough Council*

See Chapter 14.

6 Constructive Trusts

Agip (Africa) Ltd v Jackson and Others [1991] 3 WLR 116 Court of Appeal (Fox, Butler-Sloss and Beldam LJJ)

• *Knowing assistance – degree of knowledge*

Facts

The defendants were directors of companies set up to launder money received fraudulently from Agip. The companies received the money from Tunisia and paid it on to other companies. Jackson, a chartered accountant, set up the arrangements and Griffin, his employee, carried them out. Agip also claimed that Bowers, Jackson's partner, was vicariously liable and sought to make all three constructive trustees.

Held

All three defendants were liable to account as constructive trustees.

Fox LJ:

'Both common law and equity accepted the right of the true owner to trace his property into the hands of others while it was in an identifiable form. The common law treated property as identified if it had not been mixed with other property. Equity, on the other hand, will follow money into a mixed fund and charge the fund. There is, in the present case, no difficulty about the mechanics of tracing in equity. The money can be traced through the various bank accounts to Baker Oil and onwards. It is, however, a prerequisite to the operation of the remedy in equity that there must be a fiduciary relationship which calls the equitable jurisdiction into being. There is no difficulty about that in the present case since

Zdiri must have been in a fiduciary relationship with Agip. He was the chief accountant of Agip and was entrusted with the signed drafts or orders upon BdS.

I come then to the circumstances in which strangers to the trust relationship (the defendants) may be made liable in equity. They are, broadly, as follows:

(1) Knowing receipt of or dealing with the trust property. The judge held that Mr Griffin did not receive the money at all and that Mr Jackson and Mr Bowers did not receive or apply it for their benefit. Accordingly, he held that none of them could be held liable as constructive trustees on the basis of knowing receipt of the money. There is no cross-appeal as to that.

(2) Knowing assistance. A person may be liable, even though he does not himself receive the trust property, if he knowingly assists in a fraudulent design on the part of a trustee (including a constructive trustee). Liability under this head is not related to the receipt of trust property by the person sought to be made liable (*Barnes* v *Addy*).

The degree of knowledge required was described by Ungoed-Thomas J in *Selangor United Rubber Estates Ltd* v *Cradock* as knowledge of circumstances which would indicate to an honest and reasonable man that such a design was being committed or would put him on inquiry whether it was being committed.

Peter Gibson J in *Baden* v *Société Generale pour Favoriser le Developpement du Commerce et de l'Industrie en France SA* gave a more expanded description of the circumstances constituting the necessary knowledge under five heads as follows:

(1) actual knowledge;

(2) wilfully shutting one's eyes to the obvious;

(3) wilfully and recklessly failing to make

such inquiries as an honest and reasonable man would make;

(4) knowledge of any circumstances which would indicate the facts to an honest and reasonable man; and

(5) knowledge of circumstances which would put an honest and reasonable man on inquiry.

I accept that formulation. It is, however, only an explanation of the general principle and is not necessarily comprehensive.

The judge held, and it is not challenged, that Mr Bowers did not participate in the furtherance of the fraud at all; although he was a partner in Jackson and Co he played no part in the movement of the money and gave no instructions about it.

Mr Jackson and Mr Griffin are in quite a different position. Mr Jackson set up the company structures. Mr Jackson and Mr Griffin controlled the movement of the money from the time it reached Baker Oil to the time it was paid out of the account of Jackson & Co in the Isle of Man Bank.

On the evidence (and in the absence of evidence from Mr Jackson and Mr Griffin) I agree with the judge that both of them must be regarded as having assisted in the fraud.

That, however, by no means concludes the matter. There remains the question of their state of mind. Did they have the necessary degree of knowledge?

The first inquiry is what did they know. (1) They knew that a very large amount of money was involved. It was $US10million in under two years. It had all come along the same track. (2) They knew the origin of the money and its destination. Its origin was Agip and the destination of most of it was Kinz. (3) Agip was an oil company with operations in Tunisia. Kinz were jewellers in France. (4) There was nothing to suggest that there was any commercial reason why Agip should be paying such sums to Kinz. (5)As the judge said, they must have realised that the only function of the payee companies or of Euro-Arabian was to act as "cut-outs" in order to conceal the true destination of the moneys from Agip. And the purpose of having two cut-outs instead of one was to bar any connection between Agip and Kinz without reference to the records of Lloyds Bank.

There is also some documentary evidence. First, there is the letter of 14 August 1984 from Mr Smyth of Knapp Fishers to Mr Jackson. That contains advice directed to the possibility that "Agip may be able to establish a cause of action by claiming that the payments were obtained by fraud."

The letter further contains the statement:

"Because of the general principle of banking confidentiality, it would be extremely difficult for the Tunisian Government or Agip to obtain an Order requiring Lloyds Bank to disclose banking transactions …"

This shows that the question of fraud was being considered and some anxiety being felt at the possibility that Agip might obtain access to bank records. The significance of the bank records is that they are or may be a signpost to the ultimate destination of the money.

Why was concern being felt about what Agip might discover?

If there were doubts about fraud they could be set at rest by getting in touch with Agip and disclosing what was known.

It is of course possibly that Mr Jackson and Mr Griffin were honest men and that there are facts which we do not know which would demonstrate that. But, if so, they could have attended the trial and explained their position in the witness box. They did not do so. One can only infer that they were not prepared to submit their activities to critical examination.

In the circumstances I think that the judge rightly came to the conclusion that they must have known they were laundering money, and were consequently helping their clients to make arrangements to conceal some disposition of money which had such a degree of impropriety that neither they nor their clients could afford to have them disclosed.'

Comment

Leave to appeal to the House of Lords was

refused – a pity in view of the conflict between Millett J's finding at first instance that strangers must have more than constructive notice of the breach of trust, and the fact that Bowers was held to be vicariously liable, ie liable without the requisite knowledge.

Attorney-General v *Blake (Jonathan Cape Ltd, Third Party)* [2000] 4 All ER 385 House of Lords (Lords Nicholls of Birkenhead, Goff of Chieveley, Browne-Wilkinson, Steyn and Hobhouse of Woodborough)

• *Breach of fiduciary duty – breach of Official Secrets Act 1911 by publication of autobiography – restitution*

Facts
Blake was a member of the British Secret Intelligence Service from 1944 until 1961. From 1951 onwards he was also a Russian spy and in 1961 he was sentenced to 42 years imprisonment for breach of the Official Secrets Act. In 1966 he escaped from prison and went to live in Moscow where he wrote his autobiography, much of which was based on information received by him as a member of SIS. The book was published in the United Kingdom without the licence or permission of the Crown. The Crown, through the Attorney-General, claimed that publication of the autobiography was a breach of Blake's fiduciary duty, that the Crown was the beneficial owner of the copyright of the book, and that the defendant was accountable to the Crown for all sums received or receivable from the publishers. The judge at first instance dismissed the action and the Attorney-General appealed to the Court of Appeal. Sir Richard Scott V-C, at first instance had identified two issues for the court:

'First, there is the question, whether, in writing and authorising the publication of the book, the defendant was in breach of duties he owed to the Crown. Second, there is the question whether, if the defendant was in breach of duty as alleged, the proprietary consequences for which the plaintiff contends, namely, that the copyright in the book and the profits derived therefrom belong in equity to the Crown ...'

The Court of Appeal dismissed the Crown's appeal and refused an injunction, but on further appeal the Attorney-General sought restitutionary damages for breach of contract.

Held
By a majority of four to one (Lord Hobhouse dissenting) on an analogy with the grant of an order for specific performance, there was no reason why the court could not order an account of profits when it was just and equitable that the defendant should retain no benefit from his breach of contract.

Lord Nicholls:

'Recently there has been a move towards applying the label of restitution to awards of this character ... However that may be, these awards cannot be regarded as conforming to the strictly compensatory measure of damage for the injured person's loss unless loss is given a strained and artificial meaning. The reality is that the injured person's rights were invaded but, in financial terms, he suffered no loss. Nevertheless the common law has found a means to award him a sensibly calculated amount of money. Such awards are probably best regarded as an exception to the general rule.

Courts of equity went further than the common law courts. In some cases, equity required the wrongdoer to yield up all his gains. In respect of certain wrongs which originally or ordinarily were the subject of proceedings in the Court of Chancery, the standard remedies were injunction and, incidental thereto, an account of profits. These wrongs included passing off, infringement of trade marks, copyrights and patents, and breaches of confidence. Some of these subjects are now embodied in statutory codes. An injunction restrained the continuance of the wrong, and the wrongdoer was required to account for the profits or benefits he had obtained from breaches or infringements which had already occurred. The court always had a discretion regarding the grant of the remedy of an account of profits and this remains the position. Further, the circumstances in which an account of profits is available under the statutes vary. For instance, an account of profits may not be ordered against a defendant in a patent infringement action who proves that at the date of the infringement he was not aware, and had no reasonable grounds for supposing, that the patent existed (Patents Act 1977, s62(1)).

In these cases the courts of equity appear to have regarded an injunction and account of profits as more appropriate remedies than damages because of the difficulty of assessing the extent of the loss. Thus, in 1803, Lord Eldon LC stated, in *Hogg* v *Kirby*, a passing off case:

> "What is the consequence in Law and Equity … a Court of Equity in these Cases is not content with an Action for Damages, for it is nearly impossible to know the extent of the damage; and therefore the remedy here, though not compensating the pecuniary damage except by an account of profits, is the best: the remedy by an Injunction and Account."

Whether this justification for ordering an account of profits holds good factually in every case must be doubtful. Be that as it may, in these types of case equity considered that the appropriate response to the violation of the plaintiff's right was that the defendant should surrender all his gains, and that he should do so irrespective of whether the violation had caused the plaintiff any financially measurable loss. Gains were to be disgorged even though they could not be shown to correspond with any disadvantage suffered by the other party. This lack of correspondence was openly acknowledged. In *Lever* v *Goodwin* Cotton LJ stated it was "well known" that in trade mark and patent cases the plaintiff was entitled, if he succeeded in getting an injunction, to take either of two forms of relief: he might claim from the defendant either the damage he had sustained from the defendant's wrongful act

or the profit made by the defendant from the defendant's wrongful act.

Considered as a matter of principle, it is difficult to see why equity required the wrongdoer to account for all his profits in these cases, whereas the common law's response was to require a wrongdoer merely to pay a reasonable fee for use of another's land or goods. In all these cases rights of property were infringed. This difference in remedial response appears to have arisen simply as an accident of history.

In some instances the common law itself afforded a wronged party a choice of remedies. A notable example is the wrong of conversion. A person whose goods were wrongfully converted by another had a choice of two remedies against the wrongdoer. He could recover damages, in respect of the loss he had sustained by the conversion. Or he could recover the proceeds of the conversion obtained by the defendant … Historically, the latter alternative was achieved by recourse to an element of legal fiction, whereby the innocent party "waived the tort". The innocent party could suppose that the wrongful sale had been made with his consent and bring an action for money "had and received to his use". Holt CJ observed that these actions "crept in by degree".

Breach of trust and fiduciary duty
I should refer briefly to breach of trust and breach of fiduciary duty. Equity reinforces the duty of fidelity owed by a trustee or fiduciary by requiring him to account for any profits he derives from his office or position. This ensures that trustees and fiduciaries are financially disinterested in carrying out their duties. They may not put themselves in a position where their duty and interest conflict. To this end, they must not make any unauthorised profit. If they do, they are accountable. Whether the beneficiaries or persons to whom the fiduciary duty is owed suffered any loss by the impugned transaction is altogether irrelevant. The accountability of the army sergeant in *A-G* v *Reading* is a familiar

application of this principle to a servant of the Crown. …

The present case
The present case is exceptional. The context is employment as a member of the security and intelligence services. Secret information is the lifeblood of these services. In the 1950's Blake deliberately committed repeated breaches of his undertaking not to divulge official information gained as a result of his employment. He caused untold and immeasurable damage to the public interest he had committed himself to serve. In 1990 he published his autobiography, a further breach of his express undertaking. By this time the information disclosed was no longer confidential. In the ordinary course of commercial dealings the disclosure of non-confidential information might be regarded as venial. In the present case disclosure was also a criminal offence under the Official Secrets Acts, even though the information was no longer confidential. Section 1 of the 1989 Act draws a distinction in this regard between members of the security and intelligence services and other Crown servants. Under s1(3) a person who is or has been a Crown servant is guilty of an offence if without lawful authority he makes "a damaging disclosure" of information relating to security or intelligence. The offence is drawn more widely in the case of a present or past member of the security and intelligence services. Such a person is guilty of an offence if without lawful authority he discloses "any information" relating to security or intelligence which is or has been in his possession by virtue of his position as a member of those services. This distinction was approved in Parliament after debate when the legislation was being enacted.

Mr Clayton [counsel for Blake] submitted that s1(1) is drawn too widely and infringes art 10 of the Convention for the Protection of Human Rights and Fundamental Freedoms … Section 1(1) of the 1989 Act criminalises disclosure of information when no damage results. It focuses on the status of the individual who makes the disclosure, rather than on the nature of the information

itself. A non-damaging disclosure by a member of the security and intelligence service is criminal, but the identical non-damaging disclosure by a Crown servant is not.

This argument was raised for the first time in this House. Your Lordships are not equipped with the material necessary to decide the point. In the event this does not matter, because there is in the present case another consideration which is sufficient for the purposes of the Attorney-General. When he joined the SIS, Blake expressly agreed in writing that he would not disclose official information, during or after his service, in book form or otherwise. He was employed on that basis. That was the basis on which he acquired official information. The Crown had and has a legitimate interest in preventing Blake profiting from the disclosure of official information, whether classified or not, while a member of the service and thereafter. Neither he, nor any other member of the service, should have a financial incentive to break his undertaking. It is of paramount importance that members of the service should have complete confidence in all their dealings with each other, and that those recruited as informers should have the like confidence. Undermining the willingness of prospective informers to co-operate with the services, or undermining the morale and trust between members of the service when engaged on secret and dangerous operations, would jeopardise the effectiveness of the service. An absolute rule against disclosure, visible to all, makes good sense.

In considering what would be a just response to a breach of Blake's undertaking the court has to take these considerations into account. The undertaking, if not a fiduciary obligation, was closely akin to a fiduciary obligation, where an account of profits is a standard remedy in the event of breach. Had the information which Blake has now disclosed still been confidential, an account of profits would have been ordered, almost as a matter of course. In the special circumstances of the intelligence services, the same conclusion should follow even though the information is no longer confidential. That would be a just response to the breach. I am reinforced in this view by noting that most of the profits from the book derive indirectly from the extremely serious and damaging breaches of the same undertaking committed by Blake in the 1950's. As already mentioned, but for his notoriety as an infamous spy his autobiography would not have commanded royalties of the magnitude Jonathan Cape Ltd agreed to pay.'

Lord Hobhouse (dissenting):

'The concepts of restitution and compensation are not the same though they will on occasion fulfil the same need. Restitution is analogous to property: it concerns wealth or advantage which ought to be returned or transferred by the defendant to the plaintiff. It is a form of specific implement. Its clearest form is an order for the return or transfer of property which belongs in law or in equity to the plaintiff. Property includes an interest in property. Then there are rights recognised in equity such as those which arise from a fiduciary relationship. These rights give rise to restitutionary remedies including the remedy of account which, depending on the circumstances, could also derive from a common law relationship such as agency. Then again, there are the rights now grouped under the heading of the law of restitution or unjust enrichment. These are still truly restitutionary concepts leading to restitutionary remedies. Typically they require the payment of money by the person unjustly enriched to the person at whose expense that enrichment has taken place. In so far as the appropriate remedy is the payment of money or the delivery up of a chattel or goods is concerned the common law could provide it; in so far as it required some other remedy or the recognition of an equitable right, the chancery jurisdiction had to be invoked.

The essential of such rights and their enforcement was the procuring by the courts of the performance by the defendant of his obligations. The plaintiff recovers what he is actually entitled to, not some monetary substitute for it. If what the plaintiff is entitled to is wealth expressed in monetary terms, the order will be for the payment of money but this does not alter the character of the remedy or of the right being recognised. He gets the money because it was his property or he was in some other way entitled to it. It is still the enforced performance of an obligation. The same is the case where an injunction is granted or a decree of specific performance or the ordering of an account.

It is this class of rights which the Crown is unable to invoke as a result of the judgment of Sir Richard Scott V-C upheld by the Court of Appeal. There is no obligation on Blake left to perform or which now can be enforced. That time passed with the failure to apply for an injunction in 1989 or 1990. The Crown has no right to an injunction to stop the payment of the royalty to Blake and procure its payment to the Crown instead. The Crown has no right to the royalty and does not now assert one.

The law, including equity, provides extensive and effective remedies for protecting and enforcing property rights. It is no criticism of the law that they are not available now to the Crown. The Crown does not have the substantive rights to support such remedies.'

Comment
Lord Hobhouse was concerned that the House of Lords was stretching the application of an account of profits too far and that this would create an inappropriate precedent for future cases.

Attorney-General for Hong Kong v *Charles Warwick Reid and Others*
[1993] 3 WLR 1143 Privy Council (Lords Templeman, Goff of Chieveley, Lowry, Lloyd of Berwick and Sir Thomas Eichelbaum)

• *Payment of a bribe – debtor/creditor relationship or constructive trustee*

Facts

Whilst a Crown servant in Hong Kong, R received bribes in breach of his fiduciary duty. This money was used to purchase two properties in New Zealand conveyed to R and his wife and a third property conveyed to his solicitor. The Attorney-General for Hong Kong obtained caveats against title for the three properties after R pleaded guilty to offences under the Prevention of Bribery Ordinance and was sentenced to eight years' imprisonment and fined HK$12.4 million.

The Attorney-General appealed to the Privy Council after the Court of First Instance and Court of Appeal of New Zealand refused an application by the Attorney-General to renew the caveats on the basis that the Crown had no equitable interest in the three properties.

Held

The Attorney-General's application was upheld.

Lord Templeman:

'A bribe is a gift accepted by a fiduciary as an inducement to him to betray his trust. A secret benefit [or profit] which may or may not constitute a bribe, is a benefit which the fiduciary derives from trust property or obtains from knowledge which he acquires in the course of acting as a fiduciary. A fiduciary is not always accountable for a secret benefit but he is undoubtedly accountable for a secret benefit which consists of a bribe ...

Equity, however, acts in personam, insists that it is unconscionable for a fiduciary to obtain and retain a benefit in breach of duty ... The false fiduciary who received the bribe in breach of duty must pay and account for the bribe to the person to whom that duty was owed ...

... it is said that if the fiduciary is in equity a debtor to the person injured, he cannot also be a trustee of the bribe. But there is no reason why equity should not provide two remedies, so long as they do not result in double recovery. ...

The decision in *Lister & Co* v *Stubbs* is not consistent with the principles that a fidu-ciary must not be allowed to benefit from his own breach of duty, that the fiduciary should account for the bribe as soon as he receives it and that equity regards as done that which ought to be done. From these principles it would appear to follow that the bribe and the property from time to time representing the bribe are held on a constructive trust for the person injured. A fiduciary remains personally liable for the amount of the bribe [on a debtor-creditor basis] if, in the event, the value of the property then recovered by the injured person proved to be less than that amount.'

Comment

This application of the constructive trust is founded on the equitable maxim 'equity looks on as done that which ought to be done' and this case effectively overrules *Lister* v *Stubbs*.

Bank of Credit and Commerce International (Overseas) Ltd (In Liquidation) and Another v *Akindele* [2000] 3 WLR 1423 Court of Appeal (Nourse, Ward and Sedley LJJ)

- *Constructive trust – knowing receipt – requirement of dishonesty – requirement of knowledge*

Facts

Chief Akindele, a Nigerian businessman, purchased shares in ICIC, a wholly owned subsidiary of BCCI, for $US 10 million under a fraudulent scheme which enabled the company to purchase its own shares. In the BCCI liquidation, the liquidator claimed that Chief Akindele had was liable to account as constructive trustee for $US 6,679,226.33 plus interest under the heads of knowing receipt and knowing assistance. Carnwath J held at first instance that Chief Akindele had not been aware of the fraud and had not been dishonest. The bank's claim was dismissed whereupon they appealed to the Court of Appeal on two issues: what state of knowledge was required to establish a claim of knowing receipt and whether dishonesty was an essential ingredient of such a claim.

Held

The state of knowledge required to establish knowing receipt was knowledge which would make it unconscionable for the defendant to retain the benefit of the receipt. Carnwath J was entitled to find that Chief Akindele had acted honestly and thus the claim of knowing assistance failed., as did the claim of knowing receipt, since he did not have knowledge which would make it unconscionable for him to retain the benefits received.

Nourse LJ:

'The essential requirements of knowing receipt were stated by Hoffmann LJ in *El Ajou* v *Dollar Land Holdings plc*:

"For this purpose the plaintiff must show, first, a disposal of his assets in breach of fiduciary duty; secondly, the beneficial receipt by the defendant of assets which are traceable as representing the assets of the plaintiff; and thirdly, knowledge on the part of the defendant that the assets he received are traceable to a breach of fiduciary duty."

In the present case the first two requirements were satisfied in relation to the defendant's receipt of the 6.679 million paid to him pursuant to the divestiture agreement. But the satisfaction of the third requirement, knowledge on the part of the defendant that the sum received by him was traceable to a breach or breaches of fiduciary duty by Messrs Naqvi, Hafeez and Kazmi is problematical.

So far as the law is concerned, the comprehensive arguments of Mr Sheldon and Mr Moss have demonstrated that there are two questions which, though closely related, are distinct: first, what, in this context, is meant by knowledge, second, is it necessary for the recipient to act dishonestly? Because the answer to it is the simpler, the convenient course is to deal with the second of those questions first.

Knowing receipt – dishonesty

As appears from the penultimate sentence of his judgment, Carnwath J proceeded on an assumption that dishonesty in one form or another was the essential foundation of the claimants' case, whether in knowing assistance or knowing receipt. That was no doubt caused by the acceptance before him (though not at any higher level) by Mr Sheldon ... that the thrust of the recent authorities at first instance was that the recipient's state of knowledge must fall into one of the first three categories listed by Peter Gibson J in *Baden* v *Société Generale pour Favoriser le Developpement du Commerce et de l'Industrie en France SA*, on which basis, said Carnwath J, it was doubtful whether the test differed materially in practice from that for knowing assistance. However, the assumption on which the judge proceeded, derived as I believe from an omission to distinguish between the questions of knowledge and dishonesty, was incorrect in law. While a knowing recipient will often be found to have acted dishonestly, it has never been a prerequisite of the liability that he should.

An authoritative decision this this question, the complexity of whose subject transactions has sometimes caused it to be overlooked, in this particular context, is *Belmont Finance Corp* v *Williams Furniture Ltd (No 2)* where the plaintiff (Belmont) was the wholly-owned subsidiary of the second defendant (City) which in turn was the wholly-owned subsidiary of the first defendant (Williams). The chairman of all three companies and the sole effective force in the management of their affairs was Mr John James. Reduced to its essentials, what had happened there was that the shareholders of a fourth company (Maximum) had agreed to sell its shares to Belmont for £500,000 and to buy the share capital of Belmont fro City for £489,000, a transaction which, as carried out, constituted a contravention of s54 of the Companies Act 1948 (prohibition of provision of financial assistance by a company for the purchase of its own shares) and was thus a misapplication of Belmont's funds.

Belmont having subsequently become insolvent, its receiver obtained an independent valuation of the shares in Maximum as at the date of the transaction which suggests that, instead of being worth £500,000, they were only worth £60,000. The receiver brought an action in Belmont's name principally against Williams, City and the shareholders of Maximum, claiming that they were liable to Belmont, first, for damages for conspiracy and secondly, as constructive trustees on the grounds of both knowing assistance and knowing receipt. At the trial, Foster J found that Mr James genuinely believed that to buy the capital of Maximum for £500,000 was a good commercial proposition for Belmont. He held that there had been no contravention of s54 and dismissed the action.

On Belmont's successful appeal to this court, Buckley LJ is recorded as having pointed out that Mr James had genuinely believed that the transaction was a good commercial proposition for Belmont without having any good grounds for that belief. He continued:

> "After careful consideration I do not feel that we should be justified in disturbing the judge's finding that Mr James genuinely believed that the agreement was a good commercial proposition for Belmont. It was a belief which, on his view of the commercial aspects of the case, Mr James could have sincerely held."

Having observed that Mr James as a director of both Williams and City knew perfectly well what the objects of the transaction were, that other officers of City had the same knowledge and that their knowledge must be "imputed" to the respective companies, and, having referred to the judgment of Lord Selbourne LC in *Barnes* v *Addy*, Buckley LJ dealt with the claim in constructive trust:

> "In the present case, the payment of the £500,000 by Belmont to [the shareholders of Maximum], being an unlawful contravention of s54, was a misapplication of

Belmont's money and was in breach of the duties of the directors of Belmont. £489,000 of the £500,000 so misapplied found their way into the hands of City with City's knowledge of the whole circumstances of the transaction. It must follow, in my opinion, that City is accountable to Belmont as a constructive trustee of the £489,000 under the first of Lord Selbourne LC's two heads. There remains the question whether City is chargeable as a constructive trustee under Lord Selbourne LC's second head, a stranger to a trust notwithstanding that he may not have received any of the trust fund which as been misapplied will be treated as accountable as a constructive trustee if he has knowingly participated in a dishonest design on the part of the trustees to misapply the fund; he must himself have been in some way a party to the dishonesty of the trustees. It follows from what I have already held that the directors of Belmont were guilty of misfeasance but not that they acted dishonestly." …

Though the claim in knowing assistance failed because the directors of Belmont did not act dishonestly, the claim in knowing receipt succeeded. I will return to that decision when dealing with the question of knowledge.

The decision in *Belmont (No 2)* is clear authority for the proposition that dishonesty is not a necessary ingredient of liability in knowing receipt. There have been other, more recent, judicial pronouncements to the same effect. Thus in *Polly Peck International plc* v *Nadir (No 2)* Scott LJ said that liability in a knowing receipt case did not require that the misapplication of the trust funds should be fraudulent. While in theory it is possible for a misapplication not to be fraudulent and the recipient to be dishonest, in practice such a combination must be rare. Similarly, in *Agip (Africa) Ltd* v *Jackson* Millett J said that in knowing receipt it was immaterial whether the breach of trust was fraudulent or not. The point was made most clearly by Vinelott J in *Eagle Trust* v *SBC Securities Ltd*:

"What the decision in *Belmont (No 2)* shows is that in a 'knowing receipt' case it is only necessary to show that the defendant knew that the moneys paid to him were trust moneys and of circumstances which made the payment a misapplication of them. Unlike a 'knowing assistance' case it is not necessary, and never has been necessary, to show that the defendant was in any sense a participator in a fraud."

Knowing receipt – the authorities on knowledge

With the proliferation in the last twenty years or so of cases in which the misapplied assets of companies have come into the hands of third parties, there has been a sustained judicial and extra-judicial debate as to the knowledge on the part of the recipient which is required in order to found liability in knowing receipt. Expressed in its simplest terms, the question is whether the recipient must have actual knowledge (or the equivalent) that the assets received are traceable to a breach of trust or whether constructive knowledge is enough. The instinctive approach of most equity judges, especially in this court, has been to assume that constructive knowledge is enough. But there is now a series of decisions of eminent first instance judges who, after considering the question of greater depth, have come to the contrary conclusion, at all events when commercial transactions are in point. In the Commonwealth, on the other hand, the preponderance of authority has been in favour of the view that constructive knowledge is enough.

In *Karak Rubber Co Ltd v Burden (No 2)* Brightman J referred to a person:

"who is a constructive trustee because (though not nominated as a trustee) he has received trust property with actual or constructive notice that it is trust property transferred in breach of trust …"

In *Belmont (No 2)* Buckley LJ referred to the principle established by the decision of this court in *Re Lands Allotment Co* that the directors of a company are treated as if they were actual trustees of the assets of the company which are in their hands or under their control. He continued:

"So, if the directors of a company in breach of their fiduciary duties misapply the funds of their company so that they come into the hands of some stranger to the trust who receives them with knowledge (actual or constructive) of the breach, he cannot conscientiously retain those funds against the company unless he has some better equity. He becomes a constructive trustee for the company of the misapplied funds."

Goff LJ said that what Belmont had to show, amongst other things was that City received all or part of the £500,000 "knowing, or in circumstances in which it ought to know, that it was a breach of trust". He answered the question saying:

"In my judgment the answer to that question must plainly be Yes, for they are fixed with all the knowledge that Mr James had. Now, he had actual knowledge of all the facts which made the agreement illegal and his belief that the agreement was a good commercial proposition for Belmont can be no more a defence to City's liability as constructive trustees than in conspiracy. Apart from this, clearly, in my judgment, Mr James knew or ought to have known all the facts that I have rehearsed, showing that there was in any event a misfeasance apart from illegality."

Similarly, in *Rolled Steel Products (Holdings) Ltd v British Steel Corporation* Browne-Wilkinson LJ said:

"A third party who has notice (actual or constructive) that a transaction, although intra vires the company, was entered into in excess or abuse of the powers of the company, cannot enforce such transaction against the company and will be accountable as constructive trustee for any money or property of the company received by [him]."

In *Agip (Africa) Ltd v Jackson*, Millett J, in reference to a person who receives for his own benefit trust property transferred to him in breach of trust, said:

"He is liable as a constructive trustee if he received it with notice, actual or constructive, that it was a trust property and that the transfer to him was a breach of trust …"

In *Houghton* v *Fayers* I myself said that it was enough for the claimant company to establish that the second defendant

"knew or ought to have known that the money had been paid to him in breach of [the first defendant's] ~~fiduciary duty to~~ [the claimant]."

Collectively, those observations might be though to provide strong support for the view that constructive knowledge is enough. But it must at once be said that in each of the three cases in this court (including, despite some apparent uncertainty in the judgment of Goff LJ, *Belmont (No 2)*, actual knowledge was found and, further, that the decisions in the *Karak* case and the *Agip* case were based on knowing assistance, not knowing receipt. Thus in none of the five cases was it necessary for the question to be examined in any depth and there appears to be no case in which such an examination has been conducted in this court. The groundwork has been done in other cases at first instance. I will refer to those of them in which the question has been considered in depth.

The seminal judgment, characteristically penetrative in its treatment of authority and, in the best sense, argumentative, is that of Megarry V-C in *Re Montagu's Settlement Trusts, Duke of Manchester* v *National Westminster Bank Ltd*. It was he who first plumbed the distinction between notice and knowledge. It was he who, building on a passage in the judment of this court in *Re Diplock's Estates, Diplock* v *Wintle*, first emphasised the fundamental difference between the questions which arise in respect of the doctrine of purchaser without notice on the one hand and the doctrine of constructive trusts on the other. Reading from his earlier judgment in the same case, he said:

"The former is concerned with the question whether a person takes property subject to or free from some equity. The latter is concerned with whether or not a person is to have imposed upon him the personal burdens and obligations of trusteeship. I do not see why one of the touchstones for determining the burdens on property should be the same as that for deciding whether to impose a personal obligation on a [person]. The cold calculus of constructive and imputed notice does not seem to me to be an appropriate instrument for deciding whether a [person's] conscience is sufficiently affected for it to be right to bind him by the obligations of a constructive trustee."

He added that there is more to being made a trustee than merely taking property subject to an equity.

The practical importance of that distinction had been explained by Megarry V-C in his earlier judgment. The question in that case was whether the widow and executrix of the will of the tenth Duke of Manchester was liable to account to the eleventh duke in respect of certain settled chattels or the proceeds of sale thereof. Having found that the tenth duke had had no knowledge that the chattels received by him were still subject to any trust and that he believed that they had been lawfully and properly released to him by the trustees, Megarry V-C continued:

"If liability as a constructive trustee depended on his knowledge, then he was not liable as a constructive trustee, and his estate is not liable for any chattels that have been disposed of, as distinct from any traceable proceeds of them. Even if he was not a constructive trustee and was a mere volunteer, his estate is liable to yield up any chattels that remain, or the traceable proceeds of any that have gone … But, unless he was a constructive trustee, there appears to be no liability if the chattels have gone and there are no traceable proceeds."

Megarry V-C summarised his conclusions in eight sub-paragraphs. I read the first three:

"1. The equitable doctrine of tracing and the imposition of a constructive trust by reason of the knowing receipt of trust property are governed by different rules and must be kept distinct. Tracing is primarily a means of determining the rights of property, whereas the imposition of a constructive trust creates personal obligations that go beyond mere property rights.

2. In considering whether a constructive trust has arisen in a case of the knowing receipt of trust property, the basic question is whether the conscience of the recipient is sufficiently affected to justify the imposition of such a trust.

3. Whether a constructive trust arises in such a case primarily depends on the knowledge of the recipient, and not on notice to him; and for clarity it is desirable to use the word 'knowledge' and avoid the word 'notice' in such cases."

The effect of Megarry V-C's decision, broadly stated, was that, in order to establish liability in knowing receipt, the recipient must have actual knowledge (or the equivalent) that the assets received are traceable to a breach of trust and that constructive knowledge is not enough.

In *Eagle Trust plc* v *SBC Securities Ltd*, Vinelott J did not think it would be right to found a decision that the statement of claim in that case disclosed no cause of action solely on the authority of *Re Montagu's Settlement Trusts*. However, on the ground that he (unlike Megarry V-C) was dealing with a commercial transaction, he arrived at the same conclusion and held that in such a transaction constructive knowledge is not enough. He cited a well-known passage in the judgment of Lindley LJ in *Manchester Trust* v *Furness*, the latter part of which reads thus:

"In dealing with estates in land title is everything, and it can be leisurely investigated; in commercial transactions possession is everything, and there is no time to investigate title, and if we were to extend the doctrine of constructive notice to commercial transactions we should be doing infinite mischief and paralysing the trade of the country."

The decision of Vinelott J was followed by

Knox J in *Cowan de Groot Properties Ltd* v *Eagle Trust plc* (another case of a commercial transaction) and the decisions of both of them by Arden J at the trial of the action in *Eagle Trust plc* v *SBC Securities Ltd (No 2)* ...

The Baden *rule*

It will have been observed that up to this stage I have made no more than a passing reference to the fivefold categorisation of knowledge accepted by Peter Gibson J in the *Baden* case:

(1) Actual knowledge.

(2) Wilfully shutting one's eyes to the obvious.

(3) Wilfully and recklessly failing to make such inquiries as an honest and reasonable man would make.

(4) Knowledge of circumstances which would indicate the facts to an honest and reasonable man.

(5) Knowledge of circumstances which will put an honest and reasonable man on enquiry.

Reference to the categorisation has been made in most of the knowing receipt cases to which I have referred from *Re Montagu's Settlement Trusts* onwards. In many of them it has been influential in the decision. In general, the first three categories have been taken to constitute actual knowledge (or its equivalent) and the last two constructive knowledge.

Two important points must be made about the *Baden* categorisation. First, it appears to have been propounded by counsel for the plaintiffs, accepted by counsel for the defendant and then put to the judge on an agreed basis. Secondly, though both counsel accepted that all five categories of knowledge were relevant and neither sought to submit that there was any distinction for that purpose between knowing receipt and knowing assistance (a view with which the judge expressed his agreement, the claim in constructive trust was based squarely on knowing assistance and not on knowing receipt. In the circumstances, whatever may have been agreed between counsel, it is natural to assume that the categorisation was not formulated with knowing receipt primarily in mind. This, I think, may be confirmed by the references to "an honest and reasonable man" in categories (4) and (5). Moreover, in the *Agip* case, Millett J warned against over refinement or a too ready assumption that categories (4) and (5) are necessarily cases of constructive knowledge only ...

Knowing receipt – the recipient's state of knowledge
In *Royal Brunei Airlines Sdn Bhd* v *Tan* which is now the leading authority on knowing assistance, Lord Nicholls of Birkenhead, in delivering the judgment of the Privy Council, said that "knowingly" was better avoided as a defining ingredient of the liability, and that in that context the *Baden* categorisation was best forgotten. ... Although my own view is that the categorisation is often helpful in identifying different states of knowledge which may or may not result in a finding of dishonesty for the purposes of knowing assistance, I have grave doubts about its utility in cases of knowing receipt. Quite apart from its origins in a context of knowing assistance and the reservations of Millett and Knox JJ, any categorisation is of little value unless the purpose it is to serve is adequately defined, whether it be fivefold, as in the *Baden* case, or twofold, as in the classical division between actual and constructive knowledge, a division which has itself become blurred in recent authorities.

What then, in the context of knowing receipt, is the purpose to be served by a categorisation of knowledge? It can only be to enable the court to determine whether, in the words of Buckley LJ in *Belmont (No 2)* the recipient can "conscientiously retain [the] funds against the company" or, in the words of Megarry V-C in *Re Montagu's Settlement Trusts* "[the recipient's] conscience is sufficiently affected for it to be right to bind him by the obligations of a constructive trustee". But if that is the purpose, there is no need for categorisation. All that is necessary is that the recipient's state of knowledge

should be such as to make it unconscionable for him to retain the benefit of the receipt.

For these reasons I have come to the view that, just as there is now a single test of dishonesty for knowing assistance, so ought there to be a single test of knowledge for knowing receipt. The recipient's state of knowledge must be such as to make it unconscionable for him to retain the benefit of the receipt. A test in that form, though it cannot, any more than any other, avoid difficulties of application, ought to avoid those of definition and allocation to which the previous categorisations have led. Moreover, it should better enable the courts to give commonsense decisions in the commercial context in which claims in knowing receipt are now frequently made ...

Knowing receipt – a footnote
We were referred in argument to "Knowing Receipt: The Need for a New Landmark", an essay by Lord Nicholls in Cornish, Nolan, O'Sullivan and Virgo (ed) *Restitution, Past, Present and Future: Essays in Honour of Gareth Jones* (1998) ...

Most pertinent to present purposes is the suggestion made by Lord Nicholls (at 238–239) to the decision of the House of Lords in *Lipkin Gorman (A Firm)* v *Karpnale*:

"In this respect equity should now follow the law. Restitutionary liability applicable regardless of fault but subject to a defence of change of position, would be a better-tailored response to the underlying mischief of misapplied property than personal liability which is exclusively fault-based. Personal liability would flow from having received the property of another, from having been unjustly enriched at the expense of another. It would be triggered by the mere fact of receipt, thus recognising the endurance of property rights. But fairness would be ensured by the need to identify a gain, and by making change of position available as a default in suitable cases when, for instance, the recipient had changed his position in reliance on the receipt."

Lord Nicholls goes on to examine the *Diplock* principle, suggesting (at 241) that it could be reshaped by being extended to all trusts but in a form modified to take proper account of the decision in *Lipkin Gorman (A Firm) v Karpnale Ltd* …

No argument before us was based on the suggestions made in Lord Nicholls' essay. Indeed, at this level of decision, it would have been a fruitless exercise. We must continue to do our best with the accepted formulation of the liability in knowing receipt, seeking to simplify and improve it where we may. While in general it may be possible to sympathise with a tendency to subsume a further part of our law of restitution under the principles of unjust enrichment, I beg leave to doubt whether strict liability coupled with a change of position defence would be preferable to fault-based liability in many commercial transactions, for example, where, as here, the receipt is of a company's funds which have been misapplied by the directors. Without having heard argument it is unwise to be dogmatic, but in such a case it would appear to be commercially unworkable and contrary to the spirit of the rule in *Royal British Bank v Turquand*, that, simply on proof of an internal misapplication of the company's funds, the burden should shift to the recipient to defend the receipt either by change of position or perhaps in some other way. Moreover, if the circumstances of the receipt are such as to make it unconscionable for the recipient to retain the benefit of it, there is an obvious difficulty in saying that it is equitable for a change of position to afford a defence.'

Comment

Nourse LJ gives a comprehensive review of the nature and extent of recipient liability. He calls into question the validity of the five *Baden Delvaux* categories of knowledge and approves the analysis of Megarry V-C in *Re Montagu's Settlement Trusts*. This case is essential reading.

Banner Homes Group plc v Luff Developments Ltd and Another
[2000] 2 All ER 117 Court of Appeal (Stuart Smith, Evans and Chadwick LJJ)

• *Constructive trust – agreement in principle to form joint venture – subsequent purchase by one party*

Facts

Luff was given the opportunity to acquire development land at White Waltham, Berkshire, but, because of the scale of the development, preferred to proceed on the basis of a joint venture. Banner had previously been interested in the site but were deterred by planning concerns. They met with Luff and agreed in principle to proceed with the joint venture. After the meeting, Luff made an offer to purchase the site subject to detailed planning permission and it was confirmed in correspondence that the joint venture should proceed with both parties contributing equally and sharing profits and losses equally. It was agreed that the terms of the shareholders' agreement should be recorded in the memorandum and articles of the joint venture company. Negotiations continued through correspondence and meetings; solicitors were instructed to draw up the documentation and Banner's solicitors prepared a draft shareholders' agreement. The vendors of the land pressed for exchange of contracts but Banner were concerned that there should be some formal documentation of the joint venture agreement before contracts were exchanged. Luff's solicitor was on holiday and, with Banner's knowledge, contracts were exchanged without the formal agreement, although both parties intended at that time to complete the formal agreement as soon as possible. The points of difference on the agreement were resolved but Luff then raised concerns about clause 19 which provided for the transfer of the shares of the joint venture company from one party to the other in the event of breach or insolvency. At this point, unknown to Banner, Luff was having second thoughts about the joint venture and consulted a solicitor with expertise in joint ventures who expressed serious doubts as to the commercial benefit to Luff of the agreement as negotiated. The purchase was completed of the development land to Stowhelm, a wholly owned subsidiary of Luff. Luff decided to withdraw from the joint venture but did not communicate this decision to Banner. The purchase was funded by Luff and Banner learned of the completion a few days later. Banner brought proceedings, claiming an interest in the land under a constructive trust in their favour over half the shares in Stowhelm. The judge dismissed the claim on the grounds that there was no binding agreement between Banner and Luff and that either party could have withdrawn at any time and, further, that Banner had suffered no detriment, rejecting Banner's contention that, if they had known that Luff intended to abandon the joint venture, they would have entered the market to acquire the land. Banner appealed to the Court of Appeal.

Held

The appeal was allowed. Chadwick LJ held that the judge at first instance had misunderstood the principles under which equity will intervene and was wrong to reject the claim that a constructive trust had arisen. Further, he was wrong to have held that Banner had suffered no detriment.

Chadwick LJ:

'*Constructive trusts*
The judge was referred – as we have seen – to a number of cases at first instance which illustrate the circumstances in which equity will impose a constructive trust on property acquired by one person, say A, in furtherance of some pre-acquisition arrangement or understanding with another, say B, that upon the acquisition of the property by A in circumstances in which B kept out of the market, B would be granted some interest in the property; notwithstanding that the arrangement or understanding falls short of

creating contractual obligations enforceable at law. It is helpful, I think, to preface an examination of those cases with the overview, recently provided by Millett LJ in *Paragon Finance plc* v *D B Thakerar & Co (A Firm), Paragon Finance plc* v *Thimbleby & Co (A Firm)*, of the underlying principles applicable in this area. He said:

"… the expression 'constructive trust' and 'constructive trustee' have been used by equity lawyers to describe two entirely different situations. The first covers those cases … where the defendant, though not expressly appointed as trustee, has assumed the duties of a trustee by a lawful transaction which was independent of and preceded the breach of trust and is not impeached by the plaintiff. The second covers those cases where the trust obligation arises as a direct consequence of the unlawful transaction which is impeached by the plaintiff. A constructive trust arises by operation of law whenever the circumstances are such that it would be unconscionable for the owner of property (usually but not necessarily the legal estate) to assert his own beneficial interest in the property and deny the beneficial interest of another. In the first class of case, however, the constructive trustee really is a trustee. He does not receive the trust property in his own right but by a transaction by which both parties intend to create a trust from the outset and which is not impugned by the plaintiff. His possession of the property is coloured from the first by the trust and confidence by means of which he obtained it, and his subsequent appropriation of the property to his own use is a breach of trust. Well-known examples of such a constructive trust are *McCormick* v *Grogan* (a case of a secret trust) and *Rochefoucald* v *Boustead* (where the defendant agreed to buy property for the plaintiff but the trust was imperfectly recorded). *Pallant* v *Morgan* (where the defendant sought to keep for himself property which the plaintiff trusted him to buy for both parties) is another. In these cases the plaintiff does not impugn the transaction by which the defendant obtained control of the property. He alleges that the circumstances in which the defendant obtained control make it unconscionable for him thereafter to assert a beneficial interest in the property."

Robert Walker LJ pointed out in *Yaxley* v *Gotts* ... that the principles upon which equity acts in what Millett LJ has described in the *Paragon Finance* case, as the first class of constructive trust case have much in common with those of proprietary estoppel. He said:

"Plainly, there are large areas where the two concepts do not overlap .... But in the area of a joint enterprise for the acquisition of land (which may be, but is not necessarily, the matrimonial home) the two concepts coincide. Lord Diplock's very well-known statement in *Gissing* v *Gissing* ... brings this out: 'A resulting, implied or constructive trust – and it is unnecessary for present purposes to distinguish between these three classes to trust – is created by a transaction between the trustee and cestui que trust in connection with the acquisition by the trustee of a legal estate in land, whenever the trustee has so conducted himself that it would be inequitable to allow him to deny to the cestui que trust a beneficial interest in the land acquired. And he will be held to have so conducted himself if by his words or conduct he has induced the cestui que trust to act to his own detriment in the reasonable belief that by so acting he was acquiring a beneficial interest in the land'."

Robert Walker LJ drew attention to the observations of Lord Bridge of Harwich in *Lloyds Bank plc* v *Rosset* ... also a matrimonial home case. Lord Bridge identified the need, first, to find "at any time prior to the acquisition, or exceptionally at some later date ... an agreement, arrangement or understanding reached between them that the property is to be shared beneficially". He went on:

"Once a finding to this effect is made it will only be necessary for the party asserting a claim to a beneficial interest against the partner entitled to the legal estate to

show that he or she has acted to his or her detriment or significantly altered his or her position in reliance on the agreement in order to give rise to a constructive trust or proprietary estoppel."

Browne-Wilkinson V-C had expressed the same view as to the common foundation on which proprietary estoppel and this class of constructive trust are based in *Grant* v *Edwards*. In a passage to which Robert Walker LJ was to refer in *Yaxley* v *Gotts*, Browne-Wilkinson V-C said:

"I suggest that in other cases of this kind, useful guidance may in the future be obtained from the principles underlying the law of proprietary estoppel which in my judgment are closely akin to those laid down in *Gissing* v *Gissing* ... In both, the claimant must to the knowledge of the legal owner have acted in the belief that the claimant has or will obtain an interest in the property. In both, the claimant must have acted to his or her detriment in reliance on such belief. In both, equity acts on the conscience of the legal owner to prevent him from acting in an unconscionable manner by defeating the common intention. The two principles have been developed separately without cross-fertilisation between them; but they rest on the same foundation and have on all other matters reached the same conclusions."

Browne-Wilkinson V-C went on to consider the extent to which the burden was on the claimant to establish the link between the acts done by the claimant and her belief that she had, or would obtain, an interest in the property. He said:

"As at present advised, once it has been shown that there was a common intention that the claimant should have an interest in the house any act done by her to her detriment relating to the joint lives of the parties is, in my judgment, sufficient detriment to qualify. The acts do not have to be inherently referably to house ... The holding out to the claimant that she had a beneficial interest in the house is an act of such nature as to be part of the inducement to her to do the acts relied on.

Accordingly, in the absence of evidence to the contrary, the right inference is that the claimant acted in reliance on such holding out and the burden lies on the legal owner to show that she did not do so: see *Greasley* v *Cooke.*" ...

The Pallant *v* Morgan *equity*

I have thought it appropriate to analyse the decisions at first instance in more detail than might otherwise have been necessary in the circumstances that the present appeal provides the first opportunity, so far as I am aware, for this court to consider the basis and scope of what may be called the *Pallant* v *Morgan* equity in a case in which reliance has to be placed upon it by the appellant. In my view there is no doubt that such an equity does exist and is firmly based. It is an example of the wider equity to which Millett J referred in *Lonrho plc* v *Fayed (No 2)*:

> "Equity will intervene by way of constructive trust, not only to compel the defendant to restore the plaintiff's property to him, but also to require the defendant to disgorge property which he should have acquired, if at all, for the plaintiff. In the latter category of case, the defendant's wrong lies not in the acquisition of the property, which may or may not have been lawful, but in his subsequent denial of the plaintiff's beneficial interest. For such to be the case, however, the defendant must either have acquired property which but for his wrongdoing would have belonged to the plaintiff, or he must have acquired property in circumstances in which he cannot conscientiously retain it as against the plaintiff."

Or, as the same judge was to say in this court in the passage in *Paragon Finance plc* v *D B Thakerar & Co (A Firm)* to which I have already referred:

> "His [the defendant's] possession of the property is coloured from the first by the trust and confidence by means of which he obtained it, and his subsequent appropriation of the property to his own use is a breach of that trust."

It is important, however, to identify the features which will give rise to a *Pallant* v *Morgan* equity and to define its scope; while keeping in mind that it is undesirable to attempt anything in the nature of an exhaustive classification. As Millett J pointed out in *Lonrho plc* v *Fayed (No 2)*, in a reference to the work of distinguished Australian commentators, equity must retain its "inherent flexibility and capacity of adjust to new situations by reference to mainsprings of the equitable jurisdiction". Equity must never be deterred by the absence of a precise analogy, provided that the principle invoked is sound. Mindful of this caution, it is, nevertheless, possible to advance the following propositions.

1. A *Pallant* v *Morgan* equity may arise where the arrangement or understanding on which it is based precedes the acquisition of the relevant property by one of those parties to that arrangement. It is the pre-acquisition arrangement which colours the subsequent acquisition by the defendant and leads to his being treated as a trustee if he seeks to act inconsistently with it. Where the arrangement or understanding is reached in relation to property already owned by one of the parties, he may (if the arrangement is of sufficient certainty to be enforced specifically) thereby constitute himself trustee on the basis that "equity looks on that as done which ought to be done", or an equity may arise under the principles developed in the proprietary estoppel cases. As I have sought to point out, the concepts of constructive trust and proprietary estoppel have much in common in this area. ...

2. It is unnecessary that the arrangement or understanding should be contractually enforceable. Indeed, if there is an agreement which is enforceable as a contract, there is unlikely to be any need to invoke the *Pallant* v *Morgan* equity; equity can act through the remedy of specific performance and will recognise the existing of a corresponding trust. ... In particular it is no bar to a *Pallant* v *Morgan* equity that the pre-acquisition arrangement is too uncertain to be enforced as a contract ... nor that it is plainly not intended to have contractual effect ...

3. It is necessary that the pre-acquisition arrangement or understanding should contemplate that one party (the acquiring party) will take steps to acquire the relevant property; and that, if he does so, the other party (the non-acquiring party) will obtain some interest in that property. Further it is necessary that (whatever private reservations the acquiring party may have) he has not informed the non-acquiring party before the acquisition (or, more accurately, before it is too late for the parties to be restored to a position of no advantage/no detriment) that he no longer intends to honour the arrangement or understanding.

4. It is necessary that, in reliance on the arrangement or understanding, the non-acquiring party should do (or omit to do) something which confers an advantage on the acquiring party in relation to the acquisition of the property; or is detrimental to ability of the non-acquiring party to acquire the property on equal terms. It is the existence of the advantage to the one, or detriment to the other, gained or suffered as a consequence of the arrangement or understanding, which leads to the conclusion that it would be inequitable or unconscionable to allow the acquiring party to retain the property for himself, in a manner inconsistent with the arrangement or understanding which enabled him to acquire it. ... In many cases the advantage/detriment will be found in the agreement of the non-acquiring party to keep out of the market. That will usually be both the advantage of the acquiring party – in that he can bid without competition from the non-acquiring party – and to the detriment of the non-acquiring party – in that he loses the opportunity to acquire the property for himself. But there may be advantage to the one without corresponding detriment to the other.

5. That leads, I think, to the further conclusions:

(i) that, although, in many cases, the advantage/detriment will be found in the agreement of the non-acquiring party to keep out of the market, that is not a necessary feature; and

(ii) that, although there will usually be advantage to the one and co-relative disadvantage to the other, the existence of both advantage and detriment is not essential – either will do.

What is essential is that the circumstances make it inequitable for the acquiring party to retain the property for himself in a manner inconsistent with the arrangement or understanding on which the non-acquiring party has acted. Those circumstances may arise where the non-acquiring party was never "in the market" for the whole of the property to be acquired but (on the faith of the arrangement or understanding that he shall have a part of that property) provides support in relation to the acquisition of the whole which is of advantage to the acquiring party. They may arise where the assistance provided to the acquiring party (in pursuance of the arrangement or understanding) involves no detriment to the non-acquiring party; or where the non-acquiring party acts to his detriment (in pursuance of the arrangement or understanding) without the acquiring party obtaining any advantage therefrom.

The present appeal

... I am satisfied, also, that the judge was wrong to reject the constructive trust claim on the grounds that Banner had failed to show that it had acted to its detriment in reliance on the arrangement agreed on 14th July 1995. There was evidence, to which I have referred, that the existence of the arrangement led Banner to regard the site as "out of play"; that is to say, the existence of the arrangement made it unnecessary, and inappropriate, for Banner to consider the site as a potential acquisition for its own commercial portfolio. But, as the judge himself recognised, one of the reasons why Luff wanted Banner kept "on board" – and so did not disclose its own doubts as to the future of the joint venture – was that "if dropped, Banner might emerge as a rival for the site". In other words, Luff saw it as an advantage that Banner's belief that the site was out of play should be maintained. Luff wanted to keep Banner out of the market. In those circumstances, it does not lie easily in Luff's mouth to say that Banner suffered no detriment. But whether or not Banner suffered detriment from the fact that it never regarded itself as free to consider the site as a potential acquisition of its own does not seem to me conclusive. Luff obtained the advantage which it sought. Further, Luff obtained the advantage of knowing that it had Banner's support, as a potential joint venturer whose commitment was not in doubt, in an acquisition on which it had not been willing to embark on its own.

As I have sought to show, the *Pallant* v *Morgan* equity is invoked where it would be inequitable to allow the defendant to treat the property acquired in furtherance of the arrangement or understanding as his own. It may be just as inequitable to allow the defendant to treat the property as his own when it has been acquired by the use of some advantage which he has obtained under the arrangement or understanding as it is to allow him to treat the property as his own when the plaintiff has suffered some detriment under the arrangement or understanding. That, as it seems to me, is the case.'

Comment
This case is another illustration of a constructive trust imposed in the absence of a binding agreement between the parties. Here Chadwick LJ analyses very clearly the requisite advantage/detriment between the parties.

Barnes v *Addy* (1874) 9 Ch App 244 Court of Appeal in Chancery (Lord Selbourne LC, James and Mellish LJJ)

• *Strangers to the trust dealing honestly not constructive trustees*

Facts
A settlor settled funds on trust as to one-half for A's wife and children and as to one-half for B's wife and children. A was the sole surviving trustee and in exercising a power of appointing new trustees he appointed B sole trustee for that half of the fund held on trust for B's wife and children. In making the appointed A acted on the advice of a solicitor, Duffield, who executed a deed of appointment and indemnity. B acted on the advice of another solicitor, Preston, who warned B's wife of the risk of a sole trustee being appointed. However, she consented to the appointment of B and the deed of indemnity in favour of A was sealed accordingly. B later misapplied the trust funds and was declared bankrupt. B's children sought to make A liable for a breach of trust in appointing B sole trustee on the ground that it was a fraud on the power of appointing new trustees. They also sought to make both solicitors liable for the loss of the fund. A died two years before the action.

Held
The estate of A was liable to make good the loss but the solicitors were not liable.

Lord Selbourne LC:

'Strangers are not made constructive trustees merely because they act as the agents of trustees in transactions within their legal powers, transactions, perhaps, of which a Court of Equity may disapprove, unless those agents receive and become chargeable with some part of the trust property, or unless they assist with knowledge in a dishonest and fraudulent design on the part of the trustees. Those are the principles as it seems to me, which we must bear in mind in dealing with the facts of the case. If those principles were disregarded, I know not how anyone could, in transactions admitting of doubt, as to the view which a Court of Equity might take of them, safely discharge the office of a solicitor, of banker, or of agent of any sort to trustees. But on the other hand, if persons, dealing honestly as agents, are at liberty to rely on the legal power of the trustees, and are not to have the character of trustees constructively imposed upon them, then the transactions of mankind can safely be carried through; and I apprehend those who create trusts do expressly intend, in the absence of fraud and dishonesty, to exonerate such agents of all classes from the responsibilities which are expressly incumbent, by reason of the fiduciary relation upon the trustees.'

Comment
This is the seminal case on the liability of strangers as constructive trustees.

Binions v *Evans* [1971] Ch 359
Court of Appeal (Lord Denning MR, Megaw and Stephenson LJJ)

- *Constructive trust as a method of protecting equitable interests in licences*

Facts
The defendant's husband had worked for the landlords all his life. Until the husband's death, he and the defendant had lived in a cottage owned by the landlords. After his death, the landlords made a written agreement with the defendant by which 'in order to provide a temporary home' for her, they agreed to permit her to reside in and occupy the cottage 'as Tenant at will of them free of rent for the remainder of her life or until determined as hereinafter provided'. The agreement provided that the defendant might determine the 'tenancy hereby created' by giving the landlords four weeks' notice in writing. It further provided that she should personally occupy and live in the cottage as a private residence and not assign or sublet it and 'upon ceasing personally to live there vacant possession shall forthwith be given to the Landlords'. The agreement contained obligations on the defendant to keep and maintain the cottage in a proper condition and on the landlords to pay all rates, taxes and outgoings and concluded 'the tenancy hereby created shall unless previously determined forthwith determine on the death of the (defendant)'. Two years later, the landlords sold their estate, which included the cottage, to the plaintiffs. In the contract of sale they inserted a clause which stated that the property was sold subject to the defendant's tenancy of the cottage (with which the landlords had provided the plaintiffs a copy) and continued: 'The plaintiffs, having been supplied with a copy of the … Tenancy Agreement … shall purchase with the full knowledge thereof and shall not be entitled to raise any requisitions or objections in respect of any matters contained therein or arising thereout'. By reason of that, the plaintiffs paid a reduced price for the property. Seven months after completion of the conveyance, the plaintiffs gave the defendant notice to quit and subsequently brought proceedings, claiming that the defendant was a tenant at will and that, her tenancy having determined, she was a trespasser.

Held
The plaintiffs were not entitled to possession of the cottage for the following reasons:

1. Although the words 'tenant at will' were used in the agreement, the rest of the agreement contained terms which were quite inconsistent with a tenancy at will; thus, the defendant was to be permitted to stay for the remainder of her life and the landlords could not turn her out at will; the defendant was not, therefore, a tenant at will.

2. (Per Lord Denning MR): Although the agreement did not constitute a tenancy, it did confer on the defendant a contractual licence to occupy the cottage for the rest of her life; where an owner sold land to a purchaser and at the same time stipulated that he should take it 'subject to' a contractual licence, the court would impose on the purchaser a constructive trust in favour of the licensee; accordingly, the defendant as a contractual licensee, had acquired an equitable interest in the cottage which the court would protect by granting an injunction to restrain the landlord from turning her out; when the plaintiffs bought the cottage 'subject to' the defendant's rights under the agreement, they took it on a constructive trust to permit the defendant to reside there during her life or as long as she might desire.

3. (Per Megaw and Stephenson LJJ): The effect of the agreement was that the landlords held the cottage on trust to permit the defendant to occupy it so long as she might desire; she was, therefore, a tenant for life within the meaning of the Settled Land Act 1925; since the plaintiffs took with express notice of the agreement which gave rise to the trust, they could not turn her out of the cottage against her will.

4. (Per Lord Denning MR): Even if a purchaser does not take expressly 'subject to' the rights of a licensee, he may do so impliedly, at any rate when the licensee is in actual occupation of the land. Whenever the purchaser takes the land impliedly subject to the rights of the contractual licensee, a court of equity will impose a constructive trust for the beneficiary.

Lord Denning MR:

'Seeing that the defendant has no legal estate or interest in the land, the question is what rights has she? At any rate, she has a contractual right to reside in the house for the remainder of her life or as long as she pleases to stay. I know that in the agreement it is described as a tenancy, but that does not matter. The question is: "What is it in reality?" To my mind, it is a licence and no tenancy. It is a privilege which is personal to her ... it ranks as a contractual licence and not a tenancy.

What is the status of such a licence as this? ... a right to occupy for life, arising by contract, gives to the occupier an equitable interest in the land ...

Suppose, however, that the defendant did not have an equitable interest at the outset, nevertheless it is quite plain that she obtained one afterwards when the Tredegar Estate sold the cottage. They stipulated with the plaintiffs that they were to take the house "subject to" the defendants' rights under the agreement. They supplied the plaintiffs with a copy of the contract and the plaintiffs paid less because of her right to stay there. In these circumstances, this court will impose on the plaintiffs a constructive trust for her benefit for the simple reason

that it would be utterly inequitable for the plaintiffs to turn the defendant out contrary to the stipulation subject to which they took the premises.

Wherever the owner sells the land to a purchaser and at the same time stipulates that he shall take it "subject to" a contractual licence, I think it plain that a court of equity will impose on the purchaser a constructive trust in favour of the beneficiary. It is true that the stipulation (that the purchaser shall take it subject to the rights of the licensee) is a stipulation for the benefit of one who is not a party to the contract of sale, but ... that is just the very case in which equity will "come to the aid of the common law" per Lord Upjohn in *Beswick* v *Beswick*. It does so by imposing a constructive trust on the purchaser.

In my opinion, the defendant, by virtue of the agreement, had an equitable interest in the cottage which the court would protect by granting an injunction against the landlords by restraining them from turning her out. When the landlords sold the cottage to a purchaser "subject to" her rights under the agreement, the purchaser took the cottage on a constructive trust to permit the defendant to reside there during her life or as long as she might desire. The courts will not allow the purchaser to go back on that trust.'

Comment
The court can enforce a licence by imposing a constructive trust on the licensor, which it can then enforce against a purchaser with notice.

Boardman v Phipps [1967] 2 AC 46 House of Lords (Lords Cohen, Hodson, Guest, Viscount Dilhorne and Lord Upjohn)

• *Fiduciary as constructive trustee*

Facts
The Phipps family trust owned 8,000 out of 30,000 shares in a private company. The plaintiff John Phipps was one of the beneficia-

ries under the trust and the defendants were Boardman who was a solicitor and Tom Phipps, a beneficiary. Boardman was solicitor to the trust.

The defendants were dissatisfied with the way in which the private company was run, so in 1956 they made enquiries about it on behalf of the trust and received much confidential information about its affairs. In particular they learned the value of the company's assets and the size of its profit and, while the former was high, the latter was low. The defendants realised it would be advantageous to sell some of the company's non-profit making assets. The defendants, with the trustees' consent, decided to purchase a controlling interest in the company and to implement a scheme to sell off non-profit making assets. The scheme was highly profitable and the trust gained in respect of its holding and the defendants gained in respect of the shares they had purchased themselves. The plaintiff called upon the defendants to account for the profits they had made. There was no question of any dishonesty by the defendants. They had first recommended that the trustees purchase the shares but being unable to find money for this purpose the trustees refused.

Held (Viscount Dilhorne and Lord Upjohn dissenting)
The defendants were accountable as constructive trustees for the profits which they had made. The information that the shares were a good investment and the opportunity to bid for them came as a result of their relationship with the trust. They could not have done so as ordinary members of the public.

Lord Cohen

'Information is, of course, not property in the strict sense of that word and, as I have already stated, it does not necessarily follow that because the agent acquired information and opportunity while acting in a fiduciary capacity he is accountable to his principals for any profit that comes his way as the result of the use he makes of that information and opportunity. His liability to account

must depend on the facts of the case. In the present case much of the information came the appellant's way when Mr Boardman was acting on behalf of the trustees on the instructions of Mr Fox and the opportunity of bidding for the shares came because he purported for all purposes except for making the bid to be acting on behalf of the owners of the 8,000 shares in the company. In these circumstances it seems to me that the principle of the *Regal* case applies and the courts below came to the right conclusion.

That is enough to dispose of the case but I would add that an agent is, in my opinion, liable to account for profits he makes out of trust property if there is a possibility of conflict between his interest and his duty to his principal. Mr Boardman and Tom Phipps were not general agents of the trustees but they were their agents for certain limited purposes. The information they had obtained and the opportunity to purchase the 21,986 shares afforded them by their relations with the directors of the company – an opportunity they got as a result of their introduction to the directors by Mr Fox – were not property in the strict sense but that information and that opportunity they owed to their representing themselves as agents for the holders of the 8,000 shares held by the trustees. In these circumstances they could not, I think, use that information and that opportunity to purchase the shares for themselves if there was any possibility that the trustees might wish to acquire them for the trust.'

Lord Upjohn:

'Rules of equity have to be applied to such a great diversity of circumstances that they can be stated only in the most general terms and applied with particular attention to the exact circumstances of each case. The relevant rule for the decision of this case is the fundamental rule of equity that a person in a fiduciary capacity must not make a profit out of a trust which is part of the wider rule that a trustee must not place himself in a position where his duty and his interest may conflict. ...

The phrase "possibly may conflict"

requires consideration. In my view it means that the reasonable man looking at the relevant facts and circumstances of the particular case would think that there was a real sensible possibility of conflict; not that you could imagine some situation arising which might, in some conceivable possibility in events not contemplated as real sensible possibilities by any reasonable person, result in a conflict ...

... In general, information is not property at all. It is normally open to all who have eyes to read and ears to hear. The true test is to determine in what circumstances the information has been acquired. If it has been acquired in such circumstances that it would be a breach of confidence to disclose it to another then courts of equity will restrain the recipient from communicating it to another. In such cases such confidential information is often and for many years has been described as the property of the donor, the books of authority are full of such references; knowledge of secret processes, "know how", confidential information as to the prospects of a company or of someone's intention or the expected results of some horse race based on stable or other confidential information. But in the end the real truth is that it is not property in any normal sense but equity will restrain its transmission to another if in breach of confidential relationship.

With all respect to the views of Russell LJ, I protest at the idea that information acquired by trustees in the course of their duties as such is necessarily part of the assets of the trust which cannot be used by the trustees except for the benefit of the trust. Russell LJ referred to the fact that two out of three of the trustees could have no authority to turn over this aspect of trust property to the appellants except for the benefit of the trust; this I do not understand, for if such information is trust property not all the trustees acting together could do it for they cannot give away trust property.

We heard much argument upon the impact of the fact that the testator's widow was at all material times incapable of acting in the trust owing to disability. Of course

trustees must act all of them and unanimously in matters affecting trust affairs, but in this case they never performed any relevant act on behalf of the trust at all ... At no time after going to the meeting in December 1956 did Mr Boardman or Tom rely on any express or implied authority or consent of the trustees in relation to trust property. They understood rightly that there was no question of the trustees acquiring any further trust property by purchasing further shares in the company, and it was only in the purchase of other shares that they were interested.

There is, in my view, and I know of no authority to the contrary, no general rule that information learnt by a trustee during the course of his duties is property of the trust and cannot be used by him. If that were to be the rule it would put the Public Trustee and other corporate trustees out of business and make it difficult for private trustees to be trustees of more than one trust. This would be the greatest possible pity for corporate trustees and others may have much information which they may initially acquire in connection with some particular trust but without prejudice to that trust can make it readily available to other trusts to the great advantage of those other trusts.

The real rule is, in my view, that knowledge learnt by a trustee in the course of his duties as such is not in the least property of the trust and in general may be used by him for his own benefit or for the benefit of other trusts unless it is confidential information which is given to him:

(1) in circumstances which, regardless of his position as a trustee, would make it a breach of confidence for him to communicate to anyone for it has been given to him expressly or impliedly as confidential; or

(2) in a fiduciary capacity, and its use would place him in a position where his duty and interest might possibly conflict.'

Comment

This is the key case on the duties of fiduciaries. Lord Upjohn, in his dissenting judgment, points out that there is no real possibility of conflict between the duty and interest of the fiduciaries in this case, but others have noted that, if the fiduciaries owned shares in the family company from which they derived a personal benefit, this might affect their impartiality in future advice to the trust on matters relating to the company.

Brinks Ltd v *Abu Saleh and Others (No 3)* [1996] CLC 133 Chancery Division (Rimer J)

• *Accessory liability – knowledge of trust required*

Facts

This is one of the cases arising out of the Brinks Matt bullion robbery and the subsequent money laundering operations. This case was brought by Brinks against Mrs Elcombe who assisted in the laundering of money by accompanying her husband to Switzerland on six occasions, ostensibly on a family holiday, in order to deposit some of the proceeds of the robbery in a Swiss bank account for one of the convicted robbers. Brinks' claim was that the gold had been stolen with the assistance of a dishonest fiduciary and that Mrs Elcombe knew that the money her husband was carrying was the proceeds of the robbery, or, alternatively, that she at least believed he was engaged in a dishonest transaction.

Held

The court accepted that Mr and Mrs Elcombe believed they were carrying money in order to defraud the Inland Revenue. In order to be held liable as a constructive trustee, it was essential that Mrs Elcombe had knowledge of the existence of the trust.

Rimer J's judgment was reported as follows:

'Mr Tugendhat submitted that as a result of *Royal Brunei Airlines* v *Philip Tan Kok Ming* in the Privy Council, in order to fix Mrs Elcombe with liability as an accessory, all he needed to do was to prove (1) that she had rendered assistance in what, objectively

assessed, was a dishonest transaction and (2) that the transaction involved a breach of trust.

The assistance he alleged she provided was to cloak what she knew to be an illegal operation with the apparent innocence of a family holiday or an antique buying trip; to provide an important element of cover intended to deter the suspicious from regarding the various journeys as other than commonplace and honest.

Mr Sisley disputed that Mrs Elcombe had provided any relevant assistance in furtherance of Mr Black's breach of trust on the basis of *Baden and Others* v *Société Generale pour Favoriser le Developpement du Commerce et de l'Industrie en France SA* ...

His lordship held that the only conclusion which he could properly draw from the evidence was that Mrs Elcombe went on the trips in the capacity of Mr Elcombe's wife. While not wishing to minimise the benefit to a husband of being able to enjoy the company of his wife, he did not regard her presence on such trips as constituting relevant 'assistance' in the furtherance of the breach of trust.

Having come to that conclusion, it was not strictly necessary to decide the issue as to whether or not it was sufficient to fix Mrs Elcombe with liability as an accessory to the breach of trust merely to prove that she had provided her assistance to the furtherance of a dishonest transaction, regardless of whether she knew that it involved a breach of trust or whether she also had to have had knowledge of the trust which was being breached.

His lordship considered *Royal Brunei Airlines* ... and said that he did not consider that the Privy Council intended to suggest that an accessory could be made accountable to the beneficiaries as a constructive trustee regardless of whether he had any knowledge of the existence of the trust.

In *Royal Brunei Airlines* the claim was one against the director of the trustee company which had committed the breach, and he had conceded that there had been a breach of trust in which he had assisted with actual knowledge. Thus that case was one where the accessory did have the relevant knowledge.

Further, in the analysis of the basis on which accessories had in the past been held liable for assisting in breaches of trust, the judgment made it clear ... that the law had never gone so far as to give a beneficiary a remedy against an accessory who dealt with a trustee in ignorance that he was a trustee, or who knew that he was a trustee but had no reason to know or suspect that the transaction in which he was assisting was a breach of trust. The judgment made no suggestion that in that respect the earlier authorities were wrong.

In his lordship's view, the judgment proceeded on the basis that a claim based on accessory liability could only be brought against someone who knew of the existence of the trust, or at least of the facts giving rise to the trust; and all that the judgment was directed at clarifying was what further was also needed to be shown in order to make the accessory liable.

The only further ingredient was dishonesty on the part of the accessory, and that was a sufficient ingredient. It was unnecessary that there should also be any dishonesty on the part of the trustee. In his lordship's view that was all the judgment said.

But as his lordship had already held that Mrs Elcombe's accompanying her husband was not sufficient to constitute assistance in the breach of trust, Brinks' claim against her would be dismissed.'

Comment
Following on from the change of the test of liability of strangers in *Royal Brunei Airlines* (see below), this case establishes that it is still necessary to prove that the stranger knew of the existence of the trust, or of the facts on which the trust arose, in order to be held liable as a constructive trustee.

Dubai Aluminium Co Ltd v *Salaam and Others (Livingstone and Others, Third Parties)* [2003] 1 All ER 97
House of Lords (Lord Nicholls of Birkenhead, Slynn of Hadley, Hutton, Hobhouse of Woodborough and Millett)

• *Partnership – vicarious liability of partners for dishonest assistance*

Facts
The facts and the history of the case are given in Lord Nicholls' opinion:

'My Lords, these proceedings arise out of an elaborate fraud by which the plaintiff, Dubai Aluminium Co Ltd., was induced to pay out $US50m between September 1987 and March 1993 under a bogus consultancy agreement with Marc Rich & Co AG. The proceeds were shared out among the principal participants in the fraud under several equally bogus sub-agreements. Mr Harry Mohamed Salaam and His Excellency Mahdi Mohamed Al Tahir were found by the trial judge, Rix J ... to have been dishonest participants in the scheme, together with Dubai Aluminium's chief executive, Mr Ian Livingstone. They benefited either directly or through companies controlled by them to the extent of about $20.3m in the case of Mr Salaam, $16.5m in the case of Mr Al Tajir and $6.3m in the case of Mr Livingstone.

Mr Salaam was a client of two successive firms of solicitors, Amhurst Brown Martin & Nicholson and Amhurst Brown Colombotti. Nothing turns on the distinction between these two firms and it will be convenient to refer to them simply as "the Amhurst firm". Mr Salaam's affairs were dealt with mainly by Mr Amhurst, the senior partner in the Amhurst firm. Dubai Aluminium claimed that Mr Amhurst dishonestly assisted in the fraud. He did not benefit from the fraud, apart from comparatively modest amounts paid to his firm by way of fees. In addition to suing Mr

Amhurst, Dubai Aluminium sued the Amhurst firm, on the basis that the firm was vicariously liable in respect of some of Mr Amhurst's activities.

It has always been common ground that Mr Amhurst's partners were personally innocent of any dishonesty. It is also right to note at the outset that, for a reason which will appear, the case has proceeded on the assumption that Mr Amhurst was guilty of dishonesty as alleged. He has always denied this allegation. This issue has never been tried, and there has never been any finding by a court that he acted dishonestly in any respect.

At various stages in the course of the trial all the defendants settled with Dubai Aluminium on agreeing to make substantial payments. The claims against Mr Amhurst and the Amhurst firm were settled on payment by the Amhurst firm of $10m. These settlements left outstanding and unresolved contribution claims brought by some of the defendants against each other and against third parties. So the contribution claims had to be decided by the judge, Rix J. The effect of the judge's decision was that the Amhurst firm, in respect of its payment of $10m, received contribution amounting to a full indemnity from Mr Salaam and Mr Al Tajir. More precisely, Rix J gave judgment in favour of the Amhurst firm for $7,781,093 jointly and severally against Mr Salaam and Mr Al Tajir, and in the further amount of $2,651,253 against Mr Salaam.

Mr Salaam and Mr Al Tajir appealed to the Court of Appeal … The Court of Appeal, comprising Evans, Aldous LJJ and Turner J, allowed the appeal. The court held that the Amhurst firm was not vicariously liable for Mr Amhurst's alleged wrongful acts. So there was no basis on which it could obtain contribution from Mr Salaam or Mr Al Tajir in respect of its payment to Dubai Aluminium. The Amhurst firm then brought this further appeal to your Lordships' House, seeking restoration of the order of Rix J.'

Held

The Amhurst firm's appeal was allowed. The blamelessness of the employer was immaterial in the context of vicarious liability – the employer stood in the shoes of the employee who had done wrong. Although the personal innocence of the partners should not have been taken into account by Rix J, he was entitled to take into account the undisgorged profits of those who had perpetrated the fraud.

Lord Millett:

'In the present case the principal participants in the fraud needed a solicitor to draw the agreements which were to be the instrument of carrying out their scheme. They instructed Mr Amhurst, a partner in the Amhurst firm, and he is to be assumed to have carried out his instructions "in his role as a solicitor in the firm", that is to say he was not moonlighting but acting in the course of the firm's business. Drawing such agreements honestly and for a proper purpose would plainly be in the ordinary course of the firm's business. By drawing them dishonestly for an improper purpose and for his own benefit or the benefit of his confederates, the court might, on an overall assessment of the evidence at trial, have concluded that Mr Amhurst had sufficiently departed from the ordinary course of the firm's business to defeat Dubai's claim against Amhursts. He would have been engaged "on a frolic of his own" and not "acting in his role as a partner in the firm". But such a conclusion would not have been inevitable; deliberate and dishonest conduct committed by a partner for his own sole benefit is legally capable of being in the ordinary course of the business of his firm.

Accordingly, and subject only to the Court of Appeal's decision in *Mara* v *Browne*, with which I shall deal in the next section, the conclusion that Mr Amhurst was acting in the ordinary course of the firm's business would have been legally open to the trial judge had the case proceeded to trial. The case having settled, and this being the factual basis of the claim against Amhursts, the judge was entitled and bound to proceed on the assumption that it would have been established.

Mr Salaam and Mr Al Tajir submitted that, as a matter of law, it is no part of the business of a solicitor to constitute himself a constructive trustee. For this proposition they cited *Mara*'s case ... where Lord Herschell said that "it is not within the scope of the implied authority of a partner in ... [a solicitor's] business that he should so act as to make himself a constructive trustee, and thereby subject his partner to the same liability". Rigby LJ spoke in similar terms and A L Smith LJ though he used the more specific expression "trustee de son tort" and not "constructive trustee".

These observations were obiter, since the Court of Appeal dismissed the claim against the partner personally responsible, so that there could be no question of vicarious liability. But they certainly represented the general understanding at that time. Although implicit, the reasoning would have been well understood in 1896. The courts distinguished between the acts of a solicitor when acting as solicitor to the trustees and acts done by him as an express trustee. The former were within the scope of the ordinary business of a solicitor, the latter were not ... If so, it was equally no part of such a business for him to constitute himself "a constructive trustee" in the sense in which the Court of Appeal were using that term.

For my part, I do not think that these cases can be disposed of by saying that the scope of a solicitor's practice has changed since 1896. No doubt it has, but not in the requisite direction. The nineteenth century was the heyday of the family solicitor. Conveyancing and private client business formed the bulk of his work. He could expect to be appointed an executor and trustee of his clients' wills and settlements. This is much less common today. Solicitors' work has become more commercial. Private client business forms a far smaller part of their work than it did; many large firms undertake none at all. Trusteeship too has become more professinal. Clients no longer look to their trustees to be philosophers, guides and friends. They expect them to be professional fund-managers and even, sometimes, businessmen. It is part of a solicitor's business to advise whether trust money may lawfully be invested in an overseas hedge fund or used to pay a discretionary beneficiary's school fees. It is still not part of his business to make the decision whether to do so or not. If it was not part of the ordinary business of a solicitor to act as an express trustee in 1857, I do not see how it can be part of it today.

But every statement in a judgment must be understood in the context in which it is made, and this is particularly the case if it employs expressions such as "constructive trust" or "constructive trustee", for they have more than one meaning, and meanings have changed over time. *Mara v Browne* cannot be understood unless the sense in which Lord Herschell and Rigby LJ were using the expression "constructive trustee" is appreciated.

The case concerned a marriage settlement. The first defendant, whom I shall call HB, was a solicitor. He advised the persons who were acting as trustees, though not yet formally appointed as such. He suggested a series of investments for the trust funds. They were not proper investments for a trustee to make. The money was to be lent on building property of a speculative character and the margin was unsatisfactory. The investments were made and the money was lost. Lord Herschell considered that, if the claimants had charged HB with negligence as a solicitor and brought the action in time, they might well have succeeded, in which case both HB and his partner would have been liable. But any such action was barred by the Statute of Limitations. Accordingly, the claimants alleged that HB had intermeddled with the trust and was liable as a trustee de son tort. They alleged that he had laid out the trust moneys at a time when there were no trustees, and therefore must be taken to have acted as a principal in the matter and not as a mere agent for the trustees. Such a claim was not statute-barred. The judge agreed with this analysis and held that both HB and his partner were liable.

The Court of Appeal took a different view of the facts. They held that it was not correct to say that at the relevant dates there were no trustees. But even if there had been none HB would not have been liable. He did not intend or purport to act as a trustee, and no one supposed that he was so acting. He purported to act throughout only as solicitor to the trustees and was understood by all concerned to be acting as such.

This summary is sufficient to show what Lord Herschell and Rigby LJ meant by "constructive trustee". They meant "trustee de son tort", that it to say, a person who, though not appointed to be a trustee, nevertheless takes it upon himself to act as such and to discharge the duties of a trustee on behalf of others. In *Taylor* v *Davies* Viscount Cave described such persons as follows:

> "... though not originally trustees, [they] had taken upon themselves the custody and administration of property on behalf of others; and though sometimes referred to as constructive trustees, they were, in fact, actual trustees, though not so named."

Substituting dog Latin for bastard French, we would do better today to describe such persons as de facto trustees. In their relations with the beneficiaries they are treated in every respect as if they had been duly appointed. They are true trustees and are fully subject to fiduciary obligations. Their liability is strict; it does not depend on dishonesty. Like express trustees they could not plead the Limitation Acts as a defence to a claim for breach of trust. Indeed, for the purposes of the relevant provision (s25(3) of the Supreme Court of Judicature Act 1873), which distinguished between property held on express trusts and other trusts, they were treated by the courts as express trustees. That is why the action in *Mara*'s case was not statute-barred.

In the same case, however, Viscount Cave identified a very different kind of "constructive trustee":

> "But the position ... of a constructive trustee in the usual sense of the words –

that is to say, of a person who, though he had taken possession in his own right, was liable to be declared a trustee in a Court of equity – was widely different ...."

Taylor's case was not a case of fraud but it was followed and applied in *Clarkson* v *Davies*, which was. In the latter case the Lord Justice-Clerk explained that the distinction was between a trust which arose before the occurrence of the transaction impeached and a claim which arose only by reason of that transaction. In the former case the defendant is treated as a trustee even though not expressly appointed as such; in the latter case he is a stranger to the trust at the time of the transaction.

Referring to these cases in *Paragon Finance plc* v *DB Thakerar & Co (A Firm)* in the Court of Appeal, I drew attention to the fact, which was becoming increasingly overlooked, that the expressions "constructive trust" and "constructive trustee" were used by equity lawyers to describe two entirely different situations. One was the situation which the claimants unsuccessfully contended had arisen in *Mara* v *Browne*. The other is the situation which arose in the present case.

Unlike HB in *Mara*'s case, Mr Amhurst did not assume the position of a trustee on behalf of others. He never had title to the trust funds or claimed the right to deal with them on behalf of those properly entitled to them. He acted throughout on his own or his confederates' behalf. The claim against him is simply that he participated in a fraud. Equity gives relief against fraud by making any person sufficiently implicated in the fraud accountable in equity. In such a case he is traditionally (and I have suggested unfortunately) described as a "constructive trustee" and is said to be "liable to account as a constructive trustee". But he is not in fact a trustee at all, even though he may be liable to account as if he were. He never claims to assume the position of trustee on behalf of others, and he may be liable without ever receiving or handling the trust property. If he receives the trust property at all he receives it adversely to the claimant and by an unlawful transaction which is impugned by the claimant. He is not a fiduciary or subject to fiduciary obligations and he could plead the Limitation Acts as a defence to the claim.

In this second class of case the expressions "constructive trust" and "constructive trustee" create a trap. As Jules Sher QC, sitting as a deputy judge in the Chancery Division, recently observed in *Coulthard* v *Disco Mix Club Ltd* this "type of ... trust is merely the creation by the court ... to meet the wrongdoing alleged: there is no real trust and usually no chance of a proprietary remedy". The expressions are "nothing more than a formula for equitable relief" (see *Selangor United Rubber Estates* v *Cradock (A Bankrupt) (No 3)* ... per Ungoed-Thomas J). I think that we should now discard the words "accountable as a constructive trustee" in this context and substitute the words "accountable in equity".

The distinction between the two kinds of constructive trustee is of critical importance in the present context. If, as I think, it is still not within the ordinary scope of a solicitor's practice to act as a trustee of an express trust, it is obviously not within the scope of such a practice voluntarily to assume the obligations of a trustee and so incur liability as a de facto trustee or a constructive trustee of the first kind. But given that a solicitor may be guilty of deliberate and dishonest conduct while acting within the ordinary scope of his practice, there is no conceivable reason why his firm should not thereby incur vicarious liability for loss caused by the conduct which constituted him a constructive trustee of the second kind ...

I would allow Amhursts' appeal and uphold the judge's conclusion that Amhursts are entitled to claim a contribution towards the $10m they paid in settlement of Dubai's claim.'

Comment
Lord Millett's analysis of *Mara* v *Browne* makes a useful distinction between the concept of trustee de son tort and constructive

trustee. He renames the liability of strangers to the trust 'liability in equity'. Is this a more accurate description of the liability which arises in such cases?

El Ajou v *Dollar Land Holdings plc and Another* [1994] 2 All ER 685 Court of Appeal (Nourse, Rose and Hoffmann LJJ)

• *Knowing receipt – knowledge to be attributed to a company*

Facts
The plaintiff owned funds and securities which were the under control of an investment manager in Geneva who was bribed to invest the plaintiff's money, without the plaintiff's authority, in fraudulent share-selling schemes operated by three Canadians through the medium of two Dutch companies. The proceeds of these schemes were ultimately invested in DLH. The plaintiff was able to trace his funds into the hands of DLH and sought to recover them on the ground that DLH received his funds with knowledge that they were the proceeds of fraud.

Held
DLH had knowledge of the relevant facts. The person who was the 'directing mind and will of the company' had such knowledge and this made the company a constructive trustee of the funds, even though that person was not a director of the company. Decision of the High Court reversed and appeal allowed.

Nourse LJ:

> '*Knowledge*
> It having been established that DLH received assets representing proceeds of the fraud, I come to the question of knowledge. By the end of the hearing there could have been no doubt that Mr Ferdman himself had the requisite knowledge. The judge said of him:
>
> > "He freely admitted that he knew that the persons who were providing the money

for the Nine Elms project were the persons who had been behind the fraud in Amsterdam; and that by 7 April 1987, when he signed the letter to Yulara, he knew (or assumed) that the money which he would be receiving into the Keristal No 2 account was part of the proceeds of the fraud."

Thus arises the most important question remaining in dispute, which is whether Mr Ferdman's knowledge can be treated as having been the knowledge of DLH. The plaintiff contends that it can and ought to be, first, on the ground that Mr Ferdman was, in relation to DLH's receipt of the assets representing the moneys fraudulently misapplied, its directing mind and will; secondly and alternatively, on the ground that he was its agent in the transaction. Because a company's directing mind and will are often the mind and will of one or more of its directors and because a director is for many purposes an agent of the company, there is a danger of confusion between the two grounds on which the plaintiff relies. But they are, as the judge made clear, quite separate. The plaintiff can succeed on either. The convenient course is to deal with the law and the facts in regard to each of them in turn.

Directing mind and will
This doctrine, sometimes known as the alter ego doctrine, had been developed, with no divergence of approach, in both criminal and civil jurisdictions, the authorities in each being cited indifferently in the other. A company having no mind or will of its own, the need for it arises because the criminal law often requires mens rea as a constituent of the crime, and the civil law intention or knowledge is an ingredient of the cause of action or defence. In the oft-quoted words of Viscount Haldane LC in *Lennards Carrying Co Ltd* v *Asiatic Petroleum Co Ltd*:

"My lords, a corporation is an abstraction. It has no mind of its own any more than it has a body of its own; its active and directing will must consequently be sought in the person of somebody who for some purposes may be called an agent, but who is really the directing mind and will of the corporation, the very ego and centre of the personality of the corporation."

The doctrine attributes to the company the mind and will of the natural person or persons who manage and control its actions. At that point, in the words of Millett J: "Their minds are its mind; their intention is its intention; their knowledge is its knowledge." It is important to emphasise that management and control is not something to be considered generally or in the round. It is necessary to identify the natural person or persons having management and control in relation to the act or omission in point. This was well put by Eveleigh J in delivering the judgment of the Criminal Division of this court in *R* v *Andrews Weatherfoil Ltd*:

"It is necessary to establish whether the natural person or persons in question have the status and authority which in law makes their acts in the matter under consideration the acts of the company so that the natural person is to be treated as the company itself."

Decided cases show that, in regard to the requisite status and authority, the formal position, as regulated by the company's articles of association, service contracts and so forth, though highly relevant, may not be decisive. Here Millett J adopted a pragmatic approach. In my view he was right to do so, although it has led me, with diffidence, to a conclusion different from his own.'

Nourse LJ quoted the passage from Millett J's judgment with which he disagreed and continued:

'In disagreeing with the judge on this question, I start from the point that the transactions to be considered are those by which DLH received assets representing the moneys fraudulently misapplied. The responsibility for the management and control of those transactions is not to be determined by identifying those who were responsible for deciding that DLH would participate in the Nine Elms project and the nature and extent of that participation, far less by identifying those who were responsible for business decisions generally. Neither Mr Stern nor the Americans made any of the arrangements for the receipt or disbursement of the moneys by Grangewoods. Nor did they commit DLH to the obligations correlative to their receipt. None of them had the authority to do so. That was the responsibility of Mr Ferdman. The crucial considerations are that Mr Ferdman made all the arrangements for the receipt and disbursement of the £270,000 and the £1,030,000; that it was he who signed the letter of 20 March to Roth; that it was he who signed and dispatched the letter of 7 April to Yulara; and that it was those steps that caused DLH to become involved in the project and enabled it later to acquire the assets representing the moneys fraudulently misapplied.

Each of the steps taken by Mr Ferdman was taken without the authority of a resolution of the board of DLH. That demonstrates that as between Mr Ferdman on the one hand and Mr Favre and Mr Jaton on the other it was Mr Ferdman who had the de facto management and control of the transactions. It may be that that state of affairs involved some breach of the directors' duties to DLH. But that would not enable DLH to say that Mr Favre and Mr Jaton were parties to its directing mind and will in any relevant respect. Mr Tager sought to show that they did perform duties as directors of DLH. No doubt they did. But there is no real evidence that they had any responsibility for the transactions in question. In my view the directing mind and will of DLH in relation to the relevant transactions between March and June 1986 were the mind and will of Mr Ferdman and none other. That means that DLH had the requisite knowledge at that time.

Next, I must consider whether the plaintiff's right to recover is affected by Mr Ferdman's having ceased to be a director of DLH in June 1987...'

Nourse LJ referred to the view of Millett J in the lower court and continued:

'While I might agree with the judge that the knowledge of a director, who had known of a misapplication of trust moneys at the time of their misapplication but had genuinely forgotten all about it by the time that they were received by the company, could not be attributed to the company, I am unable to see how that can assist DLH here. The steps that caused DLH to become involved in the project and enabled it later to acquire the asset representing the £1,030,000 were all taken between March and June 1986 ... In the circumstances, DLH, having had the requisite knowledge at the time that it became involved in the project and when the £1,030,000 was disbursed as it directed, it would in my view be unrealistic to hold that it ceased to have that knowledge simply because the mind and will that had been the source of it played no part in the receipt of the asset itself. I am therefore of the opinion that DLH is on this ground liable to the plaintiff in constructive trust.'

Comment
The mens rea of the investment manager, attributable to the company because for the purposes of this transaction he was its directing mind and will, supplies the necessary guilty knowledge for the company to be made a constructive trustee.

Gillett v *Holt and Another* [2000] 2 All ER 289 Court of Appeal (Beldam, Waller and Robert Walker LJJ)

• *Proprietary estoppel – requirement of detrimental reliance*

Facts
From 1956 until 1995 Gillett worked on Holt's farm. Over the years, Holt gave Gillett to understand that he intended to leave him the bulk of his estate and he made wills accordingly. In 1995 Gillett and Holt had a disagreement which resulted in the breakdown of their personal and working relationship and Holt made a new will excluding Gillett. Gillett brought an action claiming that Holt had

become subject to an obligation founded on proprietary estoppel to bequeath him substantially the whole of his estate and claiming that he had given his whole life in Holt's service on the understanding, encouraged by Holt, that Gillett would inherit the estate.

Held

Allowing the appeal from the judgment of Carnwath J, the doctrine of proprietary estoppel cannot be divided into three or four watertight compartments – the court must look at the matter in the round. Robert Walker LJ accepted William Swadling's view (see [1998] Restitution Law Review 220) that the whole point of estoppel claims was that they concerned promises which were unsupported by consideration and that it was the detrimental reliance of the promisee which gave the promise its binding force. Had the judge looked at the matter in the round he would have recognised that Mr Gillett's claim of detriment was 'an unusually compelling one'.

Robert Walker LJ:

'*Proprietary estoppel*
It is important to note at the outset that the doctrine of proprietary estoppel cannot be treated as subdivided into three or four watertight compartments. Both sides are agreed on that, and in the course of the oral argument in this court it repeatedly became apparent that the quality of the relevant assurances may influence the issue of reliance, that reliance and detriment are often intertwined, and that whether there is a distinct need for a "mutual understanding" may depend on how the other elements are formulated and understood. Moreover, the fundamental principle that equity is concerned to prevent unconscionable conduct permeates all the elements of the doctrine. In the end the court must look at the matter in the round.

In his discussion of the law the judge took as his starting point the decision of Mr Edward Nugee QC in *Re Basham (deceased)*. In that case, the claimant and her husband had helped her mother and her stepfather in all sorts of ways throughout the

claimant's adult life. She received no remuneration but understood that she would inherit her stepfather's property when he died. After her mother's death in 1976, and until her stepfather's death in 1982, she and her husband lived near the cottage to which her stepfather had moved (but never lived in the cottage). The claimant was told by her stepfather that "she would lose nothing" by her help and (a few days before his death) that she was to have the cottage. The deputy judge held that she was entitled, by proprietary estoppel, to the whole of the estate of her stepfather (who died intestate). He rejected the submission that the principle could not extend beyond cases where the claimant already had enjoyment of an identified item of property … In that context he referred to the well-known judgment of Oliver J in *Taylor Fashions Ltd* v *Liverpool Victoria Trustees Co Ltd*. That judgment has been described as "a watershed in the development of proprietary estoppel" (Gray *Elements of Land Law* (2nd edn, 1993). In it Oliver J stated that in the light of the more recent cases the principle

"requires a very much broader approach which is directed to ascertaining whether, in particular individual circumstances it would be unconscionable for a party to be permitted to deny that which, knowingly unknowingly, he has allowed or encouraged another to assume to his detriment than to inquiring whether the circumstances can be fitted within the confines of some preconceived formula serving as a universal yardstick for every form of unconscionable behaviour."

The other case in which *Re Basham* has been referred to in this court is *Wayling* v *Jones*. It concerned an assurance ("It'll all be yours one day") given by the elder partner in a male homosexual relationship to his younger partner. Balcombe LJ cited Mr Nugee's statement of principle in *Re Basham* as having been accepted by the parties:

"The plaintiff relies on proprietary estoppel, the principle of which in its broadest form may be stated as follows: where one person (A) has acted to his detriment on the faith of a belief which was known and encouraged by another person (B) that he either has or is going to be given a right in or over B's property B cannot insist on his strict legal rights if to do so would be inconsistent with A's belief."

Balcombe LJ went on to state the relevant principles as to reliance and detriment:

"(1) There must be a sufficient link between the promises relied upon and the conduct which constitutes the detriment – see *Eves* v *Eves* and *Grant* v *Edwards* … per Browne-Wilkinson V-C, in particular the passage where he equates the principles applicable in cases of constructive trust to those of proprietary estoppel.

(2) The promises relied upon do not have to be the sole inducement for the conduct: it is sufficient if they are an inducement (*Amalgamated Investment and Property Co Ltd (In Liquidation)* v *Texas Commerce International Bank Ltd*).

(3) Once it has been established that promises were made, and that there has been conduct by the plaintiff of such a nature that inducement may be inferred then the burden of proof shifts to the defendant to establish that he did not rely on the promises (*Greasley* v *Cooke*; *Grant* v *Edwards* …)."

Irrevocability of assurances
The judge referred to these authorities and then to the decision of Judge Weeks QC in *Taylor* v *Dickens* (which has since been compromised on appeal). That was the case of the elderly lady who said that she would leave her estate to the gardener and did so, but then changed her mind (without telling him) after he stopped charging her for his help with gardening and odd jobs. Judge Weeks rejected the claim and criticised *Re Basham* in two respects. The first criticism was that Mr Nugee's judgment omitted the requirement of unconscionability. The criticism seems misplaced … The second criticism was that

"… it is not sufficient for A to believe that he is going to be given a right over B's property if he knows that B has reserved

the right to change his mind. In that case, A must show that B created or encouraged a belief on A's part that B would not exercise the right."

Taylor v *Dickens* has itself attracted a good deal of criticism: see for instance [1998] Conv 210 (Professor M P Thompson) and [1998] Restitution Law Review 220 (W J Swadling); but compare the contrary view [1999] Conv 46 (M Dixon). Mr Swadling's comment is short and pithy:

"This decision is clearly wrong, for the judge seems to have forgotten that the whole point of estoppel claims is that they concern promises which, since they are unsupported by consideration, are initially revocable. What later makes them binding, and therefore irrevocable, is the promissee's detrimental reliance on them. Once that occurs, there is simply no question of the promisor changing his mind."

… In my judgment these criticisms of *Taylor* v *Dickens* are well-founded. The actual result in the case may be justified on the other ground on which it was put (no unconscionability on the facts); or (as Mr Swadling suggests later in his note) the gardener's unremunerated services might have merited some modest restitutionary relief. But the inherent revocability of testamentary dispositions (even if well understood by the parties, as Mr Gillett candidly accepted that it was by him) is irrelevant to a promise or assurance that "all this will be yours" … Even when the promise or assurance is in terms linked to the making of a will … the circumstances may make clear that the assurance is more than a mere statement of present (revocable) intention, and is tantamount to a promise. …

Mutual understandings and reliance
The judge's approach seems also to have been influenced by the need to find what he called

"a mutual understanding – which may be expressed or inferred from conduct – between promisor and promisee, both as to the content of the promise and as to what the promisee is doing, or may be expected to do, in reliance on it."

Similarly, he set out his view that "the *Re Basham* principle requires some mutual 'understanding' as to the quid pro quo (ie the consideration) for the promise … ."

Here again I think the judge may have been too influenced by the cases on mutual wills in which a definite agreement is an essential part of the doctrine. There is of course a kernel of truth, indeed a considerable nugget of truth in this approach because, as Balcombe LJ said in *Wayling* v *Jones* and other distinguished judges said in the earlier cases which he cited), there must be a sufficient link between the promises relied on and the conduct which constitutes the detriment. In cases where the detriment involves the claimant moving house (as in *Watts* v *Storey*) or otherwise taking some particular course of action at the other party's request, the link is, in the nature of things, going to have some resemblance to the process of offer and acceptance, leading to a mutual understanding. But in other cases well within the mainstream of proprietary estoppel, such as *Inwards* v *Baker* and the nineteenth century decisions which this court applied in that case, there is nothing like a bargain as to what particular interest is to be granted, or when it is to be granted, or by what type of disposition it is to be granted. The link is provided by the bare fact of A encouraging B to incur expenditure on A's land …

Detriment

It is therefore necessary to go on to consider detriment. The judge would have decided the case against Mr Gillett on this point also, as he indicated at the end of his judgment in the main action … The judge devoted almost all of this part of his judgment to an analysis of whether Mr Gillett was substantially underpaid between 1965 and 1995. He dealt with the other matters relied on as detriment in a manner which Mr McDonnell has described as perfunctory …

The judge then said:

"Various other matters were relied on by Mr Gillett in support of his case of 'detriment': for example his refusal of inquiries from other employers, the limited provi-

sion made for his pension, the domestic tasks undertaken by him and Sally for Mr Holt, and the money spent by him on improving The Beeches. Against that, he acknowledges that Mr Holt was generous with gifts to the family, in paying Robert's school fees, and in other ways. It is impossible and inappropriate to attempt to weigh the balance of advantage and disadvantage. The Gilletts decided at an early stage that their future lay with Mr Holt, and as with most human relationships that involved obligations and compensations. I cannot find in them such a balance of 'detriment' as to support the case for a legally enforceable obligation."

Both sides agree that the element of detriment is an essential ingredient of proprietary estoppel. There is one passage in the judgment of Lord Denning MR in *Greasley* v *Cooke* which suggests that any action in reliance on an assurance is sufficient, whether or not the action is detrimental. In *Watts* v *Storey* Dunn LJ (who was a party to the decision in *Greasley* v *Cooke*) explained Lord Denning's observations as follows:

"Nor, if that passage from Lord Denning MR's judgment is read as a whole, was he stating any new proposition of law. As the judge said, it matters not whether one talks in terms of detriment or whether one talks in terms of it being unjust or inequitable for the party giving the assurance to go back on it. It is difficult to envisage circumstances in which it would be inequitable for the party giving an assurance alleged to give rise to a proprietary estoppel, ie an estoppel concerned with the positive acquisition of rights and interests in the land of another, unless the person to whom the assurance was given had suffered some prejudice or detriment."

The overwhelming weight of authority shows that detriment is required. But the authorities also show that it is not a narrow or technical concept. The detriment need not consist of the expenditure of money or other quantifiable financial detriment so long as it is something substantial. The requirement must be approached as part of a broad inquiry as to whether repudiation of an assurance is or is not unconscionable in all the circumstances.

There are some helpful observations about the requirement for detriment in the judgment of Slade LJ in *Jones* v *Watkins*. There must be sufficient causal link between the assurance relied on and the detriment asserted. The issue of detriment must be judged at the moment when the person who has given the assurance seeks to go back on it. Whether the detriment is sufficiently substantial is to be tested by whether it would be unjust or inequitable to allow the assurance to be disregarded – that is, again, the essential test of unconscionability. The detriment alleged must be pleaded and proved.

... In my judgment the cumulative effect of the judge's findings and of the undisputed evidence is that by 1975 (the year of The Beeches incident) Mr Gillett had an exceptionally strong claim on Mr Holt's conscience. Mr Gillett was then 35. He had left school before he was 16, without taking any of the examinations which might otherwise have given him academic qualifications, against the advice of his headmaster and in the face of his parents' doubts, in order to work for and live with a 42 year old bachelor who was socially superior to, and very much wealthier than, his own parents. Mr Holt seriously raised the possibility of adopting him. Mr Holt's influence extended to Mr Gillett's social and private life and it seems to have been only through the diplomacy of Miss Sally Wingate (as she then was) that Mr Holt came to tolerate, and then accept, the notion of Mr Gillett having a girlfriend. Mr Holt had said that he would arrange for Mr Gillett to go to agricultural college but then did not arrange it, and it was only through Mr Gillett's own hard work and determination that he learned additional skills at evening classes. He proved himself by getting in the harvest in 1964 when Mr Holt was away fishing. All these matters preceded the first of the seven assurances on which Mr Gillett relied, so they are in a sense no more than background

because they refute Mr Martin's suggestion ... that Mr Gillett's claim should be regarded as a "startling" claim by someone who was no more than an employee. On the contrary ... Mr and Mrs Gillett and their sons provided Mr Holt with a sort of surrogate family.

However, a surrogate family of that sort is not the same as a birth family, and it is clear that Mr Gillett and his wife must often have been aware of the ambivalence of their position. Mr Holt was generous but it was the generosity of the patron; his will prevailed; Mr and Mrs Gillett were expected to and did subordinate their wishes to his ...

Mr Gillett also incurred substantial expenditure on the farmhouse at The Beeches, most of it after the clear assurance which Mr Holt gave him when, in 1975, he ventured to ask for something in writing "... That was not necessary as it was all going to be ours anyway." This was after the Gilletts had sold their own small house at Thimbleby and so had stepped off the property owning ladder which they had got on to in 1964.

It is entirely a matter of conjecture what the future might have held for the Gilletts if in 1975 Mr Holt had (in spite of what he actually said) told the Gilletts frankly that his present intention was to make a will in their favour, but that he was not bound by that and that they should not count their chickens before they were hatched. Had they decided to move on, they might have done no better. They might ... have found themselves working for a less generous employer. The fact is that they relied on Mr Holt's assurance, because they thought he was a man of his word, and so they deprived themselves of the opportunity of trying to better themselves in other ways. Although the judge's view, after seeing and hearing Mr and Mrs Gillett, was that detriment was not established, I find myself driven to the conclusion that it was amply established. I think that the judge must have taken too narrowly financial a view of the requirement for detriment, as his reference to "the balance of advantage and disadvantage" suggests. Mr Gillett and his wife devoted the best years of their lives to working for Mr Holt and his company, showing loyalty and devotion to his business interests, his social life and his personal wishes, on the strength of clear and repeated assurances of testamentary benefits. They received (in 1983) 20 per cent of the shares in KAHL, which must be regarded as received in anticipation of, and on account of, such benefits. Then in 1995, they had the bitter humiliation of summary dismissal and a police investigation of alleged dishonesty which the defendants called no evidence to justify at trial. I do not find Mr Gillett's claim startling … I would find it startling if the law did not give a remedy in such circumstances.'

Comment
The Court of Appeal awarded Mr and Mrs Gillett the freehold of The Beeches, the land occupied by Countryside Companions, their tree nursery business, and land they farmed under contract together with £100,000, the purpose of the award being to give them the 'minimum required to do justice between the parties' and to achieve a clean break. Robert Walker LJ makes it clear that the question of detriment is not only financial detriment and the circumstances in which the claim of estoppel arose must be viewed as a whole.

Inwards v *Baker* [1965] 2 QB 29
Court of Appeal (Lord Denning MR, Danckwerts and Salmon LJJ)

• *Proprietary estoppel – nature of relief*

Facts
In 1931 a father suggested to his son, who was looking for a site for a bungalow, that he should build it on some land owned by the father. The father said: 'Why don't you build the bungalow on my land and make it a bit bigger?' Encouraged by this the son did not look further for a site and built a bungalow on the father's land by his own labour. The son went into occupation and was visited at the bungalow by the father on several occasions. The father died in 1951 and by his will made in 1922 his land was vested in trustees for a person other than his son. It was clear that the father had forgotten to make provision for his son. The trustees of the will brought proceedings for possession of the bungalow. The county court judge granted them possession. The son appealed.

Held
As the son had expended money on the land of his father in the expectation, fostered and encouraged by the father, that he would be allowed to remain in occupation as long as he wished, there was an equity created in favour of the son under which he could occupy the bungalow as long as he desired.

Lord Denning MR:

'So in this case, even though there is no binding contract to grant any particular interest to the licensee, nevertheless the court can look at the circumstances and see whether there is an equity arising out of the expenditure of money. All that is necessary is that the licensee should, at the request or with the encouragement of the landlord, have spent the money in the expectation of being allowed to stay there. If so, the court will not allow that expectation to be defeated where it would be inequitable so to do. In this case it is quite plain that the father allowed an expectation to be created in the son's mind that this bungalow was to be his home. It was to be his home for his life or, at all events, his home as long as he wished to remain his home. It seems to me, in the light of that equity, that the father could not in 1932 have turned to his son and said: "You are to go. It is my land, my house." Nor could he at any time thereafter so long as the son wanted it as his home.

Mr Goodhart put the case of a purchaser. He suggested that the father could sell the land to a purchaser who could get the son out. But I think that any purchaser who took with notice would clearly be bound by the equity. So here, too, the present plaintiffs, the successors in title of the father, are clearly themselves bound by this equity. It is an equity well recognised in law. It arises from the expenditure of money by a person in actual occupation of land when he is led to believe that, as the result of that expenditure, he will be allowed to remain there. It is for the court to say in what way the equity can be satisfied. I am quite clear in this case it can be satisfied. I am quite clear in this case it can be satisfied by holding that the defendant can remain there as long as he desires to as his home ...'

Comment

In this case the intention of the father was sufficiently clear from the representations made to the son for the court to find that his executors were estopped from claiming the property for the estate.

James v *Williams* [1999] 3 WLR 451 Court of Appeal (Sir Stephen Browne P, Swinton-Thomas and Aldous LJJ)

• *Fiduciary duty – executor de son tort as constructive trustee*

Facts

The plaintiff's father (who was the defendant's grandfather) died intestate so that the family home went on the statutory trusts to her mother who subsequently died intestate, by which time the plaintiff had become estranged from her brother and sister who lived in the house. The three surviving children were entitled to the house under the rules of intestacy. William, the plaintiff's brother, did not take out letters of administration and treated the property as his own. On his own death, he purported to leave the house by will to Thirza, the sister with whom he lived, and her daughter, the defendant in this case. He was able to do this because the property was still held in the name of his father which was identical to his own name. On Thirza's death, the defendant claimed to be solely entitled to the house. The plaintiff claimed a one-third share in the house. At first instance the judge

held that the plaintiff's brother was an executor de son tort, having dealt with the property as his own, but that an executor de son tort could not be liable as a constructive trustee. This meant that the plaintiff was making her claim outside the limitation period and could not succeed. The plaintiff appealed.

Held

The appeal was allowed. In the circumstances of this case, an executor de son tort could be a constructive trustee. A constructive trust had arisen on the plaintiff's mother's death. The brother had known that he was not solely entitled to the property. Had he taken out letters of administration, he would have become his mother's personal representative and would have owed his sisters a fiduciary duty. It would be inequitable to allow him to take advantage of his own decision not to take out letters of administration and to claim the property as his own. Through him, the defendant held the property on constructive trust for the plaintiff and her claim was not statute-barred.

Aldous LJ:

'Mr Ainger, in his clear and concise submission on behalf of the defendant submitted that this was not a case where a constructive trust should be imposed. He took us to Underhill and Hayton *Law of Trusts and Trustees* (15th edn, 1995) and drew to our attention arts 33 to 38. He submitted that the facts of this case do not fit any of the categories enumerated in Underhill and Hayton. He is right. But that, in my view, is not surprising as there is no direct authority upon the issue raised, namely whether an executor de son tort being one of three adult children subsisting at the date of the death of an intestate parent became a constructive trustee. That issue has to be, in my view, decided upon general principles.

As a general rule a constructive trust attaches by law to property which is held by a person in circumstances where it would be inequitable to allow him to assert full beneficial ownership of the property. Is this such a case?

Mr Parker, who appeared for the plaintiff,

submitted that in the present case the concept of constructive trust should apply. He relied on the fact that William junior took possession knowing his parents had died intestate and that his sisters were entitled to a share of the property. Further, he submitted that this was a case where there had been concealment by William junior and perhaps Thirza of the plaintiff's right to a share and deliberate exclusion of the plaintiff. The judge did not find that there had been concealment and I do not believe that it would be right for this court to conclude there was, particularly as the plaintiff continued to communicate with her mother for about 20 years after the grandfather had purchased the property. If she had wanted to know the true position then she could have asked her mother.

In the present case, William junior knew that the grandfather had purchased the house and that on his death the grandmother had acquired his interest. He also knew that the grandmother had died intestate. In those circumstances, he could not have believed that he alone was entitled to the property. He must have known that the plaintiff was entitled to a share. If he had taken out letters of administration, then he would have become a personal representative and would have taken on the duties incident to that office. The result, in my view, would have been that there would have been a trust within the definition of s68 of the Trustee Act 1925 and he would have owed a fiduciary duty to his sisters. It is the fact that letters of administration were not taken out, that makes it possible for the defendant to contend that no fiduciary duty was owed. I accept that there is no duty upon a person to become a personal representative, but I believe that the failure by William junior to take out letters of administration is relevant when considering what is the equitable position in this case as equity envisages that what should have been done has been done.

In my view the circumstances of this case are such that the constructive trust arose in about 1972 on the death of the grandmother. William junior knew that he was not solely entitled to the property. He took it upon himself to take possession of the property as if he owned it and assumed responsibility for its upkeep. In my view he was under an equitable duty to hold the property for himself and his sisters. Looking at the state of affairs as at the grandmother's death, the law envisaged that the property would be held upon a statutory trust for the children. It would be inequitable to allow William junior and, through him, the defendant, to take advantage of his decision not to take out letters of administration and to act as if he was the owner with the full knowledge that he was not. This is an unusual case and ... there are many cases where executors de son tort could not be constructive trustees. Each case will depend upon its own facts. But in my view this is a case where there was a constructive trust. It follows that the defendant's title is that of constructive trustee with the result that the plaintiff's case is not statute barred. That being so, the plaintiff must obtain a grant of letters of administration (see *Jackson* v *Sutcliffe*).

The defendant contends in her respondent's notice that if the plaintiff's claim depends upon a constructive trust then she should be able to deduct from the proceeds of sale of 2 Rose Cottages a sum to reflect either the expenditure on the property in 1985 or a sum equal to the extent by which its value was enhanced.

The plaintiff accepted that a constructive trustee could recover expenditure properly incurred but not that which was not. She submitted that the money spent in 1985 was not spent with the intention of preserving the trust property but was spent so as to benefit William junior. Further, William junior was not entitled to recover the money spent as he did not have clean hands.

Mr Ainger did not dispute that money spent improperly by a trustee could not be recovered from the trust property. He submitted that costs such as that spent on the roof had been properly spent and were recoverable.

I have no doubt that expenditure on repairs and maintenance of a property are in general proper expenses of the trustee and therefore they are properly to be paid out of the trust property; in this case deductible from the proceeds of sale. This court cannot work out whether any particular payment is properly deductible from the proceeds of sale. To do that the case must be remitted to a district judge who will give directions for the sale of the property and how the necessary account should be conducted. In view of the money already spent in resolving this dispute, I hope that all remaining issues can be decided by agreement.

For the reasons I have given I would allow this appeal.'

Comment

It would be unconscionable to allow William to rely on his own omission to take out letters of administration and claim fully entitlement to the property. The Court of Appeal applied the equitable maxim 'Equity envisages that which should have been done as done' and puts him in the position of personal representative and thus in a fiduciary relationship with his sisters. Note that the defendant was able to counterclaim for expense properly incurred on the maintenance of the property.

Jennings v *Rice* [2003] 1 P & CR 8
Court of Appeal (Aldous, Mantell and Robert Walker LJJ)

• *Proprietary estoppel – relationship of sum awarded to detriment suffered*

Facts

Jennings had been Mrs Royle's part-time gardener and odd job man since 1970. She died childless and intestate in 1997 leaving an estate of £1,285,000. Jennings worked unpaid from about 1980 onwards, having been assured by Mrs Royle that "he would be all right" and "this will all be yours one day". As Mrs Royle became more and more infirm, Jennings stayed in the house, helped her wash, dress and go to the lavatory and did her shopping. He believed that he would receive all or part of Mrs Royle's property on her death. The judge at first instance awarded him £200,000

on the basis that this would have been the cost of full time care for Mrs Royle. Jennings appealed, claiming to be entitled to £435,000, the estimated value of the house and furniture.

Held

The appeal was dismissed. The value of the award will depend on all the circumstances, including the expectation of the claimant and the detriment suffered. The court must do what is necessary to avoid an unconscionable result. There must be proportionality between expectation and the detriment.

Robert Walker LJ:

'The court was referred to two recent articles which contain a full and illuminating discussion of this area: "Estoppel and the Protection of Expectations" by Elizabeth Cooke [1997] 17 LS 258 and "The Remedial Discretion in Proprietary Estoppel" by Simon Gardner (1999) 115 LQR 438. Those articles could with advantage have been cited in *Gillett* v *Holt*. Both are concerned with whether the fundamental aim of this form of estoppel is to fulfil the claimant's expectations, or to compensate him for his detrimental reliance on the defendant's non-contractual assurances, or is some intermediate objective; and (following on from the identification of the correct principle) the nature of the discretion which the court exercises in granting a remedy to the claimant. The articles amply demonstrate that the range of English authorities provides some support for both theories and for a variety of intermediate positions; and that recent Australian authority (especially the decision of the High Court in *Commonwealth* v *Verwayen* has moved in favour of the reliance loss theory.

It cannot be doubted that in this as in every other area of the law, the court must take a principled approach, and cannot exercise a completely unfettered discretion according to the individual judge's notion of what is fair in any particular case. Dr Gardner's fourth hypothesis ("the approach is for the court to adopt whatever style and measure of relief it thinks fit, for whatever reason it thinks fit") cannot be right. I do not think that the judgment of Hobhouse LJ in *Sledmore* v *Dalby* (to which I shall return) can possibly be regarded as adopting or advocating an unfettered judicial discretion.

The need to search for the right principles cannot be avoided. But it is unlikely to be a short or simple search, because (as appears from both the English and the Australian authorities) proprietary estoppel can apply in a wide variety of factual situations, and any summary formula is likely to prove to be an over-simplification. The cases show a wide range of variation in both of the main elements, that is the quality of the assurances which give rise to the claimant's expectations and the extent of the claimant's detrimental reliance on the assurances. The doctrine applies only if these elements, in combination, make it unconscionable for the person giving the assurances (whom I will call the benefactor, although that may not always be an appropriate label) to go back on them.

Sometimes the assurances, and the claimant's reliance on them, have a consensual character falling not far short of an enforceable contract (if the only bar to the formation of a contract is non-compliance with s2 of the Law of Property (Miscellaneous Provisions) Act 1989, the proprietary estoppel may become indistinguishable from a constructive trust: *Yaxley* v *Gotts*). In a case of that sort both the claimant's expectations and the element of detriment to the claimant will have been defined with reasonable clarity. A typical case would be an elderly benefactor who reaches a clear understanding with the claimant (who may be a relative, a friend, or a remunerated companion or carer) that if the claimant resides with and cares for the benefactor, the claimant will inherit the benefactor's house (or will have a home for life). In a case like that the consensual element of what has happened suggests that the claimant and the benefactor probably regarded the expected benefit and the accepted detriment as being (in a general, imprecise way) equivalent, or at any rate not

obviously disproportionate. Cases of that sort, if free from other complications, fit fairly comfortably into Dr Gardner's first or second hypothesis (both of which aim to vindicate the claimant's expectations as far as possible, and if possible by providing the claimant with the specific property which the benefactor has promised).

However, the claimant's expectations may not be focused on any specific property. In *Re Basham* the deputy judge (Mr Edward Nugee QC) rejected the submission that there must be some clearly identified piece of property, and that decision has been approved more than once in this court. Moreover, (as the judge's findings in this case vividly illustrate), the claimant's expectations may have been formed on the basis of vague and inconsistent assurances. The judge said of Mrs Royle that she:

"... was prone to saying different things at different times and, perhaps deliberately, couched her promises in non-specific terms."

He made that observation in relation to the failure of the contract claim, but it is relevant to the estoppel claim also.

If the claimant's expectations are uncertain (as will be the case with many honest claimants) then their specific vindication cannot be the appropriate test. A similar problem arises if the court, although satisfied that the claimant has a genuine claim, is not satisfied that the high level of the claimant's expectations is fairly derived from his deceased patron's assurances, which may have justified only a lower level of expectation. In such cases the court may still take the claimant's expectations (or the upper end of any range of expectations) as a starting point, but unless constrained by authority I would regard it as no more than a starting point.

I do not see that approach as being inconsistent with authority. On the contrary, I think it is supported by a substantial body of English authority. Scarman LJ's well-known reference to "the minimum equity to do justice to the plaintiff" (*Crabb* v *Arun District Council*) must no doubt be read in the context of the rather unusual facts of that case, but it does not stand alone. As Scarman LJ recognised, the line of authority goes back to nineteenth-century cases such as *Duke of Beaufort* v *Patrick* and *Plimmer* v *Wellington Corporation*. A passage in the opinion of the Privy Council (delivered by Sir Arthur Hobhouse) in *Plimmer*'s case … is particularly instructive. The conclusion of the passage is that:

> "… in fact, the court must look at the circumstances in each case to decide in what way the equity can be satisfied."

Scarman LJ's reference to the minimum does not require the court to be constitutionally parsimonious, but it does implicitly recognise that the court must also do justice to the defendant.

It is no coincidence that these statements of principle refer to satisfying the equity (rather than satisfying, or vindicating, the claimant's expectations). The equity arises, not from the claimant's excpectations alone, but from the combination of expectations, detrimental reliance, and the unconscionableness of allowing the benefactor (or the deceased benefactor's estate) to go back on the assurances. There is a faint parallel with the old equitable doctrine of part performance, of which Lord Selborne said in *Maddison* v *Alderson*:

> "In a suit founded on such part performance, the defendant is really 'charged' upon the equities resulting from the acts done in execution of the contract, and not (within the meaning of the statute) upon the contract itself."

So with proprietary estoppel the defendant is charged with satisfying the equity which has arisen from the whole sequence of events. But the parallel is only faint since in the case of estoppel there is no contract and the nexus between the benefactor's assurances and the resulting equity is less direct; the assurances are only half the story. In *Dillwyn* v *Llewelyn* Lord Westbury expressed the point in terms which anticipated Lord Selborne:

> "The equity of the donee and the estate to be claimed by virtue of it depend on the transaction, that is, on the acts done, and not on the language of the memorandum [which amounted to an imperfect gift}."

To recapitulate, there is a category of case in which the benefactor and the claimant have reached a mutual understanding which is in reasonably clear terms but does not amount to a contract. I have already referred to the typical case of a carer who has the expectation of coming into the benefactor's house, either outright or for life. In such a case the court's natural response is to fulfil the claimant's expectations. But if the claimant's expectations are uncertain, or extravagant, or out of all proportion to the detriment which the claimant has suffered, the court can and should recognise that the claimant's equity should be satisfied in another (and generally more limited) way.

But that does not mean that the court should in such a case abandon expectations completely, and look to the detriment suffered by the claimant as defining the appropriate measure of relief. Indeed in many cases, the detriment may be even more difficult to quantify, in financial terms, than the claimant's expectations. Detriment can be quantified with reasonable precision if it consists solely of expenditure on improvements to another person's house, and in some cases of that sort an equitable charge for the expenditure may be sufficient to satisfy the equity (see *Snell's Equity*, 30th ed, para 39–21 and the authorities mentioned in that paragraph). But the detriment of an ever-increasing burden of care for an elderly person, and having to be subservient to his or her moods and wishes, is very difficult to quantify in money terms. Moreover the claimant may not be motivated solely by reliance on the benefactor's assurances, and may receive some countervailing benefits (such as free bed and board). In such circumstances the court has to exercise a wide judgmental discretion.

It would be unwise to attempt any comprehensive enumeration of the factors relevant to the exercise of the court's discretion or to suggest any hierarchy of factors. In my view they include, but are not limited to, the factors mentioned in Dr Gardner's third hypothesis (misconduct of the claimant, or particularly oppressive conduct on the part of the defendant). To these can safely be added the court's recognition that it cannot compel people who have fallen out to live peaceably together, so that there may be a need for a clean break; alterations in the benefactor's assets and circumstances, especially where the benefactor's assurances have been given , and the claimant's detriment has been suffered, over a long period of years, the likely effect of taxation; and (to a limited degree) the other claims (legal or moral) on the benefactor or his or her estate. No doubt there are many other factors which it may be right for the court to take into account in particular factual situations.

The judge did in this case consider, although not in detail, what Jennings might reasonably have earned in the way of arm's length remuneration for his services. He also considered what professional nursing care might have cost during the last eight years of Mrs Royle's life. A detailed computational approach was adopted (but with a different outcome, limited to compensation of reliance loss) by the Supreme Court of Tasmania in *Public Trustee* v *Wadley*, in which the court discussed the appropriate hourly rate and the total number of hours of housework undertaken by a daughter who (as it was put in the dissenting judgment of Wright J):

> "… had subordinated her own life to that of her father and whose attentive and affectionate service, often no doubt at considerable inconvenience to herself, put her assistance on a higher plane of that of a domestic servant."

That illustrates the Australian preference for compensating the reliance loss only. Under English law that approach may sometimes be appropriate but only where, on the facts, a higher measure would amount to over-compensation. In my view it would rarely if ever be appropriate to go into detailed inquiries as to hours and hourly rates when

the claim was based on proprietary estoppel (rather than a restitutionary claim for services which were not gratuitous). But the going rate for live in carers can provide a useful cross-check in the exercise of the court's discretion.

I have made some references to the general trend of Australian jurisprudence in this area. It is unnecessary to attempt any detailed study of the different views expressed by the High Court in the *Verwayen* case (which was concerned with estoppel in the very different context of litigation arising out of personal injuries suffered in a collision between two warships) or of Australian cases since then.

However, I respectfully agree with the view expressed by Hobhouse LJ in *Sledmore* v *Dalby* that the principle of proportionality (between remedy and detriment) … is relevant in England also. As Hobhouse LJ observes, to recognise the need for proportionality:

> "… is to say little more than that the end result must be a just one having regard to the assumption made by the party asserting the estoppel and the detriment which he has experienced."

The essence of the doctrine of proprietary estoppel is to do what is necessary to avoid an unconscionable result, and a disproportionate remedy cannot be the right way of going about that. Cases on interim injunctive relief have recognised the importance of proportionality in the granting of equitable remedies … Where the court is granting final relief after investigating all the facts, proportionality is even more important .

I do not consider that the judge made any error of law in his approach to the exercise of his discretion, or that it was otherwise flawed. He did make an error in his reference to the quantum of the relief granted in *Gillett* v *Holt* (the claimant was awarded a farmhouse and 42 hectares of land as well as £100,000). But every case depends on its own facts and that slip cannot in my view have played a significant part in the judge's disposal of the case.

I would therefore dismiss this appeal.'

Comment
Robert Walker LJ again emphasised the principled nature of equitable remedies – that they are granted according to a recognised set of principles. In cases of proprietary estoppel, he emphasises the need for proportionality between the detriment suffered and the amount awarded by the court.

Keech v *Sandford* (1726) Sel Cas t King 61 Lord Chancellor's Court (Lord King LC)

• *Duty of fiduciary not to profit from his position of trust*

Facts
A owned a market lease which he bequeathed to B in trust for an infant. B before the expiration of the term applied to the lessor for a renewal for the benefit of the infant. The lessor refused to grant such renewal so B got the lease made to himself. On a bill to have the lease assigned to the infant:

Held
B was a trustee of the lease for the infant, and must assign it to him and account for the profits.

Lord King LC:

'I must consider this as a trust for the infant, for I very well see, if a trustee, on the refusal to renew, might have a lease for himself, few trust estates would be renewed to a cestui que trust. Though I do not say there is a fraud in this case, yet he (the trustee) should rather have let it run out than to have had the lease to himself. This may seem hard that the trustee is the only person of all mankind who might not have the lease, but it is very proper that the rule should be strictly pursued, and not in the least relaxed; for it is very obvious what would be the consequence of letting trustees have the lease on refusal to renew to cestui que trust.'

Comment
This is the statement of fiduciary duty on which all future cases rest.

Lipkin Gorman v *Karpnale Ltd*
[1991] 3 WLR 10 House of Lords (Lords Bridge of Harwich, Templeman, Griffiths, Ackner and Goff of Chieveley)

• *Constructive trust – position of 'strangers' to a trust – conversion*

Facts
Cass, a partner in a firm of solicitors, misappropriated clients' money which he used in gambling. Cass was subsequently convicted of theft. The firm sought to recover the money from the casino where he gambled and from the firm's bank on the basis, inter alia, that each was a constructive trustee. The claim against the casino on the basis of knowing receipt failed at first instance as the staff there did not have actual knowledge that Cass was gambling with trust funds; nor did they have constructive knowledge of his misuse of trust funds. But the claim against the bank on the basis of knowing assistance succeeded at first instance as the bank manager was, on the judge's findings at first instance, aware that Cass's gambling was out of control, that his personal accounts were operating irregularly and that he had access to clients' accounts but either shut his eyes to the obvious or wilfully and recklessly failed to make proper enquiries. However, it was held on appeal to the Court of Appeal that the evidence did not justify the judge's findings concerning the bank manager's knowledge. Since it was on the footing of these findings that the judge had found the bank to be liable as constructive trustee, the Court of Appeal ruled that the bank's appeal must be allowed. Further, as the Court of Appeal pointed out, the relationship between a bank and its customer is contractual and, accordingly, the bank cannot be liable as a constructive trustee of funds in its cus-

tomer's account unless it is also in breach of its contractual duty of care towards its customers. In this case the Court of Appeal concluded that the evidence did not disclose a breach of the bank's duty of care towards its customer. There was a further appeal to the House of Lords.

Held

The solicitors' claim against the casino must be allowed to the extent of the balance after taking into consideration the gambler's winnings – ie making allowance for the gambler's winnings in favour of the casino. Although it was fully accepted that the casino had acted innocently and in good faith throughout, its case for retaining the money as against the solicitors depended on contracts which were rendered void by s18 of the Gaming Act 1845 for lack of consideration.

Lord Templeman:

'In the course of argument there was a good deal of discussion concerning tracing in law and in equity. In my opinion, in a claim for money had and received by a thief, the plaintiff victim must show that money belonging to him was paid by the thief to the defendant and that the defendant was unjustly enriched and remained unjustly enriched. An innocent recipient of stolen money may not be enriched at all; if Cass had paid £20,000 derived from the solicitors to a car dealer for a motor car priced at £20,000, the car dealer would not have been enriched. The car dealer would have received £20,000 for a car worth £20,000. But an innocent recipient of stolen money will be enriched if the recipient has not given full consideration. If Cass had given £20,000 of the solicitors' money to a friend as a gift, the friend would have been enriched and unjustly enriched because a donee of stolen money cannot in good conscience rely on the bounty of the thief to deny restitution to the victim of the theft. Complications arise if the donee innocently expends the stolen money in reliance on the validity of the gift before the donee receives notice of the victim's claim for restitution.

Thus, if the donee spent £20,000 in the purchase of a motor car which he would not have purchased but for the gift, it seems to me that the donee has altered his position on the faith of the gift and has only been unjustly enriched to the extent of the second hand value of the motor car, at that date when the victim of the theft seeks restitution. If the donee spends £20,000 in a trip round the world, which he would not have undertaken without the gift, it seems to me that the donee has altered his position on the faith of the gift and that he is not unjustly enriched when the victim of the theft seeks restitution. In the present case Cass stole and the club received £229,908.48 of the solicitors' money. If the club was in the same position as a donee, the club nevertheless in good faith allowed Cass to gamble with the solicitors' money and paid his winnings from time to time so that, when the solicitors sought restitution, the club only retained £154,695 derived from the solicitors. The question is whether the club which was enriched by £154,695 at the date when the solicitors sought restitution was unjustly enriched.

The club claims that it gave consideration for the sum of £154,695 by allowing Cass to gamble and agreeing to pay his winnings and therefore the club was not enriched or, alternatively, was not unjustly enriched. The solicitors claim that the club acquired £154,695 under void contracts and that, as between the club and the solicitors from whom the money was derived, the club is in no better position than an innocent donee from the thief, Cass. The resolution of this dispute depends on the true construction of s18 of the Gaming Act 1845, an analysis of the relationship between the club and Cass and a consideration of the authorities dealing with gaming and the authorities dealing with unjust enrichment.

Section 18 of the Gaming Act, so far as material provides:

"... all contracts or agreements, whether by parole or in writing, by way of gaming or wagering, shall be null and void; and ... no suit shall be brought or maintained in any court of law or equity for recovering any sum of money or valuable thing alleged to be won upon any wager, or which shall have been deposited in the hands of any person to abide the event on which any wager shall have been made ..."

The club contends that the club received money from Cass under a contract with him which was not a contract "by way of gaming or wagering" and is not rendered null and void by s18 of the 1845 Act. Alternatively, even if the club received the money under a contract by way of gaming nevertheless, it is argued, the club was not unjustly enriched because, in the belief that the money tendered by Cass was his own personal money, the club accepted the money and altered the position of the club to the detriment of the club by allowing Cass to gamble and by paying his winnings when he won; the club, it is said, was enriched, but not unjustly enriched, and may retain the money which the club fairly and lawfully won. It is well settled that s18 of the 1845 Act does not enable a gambler to recover money which he has lost and paid ...

My lords, when Cass paid money to the cashier, he was issued with a receipt in the form of a credit voucher and then in the form of a chip. The chip did not oblige Cass to avail himself of the facilities of the club and did not oblige the club to allow Cass to gamble or take advantage of any other facilities of the club. If a thief deposits stolen money in a building society, the victim is entitled to recover the money from the building society without producing the pass book issued to the thief. As against the victim, the building society cannot pretend that the building society have good consideration for the acceptance of the deposit. The building society has been unjustly enriched at the expense of the victim. Of course the building society has a defence if the building society innocently pays out the deposit before the building society realises that the deposit was stolen money. But in the present case the club retained some of the stolen money. The club cannot as against the solicitors retain the stolen money save by relying on the gaming contracts which, as

between the club and Cass, entitled the club to retain the solicitors' money which Cass lost at the gaming table. Those gaming contracts were void. The club remains unjustly enriched to the extent of £154,695.'

Comment

The Court of Appeal's ruling makes clear, in particular, the basis of the relationship between a bank and its customer in respect of paying that customer's cheques drawn on a current account in credit. Note also that in this case May LJ stated that in his opinion:

'... there is at least strong persuasive authority for the proposition that nothing less than knowledge, as defined in one of the first three categories stated by Peter Gibson J in *Baden, Delvaux and Lecuit* (ie (1) actual knowledge; (2) wilfully shutting one's eyes to the obvious; (3) wilfully and recklessly failing to make such inquiries as an honest and reasonable man would make) of an underlying dishonest design is sufficient to make a stranger a constructive trustee of the consequences of that design.'

In allowing the solicitors' appeal against the casino to the extent of the casino's winning balance as against the gambler, the House of Lords recognised, per Lord Goff, that 'bona fide change of position should of itself be a good defence.'

Accordingly, as Lord Goff also pointed out :

'... it would be inequitable to require the casino to repay in full without bringing into account winnings paid by it to the gambler on any one or more of the bets so placed with it.'

Lord Goff's judgment is quoted at length by Robert Walker LJ in *Scottish Equitable plc* v *Derby* in Chapter 15.

Lloyds Bank plc v Rosset [1990] 2 WLR 867 House of Lords (Lords Bridge, Griffiths, Ackner, Oliver and Jauncey)

• *Extent of contribution necessary to raise a constructive trust*

Facts

The husband provided funds from a trust of which he was beneficiary to purchase a house which was conveyed into his name. He then took a substantial overdraft to pay for considerable renovation work, and the charge was secured on the house. Repayment was demanded and not made, and the bank sued for possession. The husband had left and did not contest the claim, but the wife claimed an equitable interest, both under the Land Registration Act 1925 and as a beneficiary under a constructive trust as a result of work which she had done in the renovation.

Held

Following the decision the same day in *Abbey National Building Society* v *Cann*, the wife failed in the claim under the Land Registration Act. She based her claim to a property interest on either a resulting or a constructive trust in her favour. On this point the Court held that, since the work she had done did not amount to more than that which any wife would have done as part of her normal activities, and particularly as the evidence showed that much of it had been because she was anxious for the house to be ready by Christmas, her contribution was insufficient to give rise to a constructive trust.

Lord Bridge:

'On any view the monetary value of Mrs Rosset's work expressed as a contribution to a property acquired at a cost exceeding £70,000 must have been so trifling as to be de minimis. I should myself have had considerable doubt whether Mrs Rosset's contribution to the work of renovation was sufficient to support a claim to a constructive

trust in the absence of writing to satisfy the requirements of s51 of the Law of Property Act 1925 even if her husband's intention to make a gift to her of half or any other share in the equity of the property had been clearly established or if he had clearly represented to her that that was what he intended. But here the conversations with her husband on which Mrs Rosset relied, all of which took place before November 1982, were incapable of lending support to the conclusion of a constructive trust in the light of the judge's finding that by that date there had been no decision that she was to have any interest in the property. The finding that the discussions "did not exclude the possibility" that she should have an interest does not seem to me to add anything of significance.

... In the course of the argument your Lordships had the benefit of elaborate submissions as to the test to be applied to determine the circumstances in which the sole legal proprietor of a dwelling house can properly be held to have become a constructive trustee of a share in the beneficial interest in the house for the benefit of a partner with whom he or she has cohabited in the house as their shared home.

... The first and fundamental question which must always be resolved is whether, independently of any inference to be drawn from the conduct of the parties in the course of sharing the house as their home and managing their joint affairs, there has at any time prior to acquisition or exceptionally at some later date, been any agreement, arrangement or understanding reached between them that the property is to be shared beneficially. The finding of an agreement or arrangement to share in this sense can only, I think, be based on evidence of express discussion between the partners, however imperfectly remembered and however imprecise the terms may have been. Once a finding to this effect is made it will only be necessary for the partner asserting a claim to a beneficial interest against the partner entitled to the legal estate to show that he or she has acted to his or her detriment or significantly altered his or her position in reliance on the agreement in order to give rise to a constructive trust or proprietary estoppel.

In sharp contrast with this situation is the very different one where there is no evidence to support a finding of an agreement or arrangement to share, however reasonable it might have been for the parties to reach such an arrangement if they had applied their minds to the question, and where the court must rely entirely on the conduct of the parties both as the basis from which to infer a common intention to share the property beneficially and as the conduct relied on to give rise to a constructive trust. In this situation direct contributions to the purchase price by the partner who is not the legal owner, whether initially or by payment of mortgage instalments, will readily justify the inference necessary to the creation of a constructive trust. But, as I read the authorities, it is at least extremely doubtful whether anything less will do. ...

Outstanding examples on the other hand of cases giving rise to situations in the first category are *Eves* v *Eves* and *Grant* v *Edwards*. In both these cases, where the parties who had cohabited were unmarried, the female partner had been clearly led by the male partner to believe, when they set up home together, that the property would belong to them jointly. In *Eves* v *Eves* the male partner had told the female partner that the only reason why the property was to be acquired in his name alone was because she was under 21 and that, but for her age, he would have had the house put into their joint names. He admitted in evidence that this was simply an "excuse". Similarly, in *Grant* v *Edwards* the female partner was told by the male partner that the only reason for not acquiring the property in joint names was because she was involved in divorce proceedings and that, if the property were acquired jointly, this might operate to her prejudice in those proceedings. As Nourse LJ put it:

"Just as in *Eves* v *Eves*, these facts appear to me to raise a clear inference that there was an understanding between the plaintiff and the defendant, or a common intention, that the plaintiff was to have some

sort of proprietary interest in the house; otherwise no excuse for not putting her name onto the title would have been needed."

The subsequent conduct of the female partner in each of these cases, which the court rightly held sufficient to give rise to a constructive trust or proprietary estoppel supporting her claim to an interest in the property fell far short of such conduct as would by itself have supported the claim in the absence of an express representation by the male partner that she was to have such an interest. It is significant to note that the share to which the female partners in *Eves* v *Eves* and *Grant* v *Edwards* were held entitled were one-quarter and one-half respectively. In no sense could these shares have been regarded as proportionate to what the judge in the instant case described as a "qualifying contribution" in terms of the indirect contribution to the acquisition or enhancement of the value of the houses made by the female partners.

I cannot help thinking that the judge in the instant case would not have fallen into error if he had kept clearly in mind the distinction between the effect of evidence on the one hand which was capable of establishing an express agreement or an express representation that Mrs Rosset was to have an interest in the property and evidence on the other hand of conduct alone as a basis for an inference of the necessary common intention.'

Comment
This is the definitive judgment on constructive trusts of the family home but note its application in *Midland Bank plc* v *Cooke* below.

Midland Bank plc v *Cooke and Another* [1995] 4 All ER 562 Court of Appeal (Stuart Smith, Waite and Schiemann LJJ)

• *Constructive trust of the family home*

Facts
In 1971 Mr and Mrs Cooke were married and

moved into their matrimonial home which was purchased in the sole name of the husband with the aid of a deposit which was funded by a wedding present to both of them from his parents. The property was mortgaged and subsequently remortgaged to the bank to secure Mr Cooke's business borrowing. Mrs Cooke signed a consent form. At no time was there any discussion or agreement between the parties as to the beneficial ownership of the property. The bank sought possession of the property and Mrs Cooke claimed a one-half share in the property. At first instance, the judge found that the consent form was signed under undue influence and awarded her a 6.74 per cent share under a resulting trust by virtue of her share of the deposit. Mrs Cooke appealed to the Court of Appeal and the bank cross-appealed on the ground that her signature had not been obtained by undue influence.

Held

Mrs Cooke's appeal was allowed and the bank's cross-appeal was dismissed. Once Mrs Cooke had established her initial contribution to the purchase price, the Court could look at all the circumstances when assessing her share.

Waite LJ:

'The general principle to be derived from *Gissing v Gissing* and *Grant v Edwards* can, in my judgment, be summarised in this way. When the court is proceeding, in cases like the present, where the partner without legal title has successfully asserted an equitable interest through direct contribution, to determine (in the absence of express evidence of intention) what proportions the parties must be assumed to have intended for their beneficial ownership, the duty of the judge is to undertake a survey of the whole course of dealing between the parties relevant to their ownership and occupation of the property and their sharing of its burdens and advantages. That scrutiny will not confine itself to the limited range of acts of direct contribution of the sort that are needed to found a

beneficial interest in the first place. It will take into consideration all conduct which throws light on the question what shares were intended. Only if that search proves inconclusive does the court fall back on the maxim 'equality is equity'.

The court is not bound to deal with the matter on the strict basis of the trust resulting from the cash contribution to the purchase price, and is free to attribute to the parties an intention to share the beneficial interest in some different proportions.

Equity has traditionally been a system which matches established principles to the demands of social change. The mass diffusion of home ownership has been one of the most striking social changes of our own time. When people, especially young people, agree to share their lives in joint homes they do so on a basis of mutual trust and in the expectation that their relationship will endure. For a couple embarking on a serious relationship, discussion of the terms to apply at parting is almost a contradiction of the shared hopes that have brought them together. There will inevitably be numerous couples, married or unmarried, who have no discussions about ownership and who, perhaps advisedly, make no agreement about it. It would be anomalous, against that background, to create a range of home buyers who were beyond the pale of equity's assistance in formulating a fair presumed basis for the sharing of beneficial title, simply because they had been honest enough to admit that they never gave ownership a thought or reached any agreement about it.'

Comment

In the face of express evidence from both parties to the marriage that there had never been any agreement between as to the beneficial ownership of the matrimonial home, Waite LJ was still prepared to infer one from the circumstances under which the couple shared their living expenses, having once established that the wife had made a direct initial contribution to the purchase price.

Montagu's Settlement Trusts, Re
[1987] 2 WLR 1192 Chancery
Division (Sir Robert Megarry V-C)

• *Constructive trust – knowledge*

Facts
This case concerned a settlement for the
Dukes of Manchester. In 1923 he assigned
such chattels as the trustees of the settlement
should select on a trust designed to benefit the
eleventh Duke, the plaintiff. The chattels to
be put in trust for the plaintiff were to be
selected by the trustees from a remainder
interest due to tenth Duke on the death of the
ninth Duke.

When, however, the ninth Duke died in
1947 and the chattels in question vested in the
tenth Duke the trustees failed to make the
inventory and selection of chattels envisaged
by the 1923 settlement. The trustees later
released these chattels to the tenth Duke in
1948 and allowed him to treat the chattels as
his own free of any trust.

The plaintiff, now the eleventh Duke,
claimed that the trustees in failing to make the
selection had committed a breach of trust and
also that the chattels released by the trustees to
the tenth Duke were held by him as a constructive trustee for the plaintiff. This constructive trust claim was based on the head of
knowing receipt of trust property by a third
party as originally set out in the case of *Barnes
v Addy*.

Held
No constructive trust arose in this case.

Sir Robert Megarry V-C:

'It seems to me that one must be very
careful about applying to constructive trusts
either the accepted concepts of notice or any
analogy to them. In determining whether a
constructive trust has been created, the fundamental question is whether the conscience
of the recipient is bound in such a way as to
justify equity in imposing a trust on him.
The rules concerning a purchaser without
notice seem to me to provide little guidance

on this and to be liable to be misleading.
First, they are irrelevant unless there is a
purchase . A volunteer is bound by an equitable interest even if he has no notice of it;
but in many cases of alleged constructive
trusts the disposition has been voluntary and
not for value, and yet notice or knowledge is
plainly relevant. Second, although a purchaser normally employs solicitors, and so
questions of imputed notice may arise, it is
unusual for a volunteer to employ solicitors
when about to receive bounty. Even if he
does, he is unlikely to employ them in order
to investigate the right of the donor to make
the gift or of the trustees or personal representatives to make the distribution; and until
this case came before me I had never heard
it suggested that a volunteer would be fixed
with imputed notice of all that his solicitors
would have discovered had he employed
solicitors and had instructed them to investigate his right to receive the property.

… There seems to me to be a fundamental
difference between the questions that arise
in respect of the doctrine of purchaser
without notice and constructive trusts. As I
said in my previous judgment:

"The former is concerned with the question whether a person takes property
subject to or free from some equity. The
latter is concerned with whether or not a
person is to have imposed upon him the
personal burden and obligations of
trusteeship. I do not see why one of the
touchstones for determining the burdens
on property should be the same as that for
deciding whether to impose a personal
obligation on a man. The cold calculus of
constructive and imputed notice does not
seem to me to be an appropriate instrument for deciding whether a man's conscience is sufficiently affected for it to be
right to bind him by the obligations of a
constructive trustee."

I can see no reason to resile from that statement, save that to meet possible suscepti-
bilities I would alter "man" to "person". I
would only add that there is more to being
made a trustee than merely taking a property
subject to an equity. …

There is one further general consideration

that I should mention and that is that 'the court should not be astute to impute knowledge where no actual knowledge exists': see the *Baden* case at p415, per Peter Gibson J. This approach goes back at least as far as *Barnes* v *Addy*. The view of James LJ at p256 was that the court had in some cases:

> "... gone to the very verge of justice in making good to cestui que trust the consequences of the breaches of trust of the trustees at the expense of persons perfectly honest, but who have been, in some more or less degree, injudicious."

Of the five categories of knowledge set out in the *Baden* case, Mr Chadwick, as well as Mr Taylor, accepted the first three. What was in issue was nos (iv) and (v), namely knowledge of circumstances which would "indicate the facts to an honest and reasonable man" or "would put an honest and reasonable man on inquiry". On the view that I take of the present case I do not think that it really matters whether or not categories (iv) and (v) are included, but as the matter has been argued at length, and further questions on it may arise, I think I should say something about it.

First, as I have already indicated, I think that one has to be careful to distinguish the notice that is relevant to the doctrine of purchaser without notice from the knowledge that suffices for the imposition of a constructive trust. This is shown by a short passage in the long judgment of the Court of Appeal in *In re Diplock*. There, it was pointed out that on the facts of that case persons unversed in the law were entitled to assume that the executors were properly administering the estate, and that if those persons received money bona fide believing themselves to be entitled to it, "they should not have imposed upon them the heavy obligations of trusteeship". The judgment then pointed out:

> "The principles applicable to such cases are not the same as the principles in regard to notice of defects in title applicable to transfers of land where regular machinery has long since been established for inquiry and investigation."

To that I may add the obvious point that the provisions about constructive notice in s199 of the Law of Property Act 1925 apply only to purchasers (as defined in s205 (1)(xxi)) and are not in point in relation to a beneficiary who receives trust property from the trustees.

... I shall attempt to summarise my conclusions. In doing this I make no attempt to reconcile all the authorities and dicta, for such a task is beyond me; and in this I suspect I am not alone. Some of the difficulty seems to arise from judgments that have been given without all the relevant authorities having been put before the judges. All I need do is to find a path through the wood that will suffice for the determination of the case before me and assist those who have to read this judgment.

(1) The equitable doctrine of tracing and the imposition of a constructive trust by reason of the knowing receipt of trust property are governed by different rules and must be kept distinct. Tracing is primarily a means of determining the rights of property, whereas the imposition of a constructive trust creates personal obligations that go beyond mere property rights.

(2) In considering whether a constructive trust has arisen in a case of the knowing receipt of trust property, the basic question is whether the conscience of the recipient is sufficiently affected to justify the imposition of such a trust.

(3) Whether a constructive trust arises in such a case primarily depends on the knowledge of the recipient, and not on notice to him; and for clarity it is desirable to use the word "knowledge" and avoid the word "notice" in such cases.

(4) For this purpose, knowledge is not confined to actual knowledge, but includes at least knowledge of types (ii) and (iii) in the *Baden* case, ie actual knowledge that would have been acquired but for shutting one's eyes to the obvious, or wilfully and recklessly failing to make such inquiries as a reasonable and honest man would make; for in such cases there is a want of probity which justifies imposing a constructive trust.

(5) Whether knowledge of the *Baden* types (iv) and (v) suffices for this purpose is at best doubtful; in my view, it does not, for I cannot see that the carelessness involved will normally amount to a want of probity.

(6) For these purposes, a person is not to be taken to have knowledge of a fact that he once knew but has genuinely forgotten: the test (or a test) is whether the knowledge continues to operate on that person's mind at the time in question.

(7) (a) It is at least doubtful whether there is a general doctrine of "imputed knowledge" that corresponds to "imputed notice". (b) Even if there is such a doctrine, for the purposes of creating a constructive trust of the "knowing receipt" type the doctrine will not apply so as to fix a donee or beneficiary with all the knowledge that his solicitor has, at all events if the donee or beneficiary has not employed the solicitor to investigate his right to the bounty, and has done nothing else that can be treated as accepting that the solicitor's knowledge should be treated as his own. (c) Any such doctrine should be distinguished from the process whereby, under the name "imputed knowledge" a company is treated as having the knowledge that its directors and secretary have.

(8) Where an alleged constructive trust is based not on "knowing receipt" but on "knowing assistance", some at least of these considerations probably apply; but I need not decide anything on that, and I do not do so.'

Comment
Note the court's reluctance to impose a constructive trust on one who innocently receives trust property. Contrast the US application of a remedial constructive trust as noted in *Westdeutsche Landesbank Girozentrale* v *Islington London Borough Council* (see Chapter 14).

O'Sullivan v *Management Agency*
[1985] 3 All ER 351 Court of Appeal (Waller, Dunn and Fox LJJ)

• *Fiduciary relationship – constructive trusts*

Facts
The plaintiff, a well known composer and performer of popular music, entered into several agreements with the defendants in 1970 with regard to recording, publishing and performing musical works composed by him. The agreement included, inter alia, the assignment of copyright in these works. At the time the agreements were entered into the plaintiff was a young man with no business experience and he trusted the defendants implicitly. The plaintiff did not seek independent legal advice on the agreement nor was he encouraged to do so by the defendants. Consequently, the agreements were less advantageous to the plaintiff than they might have been had they been negotiated at arm's length on independent legal advice. The plaintiff achieved considerable success; by 1972 he had several hit records and was in considerable demand as a performer throughout the world. In 1976 the relationship between the plaintiff and the defendants broke down after a series of disagreements and because the plaintiff was unhappy with his contractual arrangements. The plaintiff eventually issued proceedings against the defendants claiming that the agreements were void because they had been obtained by undue influence and were also in restraint of trade. The trial judge held that the agreements were obtained by undue influence and were in restraint of trade and he also found that there was a fiduciary relationship between the defendants and the plaintiff arising from the confidence that had been reposed by the plaintiff in the defendants. Accordingly, the agreements were set aside, the copyrights were reconveyed to the plaintiff, and accounts ordered of the profits made by the defendants from the copyrights with compound interest to be paid on such profits. The defendants

appealed against the judgment. Two issues which arose on appeal were (1) whether the defendants were in a fiduciary relationship with the plaintiff and (2) whether they were liable to account for all the profits and compound interest thereon.

Held

1. Whenever two persons stand in a relationship whereby confidence is reposed by one in the other this gives rise to a confidential relationship. Such a relationship made the party in whom confidence was reposed a fiduciary. The defendants were, accordingly, in a fiduciary relationship to the plaintiff.
2. The defendants were liable to account for the profits they had made out of the fiduciary relationship. It was no bar to setting the contracts aside that restitutio in integrum was impossible because the contracts had been fully performed. The Court would set aside the contracts if this would lead to a just solution and would order the defendants to account for the profits with due allowance being made for any work the defendants had performed under the contract and also reasonable remuneration.

Fox LJ:

'It is said on behalf of the plaintiffs that if the principle of equity is that the fiduciary must account for profits obtained through the abuse of the fiduciary relationship, there is no scope for the operation of anything resembling restitutio in integrum. The profits must simply be given up. I think that goes too far and the law has for long had regard to the justice of the matter. If, for example, a person is by undue influence persuaded to make a gift of a house to another and that other spends money on improving the house, I apprehend that a credit could be given for the improvement...

... The next question is, it seems to me, the recompensing of the plaintiffs. The rules of equity against the retention of benefits by fiduciaries have been applied with severity. In *Boardman* v *Phipps* where the fiducia-

ries though in breach of the equitable rules, acted with complete honesty throughout, only succeeded in obtaining an allowance on a liberal scale for their work and skill ...

... These latter observations ... accept the existence of a power in the court to make an allowance to a fiduciary. And I think it is clearly necessary that such a power should exist. Substantial injustice may result without it. A hard and fast rule that the beneficiary can demand the whole profit without an allowance for the work without which it could not have been created would be unduly severe. Nor do I think that the principle is only applicable in cases where the personal conduct of the fiduciary cannot be criticised. I think that the justice of the individual case must be considered on the facts of the case. Accordingly, where there has been dishonesty or surreptitious dealing or other improper conduct ... it might be appropriate to refuse relief ...

... Once it is accepted that the Court can make an appropriate allowance to a fiduciary for his skill and labour I do not see why, in principle, it should not be able to give him some part of the profit of the venture if it was thought that justice between the parties demanded that. To give the fiduciary any allowance for his skill and labour involves some reduction of the profits otherwise payable to the beneficiary. And the business reality may be that the profits could never have been earned at all, as between fully independent persons, except on a profit sharing basis ...'

Comment

As in *Boardman* v *Phipps*, a constructive trustee is entitled to make a reasonable charge for his/her services if an agreement between the parties expressly so provides. This is a separate issue from making a profit by virtue of the fiduciary relationship.

Polly Peck International plc (In Administration), Re, Marangos Hotel Co Ltd and Others v *Stone and Others* [1998] 3 All ER 813 Court of Appeal (Nourse, Potter and Mummery LJJ)

• *Remedial constructive trust*

Facts

The applicants claimed to own and to be entitled to immediate possession of land in Northern Cyprus which had been declared by the Northern Cyprus authorities to be the property of the Republic of Northern Cyprus. The applicants claimed that their property had been, with knowledge of the wrongs committed against them and their property, illegally occupied and exploited without their authority and in this action sought leave to proceed against PPI and its administrators claiming that a substantial sum received by the administrators represented the profits and proceeds of wrongdoing by PPI which had been unjustly enriched at the applicants' expense. They claimed that the sum was subject to a remedial constructive trust for their benefit. At first instance the application was granted, whereupon PPI appealed to the Court of Appeal.

Held

The appeal was allowed. Such an order would require the court to impose a remedial constructive trust retrospectively on an insolvent company and this would operate to exclude the assets from a distribution pari passu in the liquidation.

Mummery LJ:

'On its face the claim is novel: the applicants seek an order from an English court retrospectively imposing on the assets of an insolvent company in administration in England a "remedial constructive trust" giving them a proprietary interest in those assets. By decree of the court the consideration would cease to be an asset absolutely

and beneficially owned by PPI. The imposed constructive trust would operate to exclude the asset from pari passu distribution by the administrators among the unsecured creditors of PPI in accordance with the legislative scheme prescribed in the 1986 Act …

The remedial constructive trust
The conclusion of the judge was that –

"… the question whether the court should impose a remedial constructive trust in those circumstances is not one which I can properly determine on this application, but that it may well be a seriously arguable question in the circumstances which emerge at the trial of the applicants' claim."

I agree with the judge that, for the reasons given by him, there is no seriously arguable claim for an institutional constructive trust. After detailed argument from both parties on the question of a "remedial constructive trust", I also conclude that the claim of the applicants that the court should retrospectively confer a proprietary interest on them in respect of the assets of the insolvent PPI is not seriously arguable in English law.

I start with the few English cases on the topic, beginning at the highest level. In *Westdeutsche Landesbank Girozentrale* v *Islington Borough Council*, Lord Browne-Wilkinson recognised that there is a critical distinction between an institutional constructive trust and a remedial constructive trust:

"Under an institutional constructive trust, the trust arises by operation of law as from the date of the circumstances which give rise to it: the function of the court is merely to declare that such trust has arisen in the past. The consequences that flow from such trust having arisen (including the possibly unfair consequences to third parties who in the interim have received the trust property) are also determined by rules of law, not under a discretion. A remedial constructive trust, as I understand it, is different. It is a judicial remedy giving rise to an unenforceable equitable obligation: the extent to which it operates retrospectively to the prejudice of third parties lies in the discretion of the court."

In an earlier passage, Lord Browne-Wilkinson said that, whereas the New York law of constructive trusts had for a long time been influenced by the concept of a remedial constructive trust, "English law has for the most part only recognised an institutional constructive trust": see *Metall und Rohstoff AG* v *Donaldson Lufkin & Jenrette Inc*.

In the latter case the Court of Appeal, after quoting from *Snell's Principles of Equity* and Goff and Jones *The Law of Restitution* (3rd edn 1986) said:

"While we have had the benefit of very full argument on almost all other aspects of the law involved in this case, we have neither heard nor invited comprehensive argument as to the circumstances in which the court will be prepared to impose a constructive trust de novo as a foundation for the grant of and equitable remedy by way of account or otherwise. Nevertheless, we are satisfied that there is a good arguable case that such circumstances may arise and, for want of a better description, will refer to a constructive trust of this nature as a 'remedial constructive trust'."

In the *Westdeutsche* case, Lord Browne-Wilkinson concluded:

"Although the resulting trust is an unsuitable basis for developing proprietary restitutionary remedies, the remedial constructive trust, if introduced into English law, may provide a more satisfactory road forward. The court by way of remedy might impose a constructive trust on a defendant who knowingly retains property of which the plaintiff has been unjustly deprived. Since the remedy can be tailored to the circumstances of the particular case, innocent third parties would not be prejudiced and restitutionary defences, such as a change of position, are capable of being given effect. However, whether English law should follow the United States and Canada by adopting the remedial constructive trust will have to be decided in some future case when the point is directly in issue."

Later cases do not, in my view, take the matter of remedial constructive trusts any further than the statements quoted above. The other cases cited were, first *Re Goldcorp Exchange Ltd (In Receivership)* where Lord Mustill, in his opinion in the Privy Council, referred to an ill-defined "remedial restitutionary right" created by the court after the event "superior to the security created by the charge". He commented: "Although remedial restitutionary rights may prove in the future to be a valuable instrument of justice they cannot in their Lordships' opinion be brought to bear on the present case."

In *El Ajou* v *Dollar Land Holdings plc*, Millett J, after having referred to the requirement of a fiduciary relationship in order to establish a right to trace in equity, made it clear that reliance was being placed not "on some new model remedial constructive trust, but an old-fashioned institutional resulting trust." Miss Dohmann cited from the opinion of Lord Nicholls in *Royal Brunei Airlines Sdn Bhd* v *Tan* a passage dealing with the liability of a dishonest accessory to a breach of trust, in particular the comment of Lord Nicholls:

"If a person knowingly appropriates another's property, he will not escape a finding of dishonesty simply because he sees nothing wrong in such behaviour ... honest people do not knowingly take others' property."

Miss Dohmann contended that the subsidiary companies of PPI in Northern Cyprus fall within that damning description.

Finally, an earlier case cited in later decisions of the English courts (and in the Canadian Supreme Court) is *Chase Manhattan Bank NA* v *Israeli-British Bank (London) Ltd*. The interest of the case for present purposes lies in the passage of the judgment of Goulding J, who rejected the contention that in an insolvency situation the rights of a person claiming a constructive trust had been excluded by the imposition of a statutory trust under the Companies Act 1985. Goulding J held that where the claim rested on a "persistent equitable proprietary interest" the assets affected did not, at the commencement of the insolvent winding up, belong beneficially to the company and therefore never formed part of the property subject to the statutory trust arising on a winding up.

That analysis is essential to the applicants' case. They wish to claim priority over the interests of the unsecured creditors of the insolvent PPI by establishing a proprietary interest in assets which would exclude those assets from pari passu distribution to the unsecured creditors. Naturally, they prefer not to stand with their personal claim in the long (and ultimately unrewarding) wait in the queue at the check-out for the unsecured creditors of PPI. The applicants wish to apply the analysis of Goulding J in the case of a "persistent equitable proprietary interest" to the case of an equitable proprietary interest arising from the ex post facto imposition by the court, in the exercise of its discretion, of a remedial constructive trust.

In my judgment, not even the Supreme Court of Canada, which has pioneered the remedial constructive trust, has gone that far in imposing such a trust.'

Nourse LJ:

'I agree with Mummery LJ that where, as here, there would be not simply a variation of proprietary rights but a variation of the manner in which the administrators are directed to deal with PPI's assets by the Insolvency Act 1986 it is not seriously arguable, even at the highest level, that a remedial constructive trust would be imposed. For myself, I would go further and hold that it would not be seriously arguable, even if PPI was solvent. It is not that you need an Act of Parliament to prohibit a variation of proprietary rights. You need one to permit it: see the Variation of Trusts Act 1958 and the Matrimonial Causes Act 1973.'

Comment
This case gives a very useful review of the case law relating to remedial constructive trusts and gives a clear indication of the reluctance of the English courts to adopt the concept, despite the dicta of Lord Browne-Wilkinson in *Westdeutsche*.

Royal Bank of Scotland v *Etridge (No 2) and Other Appeals* [2001] 4 All ER 449 House of Lords (Lords Bingham of Cornhill, Nicholls of Birkenhead, Clyde, Hobhouse of Woodborough and Lord Scott of Foscote)

• *Undue influence – manifest disadvantage*

Facts
These cases were brought by the banks against wives who had charged the matrimonial home or guaranteed loans from the banks in connection with their husbands' businesses.

Held
The rebuttable presumption of undue influence is raised by a transaction with a party in whom the complainant has imposed trust and confidence or in which that party has gained ascendancy over the complainant and one which is not readily explicable by the relationship of the parties. In these circumstances the burden of proof rests with the party who is denying undue influence. A wife's guarantee of her husband's business debts is not to be regarded as a class of transaction which is only explicable by the exercise of undue influence.

Lord Nicholls:

'The issues raised by these appeals make it necessary to go back to first principles. Undue influence is one of the grounds of relief developed by the courts of equity as a court of conscience. The objective is to ensure that the influence of one person over another is not abused. In everyday life people constantly seek to influence the decisions of others. They seek to persuade those with whom they are dealing to enter into transactions, whether great or small. The law has set limits to the means properly employable for this purpose. To this end the common law developed a principle of duress. Originally this was narrow in its scope, restricted to the more blatant forms of physical coercion, such as personal violence.

Here, as elsewhere in the law, equity supplemented the common law. Equity extended the reach of the law to other unacceptable forms of persuasion. The law will investigate the manner in which the intention to enter into the transaction was secured: "how the intention was produced", in the oft repeated words of Lord Eldon LC, from as long ago as 1807 (*Huguenin* v *Basely*). If the intention was produced by an unacceptable means, the law will not permit the transaction to stand. The means used is regarded as an exercise of improper or "undue" influence, and hence unacceptable, whenever the consent thus procured ought not fairly to be treated as the expression of a person's free will. It is impossible to be more precise or definitive. The circumstances in which one person acquires influence over another, and the manner in which influence may be exercised, vary too widely to permit of any more specific criterion.

Equity identified broadly two forms of unacceptable conduct. The first comprises overt acts of improper pressure or coercion such as unlawful threats. Today there is much overlap with the principle of duress as this principle has subsequently developed. The second form arises out of a relationship between two persons where one has acquired over another a measure of influence, or ascendancy, of which the ascendant person then takes unfair advantage. An example from the nineteenth century, when much of this law developed, is a case where an impoverished father prevailed upon his inexperienced children to charge their reversionary interests under their parents' marriage settlement with payment of his mortgage debts (see *Bainbrigge* v *Browne*).

The evidential presumption discussed above is to be distinguished sharply from a different form of presumption which arises in some cases. The law has adopted a sternly protective attitude towards certain types of relationship in which one party acquires influence over another who is vulnerable and dependent and where, moreover, substantial gifts by the influenced or vulnerable person are not normally to be expected. Examples of relationships within this special class are parent and child, guardian and ward, trustee and beneficiary, solicitor and client and medical advisor and patient. In these cases the law presumes, irrebuttably, that one party had influence over the other. The complainant need not prove he actually reposed trust and confidence in the other party. It is sufficient for him to prove the existence of the type of relationship.

It is now well established that husband and wife is not one of the relationships to which this latter principle applies. In *Yerkey* v *Jones* Dixon J explained the reason. The Court of Chancery was not blind to the opportunities of obtaining and unfairly using influence over a wife which a husband often possesses. But there is nothing unusual or strange in a wife, from motives of affection or for other reasons, conferring substantial financial benefits on her husband. Although there is no presumption, the court will nevertheless note, as a matter of fact, the opportunities for abuse which flow from a wife's confidence in her husband. The court will take this into account with all the other evidence in the case. Where there is evidence that a husband has taken unfair advantage of his influence over his wife, or her confidence in him, "it is not difficult for the wife to establish her title to relief" (see *Re Lloyds Bank Ltd, Bomze* v *Bomze* per Maugham J).

Proof that the complainant received advice from a third party before entering into the impugned transaction is one of the matters a court takes into account when weighing all the evidence. The weight, or importance, to be attached to such advice depends on all the circumstances. In the normal course, advice from a solicitor or other outside advisor can be expected to bring home to a complainant a proper understanding of what he or she is about to do. But a person may understand fully the implications of a proposed transaction, for instance, a substantial gift, and yet still be acting under the undue influence of another. Proof of outside advice does not, of itself, necessarily show that the subsequent completion of the transaction was free from the exercise of undue influence. Whether it will be proper to infer that outside advice had an emancipating effect, so that the transaction was not brought about by the exercise of undue influence, is a question of fact to be decided having regard to all the evidence in the case.

As already noted, there are two prerequisites to the evidential shift in the burden of proof from the complainant to the other party. First, that the complainant reposed trust and confidence in the other party, or the other party acquired ascendancy over the complainant. Second, that the transaction is not readily explicable by the relationship of the parties.

Lindley LJ summarised this second prerequisite in the leading authority of *Allcard* v *Skinner*, where the donor parted with almost all her property. Lindley LJ pointed out that where a gift of a small amount is made to a person standing in a confidential relationship to the donor, some proof of the exercise of the influence of the donee must be given. The mere existence of the influence is not enough. He continued:

> "But if the gift is so large as not to be reasonably accounted for on the ground of friendship, relationship, charity, or other ordinary motives on which ordinary men act, the burden is upon the donee to support the gift."

In *Bank of Montreal* v *Stuart* Lord Macnaghten used the phrase "immoderate and irrational" to describe this concept.

The need for this second prerequisite has recently been questioned: see Nourse LJ in *Barclays Bank* v *Coleman*, one of the cases under appeal before your Lordships' House. Mr Sher QC invited your Lordships to depart from the decision of the House on this point in *Morgan*'s case [see *National Westminster Bank* v *Morgan*].

My Lords, this is not an invitation I would accept. The second prerequisite, as express by Lindley LJ, is good sense. It is a necessary limitation upon the width of the first prerequisite. It would be absurd for the law to presume that every gift by a child to a parent, or every transaction between a client and his solicitor or between a patient and his doctor, was brought about by undue influence unless the contrary is affirmatively proved. Such a presumption would be too far-reaching. The law would be out of touch with everyday life if the presumption were to apply to every Christmas or birthday gift by a child to a parent, or to an agreement whereby a client or patient agrees to be responsible for the reasonable fees of his legal or medical advisor. The law would be rightly open to ridicule, for transactions such as these are unexceptionable. They do not suggest that something may be amiss. So something more is needed before the law reverses the burden of proof, something which calls for an explanation. When that something more is present, the greater the disadvantage to the vulnerable person, the more cogent must be the explanation before the presumption will be regarded as rebutted.

This was the approach adopted by Lord Scarman in *Morgan*'s case. He cited Lindley LJ's observations in *Allcard* v *Skinner*, which I have set out above. He noted that whatever the legal character of the transaction, it must constitute a disadvantage sufficiently serious to require evidence to rebut the presumption that, in the circumstances of the parties' relationship, it was procured by the exercise of undue influence. Lord Scarman concluded:

> "The Court of Appeal erred in law in holding that the presumption of undue influence can arise from the evidence of the relationship of the parties without also evidence that the transaction itself was wrongful in that it constituted *an advantage taken of the person subject to the influence which, failing proof to the contrary, was explicable only on the basis that undue influence had been exercised to procure it.*" (my emphasis)

Lord Scarman attached the label "manifest disadvantage" to this second ingredient necessary to raise the presumption. This label has been causing difficulty. It may be apt enough when applied to straightforward transactions such as a substantial gift or a sale at an undervalue. But experience has now shown that this expression can give rise to misunderstanding. The label is being understood and applied in away which does not accord with the meaning intended by Lord Scarman, its originator.

The problem has arisen in the context of wives guaranteeing payment of their husband's business debts. In recent years judge after judge has grappled with the baffling question whether a wife's guarantee of her husband's bank overdraft, together with a charge on her share of the matrimonial home, was a transaction manifestly to her disadvantage.

In a narrow sense, such a transaction plainly ("manifestly") is disadvantageous to the wife. She undertakes a serious financial obligation, and in return she personally received nothing. But that would be to take an unrealistically blinkered view of such a transaction. Unlike the relationship of solicitor and client or medical advisor and patient, in the case of husband and wife, there are inherent reasons why such a transaction may well be for her benefit. Ordinarily, the fortunes of husband and wife are bound up together. If the husband's business is the source of the family income, the wife has a lively interest in doing what she can to support the business. A wife's affection and self-interest run hand-in-hand in inclining her to join with her husband in charging the matrimonial home, usually a jointly-owned asset, to obtain the financial facilities needed by the business. The finance may be needed to start a new business, or expand a promising business, or rescue an ailing business.

Which, then, is the correct approach to adopt in deciding whether a transaction is disadvantageous to the wife: the narrow approach, or the wider approach? The answer is neither. The answer lies in discarding a label which gives rise to this sort of ambiguity. The better approach is to adhere more directly to the test outlined by Lindley LJ in *Allcard* v *Skinner* and adopted by Lord Scarman in *Morgan*'s case in the passages I have cited.

I return to husband and wife cases. I do not think that, in the ordinary course, a guarantee of the character I have mentioned is to be regarded as a transaction which, failing proof to the contrary, is explicable only on the basis that it has been procured by the exercise of undue influence by the husband. Wives frequently enter into such transactions. There are good and sufficient reasons why they are willing to do so, despite the risks involved for them and their families. They may be enthusiastic. They may not. They may be less optimistic than their husbands about the prospects of the husbands' businesses. They may be anxious, perhaps exceedingly so. But this is a far cry from saying that such transactions as a class are to be regarded as prima facie evidence of the exercise of undue influence by husbands.

I have emphasised "in the ordinary course". There will be cases where a wife's signature of a guarantee or a charge of her share in the matrimonial home does call for explanation. Nothing I have said above is directed at such a case.

I add a cautionary note, prompted by some of the first instance judgments in the cases currently being considered by the House. It concerns the general approach to be adopted by a court when considering whether a wife's guarantee of her husband's bank overdraft was procured by her husband's undue influence. Undue influence has a connotation of impropriety. In the eye of the law, undue influence means that influence has been misused. Statements or conduct by a husband which do not pass beyond the bounds of what may be expected of a reasonable husband in the circumstances should not, without more, be castigated as undue influence. Similarly, when a husband is forecasting the future of his business, and expressing his hopes or fears, a degree of hyperbole may be only natural. Courts should not too readily treat such exaggerations as misstatements.

Inaccurate explanations of a proposed transaction are a different matter. So are cases where a husband, in whom a wife has reposed trust and confidence for the management of their financial affairs, prefers his interests to hers and makes a choice for both of them on that footing. Such a husband abuses the influence he has. He fails to discharge the obligation of candour and fairness he owes a wife who is looking to him to make the major financial decisions.'

Comment

Lord Millett looks pragmatically at the situation of wives who guarantee loans for the husband's business activities and declines to generalise on the question of undue influence. He is at pains to cover all possible circumstances arising from this relationship and rejects Lord Scarman's well-established concept of 'manifest disadvantage'.

Royal Brunei Airlines Sdn Bhd v *Philip Tan Kok Ming* [1995] 3 All ER 97 Privy Council (Lords Goff, Ackner, Nicholls, Steyn and May)

• *Intermeddlers – constructive trusts – knowing assistance*

Facts

The defendant, Tan, was the principal director in, and shareholder of, Borneo Leisure Travel (BLT), a Brunei-incorporated travel agency. BLT acted as a ticket agent for the plaintiff, RBA, holding monies from ticket sales on trust for RBA under a standard form agreement. BLT became insolvent. Despite holding monies on trust for RBA, it was BLT's usual practice to pay part of the monies into its own bank account via a standing order, drawing from it for its own business purposes.

Held (on appeal to the Privy Council)

A person who dishonestly procured or assisted in a breach of trust or fiduciary obligation was liable in equity to make good any resulting loss and, although dishonesty was both a nec-

essary and a sufficient ingredient of accessory liability, the breach of trust which was a prerequisite for accessory liability need not itself be a dishonest or fraudulent breach of trust by the trustee.

Lord Nicholls:

'In the conventional shorthand the first of these two circumstances in which third parties (non-trustees) may become liable to account in equity is "knowing receipt", as distinct from the second where liability arises from "knowing assistance". Stated even more shortly, the first limb of Lord Selborne LC's formulation is concerned with the liability of a person as a *recipient* of trust property or its traceable proceeds. The second limb is concerned with what, for want of a better compendious description, can be called the liability of an *accessory* to a trustee's breach of trust. Liability as an accessory is not dependent upon receipt of trust property. It arises even though no trust property has reached the hands of the accessory. It is a form of secondary liability in the sense that it only arises where there has been a breach of trust. In the present case the plaintiff relies on the accessory limb. The particular point in issue arises from the expression "a dishonest and fraudulent design on the part of the trustees".'

His Lordship reviewed the facts and the earlier cases and continued:

'*The honest trustee and the dishonest third party*
It must be noted at once that there is a difficulty with the approach adopted on this point in the *Belmont* case. Take the simple example of an honest trustee and a dishonest third party. Take a case where a dishonest solicitor persuades a trustee to apply trust property in a way the trustee honestly believes is permissible but which the solicitor knows full well is a clear breach of trust. The solicitor deliberately conceals this from the trustee. In consequence, the beneficiaries suffer a substantial loss. It cannot be right that in such a case the accessory liability principle would be inapplicable because of the innocence of the trustee. In

ordinary parlance, the beneficiaries have been defrauded by the solicitor. If there is to be an accessory liability principle at all, whereby in appropriate circumstances beneficiaries may have direct recourse against a third party, the principle must surely be applicable in such a case, just as much as in a case where both the trustee and the third party have been dishonest. Indeed, if anything, the case for liability of the dishonest third party seems stronger where the trustee is innocent, because in such a case the third party alone was dishonest and that was the cause of the subsequent misapplication of the trust property.

The position would be the same if, instead of *procuring* the breach, the third party dishonestly *assisted* in the breach. Change the facts slightly. A trustee is proposing to make a payment out of the trust fund to a particular person. He honestly believes he is authorised to do so by the terms of the trust deed. He asks a solicitor to carry through the transaction. The solicitor well knows that the proposed payment would be a plain breach of trust. He also well knows that the trustee mistakenly believes otherwise. Dishonestly he leaves the trustee under the misapprehension and prepares the necessary documentation. Again, if the accessory principle is not to be artificially constricted, it ought to be applicable in such a case.

These examples suggest that what matters is the state of mind of the third party sought to be made liable, not the state of mind of the trustee. The trustee will be liable in any event for the breach of trust, even if he acted innocently, unless excused by an exemption clause in the trust instrument or relieved by the court. But *his* state of mind is essentially irrelevant to the question whether the *third party* should be made liable to the beneficiaries for the breach of trust. If the liability of the third party is fault-based, what matters is the nature of his fault, not that of the trustee. In this regard dishonesty on the part of the third party would seem to be a sufficient basis for his liability, irrespective of the state of mind of the trustee who is in breach of trust. It is difficult to see why, if the third party dishonestly assisted in a

breach, there should be a further prerequisite to his liability, namely that the trustee also must have been acting dishonestly. The alternative view would mean that a dishonest third party is liable if the trustee is dishonest but if the trustee did not act dishonestly that of itself would excuse a dishonest third party from liability. That would make no sense.'

Comment

In this case, Lord Nicholls recast the tests for the liability of strangers as constructive trustees. The judgment concludes with a clear analysis of the heads of liability under *Baden* and a reformulation of the requirement of dishonesty on the part of the stranger.

Satnam Investments Ltd v *Dunlop Heywood & Co Ltd* [1999] 3 All ER 653 Court of Appeal (Nourse, Schiemann and Brooke LJJ)

• *Constructive trust – breach of fiduciary duty – whether information is property of the trust – knowing receipt of confidential information*

Facts

Satnam was a property development company which acquired an option to purchase a site. There was a provision in the option agreement allowing the site's owners to terminate the option if Satnam went into receivership. When Satnam experienced cash flow problems, their bank put them into administrative receivership and Dunlop Heywood, who were acting as Satnam's surveyors at the time the option was granted, disclosed this information to a rival developer, Morbaine, who entered into negotiations to acquire the site from the owners. Having terminated the option, the owners sold the site to Morbaine. Satnam were discharged from receivership and brought an action against Dunlop Heywood, their employee, Mr Murray, and Morbaine on the grounds that Dunlop Heywood were in breach of their fiduciary duty and Morbaine were aware of the breach and were therefore liable as constructive trustee of the site for Satnam. The judge at first instance ordered Morbaine to transfer the site to Satnam on payment of their acquistion costs. Morbaine appealed.

Held

The appeal was allowed. Morbaine were not liable as constructive trustee – mere knowledge of Dunlop Heywood's breach of fiduciary duty was not enough in itself to put Morbaine under a fiduciary duty. Nor were they liable under the head of knowing receipt of the confidential information. Even if the confidential information received could be said to be property, that property could not be traced into the site as there was an insufficient nexus between the site and the confidential information.

Nourse LJ:

'*Did Dunlop Heywood and Mr Murray owe a fiduciary duty to Satnam?*
DH and Mr Murray had undertaken to act in the interests of Satnam. They clearly had both contractual and equitable obligations to Satnam and that has not been challenged. The core obligation of this type of fiduciary relationship is the obligation of loyalty. The incidents of that duty in the circumstances of the present case are the same whether one traces its origins to the common law of contract which imposes a duty of fidelity upon an agent or to equity. As Lord Browne-Wilkinson put it in *Henderson* v *Merrett Syndicates Ltd*:

> "Although the historical development of the rules of law and equity have, in the past, caused different labels to be stuck on different manifestations of the duty, in truth the duty of care imposed on bailees, carriers, trustees, directors, agents and others is the same duty: it arises from the circumstances in which the defendants were acting, not from their status or description."

We agree with the judge that it is plain that DH and Mr Murray were persons who owed fiduciary duties to Satnam.

Were DH and Mr Murray in breach of their fiduciary duties to Satnam?
The judge found that DH and Mr Murray were in breach of their fiduciary duties to Satnam both in sending the information in the disclosure letter and in not disclosing that Morbaine was seeking to acquire an interest in the Brewery Street site. That finding is challenged by Mr Vallance QC on behalf of DH and Mr Murray. The basis of the challenge was that DH were released from their duty to Satnam upon the appointment of the receivers, alternatively that it was in the interest of Satnam when in receivership for DH to introduce potential purchasers to interests in land which Satnam was in a position to sell. We do not regard this challenge as justified. There is no reason why the appointment of receivers should in itself alter the nature of, let alone bring to an end, the duties owed by DH to Satnam. Moreover, DH were clearly acting behind the backs of the directors of Satnam and the receivers and did not assume that they had the authority of either to offer to third parties information about their client. We agree with the judge that DH and Mr Murray acted in breach of their fiduciary duties to Satnam in both respects alleged.

Did Morbaine know that DH and Mr Murray were acting in breach of their fiduciary duties to Satnam?
The judge found that Morbaine knew that, in sending the disclosure letter and in not informing Satnam of Morbaine's interest, DH were acting in breach of duty. That finding is challenged by Mr Kent QC on behalf of Morbaine. The essence of the challenge is that there was no material entitling the judge to find that Morbaine knew that DH lacked specific authority from the directors or receivers of Satnam to disclose the relevant material in the disclosure letter. While we see some force in the argument if one looks at the position as at, say, 20th July, the behaviour thereafter of DH and Morbaine in not revealing what was going on to Satnam provides ample material to justify the judge's finding that:

> "... both Mr Parle and Mr John Finlan

Junior knew perfectly well that the information given to them in the letter of 17 July 1995 was given in breach of Dunlop Heywood's obligations of confidence to their clients Satnam."

Did the breaches of fiduciary duty by DH and Mr Murray cause loss to Satnam?

... The essence of Satnam's complaint against Morbaine having been that Morbaine used the opportunity afforded to it by DH's and Mr Murray's breaches of fiduciary duty for its own purposes, Satnam's case is in the mould of those which were successful in *Regal (Hastings) Ltd* v *Gulliver* and *Boardman* v *Phipps*. Chadwick J's reference to *Boardman* v *Phipps* at the end of the section of his judgment headed "Equitable remedies: the law" suggests that he thought that the principle of those cases was applicable here. In each of them, however, the defendants owed fiduciary duties to the plaintiff, in the first as directors of the plaintiff company and in the second as persons who had placed themselves in a special position of a fiduciary character, vis-à-vis the plaintiff beneficiary. In the absence of a fiduciary duty the principle of those cases cannot apply. Mere knowledge that the opportunity has been afforded in breach of someone else's fiduciary duty is not enough.

The only other basis on which it was suggested that Satnam could recover against Morbaine was that on which the *Sunday Times*, a third party, was held liable in *A-G* v *Guardian Newspapers Ltd (No 2)*. In that case, it was held that the newspaper had been in breach of an obligation of confidentiality when it published the first serialised extract from *Spycatcher* in July 1987 and that it was liable to account for the profits resulting from that breach. Mr Hapgood also relied on the decision of this court in *Schering Chemicals Ltd* v *Falkman Ltd*. While we do not question the correctness of either of those decisions, we decline to hold Morbaine liable for an account of profits on the facts of this case.

What the judge found was that some at least of the information was confidential at the time that it was disclosed, in that its disclosure to a rival developer would or might be detrimental to Satnam. However, even assuming that but for the disclosure Morbaine would not have acquired the Brewery Street site, it does not follow that it would be a proportionate response to hold it liable for an account of profits. All the circumstances must be considered. The information, though confidential, was not of the same degree of confidentiality as the information in the *Spycatcher* case and in *Schering Chemicals Ltd* v *Falkman Ltd*. All of it was either already available to Morbaine or would have been available to it on reasonable inquiry once, as was inevitable, the news of Satnam's receivership became known. There being no other basis of recovery available, it would in our view be inequitable and contrary to commercial good sense to allow Satnam to recover simply on the basis that there was a degree of confidentiality in the information at the time that it was disclosed to Morbaine.

Comment

On the facts of the case, Satnam had failed to establish a sufficient causal link between the supply of the information to Morbaine and the loss of their potential profit on the proposed development. Satnam had been put on notice that Morbaine was in the market for the sites and, had they taken heed of this information, they might have secured the sites. In any event, the receivership would have become public knowledge and the information relied on could have become available to Morbaine by other means. The Court of Appeal recognised the breach of the fiduciary duty of loyalty by Dunlop Heywood but refused to find that Morbaine was tainted with that knowledge.

Twinsectra Ltd v *Yardley and Others*
[2002] 2 WLR 802 House of Lords
(Lords Slynn of Hadley, Steyn,
Hoffmann, Hutton and Millett)

• *Constructive trust – dishonest assistance – subjective and objective tests of dishonesty* – Quistclose *trust – resulting trust*

Facts
A solicitor, Mr Sims, gave an undertaking to the lender, Twinsectra, that they would release a £1,000,000 mortgage advance to their client, Mr Yardley, for the sole purpose of the purchase of property. A solicitor's undertaking is a solemn form of promise under which the solicitor is bound to perform the terms of the undertaking to the letter or to compensate the person to whom it is given for any breach. While Mr Sims acted on the advance of the mortgage, another solicitor, Mr Leach, acted on the property acquisition, knowing of the undertaking given by Mr Sims and having refused to give a similar undertaking himself. Mr Leach received the money, knowing that it was subject to the undertaking but used only part of the money for the purchase of property. He paid over £357,720 to Mr Yardley to be used for other purposes. Twinsectra claimed that the undertaking gave rise to a relationship of trust and that Mr Leach had dishonestly assisted in a breach of trust.

The judge at first instance did not accept that the undertaking gave rise to any trust relationship because the terms of the undertaking were too vague. Nor did he accept that Mr Leach had acted dishonestly. This decision was reversed by the Court of Appeal on both issues whereupon Mr Leach appealed to the House of Lords.

Held (Lord Millett dissenting)
The money was held on trust because it was held in Mr Sims' client account. The terms of the trust were those given in the undertaking – that the money remained the lender's money until it was applied for the acquisition of property, with power to Mr Sims to advance the money. The Court of Appeal had been correct to reverse the judge at first instance and its application of a purely subjective test for dishonesty was approved.

Lord Millett gave a new test for accessory liability: the defendant's conduct was to be judged by the ordinary standards of reasonable and honest people and that he too realised that his conduct was dishonest. Both an objective and a subjective test should be applied – not a purely subjective test.

Lord Millett went on to say that the correct analysis of the relationship between Twinsectra, the two solicitors and Mr Yardley gave rise to a *Quistclose* trust (see *Barclays Bank* v *Quistclose Investments Ltd*), which, correctly analysed, was a resulting trust:

Lord Hoffmann:

'In my opinion, the effect of the undertaking was to provide that the money in the Sims client account should remain Twinsectra's money until such time as it was applied for the acquisition of property in accordance with the undertaking. For example, if Mr Yardley went bankrupt before the money had been so applied, it would not have formed part of his estate, as it would have done if Sims had held it in trust for him absolutely. The undertaking would have ensured that Twinsectra could get it back. It follows that Sims held the money in trust for Twinsectra, but subject to a power to apply it by way of loan to Mr Yardley in accordance with the undertaking. No doubt Sims also owed fiduciary obligations to Mr Yardley in respect of the exercise of the power, but we need not concern ourselves with those obligations because in fact the money was applied wholly for Mr Yardley's benefit. ...

Whether a trust was created and what were its terms must depend upon the construction of the undertaking ... The other question is whether Mr Leach, in receiving the money and paying it to Mr Yardley without concerning himself about its application, could be said to have acted dishonestly. The judge found that in so doing he was "misguided" but not dishonest. He had "shut his eyes" to some of the problems but thought he held the money to the order of Mr Yardley without restriction. The Court of Appeal reversed this finding and held that he had been dishonest.

My noble and learned friend, Lord Millett, considers that the Court of Appeal was justified in taking this view because liability as an accessory to a breach of trust does not depend upon dishonesty in the normal sense of that expression. It is sufficient that the defendant knew all the facts which made it wrongful for him to participate in the way in which he did. In this case, Mr Leach knew the terms of the undertaking. He therefore knew all the facts which made it wrongful for him to deal with the money to the order of Mr Yardley without satisfying himself that it was for the acquisition of property.

I do not think that it is fairly open to your Lordships to take this view of the law without departing from the principles laid down by the Privy Council in the *Royal Brunei* case. For the reasons given by my noble and learned friend Lord Hutton, I consider that those principles require more than knowledge of the facts which make the conduct wrongful. They require a dishonest state of mind, that is to say, consciousness that one is transgressing ordinary standards of honest behaviour. I also agree with Lord Hutton that the judge correctly applied this test and that the Court of Appeal was not entitled, on the basis of the written transcript, to make a finding of dishonesty which the judge who saw and heard Mr Leach did not.

The ground upon which the Court of Appeal reversed the judge's finding was that he had misdirected himself in law. His finding about Mr Leach shutting his eyes to problems meant that he did not appreciate that a person may be dishonest without actually knowing all the facts if he suspects that he is about to do something wrongful and deliberately shuts his eyes to avoid finding out. As Lord Nicholls said in the *Royal Brunei* case [see *Royal Brunei Airlines Sdn*

Bhd v *Philip Tan Kok Ming*], an honest man does not "deliberately close his eyes and ears, or deliberately not ask questions, lest he learn something he would rather not know, and then proceed regardless." So the Court of Appeal said that, when the judge said that Mr Leach was not dishonest, he meant that he was not "consciously dishonest". But the finding about shutting his eyes meant that in law had had nevertheless been dishonest.

I do not believe that the judge fell into such an elementary error. ... That said, I do respectfully think it was unfortunate that the judge three times used the expression "shut his eyes" to "the details" or "the problems" or "the implications". The expression produces in judges a reflex image of Admiral Nelson at Copenhagen and the common use of this image by lawyers to signify a deliberate abstinence from inquiry in order to avoid certain knowledge of what one suspects to be the case. But, as my noble and learned friend Lord Millett points out, there were in this case no relevant facts of which Mr Leach was unaware. What I think the judge meant was that he took a blinkered approach to his professional duties as a solicitor, or buried his head in the sand (to invoke two different animal images). But neither of those would be dishonest.

Mr Leach believed that the money was at the disposal of Mr Yardley. He thought that whether Mr Yardley's use of the money would be contrary to the assurance he had given Mr Sims or put Mr Sims in breach of his undertaking was a matter between those two gentlemen. Such a state of mind may have been wrong. It may have been, as the judge said, misguided. But if he honestly believed, as the judge found, that the money was at Mr Yardley's disposal, he was not dishonest.

I do not suggest that one cannot be dishonest without a full appreciation of the legal analysis of the transaction. A person may dishonestly assist in the commission of a breach of trust without any idea of what a trust means. The necessary dishonest state of mind may be found to exist simply on the fact that he knew perfectly well that he was helping to pay away money to which the recipient was not entitled. But that was not the case here. I would therefore allow the appeal and restore the decision of Carnwath J.'

Lord Hutton:

'... I do not think that it would have been right for the Court of Appeal in this case to have come to a different conclusion from the judge and to have held that Mr Leach was dishonest in that when he transferred the moneys to Mr Yardley he knew that his conduct was dishonest by the standards of responsible and honest solicitors.

I agree with Lord Hoffmann that it is unfortunate that Carnwath J referred to Mr Leach deliberately shutting his eyes to the problems and to the implications of the undertaking, but like Lord Hoffmann I do not think it probable that having cited the passage from the judgment of Lord Nicholls [in *Royal Brunei Airlines* v *Tan*], the judge then overlooked the issue of Nelsonian dishonesty in finding that Mr Leach was not dishonest. I also consider, as Lord Millett has observed, that this was not a case where Mr Leach deliberately closed his eyes and ears, or deliberately did not ask questions, lest he learned something he would rather not know – he already knew all the facts but the judge concluded that nevertheless he had not been dishonest. I also think that Potter LJ applied too strict a test when he stated:

> "It seems to me that, save perhaps in the most exceptional circumstances, it is not the action of an honest solicitor knowingly to assist or encourage another solicitor in a deliberate breach of undertaking."

This test does not address the vital point whether Mr Leach realised that his action was dishonest by the standards of responsible and honest solicitors. In the light of the judge's finding, based as it was on an assessment of Mr Leach's evidence in cross-examination in the witness box before him, I consider the Court of Appeal should not have substituted its own finding of dishonesty.'

Lord Millett (dissenting):

'My Lords, there are two issues in this appeal. The first is concerned with the nature of the so-called "*Quistclose* trust" and the requirements for its creation ... The second arises only if the first is answered adversely to the appellant. It is whether his conduct rendered him liable for having assisted in a breach of trust. This raises two questions of some importance. One concerns the extent of the knowledge of the existence of a trust which is required before a person can be found civilly liable for having assisted in its breach. In particular, is it sufficient that he was aware of the arrangements which created the trust or must he also have appreciated that they did so? The other, which has led to a division of opinion among your Lordships, is whether, in addition to knowledge, dishonesty is required and, if so, the meaning of dishonesty in this context. For reasons which will appear, a third question, concerned with the ingredients of the equitable claim tendentiously described as being in respect of the "knowing receipt" of trust property, is no longer alive. The much needed rationalisation of this branch of the law must, therefore, await another occasion.

...

Money advanced by way of loan normally becomes the property of the borrower. He is free to apply the money as he chooses, and save to the extent to which he may have taken security for repayment the lender takes the risk of the borrower's insolvency. But it is well established that a loan to a borrower for a specific purpose where the borrower is not free to apply the money for any other purpose gives rise to fiduciary obligations on the part of the borrower which a court of equity will enforce. In the earlier cases the purpose was to enable the borrower to pay his creditors or some of them, but the principle is not limited to such cases.

Such arrangements are commonly described as creating "a *Quistclose* trust", after the well-known decision of the House ... in which Lord Wilberforce confirmed the validity of such arrangements and explained their legal consequences. When the money is advanced, the lender acquires a right, enforceable in equity, to see that it is applied for the stated purpose, or more accurately to prevent its application for any other purpose. This prevents the borrower from obtaining any beneficial interest in the money, at least while the designated purpose is still capable of being carried out. Once the purpose has been carried out, the lender has his normal remedy in debt. If for any reason the purpose cannot be carried out, the question arises whether the money falls within the general fund of the borrower's assets, in which case it passes to his trustee in bankruptcy in the event of his insolvency and the lender is merely a loan creditor, or whether it is held on a resulting trust for the lender. This depends on the intention of the parties collected from the terms of the arrangement and the circumstances of the case.

In the present case Twinsectra contends that clauses 1 and 2 of the undertaking which Mr Sims signed on 24 December 1992 created a *Quistclose* trust. Mr Leach denies this and advances a number of objections to the existence of a trust. He says that Twinsectra lacked the necessary intention to create a trust, and relies on evidence that Twinsectra looked exclusively to Mr Sims' personal undertaking to repay the loan as its security for repayment. He says that commercial life would be impossible if trusts were lightly inferred from slight material, and that it is not enough to agree that a loan is to be made for a particular purpose. There must be something more, for example, a requirement that the money be paid into a segregated account, before it is appropriate to infer that a trust has been created. In the present case the money was paid into Mr Sims' client account, but that is sufficiently explained by the fact that it was not Mr Sims' money but his client's; it provides no basis for an inference that the money was held in trust for anyone other than Mr Yardley. Then it is said that a trust requires certainty of objects and this was lacking, for the stated purpose "to be applied in the purchase of property" is too uncertain to be

enforced. Finally, it is said that no trust in favour of Twinsectra could arise prior to the failure of the stated purpose, and this did not occur until the money was misapplied by Mr Yardley's companies.

The first two objections are soon disposed of. A settlor must, of course, possess the necessary intention to create a trust, but his subjective intentions are irrelevant. If he enters into arrangements which have the effect of creating a trust, it is not necessary that he should appreciate that they do so; it is sufficient that he intends to enter into them. Whether clauses 1 and 2 of the undertaking created a *Quistclose* trust turns on the true construction of those clauses.

The fact that Twinsectra relied for its security exclusively on Mr Sims' personal liability to repay goes to Twinsectra's intention and is not relevant to the construction of the undertaking, but it is in any case not inconsistent with the trust alleged. Arrangements of this kind are not intended to provide security for repayment of the loan, but to prevent the money from being applied otherwise than in accordance with the lender's wishes. If the money is properly applied the loan is unsecured. This was true of all the decided cases, including the *Quistclose* case itself.

A *Quistclose* trust does not necessarily arise merely because money is paid for a particular purpose. A lender will often inquire into the purpose for which a loan is sought in order to decide whether he would be justified in making it. He may be said to lend the money for the purpose in question, but this is not enough to create a trust; once lent the money is at the free disposal of the borrower. Similarly payments in advance for goods or services are paid for a particular purpose, but such payments do not ordinarily create a trust. The money is intended to be at the free disposal of the supplier and may be used as part of his cash flow. Commercial life would be impossible if this were not the case.

The question in every case is whether the parties intended the money to be at the free disposal of the recipient ... His freedom to dispose of the money is necessarily excluded by an arrangement that the money shall be used exclusively for the stated purpose, for as Lord Wilberforce observed in the *Quistclose* case:

> "A necessary consequence from this, by a process simply of interpretation, must be that if, for any reason, [the purpose could not be carried out], the money was to be returned to [the lender]: the word 'only' or 'exclusively' can have no other meaning or effect."

In the present case clauses 1 and 2 of the undertaking are crystal clear. Mr Sims undertook that the money would be used solely for the acquisition of property and for no other purpose, and was to be retained by his firm until so applied. It would not be held by Mr Sims simply to Mr Yardley's order, and it would not be at Mr Yardley's free disposition. Any payment by Mr Sims of the money, whether to Mr Yardley or anyone else, otherwise than for the acquisition of property would constitute a breach of trust.

Mr Leach insisted that such a payment would, no doubt, constitute a breach of contract, but there was no reason to invoke equitable principles merely because Mr Sims was a solicitor. But Mr Sims' status as a solicitor has nothing to do with it. Equity's intervention is more principled than this. It is unconscionable for a man to obtain money on terms as to its application and then disregard the terms on which he received it. ... The duty is not contractual but fiduciary. ... The duty is fiduciary in character because a person who makes money available on terms that it is to be used for a particular purpose only and not for any other purpose thereby places his trust and confidence in the recipient to ensure that it is properly applied. This is a classic situation in which a fiduciary relationship arises, and since it arises in respect of a specific fund it gives rise to a trust.

The latter two objections cannot be so easily disposed of. They call for an exploration of the true nature of the *Quistclose* trust, and in particular the location of the beneficial interest while the purpose is still capable of being carried out.

This has been the subject of much academic debate. The starting point is provided by two passages in Lord Wilberforce's speech in the *Quistclose* case. He said:

> "That arrangements of this character for the payment of a person's creditors by a third person, give rise to a relationship of a fiduciary character or trust, in favour, as a primary trust, of the creditors, and secondarily, if the primary trust fails, of the third person, has been recognised in a series of cases over some 150 years."

Later, he said:

> "... when the money is advanced, the lender acquires an equitable right to see that it is applied for the primary designated purpose ..."

These passages suggest that there are two successive trusts, a primary trust for payment to identifiable beneficiaries, such as creditors or shareholders, and a secondary trust in favour of the lender arising on the failure of the primary trust. But there are formidable difficulties in this analysis, which has little academic support. What if the primary trust is not for identifiable persons, but as in the present case to carry out an abstract purpose? Where in such a case is the beneficial interest pending the application of the money for the stated purpose or the failure of the purpose? There are four possibilities:

(1) in the lender;
(2) in the borrower;
(3) in the contemplated beneficiary; or
(4) in suspense.

(1) The lender
In "The *Quistclose* Trust: Who Can Enforce It?" (1985) 101 LQR 269, I argued that the beneficial interest remained throughout in the lender. This analysis has received considerable, though not universal academic support ...

On this analysis, the *Quistclose* trust is a simple commercial arrangement akin ... to a retention of title clause (though with a different object) which enables the borrower to have recourse to the lender's money for a particular purpose without entrenching on the lender's property rights more than necessary to enable the purpose to be achieved. The money remains the property for the lender unless and until it is applied in accordance with his directions, and insofar as it is not so applied, it must be returned to him. I am disposed, perhaps predisposed, to think that this is the only analysis which is consistent both with orthodox trust law and with commercial reality. Before reaching a concluded view that it should be adopted, however, I must consider the alternatives.

(2) The Borrower

It is plain that the beneficial interest is not vested unconditionally in the borrower so as to leave the money at his free disposal. That would defeat the whole purpose of the arrangements, which is to prevent the money from passing to the borrower's trustee in bankruptcy in the event of his insolvency. It would also be inconsistent with all the decided cases where the contest was between the lender and the borrower's trustee in bankruptcy, as well as with the *Quistclose* case itself …

The borrower's interest pending the application of the money for the stated purpose or its return to the lender is minimal. He must keep the money separate; he cannot apply it except for the stated purpose; unless the terms of the loan otherwise provide he must return it to the lender if demanded; he cannot refuse to return it if the stated purpose cannot be achieved; and if he becomes bankrupt it does not vest in his trustee in bankruptcy. If there is any content to beneficial ownership at all, the lender is the beneficial owner and the borrower is not.

In the present case the Court of Appeal adopted a variant, locating the beneficial interest in the borrower but subject to restrictions. I shall have to return to this analysis later.

(3) In the contemplated beneficiary

In the *Quistclose* case itself, as in all the reported cases which preceded it, either the primary purpose had been carried out and the contest was between the borrower's trustee in bankruptcy or liquidator and the person or persons to whom the borrower had paid the money; or it was treated as having failed, and the contest was between the borrower's trustee in bankruptcy and the lender. It was not necessary to explore the position while the primary purpose was still capable of being carried out and Lord Wilberforce's observations must be read in that light.

The question whether the primary trust is accurately described as a trust for the creditors first arose in *Re Northern Developments (Holdings) Ltd*, where the contest was between the lender and the creditors. The borrower, which was not in liquidation and made no claim to the money, was the parent company of a group, one of whose subsidiaries was in financial difficulty. There was a danger that if it were wound up or ceased trading it would bring down the whole group. A consortium of the group's banks agreed to put up a fund of more than £500,000 in an attempt to rescue the subsidiary. They paid the money into a special account in the name of the parent company for the express purpose of "providing money for the subsidiary's unsecured creditors over the ensuing weeks" and for no other purpose. The banks' object was to enable the subsidiary to continue trading, though on a reduced scale; it failed when the subsidiary was put into receivership at a time when some £350,000 remained unexpended. Relying on Lord Wilberforce's observations [in *Quistclose*], Megarry VC held that the primary trust was a purpose trust enforceable (inter alios) by the subsidiaries' creditors as the persons for whose benefit the trust was created.

There are several difficulties with this analysis. In the first place, Lord Wilberforce's reference to *Re Rogers* makes it plain that the equitable right he had in mind was not a mandatory order to compel performance, but a negative injunction to restrain improper application of the money, for neither Lindley nor Kay LJJ recognised more than this. In the second place, the object of the arrangements was to enable the subsidiary to continue trading, an this would necessarily involve it in incurring further liabilities to trade creditors. Accordingly, the application of the fund was not confined to existing creditors at the date when the fund was established. The company secretary was given to understand that the purpose of the arrangements was to keep the subsidiary trading, and that the fund was "as good as share capital". Thus the purposes of the arrangements was not, as in other cases, to enable the debtor to avoid bankruptcy by paying off existing creditors, but to enable the debtor to continue trading by providing it with working capital with which to incur fresh liabilities. There is a powerful argument for saying that the result of the arrangements was to vest a beneficial interest in the subsidiary from the start. If so, then this was not a *Quistclose* trust at all.

In the third place, it seems unlikely that the banks' object was to benefit the creditors (who included the Inland Revenue) except indirectly. The banks had their own commercial interests to protect by enabling the subsidiary to trade out of its difficulties. If so, then the primary trust cannot be supported as a valid non-charitable purpose trust ...

The most serious objection to this approach is exemplified by the facts of the present case. In several of the cases the primary trust was for an abstract purpose with no one but the lender to enforce performance or restrain misapplication of the money. In *Edwards* v *Glyn* the money was advanced to a bank to enable the bank to meet a run ... In *General Communications Ltd* v *Development Finance Corp of New Zealand Ltd* the money was paid to the borrower's solicitors for the express purpose of purchasing new equipment. The present case is another example. It is simply not possible to hold money on trust to acquire unspecified property from an unspecified vendor at an unspecified time. There is no reason to make an arbitrary distinction between money paid for an abstract purpose and money paid for a purpose which can be said to benefit an ascertained class of beneficiaries, and the cases rightly draw no such distinction. Any analysis of the *Quistclose* trust must be able to accommodate gifts and loans for an abstract purpose.

(4) In suspense

As Peter Gibson J pointed out in *Carreras*

Rothmans Ltd v *Freeman Matthews Treasure Ltd*, the effect of adopting Megarry VC's analysis is to leave the beneficial interest in suspense until the stated purpose is carried out or fails. The difficulty with this (apart from its unorthodoxy) is that it fails to have regard to the role which the resulting trust plays in equity's scheme of things, or to explain why the money is not simply held on a resulting trust for the lender.

Lord Browne-Wilkinson gave an authoritative explanation of the resulting trust in *Westdeutsche Landesbank Girozentrale* v *Islington London Borough Council* and its basis has been further illuminated by Dr R Chambers in his book *Resulting Trusts* published in 1997. Lord Browne-Wilkinson explained that a resulting trust arises in two sets of circumstances. He described the second as follows: "Where A transfers property to B on express trusts, but the trusts declared do not exhaust the whole beneficial interest ...". The *Quistclose* case was among the cases he cited as examples. He rejected the argument that there was a resulting trust in the case before him because, unlike the situation in the present case, there was no transfer of money on express trusts. But he also rejected the argument on a wider and, in my respectful opinion, surer ground that the money was paid and received with the intention that it should become the absolute property of the recipient.

The central thesis of Dr Chambers' book is that a resulting trust arises whenever there is a transfer of property in circumstances in which the transferor (or more accurately the person at whose expense the property was provided) did not intend to benefit the recipient. It responds to the absence of an intention on the part of the transferor to pass the entire beneficial interest, not to a positive intention to retain it. In so far as the transfer does not exhaust the entire beneficial interest, the resulting trust is a default trust which fills the gap and leaves no room for any part to be in suspense. An analysis of the *Quistclose* trust as a resulting trust for the transferor with a mandate to the transferee to apply the money for the stated purpose sits comfortably with Dr Chambers' thesis, and it might be thought surprising that he does not adopt it.

(5) The Court of Appeal's analysis

The Court of Appeal were content to treat the beneficial interest as in suspense, or (following Dr Chambers' analysis) to hold that it was in the borrower, the lender having merely a contractual right enforceable by injunction to prevent misapplication. Potter LJ put it in there terms:

"The purpose imposed at the time of the advance creates an enforceable restriction on the borrower's use of the money.

Although the lender's right to enforce the restriction is treated as arising on the basis of a 'trust', the use of that word does not enlarge the lender's interest in the fund. The borrower is entitled to the beneficial use of the money, subject to the lender's right to prevent its misuse; the lender's limited interest in the fund is sufficient to prevent its use for other than the special purpose for which is was advanced."

This analysis, with respect, is difficult to reconcile with the court's actual decision in so far as it granted Twinsectra a proprietary remedy against Mr Yardley's companies as recipients of the misapplied funds. Unless the money belonged to Twinsectra immediately before the misapplication, there is no basis on which a proprietary remedy against third party recipients can be justified.

Dr Chambers' "novel view" (as it has been described) is that the arrangements do not create a trust at all; the borrower receives the entire beneficial ownership in the money subject only to a contractual right in the lender to prevent the money being used otherwise than for the stated purpose. If the purpose fails, a resulting trust in the lender springs into being. In fact, he argues for a kind of restrictive covenant enforceable by negative injunction yet creating property rights in the money. But restrictive covenants, which began life as negative easements, are part of our land law. Contractual obligations do not run with

money or a chose in action like money in a bank account.

Dr Chambers' analysis has attracted academic comment, both favourable and unfavourable. ... It provides no solution to cases of non-contractual payment; is inconsistent with Lord Wilberforce's description of the borrower's obligation as fiduciary and not merely contractual; fails to explain the evidential significance of a requirement that the money should be kept in a separate account; cannot easily be reconciled with the availability of proprietary remedies against third parties; and while the existence of a mere equity to prevent misapplication would be sufficient to prevent the money from being available for distribution to the creditors on the borrower's insolvency (because the trustee in bankruptcy has no greater rights than his bankrupt), it would not prevail over secured creditors. If the bank in the *Quistclose* case had held a floating charge (as it probably did) and had appointed a receiver, the adoption of Dr Chambers' analysis should have led to a different outcome.

Thus all the alternative solutions have their difficulties but there are two problems which they fail to solve, but which are easily solved if the beneficial interest remains throughout in the lender. One arises from the fact, well established by the authorities, that the primary trust is enforceable by the lender. But on what basis can he enforce it? He cannot do so as the beneficiary under the secondary trust, for if the primary purpose is fulfilled there is no secondary trust: the precondition of his claim is destructive of his standing to make it. He cannot do so as settlor, for a settlor who retains no beneficial interest cannot enforce the trust which he has created.

Dr Chambers insists that the lender has merely a right to prevent the misapplication of the money, and attributes this to his contractual right to specific performance of a condition of a contract of loan. As I have already pointed out, this provides no solution where the arrangement is non-contractual. But Lord Wilberforce clearly based the borrower's obligation on an equitable or fiduciary basis and not a contractual one. He was concerned to justify the co-existence of equity's exclusive jurisdiction with the common law action for debt. Basing equity's intervention on its auxiliary jurisdiction to restrain a breach of contract would not have enabled the lender to succeed against the bank, which was a third party to the contract. There is only one explanation of the lender's fiduciary right to enforce the primary trust which can be reconciled with basic principle: he can do so because he is the beneficiary.

The other problem is concerned with the basis on which the primary trust is said to have failed in several of the cases … and the *Quistclose* trust itself. Given that the money did not belong to the borrower in either case, the borrower's insolvency should not have prevented the money from being paid in the manner contemplated. A man cannot pay some only of his creditors once he has been adjudicated bankrupt, but a third party can. A company cannot pay a dividend once it has gone into liquidation, but there is nothing to stop a third party from paying the disappointed shareholders. The reason why the purpose failed in each case must be because the lender's object in making the money available was to save the borrower from bankruptcy in the one case and collapse in the other. But this in itself is not enough. A trust does not fail merely because the settlor's purpose in creating it has been frustrated: the trust must become illegal or impossible to perform. The settlor's motives must not be confused with the purpose of the trust; the frustration of the former does not by itself cause the failure of the latter. But if the borrower is treated as holding the money on a resulting trust for the lender but with power (or in some cases a duty) to carry out the lender's revocable mandate, and the lender's object in giving the mandate is frustrated, he is entitled to revoke the mandate and demand the return of money which never ceased to be his beneficially.

As Sherlock Holmes reminded Dr Watson, when you have eliminated the impossible, whatever remains, however impossible, must be the truth. I would reject all the alternative analyses, which I find unconvincing for the reasons I have endeavoured to explain, and hold the *Quistclose* trust to be an entirely orthodox example of the kind of default trust known as a resulting trust. The lender pays the money to the borrower by way of loan, but he does not part with the entire beneficial interest in the money, and in so far as he does not it is held on a resulting trust for the lender from the outset. Contrary to the opinion of the Court of Appeal, it is the borrower who has a very limited use of the money, being obliged to apply it for the stated purpose and return it. He has no beneficial interest in the money, which remains throughout in the lender subject only to the borrower's power or duty to apply the money in accordance with the lender's instructions. When the purpose fails, the money is returnable to the lender, not under some new trust in his favour which only comes into being on the failure of the purpose, but because the resulting trust in his favour is no longer subject to any power on the part of the borrower to make use of the money. Whether the borrower is obliged to apply the money for the stated purpose or merely at liberty to do so, and whether the lender can countermand the borrower's mandate, while it is still capable of being carried out, must depend on the circumstances of the particular case.'

Lord Millett then went on to review the requirements of knowing or dishonest assistance:

'The question for your Lordships is not whether Lord Nicholls was using the word dishonesty in a subjective or objective sense in the *Royal Brunei* case. The question is whether a plaintiff should be required to establish that an accessory to a breach of trust had a dishonest state of mind (so that he was subsequently dishonest in the *R* v *Ghosh* sense); or whether it should be sufficient to establish that he acted with the requisite knowledge (so that his conduct was objectively dishonest). This question is at large for us, and we are free to resolve it either way.

I would resolve it by adopting the objective approach. I would do so because

(i) consciousness of wrongdoing is an aspect of mens rea and an appropriate condition of criminal liability: it is not an appropriate condition of civil liability. This generally results from negligent or intentional conduct. For the purpose of civil liability, it should not be necessary that the defendant realised that his conduct was dishonest: it should be sufficient that it constituted intentional wrongdoing.

(ii) The objective test is in accordance with Lord Selbourne LC's statement in *Barnes* v *Addey* and traditional doctrine This taught that a person who knowingly participates in the misdirection of money is liable to compensate the injured party. While negligence is not a sufficient condition of liability, intentional wrongdoing is. Such conduct is culpable and falls below the objective standard of honesty adopted by ordinary people.

(iii) The claim for "knowing assistance" is the equitable counterpart of the economic torts. These are intentional torts; negligence is not sufficient and dishonesty is not necessary. Liability depends on knowledge. A requirement of subjective dishonesty introduces an unnecessary and unjustified distinction between the elements of the equitable claim and those of the tort of wrongful interference with the performance of a contract.

If Mr Sims' undertaking was contractual, as Mr Leach thought it was, then Mr Leach's conduct would have been actionable as a wrongful interference with the performance of the contract. Where a third party with knowledge of a contract has dealings with the contract breaker which the third party knows will amount to a breach of contract and damage results, he commits an actionable interference with the contract. ...

It would be most undesirable if we were to introduce a distinction between the equitable claim and the tort, thereby inducing the claimant to attempt to spell a contractual obligation out of a fiduciary relationship in order to avoid the need to establish that the defendant had a dishonest state of mind. It would, moreover, be strange if equity made liability depend on subjective dishonesty when in a comparable situation the common law did not. This would be a reversal of the general rule that equity demands higher standards of behaviour than the common law.

If we were to reject subjective dishonesty as a requirement of civil liability in this branch of the law, the remaining question is merely a semantic one. Should we return to the traditional description of the claim as "knowing assistance", reminding ourselves that nothing less than actual knowledge is sufficient; or should we adopt Lord Nicholls' description of the claim as "dishonest assistance", reminding ourselves that the test is an objective one?

For my own part, I have no difficulty in equating the knowing mishandling of money with dishonest conduct. But the introduction of dishonesty is an unnecessary distraction, and conducive to error. Many judges would be reluctant to brand a professional man as dishonest where he was unaware that honest people would consider his conduct to be so. If the condition of liability is intentional wrongdoing and not conscious dishonesty as understood in the criminal courts, I think that we should return to the traditional description of this head of equitable liability as arising from "knowing assistance".

The question here is whether it is sufficient that the accessory should have actual knowledge of the facts which created the trust, or must he also have appreciated that they did so? It is obviously not necessary that he should know the details of the trust or the identity of the beneficiary. It is sufficient that he knows that the money is not at the free disposal of the principal. In some circumstances it may not even be necessary that his knowledge should extend this far. It may be sufficient that he knows that he is assisting in a dishonest scheme.

That is not this case, for in the absence of knowledge that his client is not entitled to receive it there is nothing intrinsically dishonest in a solicitor paying money to him. But I am satisfied that knowledge of the arrangements which constitute the trust is sufficient; it is not necessary that the defendant should appreciate that they do so. Of course, if they do not create a trust, then he will not be liable for having assisted in a breach of trust. But he takes the risk that they do.

The gravamen of the charge against the principal is not that he has broken his word, but that, having been entrusted with the control of a fund with limited powers of disposal, he has betrayed the confidence placed in him by disposing of the money in an unauthorised manner. The gravamen of the charge against the accessory is not that he is handling stolen property, but that he is assisting a person who has been entrusted with the control of a fund to dispose of the fund in an unauthorised manner. He should be liable if he knows of the arrangements by which that person obtained control of the money and that his authority to deal with the money was limited, and participates in a dealing with the money in a manner which he knows is unauthorised. I do not believe that the man in the street would have any doubt that such conduct was culpable. ...

... From the very moment [Mr Leach] received the money he treated it as held to Mr Yardley's order and at Mr Yardley's free disposition. He did not shut his eyes to the facts, but to "the implications", that is to say the impropriety of putting the money at Mr Yardley's disposal. His explanation was that this was Mr Sims' problem, not his.

Mr Leach knew that Twinsectra had entrusted the money to Mr Sims with only limited authority to dispose of it; that Twinsectra trusted Mr Sims to ensure that the money was not used except for the acquisition of property; that Mr Sims had betrayed the confidence placed in him by paying the money to him (Mr Leach)

without seeing to its further application; and that by putting it at Mr Yardley's free disposal took the risk that the money would be applied for an unauthorised purpose and place Mr Sims in breach of his undertaking. But all that was Mr Sims' responsibility.

In my opinion this I enough to make Mr Leach civilly liable as an accessory (1) for the tort of wrongful interference with the performance of Mr Sims' contractual obligations if this had been pleaded and the undertaking was contractual as well as fiduciary; and (2) for assisting in a breach of trust. It is unnecesary to consider whether Mr Leach realised that honest people would regard his conduct as dishonest. His knowledge was that he was assisting Mr Sims to default in his undertaking to Twinsectra is sufficient.

Each of the sums which Mr Leach received for his own benefit was paid in respect of an acquisition of property, and as such was a proper disbursement. He thus received trust property but not in breach of trust. This was very properly conceded by counsel for Twinsectra before your Lordships.'

Comment

By far the most important opinion is the dissenting opinion of Lord Millett in which he analyses at length the status of the *Quistclose* trust and reintroduces the idea that this is a form of automatic resulting trust.

His analysis of knowing and dishonest assistance makes the distinction between subjective dishonesty, which merely requires that the defendant had the requisite knowledge of the breach of trust, and dishonest assistance, which provides an objective test – that a reasonable person would have regarded the assistance as dishonest.

7 Trusts of Imperfect Obligation

Astor's Settlement, Re [1952] Ch 534
Chancery Division (Roxburgh J)

- *Purpose trust – unenforceable*

Facts
In 1945 Lord Astor made an inter vivos settlement for a number of non-charitable objects, including (1) 'The maintenance ... of good understanding, sympathy and co-operation between nations, (2) The preservation of the independence and integrity of newspapers ... (3) The protection of newspapers ... from being absorbed or controlled by combines.'

Held
The trusts failed. The objects of the trust were void for uncertainty and further they were not for the benefit of individuals and were, therefore, purpose trusts which failed.

Roxburgh J:

'Let me then sum up the position so far. On the one side there are Lord Parker's two propositions with which I began. These were not new but merely re-echoed what Sir William Grant had said as Master of the Rolls in *Morice* v *Bishop of Durham* as long ago as 1804: "There must be somebody, in whose favour the court can decree performance." The position was recently restated by Harman J in *Re Wood*: "A gift on trust must have a cestui que trust", and this seems to be in accord with principle. On the other side is a group of cases relating to horses and dogs, graves and monuments – matters arising under wills and intimately connected with the deceased – in which the courts have found means of escape from these general propositions and also *Re Thompson* and *Re Price*, which I have endeavoured to explain. *Re Price* belongs to another field. The rest

may, I think, properly be regarded as anomalous and exceptional and in no way destructive of the proposition which traces descent from or through Sir William Grant, through Lord Parker to Harman J. Perhaps the late Sir Arthur Underhill was right in suggesting that they may be concessions to human weaknesses or sentiment ... They cannot, in my judgment, of themselves (and no other suggestion has been suggested to me) justify the conclusion that a Court of Equity will recognise as an equitable obligation affecting the income of large funds in the hands of trustees a direction to apply it in furtherance of enumerated non-charitable purposes in a manner which no court or department can control or enforce. I hold that the trusts here in question are void on the first of the grounds submitted by Mr Jennings and Mr Buckley.'

Comment
Although the purpose of the trust would clearly be beneficial to mankind as a whole, there is not sufficient certainty of objects for the trust to be enforceable.

Dean, Re (1889) 41 Ch D 552
Chancery Division (Cohen J)

- *Purpose trusts – animal cases*

Facts
A testator charged his estate with the payment of £750 per annum to trustees for the period of 50 years if any of his horses and hounds should so long live for the maintenance of the same.

Held
Although the gift was non-charitable and its

execution not enforceable by anyone, it was nevertheless a valid trust.

North J:

> 'The first question is as to the validity of the provision made by the testator in favour of his horses and dogs. It is said that it is not valid because (for this is the principal ground on which it is put) neither a horse nor a dog could enforce the trust; and there is no person who could enforce it. It is obviously not a charity, because it is intended for the benefit of the particular animals mentioned and not for the benefit of animals generally, and it is quite distinguishable from the gift made in a subsequent part of the will to the Royal Society for the Prevention of Cruelty to Animals, which may well be a charity. In my opinion this provision for the particular horses and hounds referred to in the will is not, in any sense, a charity, and if it were, of course the whole gift would fail because it is a gift of an annuity arising out of land alone, but in my opinion, as it is not a charity, there is nothing in the fact that the annuity arises out of land to prevent its being a good gift.
>
> Then it is said, that there is no cestui que trust who can enforce the trust, and that the Court will not recognise a trust unless it is capable of being enforced by some one. I do not assent to that view. There is not the least doubt that a man may if he pleases, give a legacy to trustees, upon trust to apply it in erecting a monument to himself, either in a church or in a churchyard, or even in unconsecrated ground, and I am not aware that such a trust is in any way invalid, although it is difficult to say who would be the cestui que trust of the monument. In the same way I know of nothing to prevent a gift of a sum of money to trustees, upon trust to apply it for the repair of such a monument. In my opinion such a trust would be good, although the testator must be careful to limit the time for which it is to last, because, as it is not a charitable trust, unless it is to come to an end within the limits fixed by the rule against perpetuities, it would be illegal. But a trust to lay out a certain sum in building a monument, and the gift of another sum in trust to apply the same to keeping that monument in repair, say for ten years, is, in my opinion, a perfectly good trust, although I do not see who could ask the Court to enforce it. If persons beneficially interested in the estate could do so, then the present Plaintiff can do so; but if such persons could not enforce the trust, still it cannot be said that the trust must fail because there is no one who can actively enforce it.
>
> Is there then anything illegal or obnoxious to the law in the nature of the provision, that is in the fact that it is not for human beings but for horses and dogs? It is clearly settled by authority that a charity may be established for the benefit of horses and dogs, and, therefore, the making of a provision for horses and dogs, which is not a charity, cannot of itself be obnoxious to the law, provided, of course, that it is not to last for too long a period ...'

Comment

Although the court bows to sentiment in recognising the validity of such trusts, they must still observe the perpetuity rules, based on a *human* life in being.

Denley's Trust Deed, Re [1969] 1 Ch 373 Chancery Division (Goff J)

• *Purpose trusts and ascertainable beneficiaries*

Facts

The instrument provided a trust for the provision of a sports or recreation ground, for a period within the perpetuity rule, for the benefit, primarily, of employees of a company, and secondarily for the benefit of such other persons as the trustees allowed to use it.

Held

A distinction must be drawn between 'purpose or object trusts which are abstract or personal' and are void, and a trust for objects which 'though expressed as a purpose, is directly or indirectly for the benefit of an individual or group of individuals'. Such a trust is outside the mischief for which purpose trusts are held invalid, that is, that there is no cestui que trust. In this case there were ascertainable beneficiaries and therefore the trust was valid.

Goff J:

'Mr Mills has argued that the trust in cl 2(c) in the present case is either a trust for the benefit of individuals, in which case he argues that they are an unascertainable class and therefore the trust is void for uncertainty, or that it is a purpose trust, that is, as trust for providing recreation, which he submits is void on the beneficiary principle, or, alternatively, that it is something of a hybrid, having the vices of both kinds.

I think there may be a purpose or object trust, the carrying out of which would benefit an individual or individuals, where the benefit is so indirect or intangible or which is otherwise so framed as not to give those persons any locus standi to apply to the court to enforce the trust, in which case the beneficiary principle would, as it seems to me, apply to invalidate the trust, quite apart from any question of uncertainty or perpetuity. Such cases can be considered if and when they arise. The present is not, in my judgment, of that character, and it will be seen that cl 2(d) of the trust deed expressly states that, subject to any rules and regulations made by the trustees, the employees of the company shall be entitled to the use and enjoyment of the land. Apart from this possible exception, in my judgment the beneficiary principle of *Re Astor's Settlement Trusts* which was approved in *Re Endacott* is confined to purpose or object trusts which are abstract or impersonal. The objection is not that the trust is for a purpose or object per se but that there is no beneficiary or cestui que trust. ...

The trust in the present case is limited in point of time so as to avoid any infringement of the rule against perpetuities and, for the reasons I have given, it does not offend against the beneficiary principle; and unless, therefore, it be void for uncertainty, it is a valid trust.'

Comment

Where possible, the court will construe a gift specifying a purpose as an outright gift if ascertainable beneficiaries are named – they can then enforce the trust.

Endacott, Re [1960] Ch 232 Court of Appeal (Lord Evershed MR, Sellers and Harman LJJ)

• *Purpose trusts*

Facts

The testator gave his residuary estate 'to North Tawton Devon Parish Council for the purposes of providing some useful memorial to myself.' The question arose as to whether the gift was valid.

Held

The gift was not charitable and as it was not beneficial to the council or the inhabitants, it was void.

Harman LJ:

'I cannot think that charity has anything to do with this bequest. As for establishing it without the crutch of charity, I applaud the orthodox sentiments of Roxburgh J in the *Astor* case, and I think, as I think he did, that though no one knows there have been decisions at times which are not really to be satisfactorily classified, but are perhaps merely occasions when Homer has nodded, at any rate, these cases stand by themselves and ought not to be increased in number, nor indeed followed, except where the one is exactly like another. Whether it would be better that some authority now should say those cases were wrong, this perhaps is not the moment to consider. At any rate, I cannot think a case of this kind, the case of providing outside a church an unspecified and unidentified memorial, is the kind of instance which should be allowed to add to those troublesome, anomalous and aberrant cases.'

Comment

The court must ascertain some useful purpose in such trusts – it will not permit memorials to be ostentatious or wasteful.

Hetherington, Re

See Chapter 8.

Leahy v *Attorney-General for New South Wales* [1959] AC 457 Privy Council (Viscount Simonds, Lords Morton, Cohen, Somervell and Denning)

- *Trusts of imperfect obligation – unincorporated associations*

Facts

By cl 3 of his will the testator left certain property 'upon trust for such order of nuns of the Catholic Church or the Christian Brothers as my executors and trustees shall select'. The trustees took out a summons to determine the effect of cl 3 since it was recognised that the words 'such order of nuns' might include contemplative orders which were not charitable in the legal sense.

Held

The gift showed an intention to create a trust not merely for the benefit of existing members of the order selected but also for the benefit of the order as a continuing society; thus the gift infringed the rule against perpetual trusts. Therefore, if the order selected were non-charitable, the gift would fail for this reason.

Viscount Simonds:

'The prima facie validity of such a gift is a convenient starting point for the examination of the relevant law. For, as Lord Tomlin ... said in *Re Ogden*, a gift to a voluntary association of persons for the general purposes of the association is an absolute gift and prima facie a good gift. He was echoing the words of Lord Parker in *Bowman*'s case that a gift to an unincorporated association

for the attainment of its purposes "may ... be upheld as an absolute gift to its members". These words must receive careful consideration, for it is to be noted that it is because the gift can be upheld as a gift to the individual members that it is valid, even though it is given for the purposes of the association. If the words "for the general purposes of the association" were held to impart a trust, the question would have to be asked "what is the trust and who are the beneficiaries?" A gift can be made to persons (including a corporation) but it cannot be made to a purpose or to an object unless the purpose or object be charitable. For a purpose or object cannot sue, but, if it is to be charitable, the Attorney-General can sue to enforce it ... It is therefore by disregarding the words "for the general purposes of the association" (which are assumed not to be charitable purposes) and treating the gift as an absolute gift to individuals that it can be sustained. The same conclusion had been reached fifty years before in *Cocks* v *Manners*, where a bequest of a share of residue to the Dominican Convent at Carisbrooke payable to the Superior for the time being was held a valid gift to the individual members of the society. In that case, no difficulty was created by the addition of words which might suggest that the community as a whole, not its members individually, should be the beneficiary. See also *Re Smith*. There the bequest was to the society or institution known as the Franciscan Friars of Clevedon (in the) County of Somerset absolutely. Joyce J had no difficulty in construing this as a gift individually to the small number of persons who had associated themselves at Clevedon under monastic vows. Greater difficulty must be felt when the gift is in such terms that though it is clearly not contemplated that the individual members shall divide it amongst themselves, yet it is prima facie a gift to the individuals and, there being nothing in the constitution in the Society to exhibit it, they can dispose of it as they think fit. Of this type of case *Re Clark* may be taken as an example. There the bequest was to the committee for the time being of the Corps of Commissionaires in London to act in the purchase of their barracks, or in any other way beneficial to the Corps. The judge ... was able to uphold this as a valid gift on the ground that all the members of the association could join together to dispose of the funds for the barracks. He assumed (however little the testator may have intended it) that the gift was to the individual members in the name of the society or of the committee of the society.'

Comment

This gift was saved by legislation.

Lipinski's Will Trusts, Re [1976] Ch 235 Chancery Division (Oliver J)

• *Trusts of imperfect obligation – unincorporated associations*

Facts

A testator left half his residuary estate upon trust 'for the Hull Judeans (Maccabi) Association in memory of my late wife to be used solely in the work of constructing new buildings for the association and/or improvements to the said buildings'. The trustees took out a summons to determine the effect of the trust.

Held

The trust was a valid trust for the members of the unincorporated association.

Oliver J:

'There would seem to me to be, as a matter of common sense, a clear distinction between the case where a purpose is prescribed which is clearly intended for the benefit of ascertained or ascertainable beneficiaries, particularly, where those beneficiaries have the power to make the capital their own, and the case where no beneficiary at all is intended (for instance, a memorial to a favourite pet) or where the beneficiaries are ascertainable (as for instance *Re Price*). If a valid gift may be made to an incor-

porated body as a simple accretion to the funds which are the subject matter of the contract which the members have made inter se and *Neville Estates* v *Madden* and *Re Recher's Will Trusts* show that it may, I do not really see why such a gift, which specifies a purpose which is within the powers of the unincorporated body and of which the members of that body are the beneficiaries, should fail. Why are not the beneficiaries able to enforce the trust or, indeed, in the exercise of their contractual rights, to terminate the trust for their own benefit? Where the donee body is itself the beneficiary of the prescribed purpose, there seems to me to be the strongest argument in common sense for saying that the gift should be construed as an absolute one within the second category, the more so where, if the purpose is carried out, the members can by appropriate action vest the resulting property in themselves, for here the trustees and the beneficiary are the same person ...

I have already said that, in my judgment, no question of perpetuity arises here, and accordingly the case appears to me to be one of the specification of a particular purpose for the benefit of ascertained beneficiaries, the members of the association for the time being. There is an additional factor. This is a case in which, under the constitution of the association, the members could, by the appropriate majority, alter their constitution so as to provide, if they wishes, for the division of the association's assets among themselves. This has, I think, a significance. I have considered whether anything turns in this case on the testator's direction that the legacy shall be used "solely" for one or other of the specified purposes. Counsel for the association has referred me to a number of cases where legacies have been bequeathed for particular purposes and in which the beneficiaries have been held entitled to override the purpose, even though expressed in mandatory terms.

Perhaps the most striking in the present context is the case of *Re Bowes*, where money was directed to be laid out in the planting of trees on a settled estate. That was a "purpose" trust, but there were ascertainable beneficiaries, the owners for the time being of the estate; and North J held that the persons entitled to the settled estate were entitled to have the money whether or not it was laid out as directed by the testator. He said:

"Then, the sole question is where this money is to go to. Of course, it is a perfectly good legacy. There is nothing illegal in the matter, and the direction to plant might easily be carried out; but it is not necessarily capable of being performed, because the owner of the estate might say he would not have any trees planted upon it at all. If that were the line he took, and he did not contend for anything more than that, the legacy would fail; but he says he does not refuse to have trees planted upon it; he is content that trees should be planted upon some part of it; but the legacy has not failed. If it were necessary to uphold it, the trees can be planted upon the whole of it until the fund is exhausted. Therefore, there is nothing illegal in the gift itself; but the owners of the estate now say 'It is a very disadvantageous way of spending this money; the money is to be spent for our benefit, and that of no one else; it was not intended for any purpose other than our benefit and that of the estate. That is no reason why it should be thrown away by doing what is not for our benefit, instead of being given to us; who want to have the enjoyment of it.' I think their contention is right. I think the fund is devoted to improving the estate, and improving the estate for the benefit of the persons who are absolutely entitled to it."

I can see no reason why the same reasoning should not apply in the present case simply because the beneficiary is an unincorporated non-charitable association. I do not think the fact that the testator has directed the application "solely" for the specified purpose adds any legal force to the direction. The beneficiaries, the members of the association for the time being, are the persons who could enforce the purpose and they must, as it seems to me, be entitled not to enforce it or, indeed, to vary it.'

Comment
The gift is valid because there are ascertainable beneficiaries to enforce it.

Neville Estates Ltd v *Madden* [1962] Ch 832 Chancery Division (Cross J)

• *Gifts to unincorporated associations*

Facts
Catford Synagogue was established in 1937, comprising a Charity Commissioners' Scheme merging five London synagogues. During its existence various funds were raised and in 1952 a site was purchased on which a synagogue was built. In 1959 the synagogue obtained permission to develop part of the unused site. A prospective purchaser was found. However, the Charity Commissioners indicated that their permission to sell was required, and then compelled the synagogue to offer the land publicly, after which higher offers than the one by now accepted were received.

Held
On application by the prospective purchaser:

1. The funds originally raised, and therefore the land, were held on trust for the synagogue as a quasi-corporation.
2. However, whilst the general presumption was that an unincorporated association would not be held to be a charity, this rule was relaxed when the purposes had a religious element. The trust was for religious purposes and therefore the Charity Commissioners' authority over it was upheld.

Cross J:

'I turn now ... to the legal issues involved. The question of the construction and effect of gifts to or in trust for unincorporated associations was recently considered by the Privy Council in *Leahy* v *Attorney-General for New South Wales*. The position as I understand it is as follows. Such a gift may take effect in one or other of three quite different ways.

In the first place, it may, on its true construction, be a gift to the members of the association at the relevant date as joint tenants, so that any member can sever his share and claim it whether or not he continues to be a member of the association. Secondly, it may be a gift to the existing members not as joint tenants, but subject to their respective contractual rights and liabilities towards one another as members of the association. In such a case a member cannot sever his share. It will accrue to the other members on his death or resignation, even though such members include persons who became members after the gift took effect. If this is the effect of the gift, it will not be open to objection on the score of perpetuity, unless there is something in its terms or in the rules of the association which precludes the members at any given time from dividing the subject of the gift between them on the footing that they are solely entitled to it in equity.

Thirdly, the terms or circumstances of the gift or the rules of the association may show that the property in question is not to be at the disposal of the members for the time being, but is to be held in trust so that it or its income may be enjoyed by the association or its members from time to time. In this case ... the gift will fail unless the association is a charitable body.'

Comment

In this case, the association was trying to avoid charitable status.

Recher's Will Trusts, Re [1972] Ch 526 Chancery Division (Brightman J)

• *Trusts of imperfect obligation – unincorporated association*

Facts

The testatrix made a bequest to 'The Anti-Vivisection Society, 76 Victoria Street, London SW1' by her will made in 1957. Until the end of 1956 a non-charitable unincorporated society, known as 'The London and Provincial Anti-Vivisection Society' had carried on its activities at 76 Victoria Street, but in 1957 it was amalgamated with the National Anti-Vivisection Society and the premises at 76 Victoria Street closed. The testatrix died in 1962 and the question arose whether the gift was valid.

Held

The gift could not be construed as a gift to the larger and amalgamated society but only as a gift to the London and Provincial Society. If this society had remained in existence until the testatrix's death, the gift could have taken effect as a legacy to the members of the society beneficially, not so as to entitle each member to receive a share but as an accretion to the funds which constituted the subject-matter of the contract by which the members bound themselves inter se.

Brightman J:

'Having reached the conclusion that the gift in question is not a gift to the members of the London and Provincial Society at the date of death, as joint tenants or tenants in common so as to entitle a member as of right to a distributive share, nor an attempted gift to present and future members beneficially, and is not a gift in trust for the purposes of the society, I must now consider how otherwise, if at all, it is capable of taking effect.

As I have already mentioned, the rules of the London and Provincial Society do not purport to create any trusts except insofar as the honorary trustees are not beneficial owners of the assets of the society, but are trustees on trust to deal with such assets according to the directions of the committee.

A trust for non-charitable purposes, as distinct from a trust for individuals, is clearly void because there is no beneficiary. It does not, however, follow that persons cannot band themselves together as an association or society, pay subscriptions and validly devote their funds in pursuit of some lawful non-charitable purpose. An obvious example is a members' social club. But it is not essential that the members should only intend to secure direct personal advantages to themselves. The association may be one in which personal advantages to the members are combined with the pursuit of some outside purpose. Or the association may be one which offers no personal benefit at all to the members, the funds of the association being applied exclusively to the pursuit of some outside purpose. Such an association of persons is bound, I would think, to have some sort of constitution; ie the rights and liabilities of the members of the association will inevitably depend on some form of contract inter se, usually evidenced by a set of rules.

In the present case, it appears to me clear that the life members, the ordinary members and the associate members of the London and Provincial Society were bound together by a contract inter se. Any such member was entitled to the rights and subject to the liabilities defined by the rules. If the committee acted contrary to the rules, an individual member would be entitled to take proceedings in the courts to compel observance of the rules or to recover damages for any loss he had suffered as a result of the breach of contract. As and when a member paid his subscription to the association, he would be subjecting his money to the disposition and expenditure thereof laid down by the rules. That is to say, the member would be bound to permit, and entitled to require, the honorary trustees and other members of the society to deal with that subscription in accordance with the lawful direction of the committee. Those directions would include the expenditure of that subscription, as part of the general funds of the association, in furthering the objects of the association. (The resultant situation, on analysis, is that the London and Provincial Society represented an organisation of individuals bound together by a contract under which their subscriptions became, as it were, mandated towards a certain type of expenditure as adumbrated in r.I.) Just as the two parties to a bipartite bargain can vary or terminate their contract by mutual assent, so it must

follow that the life members, ordinary members and associate members of the London and Provincial Society could, at any moment of time, by unanimous agreement (or by majority vote if the rules so prescribe), vary or terminate their multi-partite contract. There would be no limit to the type of variation or termination to which they all might agree. There is no private trust or trust for charitable purposes or other trust to hinder the process. It follows that if all members agreed, they could decide to wind up the London and Provincial Society and divide the net assets among themselves beneficially. No one would have any locus standi to stop them so doing. The contract is the same as any other contract and concerns only those who are parties to it, that is to say, the members of the society.

The funds of such an association may, of course, be derived not only from the subscriptions of the contracting parties but also from donations from non-contracting parties and legacies from persons who have died. In the case of a donation which is not accompanied by any words which purport to impose a trust, it seems to me that the gift takes effect in favour of the existing members of the association as an accretion to the funds which are the subject matter of the contract which such members have made inter se, and falls to be dealt with in precisely the same way as the funds which the members themselves have subscribed. So, in the case of legacy. In the absence of words which purport to impose a trust, the legacy is a gift to the members beneficially, not as joint tenants or as tenants in common so as to entitle each member to an immediate distributive share, but as an accretion to the funds which are the subject matter of the contract which the members have made inter se.'

Comment
This case sets out the contractual basis on which unincorporated associations can receive property.

Tyler, Re [1891] 3 Ch 252 Court of Appeal (Lindley, Fry and Lopes LJJ)

* *Purpose trusts – monuments*

Facts

The testator bequeathed £42,000 Russian 5 per cent stock to the trustees of the London Missionary Society and committed to their care and charge the keys of his family vault at Highgate Cemetery 'the same to be kept in good repair, and name legible, and to rebuild when it shall require: failing to comply with this request, the money to go to the Bluecoat School, Newgate Street, London'. The question arose whether the gift was valid.

Held

The condition to repair the vault was valid, the rule against perpetuities had no application to a transfer, on the occurrence of a certain event, of property from one charity to another, as in this case.

Fry LJ:

'In this case the testator has given a sum of money to one charity with a gift over to another charity, upon the happening of a certain event. That event, no doubt, is such as to create an inducement or motive on the part of the first donee, the London Missionary Society, to repair the family tomb of the testator. Inasmuch as both the donees of this fund, the first donee and the second, are charitable bodies, and are created for the purposes of charity, the rule of law against perpetuities has nothing whatever to do with the donees. Does the rule of law against perpetuities create any object to the nature of the condition? If the testator had required the first donee, the London Missionary Society, to apply any portions of the fund towards the repair of the family tomb, that would, in all probability, at any rate, to the extent of the sum required , have been void as a perpetuity which was not charity. But he has done nothing of the sort. He has given to the first donee no power to apply any part of the money. He has only created a condition that the sum shall go over to Christ's Hospital if the London Missionary Society do not keep the tomb in repair. Keeping the tomb in repair is not an illegal object. If it were, the condition tending to bring about an illegal act would itself be illegal; but to repair the tomb is a perfectly lawful thing. All that can be said is that it is not lawful to tie up property for the purpose. But the rule of law against perpetuities applies to property, not motives, and I know of no rule which says that you may not try to enforce a condition creating a perpetual inducement to do a thing which is lawful. That is the case.'

Comment

This bequest does not offend the beneficiary principle because the beneficiary of the gift over can enforce it.

8   Charitable Trusts

Attorney-General* v *Ross [1986] 1
WLR 252 Chancery Division
(Scott J)

• *Charitable trusts with ancillary objects*

Facts

A students' union was an integral part of a
polytechnic, a registered charity, but its rules
permitted its funds to be used for political purposes.

Held

The political purposes for which part of the
funds were used were ancillary to the union's
principal object, that of promoting the welfare
of its members.

Scott J:

'It is well settled that an organisation may
properly be regarded as established for charitable purposes only notwithstanding that
some of its activities in themselves promote
charitable purposes. Lord Reid in *Inland
Revenue Commissioners* v *City of Glasgow
Police Athletic Association* said:

"It is not enough that one of the purposes
of a body of persons is charitable: the Act
requires that it must be established for
charitable purposes only. This does not
mean that the sole effect of the activities
of the body must be to promote charitable purposes but it does mean that that
must be its predominant object and that
any benefit to its individual members of
a non-charitable character which result
from its activities must be of a subsidiary
or incidental character."

Lord Cohen in the same case said at p405:

"Certain principles appear to be settled.
(a) If the main purpose of the body of
persons is charitable and the only ele-

ments in its constitution and operations
which are non-charitable are merely incidental to that main purpose, that body of
persons is a charity notwithstanding the
presence of those elements ... (b) If,
however, a non-charitable object is itself
one of the purposes of the body of persons
and is not merely incidental to the charitable purpose, the body of persons is not a
body of persons formed for charitable
purposes only within the meaning of the
Income Tax Acts ... (c) If a substantial
part of the objects of the body of persons
is to benefit its own members, the body
of persons is not established for charitable
purposes only ..."

Brightman J in the *London Hospital* case,
after citing the passage that I have read from
Lord Reid's judgment commented, at p623
"In the end it seems to me that the question
is to some extent a matter of degree."

In the present case Mr Lightman has concentrated on the affiliation of the union to
the National Union of Students. This affiliation is expressly authorised under sub-
clause (d) of cl 3 but is, I think, properly to
be regarded as a means of pursuing the rep-
resentational object expressed in sub-clause
(a). Be that as it may, the union pays, it
seems, affiliation fees in excess of £15,000
per annum at the current level to the
National Union of Students. The National
Union of Students expends its funds on purposes which are plainly not charitable. It is
not, and could not be, suggested that the
National Union of Students is charitable.
How, argues Mr Lightman, can the union
then be charitable? It is empowered to
spend, and does spend, substantial sums out
of its funds on an non-charitable purpose.
But, as Brightman J observed, the question
is one of degree. There is no reason in principle why, for the purpose of achieving its
own charitable purposes, a body should not

ally itself with and contribute to the funds of a non-charitable organisation. I am sure that a number of charities do so as a matter of course.

There is, in my view, no reason in principle why a students' union being a charity should not affiliate itself to the National Union of Students, a non-charity, and pay the subscriptions or fees consequent upon the affiliation. It is an express object of this union, and consistent with an over-all charitable purpose, that it should represent its members on national student organisations. I do not, therefore, accept Mr Lightman's argument that affiliation to the National Union of Students and the payment of affiliation fees is inconsistent with the students' union having a charitable status.

A point was made by Mr Lightman concerning the reference in sub-clause (b) to political activities. The carrying on of political activities or the pursuit of political objectives cannot, in the ordinary way, be a charitable purpose. But I can see nothing the matter with an educational charity, in the furtherance of its educational purposes, encouraging students to develop their political awareness or to acquire knowledge of, and to debate, and to form views on, political issues. If the form of the encouragement involves provision of facilities for a students' Labour Club or Conservative Club, or any other political club, I can see nothing in that which is necessarily inconsistent with the furtherance of educational purposes. Here, too, the question is, perhaps, one of degree. But the proposition that an educational charity, be it a school, polytechnic or university, cannot consistently with its charitable status promote and encourage the development of political ideas among its students has only to be stated to be seen to be untenable. The reference to political activities in sub-clause (b) is, in my judgment, no obstacle to the union's charitable status.

Finally, Mr Lightman prayed in aid the activities of the union. He submitted that the activities of the union since it was founded in 1970 could be prayed in aid in order to resolve the question whether the union was or was not charitable. He submitted that, on the facts of this case, I should conclude that the union existed primarily in order to express the political views and aspirations of its student members. I am unable to accept these submissions.

The question whether under its constitution the union is or is not charitable must, in my view, be answered by reference to the content of its constitution, construed and assessed in the context of the factual background to its formation. This background may serve to elucidate the purpose for which the union was formed. But if the union was of a charitable nature when formed in 1971 it cannot have been deprived of that nature by the activities carried on subsequently in its name.

I must not be taken to be expressing the opinion that the activities of an organisation subsequent to its formation can never be relevant to the question whether the organisation was formed for charitable purposes only. The skill of Chancery draftsmen is well able to produce a constitution of charitable flavour intended to allow the pursuit of aims of a non-charitable or dubiously charitable flavour. In a case where the real purpose for which an organisation was formed is in doubt, it may be legitimate to take into account the nature of the activities which the organisation has since its formation carried on. It is, as I have remarked, settled by, among other cases, *Inland Revenue Commissioners* v *City of Glasgow Police Athletic Association* that, if the main purpose of an organisation is charitable, power to carry on incidental supplementary non-charitable activities is not fatal to charitable status. The activities of an organisation after its formation may serve to indicate that the power to carry on non-charitable activities was in truth not incidental or supplementary at all but was the main purpose for which the organisation was formed. In such a case, the organisation could not be regarded as charitable.'

Comment
The Charity Commission now issues clear

guidelines on the permitted political activities of charities.

Attorney-General of the Cayman Islands and Others v *Wahr-Hansen*
[2000] 3 All ER 643 Privy Council (Lords Browne-Wilkinson, Steyn, Clyde, Hobhouse of Woodborough and Millett)

• *Exclusively charitable purposes*

Facts
The Continental Foundation was set up in 1976 'for the benefit of worthy individuals, organisations and corporations'. The trustees were directed to pay money to 'religious charitable or educational institutions' or any 'organisations or institutions operating for the public good', the intention of the settlor being to enable the trustees to 'endeavour to act for the good or for the benefit of mankind in general or any section of mankind in particular anywhere in the world or throughout the world'. On the settlor's death, the administrator of his estate claimed that the gifts failed because they were not exclusively charitable. This was challenged on behalf of the trust by the Attorney-General of the Cayman Islands on the grounds that, despite the words used, the settlor's intention was to settle the fund for the benefit of a particular locality and that the second group of purposes was intended to read ejusdem generis with the first and was thus restricted to purposes which were exclusively charitable. The case came on appeal to the Privy Council.

Held
These arguments were rejected by the Privy Council who held that, although there was a limited class of cases where gifts in general terms for the benefit of a named locality or its inhabitants had been benevolently construed, that principle was not to be applied to all cases where there were general statements. General words were not to be artificially construed so

as to be impliedly limited to charitable purposes only. In this case there were clear indications that no such implied limitation had been intended. There were indications that there was an intention to benefit worthy individuals which could not be a charitable purpose. The wording 'to endeavour' etc demonstrated a much wider intention than to benefit objects which were exclusively charitable. The appeal was therefore dismissed.

Lord Browne-Wilkinson:

'In order to demonstrate that trusts are, in law, charitable, it must be shown that those trusts are *exclusively* charitable. If it is shown that, consistently with the provisions of the trust deed, property can be applied for purposes other than charitable purposes the trust will fail. In the present case the purposes stated by clause 4 fall into two groups. The first group consists of "any one or more religious, charitable or educational institution or institutions". The second group, crucially introduced by the word "or", consists of "any organisations or institutions operating for the public good". The objects specified in the first group are plainly charitable. But, on their literal construction, the purposes stated in the in the second group are not exclusively charitable. Applications of moneys for public philanthropic or benevolent purposes would be for the public good but would not necessarily be legally charitable ... Accordingly, unless the Attorney-General can demonstrate that the words of clause 3 are not to be given their literal meaning, the trusts and powers declared concerning the Continental Foundation are not charitable and are all void for the outset.

How then does the Attorney-General seek to restrict the meaning of the words used in the second group of purposes? First he points to the so-called locality cases. These are cases where the gift is made, for example, to a parish ... or "for the good of" a specific county ... or "for "charitable, beneficial and public works" or for "the benefit of Great Britain" ... or "unto my country England"... In all these cases the gifts were held to be valid charitable trusts, even though the breadth of the words used, literally construed, would certainly have authorised the applications of the funds for non-charitable purposes in the specified locality. The courts have held that such purposes are to be impliedly limited to charitable purposes in the specified community. So, it is argued in the present case, although the second group of purposes ("organisations or institutions operating for the public good") is not limited to a particular locality, the same principle ought to be applied and the purposes should be limited to those organisations operated for the public good by charitable means.

In the Lordships' view, this argument is fallacious. There is a limited class of cases where gifts in general terms are made for the benefit of a named locality or its inhabitants. For reasons which are obscure, such cases have been benevolently construed. They are now so long established that in cases falling within the very circumscribed description of gifts for the benefit of a specified locality they remain good law. But they have been widely criticised and indeed have been said to be wrongly decided (see, for example Albery: "Trusts for the benefit of a locality" (1940) 56 LQR 49). To apply the same principle to all cases where there are general statements of benevolent or philanthropic objects so as to restrict the meaning of the general words to such objects as are in law charitable would be inconsistent with the overwhelming body of authority which decides that general words are not to be artificially construed so as to be impliedly limited to charitable purposes only.

The Attorney-General sought to pray in aid the remarks of Russell LJ in *Incorporated Council of Law Reporting for England and Wales* v *A-G*. In considering the proper approach to the question whether or not a specific purpose fell within the fourth head in *Income Tax Special Purposes Commissioners* v *Pemsel*, ie as being a purpose for the benefit of the public at large with the spirit and intendment of the preamble to the Statute of Elizabeth I ... Russell LJ said:

"... the courts, in consistently saying that not all such are necessarily charitable in law, are in substance accepting that if a purpose is shown to be so beneficial or of such utility it is prima facie charitable in law, but have left open a line of retreat based on the equity of the statute in case they are faced with a purpose (eg a political purpose) which could not have been within the contemplation of the statute even if the then legislators had been endowed with the gift of foresight into the circumstances of later centuries. In a case such as the present, in which in my view the object cannot be thought otherwise than beneficial to the community and of general public utility, I believe the proper question to ask is whether there are any grounds for holding it to be outside the equity of the statute; and I think the answer to that is here in the negative."

The Attorney-General contends that this presumption in favour of a beneficial purpose being charitable ought to be applied in the present case so as to provide a presumption that the institutions "operating for the public good" should be restricted to such organisations as are operating in a charitable manner. Although, in the judgment of their Lordships, Russell LJ's approach has much to commend it in deciding whether or not a purpose specified by the donor falls within the spirit and intendment of the preamble to the Statute of Elizabeth I, it has no application at all to the quite different problem which is raised in the present case, viz are *general* words to be artificially restricted to purposes which are within the spirit and intendment of the statute and thereby rendered charitable. The principle has no application to such a case nor was it ever intended to.

Finally, the Attorney-General submitted that the words in the second group of purposes were to be construed as being ejusdem generis with those in the first group, ie institutions "operating for the public good" by charitable means. It is said that the word "charitable" in the first group refers only to eleemosynary charities for the relief of poverty. Then it is said that it cannot be mere chance that the draftsman in stating the purposes of the Continental Foundation reflects the same four categories as those commonly known as the four heads of charity mentioned in *Pemsel*'s case – the advancement of religion, the advancement of education, the relief of poverty and other public purposes. Therefore, it is said, the second group of objects must be construed as being of the same nature as those in the first group, ie which are in law charitable and as being limited to those purposes which fall within the fourth head in *Pemsel*'s case. This argument has only subtlety to recommend it. Their Lordships can see no reason to give this artificially limited construction to the second group of objects which are entirely general. On the contrary, there are clear indications that no such implied limitation was intended. The first recital demonstrates that the purpose of the trust was, amongst other things, to benefit "worthy" individuals, a purpose which is plainly not charitable. Moreover, even clause 3 itself states that the intention is "to endeavour to act for the good or for the benefit of mankind in general". This demonstrates a much wider intention than to benefit those objects which are strictly charitable. Their Lordships are of the view that the memorandum of agreement clearly manifests an intention to establish general welfare trusts without confining those trusts to purposes which are in law charitable.'

Comment
While the *Incorporated Council of Law Reporting* case leaves Lord McNaughten's fourth category open for further charitable purposes which are beneficial to the community, in this case no specific purpose was mentioned in the Continental Foundation trust deed. In relation to the argument based on the locality cases, can it be said that the whole world is a locality?

Chichester Diocesan Fund and Board of Finance Inc v Simpson
[1944] AC 341 House of Lords (Viscount Simonds LC, Lords Macmillan, Porter, Simonds and Wright)

- *Charitable trusts must be exclusively charitable*

Facts
Caleb Diplock who died in 1936 left a will by the terms of which his executors were directed to apply his residuary estate 'for such charitable institution or institutions or other charitable or benevolent object or objects in England' as they should in their absolute discretion think fit. The executors proceeded to distribute the estate among 139 charities of their choice. However, the next of kin challenged the validity of the gift on the grounds that it was void for uncertainty.

Held (Lord Wright dissenting)
'Charitable or benevolent' purposes resulted in the trust being not wholly and exclusively charitable. The gift was not charitable in these circumstances. Further, it was not a valid private trust either; there was uncertainty of objects.

Lord Porter:

'Technical words must be interpreted in their technical sense and "charity" or "charitable" are technical words in English law and must be so construed unless it can be seen from the wording of the will as a whole that they are used in some other than their technical sense. For this purpose and in order to discover the testator's intention, it is the duty of the court to take into consideration the whole of the terms of the will and not to confine itself to the disputed words or their immediate context.

In the present case, the words whose interpretation is contested are "charitable or benevolent". It is admitted on behalf of the appellants that, if the word "benevolent" stood alone, it would be too vague a term and the gift would be void … But it is said that, when coupled with the word "charitable" even by the disjunctive "or", it either takes colour from its associate or is merely exegetical, and the phrase is used as implying either that "charitable" and "benevolent" are the same thing or that "benevolent" qualifies "charitable" so as to limit the gift to objects which are both charitable and benevolent.

In my view, the words so coupled do not naturally bear any of the meanings suggested. The addition of "benevolent" to "charitable" on the face of it suggests an alternative purpose and I do not see why in this collocation "benevolent" should be read as "charitable benevolent". Nor do I think that it can be said to be merely exegetical. Prima facie, these are alternative objects …'

Comment

Further litigation in this matter will be found in *Re Diplock* (Chapter 14 below) and *Ministry of Health* v *Simpson* (Chapter 15 below).

Dingle v *Turner* [1972] AC 601
House of Lords (Viscount Dilhorne, Lords MacDermott, Hodson, Simon and Cross)

• *Charitable trusts for the relief of poverty – no public benefit required*

Facts

A testator directed the trustees of his will to invest £10,000 and apply the income thereof 'in paying pensions to poor employees of E Dingle & Co Ltd'. At the testator's death E Dingle & Co Ltd had 705 full-time employees and 189 part-time employees and was paying pensions to 89 ex-employees.

Held

The gift was a valid charitable gift. A gift for the relief of poverty would be charitable where, as a matter of construction, it was to relieve poverty amongst a particular description of poor persons. If, however, the trust is one to relieve poverty among named persons it is not a charitable trust but a private trust.

Lord Cross:

'Your Lordships, therefore, are now called on to give to the old "poor relations" cases and the more modern "poor employees" cases that careful consideration which, in his speech in the *Oppenheim* case, Lord Morton of Henryton said that they might one day require.

The contention of the appellant and the respondents may be stated broadly as follows. The Appellant says that in the *Oppenheim* case this House decided that in principle a trust ought not to be regarded as charitable if the benefits under it are confined either to the descendants of a named individual or individuals or the employees of a given individual or company and that although the "poor relations" cases may have to be left standing as an anomalous exception to the general rule because their validity has been recognised for so long, the exception ought not to be extended to "poor employees" trusts which had not been recognised for long before their status as charitable trusts began to be called in question. The respondents, on the other hand, say, first that the rule laid down in the *Oppenheim* case with regard to educational trusts ought not to be regarded as a rule applicable in principle to all kinds of charitable trust and, secondly, that in any case it is impossible to draw any logical distinction between "poor relation" trusts and "poor employees" trusts, and that as the former cannot be held invalid today after having been recognised as valid for so long, the latter must be regarded as valid also.

By a curious coincidence within a few months of the decision of this House in the *Oppenheim* case the cases on gifts to "poor relations" had to be considered in the Court of Appeal in *Re Scarisbrick*. Most of the cases on this subject were decided in the eighteenth or early nineteenth centuries and are very inadequately reported but two things at least were clear. First, that it never occurred to the judges who decided them that in the field of "poverty" a trust could not be a charitable trust if the class of beneficiaries was defined by reference to descent from a common ancestor. Secondly, that the courts did not treat a gift or trust as necessarily charitable because the objects of it have to be poor in order to qualify, for in some of the cases the trust was treated as a private trust and not a charity. The problem in *Re Scarisbrick* was to determine on what basis the distinction was drawn. ...

The appellant in the instant case, while of course submitting that the judges who decided the old cases were wrong in not appreciating that no gift for the relief of poverty among persons tracing descent from a common ancestor could ever have a sufficiently "public" quality to constitute a charity, did not dispute the correctness of the analysis of those cases made by the Court of Appeal in *Re Scarisbrick* ...

Indeed counsel for the appellant ventured to suggest that we should overrule the "poor relations" cases. His submission was that which was accepted by the Court of Appeal in Ontario in *Re Cox (deceased)* – namely that while the "poor relations" cases might have to be left as long standing anomalies there was no good reason for sparing the "poor employees" cases which only date from *Re Gosling* decided in 1900 and which have been under suspicion ever since the decision in *Re Compton* in 1945. But the "poor members" and the "poor employees" decisions were a natural development of the "poor relations" decisions and to draw a distinction between different sorts of "poverty" trusts would be quite illogical and could certainly not be said to be introducing "greater harmony" into the law of charity. Moreover, although not as old as the "poor relations" trusts, "poor employees" trusts have been recognised as charities for many years; there are now a large number of such trusts in existence; and assuming, as one must, that they are properly administered in the sense that benefits under them are only given to people who can fairly be said to be, according to current standards, "poor persons", to treat such trusts as charities is not open to

any practical objection. So as it seems to me it must be accepted that where ever else it may hold sway, the *Compton* rule has no application in the field of trusts for the relief of poverty and that the dividing line between a charitable trust and a private trust lies where the Court of appeal drew it in *Re Scarisbrick* ...'

Comment
Trusts for the relief of poverty have always been given special treatment because, if an individual undertakes the upkeep of the poor, there is a public benefit in the fact that the state is relieved of its obligations in this regard.

Gaudiya Mission and Others v *Brahmachary and Others* [1997] 4 All ER 957 Court of Appeal (Leggatt, Morritt and Mummery LJJ)

• *Overseas charities – jurisdiction of the English court*

Facts
Gaudiya Mission was a charity registered and functioning in India. It had a temple in London. In 1991 another organisation sought registration as a charity in England and Wales under that name. The case concerned the jurisdiction of the English court to adjudicate on a matter relating to an overseas charity.

Held
The English court had no such jurisdiction.

Mummery LJ:

'Under English law charity has always received special treatment. It often takes the form of a trust; but it is a public trust for the promotion of purposes beneficial to the community, not a trust for private individuals. It is, therefore, subject to special rules governing registration, administration, taxation and duration. Although not a state institution, a charity is subject to the constitutional protection of the Crown as *parens patriae*, acting through HM Attorney General, to the state supervision of the Charity Commissioners and to the judicial supervision of the High Court. This regime applies whether the charity takes the form of a trust or of an incorporated body.

The English courts have never sought to subject to this regime instutions or undertakings established for public purposes under other legal systems.'

Mummery LJ referred to *Dicey and Morris on the Conflict of Laws* and to the relevant case law and continued:

'The practice established so long ago has been followed in modern times. In *Re Robinson* (a gift to the German government for the benefit of disabled German soldiers) Maugham J said:

"... if the trustee is abroad there is no power in the court to direct a scheme to be settled, and the practice in such a case is to hand over the fund to the trustee to be applied according to the trusts of the will without directing a scheme."

These cases show that the courts of this country accept that they do not have the means of controlling an institution established in another country and administered by trustees there. This was recognised as the reason why courts have no authority to make a scheme ...

The practical problems were most forcefully stated by Lord Brougham in *Mayor of Lyon* v *East India Co* (1836) in a passage which merits quotation. Lord Brougham said:

"The objection, in the ordinary case, to administering a foreign charity under the superintendence of the Court is this: those who are engaged in the actual execution of it, are beyond the Court's control, and those who are within the jurisdiction are answerable to the Court for the acts of persons as to whom they can derive no aid from the Court. Such an office will not easily be undertaken by any one; and its duties cannot be satisfactorily performed;

at least the party must rely more on the local, that is, the foreign, authorities for help, than on the Court to which he is accountable."

These cases are to be contrasted with other cases in which a charity sometimes misdescribed as a "foreign charity", has been held to be subject to the control of the High Court and to its scheme-making powers. In *Re Colonial Bishoprics Fund 1841*, Luxmoore J rejected the contention that he had no jurisdiction to may a cy-près scheme because it was a "foreign charity", in the sense that all its objects were located abroad. That was a trust established in England for the endowment of bishoprics in the colonies. Luxmoore J accepted the submission of counsel for the Attorney-General Mr Danckwerts, that, as the trustees of the fund were in this country and the trusts were established here, he could direct the scheme, even though the objects of bounty were located abroad.'

Leggatt LJ:

'Charities provide a prime example of institutions which it is in the English public interest to regulate and control. But that is only so if they are English charities. Any attempt to control foreign charities would represent something akin to encroachment upon the sovereignty of a foreign state. I am quite satisfied that because, for the reasons given by Mummery LJ, the Gaudiya Mission is not established in England for charitable purposes and is not subject to the control of the High Court in the exercise of its jurisdiction in respect to charities, it is not a charity within s33 of the Charities Act 1993.'

Comment

Note the distinction made between a charity registered in England for an overseas purpose over which the court will accept jurisdiction and a charity registered overseas over which the court has no such jurisdiction.

Guild (Executor Nominate of the Late James Young Russell) v *IRC*
[1992] 2 WLR 397 House of Lords
(Lords Keith of Kinkel, Roskill, Griffiths, Jauncey of Tullichettle and Lowry)

• *Recreational Charities Act 1958 – sports facilities – Scotland*

Facts
The testator had left the residue of his estate to the council of North Berwick for 'use in connection with the sports centre in North Berwick or some similar purpose in connection with sport'. The IRC determined the transfer was not charitable and was therefore liable to capital transfer tax.

Held
It was held on appeal that the term 'charity' and 'charitable purposes' were to be determined in Scotland, for tax purposes, by their English meaning. Further, on applying s1(2)(a) of the Recreational Charities Act 1958, the provision of facilities for recreation or other leisure-time occupation could be provided with the view of improving the conditions of life of its intended recipients. This was so notwithstanding that they were not in a position of relative social disadvantage or suffering from some degree of deprivation.

Lord Keith:

'Section 1 of the 1958 Act provides:
(1) Subject to the provisions of this Act, it shall be and be deemed always to have been charitable to provide, or assist in the provision of, facilities for recreation or other leisure-time occupation, if the facilities are provided in the interests of social welfare: Provided that nothing in this section shall be taken to derogate from the principle that a trust or institution to be charitable must be for the public benefit.
(2) The requirement of the foregoing subsection that the facilities are provided in the interest of social welfare shall not be treated as satisfied unless (a) the facilities are provided with the object of improving the conditions of life for the persons for whom the facilities are primarily intended and (b) either (1) those persons have need of such facilities as aforesaid by reasons of their youth, age, infirmity or disablement, poverty or social and economic circumstances; or (2) the facilities are to be available to the members or female members of the public at large.
(3) Subject to the said requirement, subsection (1) of this section applies in particular to the provision of facilities at village halls, community centres and womens institutes, and to the provision and maintenance of grounds and buildings to be used for purposes of recreation or leisure-time occupation and extends to the provision of facilities for those purposes by the organising of any activity.
In the course of his argument in relation to the first branch of the bequest counsel for the Crown accepted that it assisted in the provision of facilities for recreation or other leisure-time occupation within the meaning of subsection (1) of s1 of the 1958 Act and also that the requirement of public benefit in the proviso to the subsection was satisfied. It was further accepted that the facilities of the sports centre were available to the public at large so that the conditions of subsection (2) were satisfied. It was maintained, however, that these facilities were not provided "in the interests of social welfare" as required by subsection (1), because they did not meet the conditions laid down in subsection (2)(a), namely that they would be provided with the object of improving the conditions of life for the persons for whom the facilities are primarily intended. The reason why it was said that this condition was not met was that on a proper construction it involved that the facilities should be provided with the object of meeting a need for such facilities in people who suffered from a position of relative social disadvantage.'

Lord Keith reviewed the case law and continued:

'It is difficult to envisage a case where,

although these essential elements are present, yet the facilities are not provided in the interests of social welfare. Nor do I consider that the reference to social welfare in subsection (1) can properly be held to colour subsection (2)(a) to the effect that the persons for whom the facilities are primarily intended must be confined to those persons who suffer from some form of social deprivation. That this is not so seems to me to follow from the alternative conditions expressed in subsection (2)(b). If it suffices that the facilities are to be available to the members of the public at large, as sub-paragraph (2) provides, it must necessarily be inferred that the persons for whom the facilities are primarily intended are not to be confined to those who have need of them by reason of one of the forms of social deprivation mentioned in sub-paragraph (1).

The fact is that persons in all walks of life and all kinds of social circumstances may have their conditions of life improved by the provision of recreational facilities of suitable character. The proviso requiring public benefit excludes facilities of an undesirable nature. In my opinion the view expressed by Bridge LJ in *IRC v McMullen* is clearly correct and that of Walton J in the same case is incorrect ...

It remains to consider the point upon which the executor was unsuccessful before the First Division, namely whether or not the second branch of the bequest of residue, referring to "some similar purpose in connection with sport", is so widely expressed as to admit of the funds being applied in some manner which falls outside the requirements of s1 of the 1958 Act. Counsel for the executor invited your Lordships , in constructing this part of the bequest, to adopt the benignant approach which has regularly been favoured in the interpretation of trusts deeds capable of being regarded as evincing a charitable intention. That approach is appropriate where the language used is susceptible of two constructions, one of which would make it void and the other effectual ... It was argued for the Crown that the benignant approach was not apt in the present case, since the question was not whether the trust was valid or invalid, but whether it qualified for exemption from tax by virtue of the 1958 Act. But the importation into Scots law, for tax purposes, of the technical English law of charities involves that a Scottish judge should approach any question of construction arising out of the language used in the relevant instrument in the same manner as would an English judge who had to consider its validity as a charitable gift. The English judge would adopt the benignant approach in setting about that task, and so the Scottish judge dealing with the tax consequences should do likewise.

The matter for decision turns upon the ascertainment of the intention of the testator in using the words he did. The adjective "similar" connotes that there are points of resemblance between one thing and another. The points of resemblance here with the sports centre cannot be related only to location in North Berwick or to connection with sport. The first of these is plainly to be implied from the fact of the gift being to the town council of North Berwick and the second is expressly stated in the words under construction. So the resemblance to the sports centre which the testator had in mind must be ascertained by reference to some other characteristics possessed by it. The leading characteristics of the sports centre lie in the nature of the facilities which are provided there and the fact that those facilities are available to the public at large. These are the characteristics which enable it to satisfy s1 of the 1958 Act. Adopting so far as necessary a benignant construction, I infer that the intention of the testator was that any other purpose to which the town council might apply the bequest or any part of it should also display those characteristics. In the result I am of opinion, the first part of the bequest having been found to be charitable within the meaning of s1 of the 1958 Act, that the same is true of the second part, so that the funds in question qualify for exemption from capital transfer tax.'

Comment
Note the approval of the benignant approach to construction adopted by the English courts and the wide definition of 'social welfare'.

Hetherington, Re, Gibbs v McDonnell [1989] 2 All ER 129
High Court (Sir Nicholas Browne-Wilkinson V-C)

• *Public benefit and advancement of religion – saying of masses*

Facts
A devout Roman Catholic and regular worshipper at church, the testatrix included in her holograph will gifts as follows:

'I wish to leave two thousand pounds to the Roman Catholic Church Bishop of Westminster for masses for the repose of the souls of my husband and my parents and my sisters and also myself when I die.'

'Whatever is left over of my estate is to be given to the Roman Catholic Church St Edwards, Golders Green for masses for my soul.'

The administrator applied for a ruling whether these gifts established a valid charitable trust.

Held
They were valid charitable trusts as they were for a religious purpose and contained the necessary element of public benefit.

Sir Nicholas Browne-Wilkinson V-C:

'The grounds on which the trust in the present case can be attacked are that there is no *express* requirement that the Masses for souls which are to be celebrated are to be celebrated in public. The evidence shows that celebration in public is the invariable practice but there is no requirement of canon law to that effect. Therefore it is said the money could be applied to saying Masses in private which would not be charitable since there would be no sufficient element of public benefit.

In my judgment the cases establish the following propositions. A trust for the advancement of education, the relief of poverty or the advancement of religion is prima facie charitable and assumed to be for the public benefit: see *National Anti-Vivisection Society* v *IRC*. This assumption of public benefit can be rebutted by showing that in fact the particular trust in question cannot operate so as to confer a legally recognised benefit on the public, as in *Gilmour* v *Coats*. The celebration of a religious rite in public does confer a sufficient public benefit because of the edifying and improving effect of such celebration on the members of the public who attend. As Lord Reid said in *Gilmour* v *Coats*:

"A religion can be regarded as beneficial without it being necessary to assume that all its beliefs are true, and a religious service can be regarded as beneficial to all those who attend it without it being necessary to determine the spiritual efficacy of that service or to accept any particular belief about it."

... The celebration of a religious rite in private does not contain the necessary element of public benefit since any benefit by prayer or example is incapable of proof in the legal sense, and any element of edification is limited to a private, not public, class of those present at the celebration ... Where there is a gift for a religious purpose which could be carried out in a way which is beneficial to the public (ie by public Masses) but could also be carried out in a way which would not have sufficient element of public benefit (ie by private Masses) the gift is to be construed as a gift to be carried out only by the methods that are charitable, all non-charitable methods being excluded ... Applying those principles to the present case, a gift for the saying of Masses is prima facie charitable, being for a religious purpose. In practice, those Masses will be celebrated in public, which provides a sufficient element of public benefit. The provision of stipends for priests saying the Masses, by relieving the Roman Catholic Church pro tanto of the liability to provide such stipends, is a further benefit. The gift is to be construed as a gift for public

Masses only on the principle of *Re White*, private masses not being permissible since it would not be a charitable application of the fund for a religious purpose.

Comment

The public benefit in trusts for the advancement of religion relies in the advantage of access by the public to people whose lives are dedicated to worthy causes. Hence enclosed religious orders cannot be charitable because access to the public is forbidden.

Income Tax Special Purposes Commissioners v *Pemsel* [1891] AC 531 House of Lords (Lord Halsbury LC, Lords Macnaghten, Watson, Bramwell, Herschell and Morris)

• *Charity in law*

Facts

Land was vested in the respondent on trust to apply the rents and profits for the missionary establishments of the Moravian Church. He applied to the Special Commissioners for Schedule A allowance extended to charitable trusts. The Commissioners refused, denying his was a charitable object, and the Queen's Bench Division refused him an order of mandamus. This was reversed in the Court of Appeal and the Commissioners appealed to the House of Lords.

Held

The appeal was dismissed.

Lord Halsbury LC:

'[The Statute of Elizabeth] is intituled "an Act to redress the misemployment of land goods and stocks of money heretofore given to charitable uses" ... [and] it is very intelligible ... that the Court of Chancery ... should have given the widest possible interpretation to an Act intended to remedy such abuses. The enumeration of charitable objects in the preamble ... was very soon interpreted not to be limited to the exact charities therein referred to. Where a purpose by analogy was deemed by the Court of Chancery to be within its spirit and intendment it was held to be "charitable".

Lord Macnaghten:

'No doubt the popular meaning of the words "charity" and "charitable" does not coincide with their legal meaning: and no doubt it is easy enough to collect from the books a few decisions which seem to push the doctrine of the Court to the extreme, and to present a contrast between the two meanings in an aspect almost ludicrous. But, still, it is difficult to fix the point of divergence, and no one has yet succeeded in defining the popular meaning to the word "charity" ... How far, then, it may be asked, does the popular meaning of the word "charity" correspond with its legal meaning? "Charity" in its legal sense comprises four principal divisions: trusts for the relief of poverty, trusts for the advancement of education, trusts for the advancement of religion and trusts for other purposes beneficial to the community, not falling under any of the preceding heads.'

Comment

Lord Macnaghten redefined the definition in the preamble to the Statute of Elizabeth into our modern definition of charitable purpose by grouping the categories of charitable purposes under four heads.

Incorporated Council of Law Reporting for England and Wales v *Attorney-General* [1972] Ch 73 Court of Appeal (Russell, Sachs and Buckley LJJ)

• *Sources of the definition of charity*

Facts

The object of the Council was 'the preparation and publication, in a convenient form, at a moderate price, and under gratuitous professional control, of Reports of Judicial Decisions of the Superior and Appellate

Courts in England.' The Council was a non-profit making body whose reports were used by judges and the legal profession and others engaged in the study of law. The Charity Commissioners refused to register the Council as a charity.

Held

The appeal against the decision of the Charity Commissioners was allowed. On the nature and definition of charity, Sachs LJ held that the Council's activities were charitable under the head of trusts for the advancement of education.

Russell LJ:

'I come now to the question whether, if the main purpose of the Association is (as I think it is) to further the sound development and administration of the law in this country, and if (as I think it is) that is a purpose beneficial to the community or of general public utility, that purpose is charitable according to the law of England and Wales. On this point the law is rooted in the Statute of Elizabeth, a statute whose object was the oversight and reform of abuses in the administration of property devoted by donors to purposes which were regarded as worthy of such protection as being charitable. The preamble to the statute listed certain examples of purposes which were regarded as worthy of such protection. These were from an early stage regarded merely as examples, and have through the centuries been regarded as examples or guide posts for the courts in the differing circumstances of a developing civilisation and economy. Sometimes recourse has been had by the courts to the instances given in the preambles in order to see whether in a given case sufficient analogy may be found with something specifically stated in the preamble, or sufficient analogy with some decided case in which already a previous sufficient analogy has been found. Of this approach perhaps the most obvious example is the provision of crematoria by analogy with the provision of grounds by analogy with the upkeep of churchyards by analogy with the repair of churches. On other occasions a decision in favour or against a purpose being charitable has been based on terms on a more general question whether the purpose is or is not within "the spirit and intendment" of the Elizabethan statute and in particular its preamble. Again (and at an early stage in development) whether the purpose is within "the equity" or within "the mischief" of the statute. Again whether the purpose is charitable "in the same sense" as purposes within the purview of the statute. I have much sympathy with those who say that these phrases do little of themselves to elucidate any particular problem. "Tell me", they say, "what you define when you speak of spirit, intendment, equity, mischief, the same sense and I will tell you whether a purpose is charitable according to law. But you never define. All you do is sometimes to say that a purpose is none of these things. I can understand it when you say that the preservation of sea walls is for the safety of lives and property, and therefore by analogy the voluntary provision of lifeboats and fire brigades are charitable. I can even follow you as far as crematoria. But these other generalities teach me nothing." I say I have much sympathy for such an approach; but it seems to me to be unduly and improperly restrictive. The Statute of Elizabeth was a statute to reform abuses; in such circumstances and in that age the courts of this country were not inclined to be restricted in their implementation of Parliament's desire for reform to particular examples given by the statute, and they deliberately kept open their ability to intervene when they thought necessary in cases not specifically mentioned, by applying as the test whether any particular case of abuse of funds or property was within the "mischief" or the "equity" of the statute.

For myself I believe that this rather vague and undefined approach is the correct one, with analogy its handmaid, and that when considering Lord Macnaghten's fourth category in *Pemsel*'s case of "other purposes beneficial to the community" (or as phrased by Sir Samuel Romilly "objects of general public utility") the courts, in consistently saying that not all such are necessarily charitable in law, are in substance accepting that if a purpose is shown to be so beneficial or of such utility it is prima facie charitable in law, but have left open a line of retreat based on the equity of the statute in case they are faced with a purpose (eg a political purpose) which could not have been within the contemplation of the statute even if the then legislators had been endowed with the gift of foresight into the circumstances of later centuries.

In a case such as the present, in which in my view the object cannot be thought otherwise than beneficial to the community and of general public utility, I believe the proper question to ask is whether there are any grounds for holding it to be outside the equity of the statute; and I think the answer to that is here in the negative. I have already touched on its essential importance to our rule of law. If I look at the somewhat random examples in the preamble to the statute I find in the repair of bridges, havens, causeways, sea banks and highways examples of matters which if not looked after by private enterprise must be a proper function and responsibility of government, which would afford strong ground for a statutory expression by Parliament of anxiety to prevent misappropriation of funds voluntarily dedicated to such matters. It cannot I think be doubted that if there were not a competent and reliable set of reports of judicial decisions, it would be a proper function and responsibility of government to secure their provision for the due administration of the law. It was argued that the specific topics in the preamble that I have mentioned are all concerned with concrete matters, and that so also is the judicially accepted opinion that the provision of a court house is a charitable purpose. But whether the search be for analogy or for the equity of the statute this seems to me to be too narrow or refined an approach. I cannot accept that the provision, in order to facilitate the proper administration of the law, of the walls and other physical facilities of a court house is a charitable purpose, but that the dissemination by accurate and selective reporting of knowl-

edge of a most important part of the law to be there administered is not.

In my judgment accordingly the purpose for which the Association is established is exclusively charitable in the sense of Lord MacNaghten's fourth category.'

Comment
This is a useful exposition of the fourth of Lord Macnaghten's categories and the way in which it can be extended within the 'spirit and intendment' of the Statute of Elizabeth. The Incorporated Council publish the official law reports and the Weekly Law Reports.

IRC v Baddeley [1955] AC 572
House of Lords (Viscount Simonds, Lords Porter, Reid, Tucker and Somervell)

• *Wholly and exclusively charitable – public benefit*

Facts
Two conveyances of land were made to trustees to permit it to be 'used by the leaders for the time being of the Stratford Newtown Methodist Mission for the promotion of the religious, social and physical well-being of persons resident in the County Boroughs of West Ham and Leyton ... by the provision of facilities ... for the social and physical training and recreation ... and by promoting and encouraging all forms of such activities as are calculated to contribute to the health and well being of such persons.' The trustees claimed a reduced rate of stamp duty on the conveyance on the ground that these purposes were charitable.

Held
The objects of the trust were not wholly and exclusively charitable; the use of the word 'social' would permit the property to be used for non-charitable purposes. Further, the trust did not satisfy the public benefit requirement in any event.

Viscount Simonds:

'It is … particularly important in cases falling within the fourth category to keep firmly in mind the necessity of the element of general public utility, and I would not relax this rule. For here is a slippery slope. In the case under appeal the intended beneficiaries are a class within a class; they are those of the inhabitants of a particular area who are members of a particular church: the area is comparatively large and populous and the members may be numerous, but if this trust is charitable for them, does it cease to be charitable as the area narrows down and the numbers diminish? Suppose the area is confined to a single street and the beneficiaries to those whose creed commands few adherents: or suppose the class is one that is determined not by religious belief but by membership of a particular profession or by pursuit of a particular trade. These were considerations which influenced the House in the recent case of *Oppenheim.* That was a case of trust which by their nominal classification depend for their validity upon general public utility.'

Comment

The court refused to accept that a 'social' purpose could be exclusively charitable. Note also the concerns of the court about the personal nexus between the members of the church.

IRC v *McMullen* [1981] AC 1 House of Lords (Lords Hailsham, Diplock, Salmon, Russell and Keith)

• *Charity for the furtherance of education*

Facts

The Football Association set up a trust known as the Football Association Youth Trust, the main objects of which were 'the furtherance of education of Schools and Universities in any part of the United Kingdom encouraging and facilitating the playing of Association Football or other games and sports at such Schools and Universities and thus assisting to ensure that due attention is given to the physical education and character development of pupils at such Schools and Universities'.

Held

The trust was a valid charitable trust for the advancement of education as the purpose of the settlor was to promote the physical education and development of pupils at schools as an addition to such part of their education as related to their mental education. Education could not be restricted to mean formal instruction in the classrooms or the playground because the idea of education as set out by the Education Act 1944 expressly recognised the contribution which extra-mural activities and voluntary societies or bodies could make to the statutory system of education.

Lord Hailsham:

'But in deciding what is or is not an educational purpose for the young in 1980 it is not irrelevant to point out what Parliament considered to be educational for the young in 1944 when, by the Education Act of that year in ss7 and 53 (which are still on the statute book), Parliament attempted to lay down what was then intended to be the statutory system of education organised by the State, and the duties of the local education authorities and the Minister in establishing and maintaining the system. Those sections are so germane to the present issue that I cannot forbear to quote them both. Section 7 provided (in each of the sections the emphasis being mine):

"The statutory system of public education shall be organised in three progressive stages to be known as primary education, secondary education and further education; and it shall be the duty of the local education authority for every area, so far as their powers extend, to contribute toward the spiritual, moral, mental and physical development of the community by securing that efficient education throughout those stages shall be available to meet the needs of the population of their area."

And in s53 of the same Act it is said:

"(1) It shall be the duty of every local education authority to secure that the facilities for primary, secondary and further
education provided for their area include
adequate facilities for recreation and
social and physical training, and for that
purpose a local education authority, with
the approval of the Secretary of State,
may establish, maintain and manage, or
assist the establishment maintenance and
management of camps, holiday classes,
playing fields, play centres and other
places (including playgrounds, gymnasi-
ums, and swimming baths not appropriated to any school or college), at which
facilities for recreation and for such training as aforesaid are available for persons
receiving primary, secondary or further
education, and may organise games,
expeditions and other activities for such
persons, and may defray or contribute
toward the expenses thereof.

(2) A local education authority, in
making arrangements for the provision of
facilities or the organisation of activities
under the powers conferred on them by
the last forgoing subsection shall, in par
ticular, have regard to the expediency of
co-operating with any voluntary societies
or bodies whose objects include the provision of facilities or the organisation of
activities of a similar character."

There is no trace in these sections of an idea
of education limited to the development of
mental vocational or practical skills, to
grounds or facilities the special prerequisite
of particular schools, or of any schools or
colleges, or term time, or particular locali-
ties, and there is express recognition of the
contribution which extra-curricular activities and voluntary societies or bodies can
play even in the promotion of the purely
statutory system envisaged by the Act. In
the light of s7 in particular I would be very
reluctant to confine the meaning of education to formal instruction in the classroom or
even the playground, and I consider them
sufficiently wide to cover all the activities
envisaged by the settlor in the present case.
One of the affidavits filed on the part of the

Crown referred to the practices of ancient
Sparta. I am not sure that this particular
precedent is an entirely happy one, but from
a careful perusal of Plato's Republic I doubt
whether its author would have agreed with
Stamp LJ in regarding "physical education
development" as an elusive phrase, or as
other than an educational charity, at least
when used in association with the formal
education of the young during the period
when they are pupils of schools or in statu
pupillari at universities.'

Comment
Note the wide definition of education afforded
by the Education Act 1944 which was Lord
Hailsham's starting point in this case.

McGovern v Attorney-General
[1982] Ch 321 Chancery Division
(Slade J)

• *Primarily political objects*

Facts
In 1977 Amnesty International, an unincorporated non-profit-making body set up to ensure
that prisoners of conscience throughout the
world were treated in accordance with the
United Nations Declaration on human rights,
set up a trust to administer those of its objects
which were believed to be charitable. The
objects of the trusts were (a) the relief of prisoners of conscience, (b) attempting to secure
the release of prisoners of conscience, (c)
procuring the abolition of torture or inhuman
or degrading treatment or punishment, (d)
research into the maintenance and observance
of human rights, (e) the dissemination of the
results of such research, and (f) doing all such
other things as would promote these charitable
objects. The trust deed then stated that the
objects were to be restricted to those things
which were charitable according the United
Kingdom law. The trustees applied to have the
trust registered as a charity. This was refused
by the Charity Commissioners so an application was made to the court seeking a declara-

tion as to whether these objects were charitable.

Held

Charitable status could not be granted because (a), (b) and (c) were essentially political objects. However, (d) and (e) were charitable but as the trust was not 'wholly and exclusively' charitable it could not be registered.

Slade J:

'Save in the case of gifts to classes of poor persons, a trust must always be shown to promote a public benefit of a nature recognised by the courts as being such, if it is to qualify as being charitable. The question whether a purpose will or may operate for the public benefit is to be answered by the court forming an opinion on the evidence before it; see *National Anti-Vivisection Society* v *Inland Revenue Commissioners* per Lord Wright. No doubt in some cases a purpose may be so manifestly beneficial to the public that it would be absurd to call evidence on this point. In many other instances, however, the element of public benefit may be much more debatable. Indeed, in some cases the court will regard this element of being incapable of proof one way or the other and thus will inevitably decline to recognise the trust as being of a charitable nature. ...

From the passages from the speeches of Lord Parker, Lord Wright and Lord Simonds which I have read, I extract the principle that the court will not regard as charitable a trust of which a main object is to procure an alteration of the law of the United Kingdom for one or both of two reasons. First, the court will ordinarily have no sufficient means of judging, as a matter of evidence, whether the proposed change will or will not be for the public benefit. Second, even if the evidence suffices to enable it to form a prima facie opinion that a change in the law is desirable, it must still decide the case on the principle that the law is right as it stands, since to do otherwise would be to usurp the functions of the legislature. I interpret the point made by Lord Simonds concerning the position of the Attorney-General as merely illustrating some of the anomalies and undesirable consequences that might ensue if the courts began to encroach on the functions of the legislature by ascribing charitable status to trusts of which a main object is to procure a change in the law of the United Kingdom as being for the public benefit ...

I now turn to consider the status of a trust of which a main object is to secure the alteration of the laws of a foreign country. The mere fact that the trust was intended to be carried out abroad would not by itself necessarily deprive it of charitable status. A number of trusts to be executed outside this country have been upheld as charities, though the judgment of Evershed MR in *Camille and Henry Dreyfus Foundation Inc* v *Inland Revenue Commissioners* illustrates that certain types of trust, for example trusts for the setting out of soldiers or the repair of bridges or causeways, might be acceptable as charities only if they were to be executed in the United Kingdom. The point with which I am at present concerned is whether a trust of which a direct or main object is to secure a change in the laws of a foreign country can ever be regarded as charitable under English law. Though I do not think that any authority cited to me precisely covers the point, I have come to the conclusion that it cannot ...

... Whatever might be its view as to the content of the relevant law from the standpoint of an English lawyer, [the court] would I think have no satisfactory means of judging such probable effects on the local community.

Furthermore, before ascribing charitable status to an English trust of which a main object was to secure the alteration of a foreign law, the court would also, I conceive, be bound to consider the consequences for this country as a matter of public policy. In a number of such cases there would arise a substantial prima facie risk that such a trust, if enforced, could prejudice the relations of this country with the foreign country concerned (*Habershon* v *Vardon*). The court would have no satisfactory means of assessing the extent of such risk, which would not be capable of being readily dealt with by evidence and would be a matter more for political than for legal judgment. For all these reasons, I conclude that a trust of which a main purpose is to procure a change in the laws of a foreign country is a trust for the attainment of political objects within the spirit of Lord Parker's pronouncement and as such is non-charitable.

Comment
Note the court's very cautious approach to an area where they must observe the separation of powers.

Niyazi's Will Trusts, Re [1978] 1 WLR 910 Chancery Division (Megarry V-C)

- *Charity for the relief of poverty implied*

Facts
A testator left the residue of his estate worth about £15,000, to be used for 'the construction of or as a contribution towards the construction of a working men's hostel' in Famagusta, Cyprus. The next of kin challenged the gift on the ground that it was not charitable and therefore failed.

Held
The terms 'working men's' and 'hostel' together had a sufficient connotation to make the residuary gift charitable. The size of the gift also implied that it would be restricted to the relief of poverty as it would only allow for the erection of a building with the basic requirements and therefore those who occupied it were likely to be impoverished.

Megarry V-C:

'Certain points seem reasonably plain. First "poverty" is not confined to destitution, but extends to those who have small means and so have to "go short". Second, a gift which in terms is not confined to the relief of

poverty may by inference be thus confined. In *Re Lucas* there was a gift of 5s per week to the older respectable inhabitants of a village. As the law then stood, Russell J was unable to hold that a gift merely to the aged was charitable; but he held that the limitation to 5s a week indicated quite clearly that only those to whom such a sum would be of importance and a benefit were to take, and so the gift was charitable as being for the relief of poverty. I do not think that it can be said that nothing save the smallness of the benefit can restrict an otherwise unrestricted benefit so as to confine it within the bounds of charity. I think that anything in the terms of the gift which by implication prevents it from going outside those bounds will suffice. In *Re Glyn's Will Trusts* Danckwerts J held that a trust for building free cottages for old women of the working classes aged 60 or more provided a sufficient context to show an intention to benefit indigent persons, and so was charitable ...

... As the argument finally emerged, Mr Mummery's main contention was that, even if neither "working men" nor "hostel", by itself, could be said to confine the trust to what in law was charity, the use of these expressions in conjunction sufficed for his purpose. They were enough to distinguish *Re Sanders' Will Trusts*, especially, as Harman J had not had the advantage which I have had of being able to consider what had been said in the *Guinness* case.

I think that the adjectival expression "working men's" plainly has some flavour of "lower income" about it, just as "upper class" has some flavour of affluence and "middle class" some flavour of comfortable means. Of course, there are some "working men" who are at least of comfortable means, if not affluence: one cannot ignore the impact of such things as football pools. But in construing a will I think that I am concerned with the ordinary or general import of words rather than exceptional cases; and, whatever may be the future meaning of "working men" or "working class", I think that by 1967 such phrases had not lost their general connotation of "lower income". I may add that nobody has suggested that any difficulty arose from the use of 'working men' as distinct from "working persons" or "working women".

The connotation of "lower income" is, I think, emphasised by the word "hostel". No doubt there are a number of hostels of superior quality; and one day, perhaps, I may even encounter the expression "luxury hostel". But without any such laudatory adjective the word "hostel" has to my mind a strong flavour of a building which provides somewhat modest accommodation for those who have some temporary need for it and are willing to accept accommodation of that standard in order to meet the need. When "hostel" is prefixed by the expression "working men's" then the further restriction is introduced of the hostel being intended for those with a relatively low income who work for their living, especially as manual workers. The need, in other words, is to be the need of working men, and not of students or battered wives or anything else. Furthermore, the need will not be the need of the better paid working men who can afford something superior to mere hostel accommodation, but the need of the lower end of the financial scale of working men who cannot compete for the better accommodation but have to content themselves with the economies and shortcomings of hostel life …

Has the expression "working men's hostel" a sufficient connotation of poverty in it to satisfy the requirements of charity? On any footing the case is desperately near the borderline, and I have hesitated in reaching my conclusion. On the whole, however, for the reasons that I have been discussing, I think that the trust is charitable, though by no great margin. This view is in my judgment supported by two further considerations. First, there is the amount of the trust fund, which in 1969 was a little under £15,000. I think one is entitled to assume that a testator has a least some idea of the probable value of his estate. The money is given for the purpose "of the construction of or a contribution towards the cost of the construction of a working men's hostel". £15,000 will not go very far in such a project, and it seems improbable that contributions from other sources towards constructing a "working men's hostel" would enable or encourage the construction of any grandiose building. If financial constraints point towards the erection of what may be called an "economy hostel", decent but catering for only the more basic requirements, then only the relatively poor would be likely to be occupants. There is at least some analogy here to the 5s per week in *Re Lucas*. Whether the trust is to give a weekly sum that is small enough to indicate that only those in straitened circumstances are to benefit, or whether it is to give a capital sum for the construction of a building which will be of such a nature that it is likely to accommodate those only who are in straitened circumstances, there will in each case be an implied restriction to poverty.

The other consideration is that of the state of housing in Famagusta. Where the trust is to erect a building in a particular area, I think that it is legitimate, in construing the trust, to have some regard to the physical condition existing in that area. Quite apart from any question of the size of the gift, I think that a trust to erect a hostel in a slum or in such an area of acute housing need may have to be construed differently from a trust to erect a hostel in an area of housing affluence or plenty. Where there is a grave housing shortage, it is plain that the poor are likely to suffer more than the prosperous, and that the provision of a "working men's hostel" is likely to help the poor and not the rich.'

Comment

This is an example of a valid English trust for an overseas purpose. Note the court's approach to the definition of poverty – they will look at the individual circumstances of the intended beneficiaries and conclude whether they are needy or 'go short'.

Oppenheim v Tobacco Securities Trust Co Ltd [1951] AC 297 House of Lords (Lords Simonds, Normand, Oaksey, Morton and MacDermott)

• *Charitable trusts must be for the public benefit*

Facts

Certain investments were held on trust by the Tobacco Securities Trust to apply the income 'in providing for the … education of children of employees or former employees of British-American Tobacco Co Ltd … or any of its subsidiary or allied companies'. The question arose whether the trust was charitable. At first instance Roxburgh J held it was not charitable as it lacked the element of public benefit. The Court of Appeal affirmed his decision.

Held (Lord MacDermott dissenting)

The appeal would be dismissed.

Lord Simonds:

'It is a clearly established principle of the law of charity that a trust is not charitable unless it is directed to the public benefit. This is sometimes stated in the proposition that it must benefit the community or a section of the community. Negatively it is said that a trust is not charitable if it confers only private benefits. In the recent case of *Gilmour* v *Coats* this principle was reasserted. It is easy to state and has been stated in a variety of ways, the earliest statement that I find being in *Jones* v *Williams*, in which Lord Hardwick LC is briefly reported as follows: "Definition of charity: a gift to a general public use, which extends to the poor as well as to the rich …". We are apt not to classify them by reference to Lord MacNaghten's decision in *Income Tax Special Purposes Commissioners* v *Pemsel,* and, as I have elsewhere pointed out, it was at one time suggested that the element of public benefit was not essential except for charities falling within the fourth class, "other purposes beneficial to the community". This is certainly wrong except in the

anomalous case of trusts for the relief of poverty, with which I must specifically deal. In the case for educational purposes the condition of public benefit must be satisfied. The difficulty lies in determining what is sufficient to satisfy the test, and there is little to help your Lordships to solve it.

If I may begin at the bottom of the scale, a trust established by a father for the education of his son is not a charity. The public element, as I will call it, is not supplied by the fact that from that son's education all my benefit. At the other end of the scale the establishment of a college or university is beyond doubt a charity. "Schools of learning and free schools and scholars of universities" are the very words of the preamble to the Charitable Uses Act 1601. So also the endowment of a college, university or school by the creation of scholarships or bursaries is a charity, and nonetheless because competition may be limited to a particular class of persons. It is on this ground, as Lord Greene MR pointed out in *Re Compton* that the so-called "founder's kin" cases can be rested. The difficulty arises where the trust is not for the benefit of any institution either then existing or by the terms of the trust to be brought into existence, but for the benefit of a class of persons at large. Then the question is whether that class of persons can be regarded as such a "section of the community" as to satisfy the test of public benefit. These words "section of the community" have no special sanctity, but they conveniently indicate (1) that the possible (I emphasise the word "possible") beneficiaries must not be numerically negligible, and (2) that the quality which distinguishes them from other members of the community, so that they form by themselves a section of it, must be a quality which does not depend on their relationship to a particular individual. It is for this reason that a trust for the education of members of a family or, as in *Re Compton*, of a number of families cannot be regarded as charitable. A group of persons may be numerous, but if the nexus between them is their personal relationship to a single propositus or to several propositi, they are neither the community nor a section of the community for charitable purposes.

I come, then, to the present case where the class of beneficiaries is numerous, but the difficulty arises in regard to their common and distinguishing quality. That quality is being children of employees of one or other of a group of companies. I can make no distinction between children of employees of one or other of a group of companies. In both cases the common quality is found in employment by particular employers.'

Comment

There were 110,000 employees whose families were potential beneficiaries of this trust but nevertheless the personal nexus test applied and the class of beneficiaries was not derived from the general public.

Resch's Will Trusts, Re [1969] AC 514 Privy Council (Lords Hodson, Guest, Donovan and Wilberforce, Sir Alfred North)

• *'Relief for the impotent', ie the sick, under the statute*

Facts

A testator died in 1963 leaving a large bequest 'to the Sisters of Charity for a period of 200 years or for so long as they shall conduct St Vincent's Private Hospital whichever shall be the shorter period, to be applied for the general purpose of such hospital'.

Held

The gift was a valid charitable bequest for the relief of the sick.

Lord Wilberforce:

'A gift for the purposes of a hospital is *prima facie* a good charitable gift. This is now clearly established both in Australia and England, not merely because of the use of the words "impotent" in the preamble to 43 Eliz. c4, though the process of referring to the preamble is one often used for reassurance, but because of the provision of medical care for the sick is, in modern times, accepted as a public benefit suitable to attract the privileges given to charitable institutions ...

In spite of this general proposition, there may be certain hospitals, or categories of hospitals, which are not charitable institutions ... Disqualifying indicia may be either that the hospital is carried on commercially, ie with a view to making profits for private individuals, or that the benefits it provides are not for the public, or a sufficiently large class of the public to satisfy the necessary tests of public character. Each class of objection is taken in the present case. As regards the first, it is accepted that the private hospital is not run for profit, in any ordinary sense, of individuals. Moreover, if the purposes of the hospital are otherwise charitable, they do not lose this character merely because charges are made to the recipients of the benefits ...

Their Lordships turn to the second objection. This, in substance, is that the private hospital is not carried on for "purposes beneficial to the community" because it provides only for persons of means who are capable of paying the substantial fees required as a condition of admission.

In dealing with this objection it is necessary first to dispose of a misapprehension. It is not a condition of validity of a trust for the relief of the sick that it should be limited to the poor sick. Whether one regards the charitable character of trusts for the relief of the sick as flowing from the word "impotent" ("aged, impotent and poor people") in the preamble to 43 Eliz c4 or more broadly as derived from the conception of benefit to the community, there is no warrant for adding to the condition of sickness that of poverty ... The proposition that relief of sickness was a sufficient purpose without adding poverty was accepted by the Court of Appeal in *Re Smith*. The appellants did not really contest this. They based their argument on the narrower proposition that a trust could not be charitable which excluded the poor from participation in its benefits. The purposes of the private hospital were, they said, to provide facilities for the well-to-do: an important section of the community was excluded: the trusts could not therefore be said to be for the benefit of the community. There was no sufficient "public element".

Lord Wilberforce referred to *Jones* v *Williams* and *Re Macduff* and continued:

'Their Lordships accept the correctness of what has been said in those cases, but they must be rightly understood. It would be a wrong conclusion from them to state that a trust for the provision of medical facilities would necessarily fail to be charitable merely because by reason of expense they could only be made use of by persons of some means. To provide, in response to public need, medical treatment otherwise inaccessible but in its nature expensive, without any profit motive, might well be charitable: on the other hand, to limit admission to a nursing home to the rich would not be so. The test is essentially one of public benefit, and indirect as well as direct benefit enters into the account. In the present case, the element of public benefit is strongly present. It is not disputed that a need exists to provide accommodation and medical treatment in conditions of greater privacy and relaxation than would be possible in a general hospital and as a supplement to the facilities of a general hospital. This is what the private hospital does and it does so at, approximately, cost price. The service is needed by all, not only by the well-to-do. So far as its nature permits it is open to all: the charges are not law, but the evidence shows that it cannot be said that the poor are excluded: : such exclusion as there is, is of some of the poor – namely, those who have (a) not contributed sufficiently to a medical benefit scheme or (b) need to stay longer in the hospital than their benefit will cover or (c) cannot get a reduction of or exemption from the charges. The general benefit to the community of such facilities results from the beds and medical staff of the general hospital, the availability of a particular type of nursing and treatment which supplements that provided by the general hospital and the benefit to the standard of medical care in the general hospital which arises from the juxtaposition of the two institutions ...'

Comment
Note that there is no requirement that charities for the sick should be only for the benefit of those who are poor.

Rowntree Housing Association v *Attorney-General* [1983] Ch 159
Chancery Division (Peter Gibson J)

• *Charity for 'the relief of aged, impotent and poor people' under the Statute of Elizabeth*

Facts
The housing association was an incorporated charity whose objects included, inter alia, the provision of housing for elderly persons in need of such accommodation. The charity wished to build small self-contained houses, flats and bungalows to be sold to elderly people on long leases in consideration of a capital sum. Five different schemes were put forward for the sale of the dwellings, these schemes merely reflecting the needs of the persons who would benefit and containing suitable conditions as to payment for the dwellings, the provision of wardens and determination of the leases. The Charity Commissioners doubted if these schemes were charitable and raised four objections, namely: (1) they made provision for the aged on a contractual basis rather than by way of bounty; (2) the benefits were not capable of being withdrawn if a beneficiary at any time ceased to qualify; (3) they were for the benefit of private individuals rather than a charitable class; and (4) they were a commercial enterprise capable of producing a profit for the beneficiary. The trustees of the charity sought the determination of the court as to whether all or any of the schemes were charitable in law.

Held
All the schemes were charitable being for the relief of the aged. As to the first objection there was nothing objectionable in giving a benefit by way of contract rather than bounty.

As to the second objection, it depended very much on the circumstances and providing housing benefits for the elderly which were capable of being withdrawn at any time could have an unsettling effect on such people. As to the third objection, this must be rejected. The scheme was for the benefit of a charitable class and the fact the trustees selected people to obtain the benefits did not defeat the charitable nature of the gift. As to the fourth objection, if the elderly tenants profited because the dwellings increased in value this was purely incidental and was not a profit at the expense of the charity.

Peter Gibson J:

'... it is appropriate to consider the scope of the charitable purpose which the plaintiffs claim the scheme carried out, that is to say in the words of the preamble to the Statute of Elizabeth (43 Eliz c4 of the Charitable Uses Act 1601) "the relief of aged persons". That purpose is indeed part of the very first set of charitable purposes contained in the preamble: "the relief of aged, impotent and poor people". Looking at those words without going to authority and attempting to give them their natural meaning, I would have thought that two inferences therefrom were tolerably clear. First, the words "aged, impotent and poor" must be read disjunctively. It would be as absurd to require that the aged must be impotent or poor as it would be to require the impotent to be aged or poor, or the poor to be aged or impotent. There will not doubt be many cases where the objects of charity prove to have two or more of the three qualities at the same time. Second, essential to the charitable purpose is that it should relieve aged, impotent and poor people. The word "relief" implies that the persons in question have a need attributable to their condition as aged, impotent or poor persons which requires alleviating themselves from their own resources. The word "relief" is not synonymous with "benefit".

Those inferences are in substance what both counsel submit are the true principles governing the charitable purpose of the relief of aged persons. Mr Nugee stresses that any benefit provided must be related to the needs of the aged. Thus a gift of money to the aged millionaires of Mayfair would not relieve a need of theirs as aged persons. Mr McCall similarly emphasises that to relieve a need of the aged attributable to their age would be charitable only if the means employed are appropriate to the need. He also points out that an element of public benefit must be found if the purpose is to be charitable ...

... I have no hesitation in preferring the approach adopted in *Re Neal* and *Re Resch's Will Trusts* that there may be a need which is to be relieved by the charitable gift, such need being attributable to the aged or impotent condition of the person to be benefitted ...'

Comment
The terms 'aged', 'impotent' and 'poor' can be read disjunctively. Note that it is possible to maintain charitable status and make a charge for hospital treatment or housing as long as the charity is non-profit making.

Scottish Burial Reform and Cremation Society Ltd v *Glasgow Corporation* [1968] AC 138 House of Lords (Lords Reid, Guest, Upjohn, Wilberforce and Pearson)

• *Charitable trusts – benefit to the community*

Facts
The appellants, a non-profit-making limited company, were established for the general purpose of promoting methods of disposal of the dead which were both inexpensive and sanitary and for the particular purpose of encouraging and providing facilities for cremation. They claimed a declaration that they were a charity in order to obtain relief from rates on their premises.

Held

This was a purpose which was beneficial to the community and within the spirit and intendment of the preamble to the Statute of Elizabeth.

Lord Reid:

'... the appellants must also show, however, that the public benefit is of a kind within the spirit and intendment of the Statute of Elizabeth. The preamble specifies a number of objects which were then recognised as charitable. But in more recent times a wide variety of other objects have come to be recognised as also being charitable. The courts appear to have proceeded first by seeking some analogy between an object mentioned in the preamble and the object with regard to which they had to reach a decision. Then they appear to have gone farther, and to have been satisfied if they could find an analogy between the object already held to be charitable and the new object claimed to be charitable. This gradual extension has proceeded so far that there are few modern reported cases where a bequest or donation was made or an institution was being carried on for a clearly specified object which was for the benefit of the public at large and not of individuals, and yet the object was held not to be within the spirit and intendment of the Statute of Elizabeth. Counsel in the present case were invited to search for any case having even the remotest resemblance to this case in which an object was held to be for the public benefit but not yet to be within the spirit and intendment, but no case could be found.

There is, however, another line of cases where the bequest did not clearly specify the precise object to which it was to be applied, but left a discretion to trustees or others to choose objects within a certain field. There the courts have been much more strict, so that if it is possible that those entrusted with the discretion could, without infringing the testator's directions, apply the bequest in any way which would not be charitable (for example, because it did not benefit a sufficiently large section of the public) then the claim that the bequest is charitable fails. That line of cases, however, can have no application to the present judicial observations made in a case where there was a discretion which could go beyond objects strictly charitable. In the present case, the appellants make a charge for the services which they provide. It has never been held, however, that objects, otherwise charitable, cease to be charitable if beneficiaries are required to make payments for what they receive. It may even be that public demand for the kind of service which the charity provides becomes so large that there is room for a commercial undertaking to come in and supply similar services on a commercial basis; but no authority and no reason has been put forward for holding that when that stage is reached the objects and activities of the non-profit earning charitable organisation ceases to be charitable.

If, then, all that is necessary to bring the objects and activities of the appellants within the spirit and intendment of the preamble to the Statute of Elizabeth is to find analogous decided cases, I think that there is amply sufficient analogy with the series of cases dealing with burial. I would therefore allow this appeal.'

Comment

The court were prepared to accept that this activity came within the 'spirit and intendment of the preamble to the Statute of Elizabeth'. They recognised that there may be cases in which commercial activity of charities should also be within that status.

9   The Cy-près Doctrine

ARMS (Multiple Sclerosis Research) Ltd, Re [1997] 1 WLR 877 Chancery Division (Neuberger J)

* *Gift to a charitable company*

Facts

Several testamentary gifts had been made to a charity which operated through a company limited by guarantee. As stated in its memorandum and articles of association, the primary objects of the charity were to promote research into the cause, cure and prevention of multiple sclerosis and the assistance of its victims. The gifts were made to the company before it formally went into liquidation. The liquidator applied to the court for directions as to how to deal with the gifts.

Held

They formed part of the company's assets and were available for distribution to its creditors.

Neuberger J:

'In the present case, at the date of Mr Dove's death, the company was still in existence: indeed, even now it has not been dissolved. Accordingly, Mr Alleyne and the trust contend that Mr Dove has effected a simple "bequest to a corporate body", namely the company, which "takes effect simply as a gift to that body beneficially". The fact that the body is in liquidation does not alter the fact that it still exists. Furthermore, they contend that there are no circumstances to suggest that the company was intended to take the gift as a trustee.

If, as a matter of construction of the will, the gift is expressed to be for a company then "unless there are circumstances which show that the recipient is to take the gift as a trustee" (per Buckley J, in *In re Vernon's Will Trusts*), it takes effect so long as the company is in existence at the date of the testator's death.

In general, one has the very strong suspicion that, where a testator makes a will leaving a gift to a company established for charitable purposes, and that company subsequently goes into insolvent liquidation, prior to his death, the testator would not have intended the gift to go to the company. However, in my judgment that is insufficient to justify a departure from the plain words of a will. If, according to their natural tenor, the words of a will provide that a specific gift is to be given to a specific company, then it is not for the court to speculate as to whether the testator would in fact have intended the gift to take effect had he known of a change in the circumstances of the company between the making of his will and his death.

In the case of Mr Dove's will, the use of the word "charities" in two places in the relevant provision does provide the Attorney-General's argument in the particular case with little assistance. It can be said with some force that the obvious inference is that the testator intended that these bequests be charitable, in the sense that the money be devoted, in one way or another, towards the charitable aims of the company. However, I do not consider that that is sufficient to enable the court to conclude that the gift fails according to its terms, merely because the company is in insolvent liquidation. The description of the company as one of two charities is not inaccurate as a matter of law, because, although it is in insolvent liquidation, it can remain registered with the Charity Commission (although I understand that it is the normal practice of the Charity Commissioners to remove a charitable company from the register if it goes into

188

insolvent liquidation). Furthermore, it is
hard to contend that the description of the
company, even after it has gone into insolvent liquidation, as a "charity" is inaccurate,
bearing in mind that s63 of the Charities Act
1993 ... clearly treats a company established for charitable purposes as a charity at
all times until it is actually dissolved.

Accordingly, while I have sympathy for
the proposition that the testator would not
have intended the gift to the company to
take effect had he known that the company
was in insolvent liquidation at the date of
his death, I reject the Attorney-General's
argument.'

Comment

A charity run through a limited company has
its own legal personality. It is therefore difficult for the court to establish that the testator
had a general charitable intention when the
gift was made and it is more likely, as in this
case, that the gift will be construed as one to
the corporate body.

Faraker, Re [1919] 2 Ch 488 Court of Appeal (Cozens-Hardy MR, Farwell and Kennedy LJJ)

• *Meaning of 'cease to exist'*

Facts

Mrs Faraker died in 1911 and by her will she
gave a legacy of £200 'to Mrs Bailey's
Charity, Rotherhithe'. There had been a
charity known as Mrs Hannah Bayly's Charity
at Rotherhithe, founded in 1756, for the
benefit of poor widows resident in the parish
of St Mary's Rotherhithe. In 1905 the Charity
Commissioners consolidated this and several
other charities in Rotherhithe into one trust
for the benefit of the poor of Rotherhithe but
made no mention to the charity. The question
arose whether the gift had lapsed (no question
was raised on the spelling: it was agreed that
Mrs Faraker intended to refer to Hannah
Bayly's Charity). On appeal:

Held

The gift had not lapsed. Hannah Bayly's
charity was still in existence subject to the
alteration which had been made by the Charity
Commissioners. The gift to the charity was
one which simply identified the charity by
name and therefore carried with it the application of it to the lawful objects of the charity
funds for the time being.

Farwell J:

'What is said is this: the Commissioners
have in fact destroyed this trust because in
the scheme which they have issued dealing
with the amalgamation of the several charities the objects are stated to be poor persons
of good character resident in Rotherhithe,
not mentioning widows in particular – not of
course excluding them, but not giving them
that preference which I agree with the
Master of the Rolls in thinking ought to
have been given. But to say that this omission has incidentally destroyed the Bayly
Trust is a very strained construction of the
language and one that entirely fails, because
the Charity Commissioners had no jurisdiction whatever to destroy the Charity.
Suppose the Charity Commissioners or this
Court were to declare that a particular existing charitable trust was at an end and
extinct, in my opinion they would go
beyond their jurisdiction in so doing. They
cannot take an existing charity and destroy
it: they are obliged to administer it. To say
that this pardonable slip (I use the word with
all respect to the draftsman) has the effect of
destroying the charity appears to me to be
extravagant. In all these cases one has to
consider not so much the means to the end
as the charitable end which is in view, and
so long as that charitable end is well established the means are only machinery, and
no alteration of the machinery can destroy
the charitable trust for the benefit of which
the machinery is provided.'

Comment

There was, in fact, no need to apply the cy-
près doctrine as the charity continued to exist
in another form.

Guild v *IRC*

See Chapter 8.

Harwood, Re [1936] Ch 285
Chancery Division (Farwell J)

• *Impossible gift*

Facts

The testatrix made a will in 1925 leaving a bequest of £200 to Wisbech Peace Society and a bequest of £300 to the Peace Society of Belfast. When the testatrix died in 1934 the Wisbech Peace Society had by that time ceased to exist. However, there was no evidence that there was a Peace Society of Belfast in existence or indeed that one had ever existed.

Held

The bequest to the Wisbech Peace Society lapsed and could not be applied cy-près, as there was no general charitable intention. But the bequest to the Peace Society of Belfast could be applied cy-près. It indicated a means of benefiting a charity: there was a general charitable intention.

Farwell J:

'Then there is the gift to the "Peace Society of Belfast". The claimant for this legacy is the Belfast Branch of the League of Nations Union. I am quite unable on the evidence to say that that was the society which this lady intended to benefit, and I doubt whether the lady herself knew exactly what society she did mean to benefit. I think she had a desire to benefit any society which was formed for the purpose of promoting peace and was connected with Belfast. Beyond that, I do not think that she had any very clear idea in her mind. That is rather indicated by the pencil note which was found after her death. At any rate I cannot say that by the description "the Peace Society of Belfast" the lady meant the Belfast Branch of the League of Nations Union, but there is enough in this case to enable me to say that, although there

is no gift to any existing society, the gift does not fail. It is a good charitable gift and must be applied cy-près. The evidence suggests that at some time or other, possibly before the last War, there may have been a society called the Peace Society of Belfast. It is all hearsay evidence; there is nothing in the least definite about it, and it does not satisfy me that there ever was any society in existence which exactly fits the description in this case, and there being a clear intention on the part of the lady, as expressed in her will, to benefit societies whose object was the promotion of peace, and there being no such society as that named in her will, in this case there is a general charitable intent, and, accordingly, the doctrine of cy-près applies.'

Comment

Where the gift is to a named organisation which existed, it is more difficult to construe the gift as a gift for a purpose.

Oldham Borough Council v *Attorney-General* [1993] 2 WLR 224
Court of Appeal (Dillon, Russell and Farquarson LJJ)

• *Cy-près doctrine – sale of land – original purposes – whether attaching to trust property – court's inherent jurisdiction*

Facts

Oldham Borough Council was left land 'on trust to preserve and manage the same as playing fields known as the "Clayton Playing Fields" for the benefit of the inhabitants of Oldham, Chatterton and Royton'.

Held

The Council was entitled to sell the site and use the proceeds to acquire a new site. The original purpose of the gift was not intended to oblige the Council to retain the land in perpetuity for use as playing fields, but to provide playing fields for the benefit of the local community.

Dillon LJ:

'I come then to what I regard as the crux of this case, viz the true construction of the words "original purposes of the charitable gift" in s13 of the Act of 1960. Do the "original purposes" include the intention and purpose of the donor that the land given should be used for ever for the purposes of the charity, or are they limited to the purposes of the charity?

Certain of the authorities cited to us can be put one one side. Thus, in *In re J W Laing Trust,* Peter Gibson J said, plainly correctly:

"It cannot be right that any provision, even if only administrative, made applicable by a donor to his gift should be treated as a condition and hence as a purpose."

In that case, however, the provision, which was held to be administrative and was plainly not a "purpose", was a provision that the capital was to be wholly distributed within the settlor's lifetime or within 10 years of his death.

Conversely, there are cases where the donor has imposed a condition, as part of the terms of his gift, which limits the main purpose of the charity in a way which, with the passage of time, has come to militate against the achievement of that main purpose. The condition is there part of the purpose, but the court has found itself able on the facts to cut out the condition by way of a cy-près scheme under the cy-près jurisdiction, on the ground that the subsistence of the condition made the main purpose impossible or impracticable of achievement: see *In re Dominion Students' Hall Trust,* where a condition of trust for the maintenance of a hostel for male students of the overseas dominions of the British Empire restricted the benefits to dominion students of European origin; and see, also, *In re Robinson, Wright* v *Tugwell,* where it was a condition of the gift of an endowment for an evangelical church that the preacher should wear a black gown in the pulpit. But unlike those conditions, the intention or purpose in the present case that the actual land given should be used as playing fields is not a condition qualifying the use of that land as playing fields.

It is necessary, in my judgment, in order to answer the crucial question of the true construction of s13, to appreciate the legislative purpose of s13. Pennycuick V-C said in *In re Lepton's Charity* that the section "in part restates the principles applied under the existing law, but also extends those principles". That section is concerned with the cy-près application of charitable funds, but sales of charitable lands have, in so far as they have been dealt with by Parliament, always been dealt with by other sections not concerned with the cy-près doctrine.

There are, of course, some cases where the qualities of the property which is the subject matter of the gift are themselves the factors which make the purposes of the gift charitable, for example, where there is a trust to retain for the public benefit a particular house once owned by a particular historical figure or a particular building for its architectural merit or a particular area of land of outstanding natural beauty. In such cases, sale of the house, building or land would necessitate an alteration of the original charitable purposes and, therefore, a cy-près scheme because after a sale the proceeds or any property acquired with the proceeds could not possibly be applied for the original charitable purpose. But that is far away from cases such as the present, where the charitable purpose – playing fields for the benefit and enjoyment of the inhabitants of the districts of the original donees, or it might equally be a museum, school or clinic in a particular town – can be carried on on other land.'

Comment

This is a significant application of the cy-près doctrine when the needs of the community change over time, or where they can make better use of the resources available by selling the original land as development land and using the proceeds to improve facilities for the community.

Peggs and Another v *Lamb* [1994] 2 WLR 1 Chancery Division (Morritt J)

• *Scheme under s13(1)(d) of the Charities Act 1960*

Facts
The bequest entitled freemen of the Borough of Huntingdon and their widows to an income generated from certain plots of land. By 1992, there were not enough beneficiaries (only fifteen) to benefit from the full income of the fund, by then some £550,000.

Held
Applying s13(1)(d) of the Charities Act 1960, a scheme could be approved under which the class of beneficiaries could be enlarged to include all the inhabitants of the borough of Huntingdon. The original class of beneficiaries had dwindled to such an extent that the ceased to be a suitable class.

Morritt J:

'I have no hesitation in rejecting the submission for the freemen that the purpose of the trust is merely the provision of income and general benefits for the freemen and their widows. Until the beginning of the 20th century, there was no question of the freemen dividing between themselves the whole of the income of the land and of the proceeds of sale of the land. They benefited either from exercising a right to pasture their own cattle or from receipt of the head money if they chose not to. The gross income was used to defray expenses and any balance was carried forward. The exercise of the rights of pasture was controlled by the borough and, either from exercising a right to pasture their own cattle or from receipt of the head money if they chose not to. The gross income was used to defray expenses and any balance was carried forward. The exercise of the rights of pasture was controlled by the borough and, in earlier times, limited rights were available for disposal to the poor inhabitants. I do not think that the usage since time immemorial

justifies the presumption that the trust existed for the purpose of benefiting the freemen individually, though the provision of such benefits might in suitable circumstances be the way in which the purpose is achieved. There is a difference between the purpose of a trust and the means by which the purpose may be achieved: cf *IRC* v *McMullen*.

Counsel for the freemen and for the Attorney-General knew of no case in which a trust to distribute the income equally amongst a class however large the income or small the class had been held to be charitable. Nor do I. The reason must be that the purpose of such a trust could not come within the spirit and intendment of the preamble.

In the case of the Lammas charity such property has been confined to the Lammas' rights. But this gives rise to no problem because, I was told, there is in the area a well recognised formula by which the value of land is divided between those who are entitled to the Lammas' rights and others interested in the land. In the case of the commons charity it seems to me that the only proper inference is that the whole interest in the land was given for the charitable purposes for the benefit of the freemen even though at the time the only way the charitable purpose could be achieved was by the exercise of grazing rights. This accords with the evidence that there seems to be no instance in which the corporation obtained and retained for itself any benefit from the land, the income from the land or from the proceeds of sale or the income thereof.

In my judgment the income of the land or of the Lammas rights, as the case may be, and of the proceeds of sale of the same is held by the trustees to be applied for exclusively charitable purposes for the benefit of qualifying freemen or their widows.

Thus the question now arises whether a scheme is necessary. For the freemen it was submitted that there was no need for or jurisdiction to order the settlement of a scheme. But the submission was on the basis that the freemen were entitled to divide the annual income between them. In my judgment, and for the reasons I have already given, that is not so. Moreover, I do not think that the settlement of a scheme would be necessary merely to make plain that the income was to be applied for the original, namely general charitable purposes only amongst the freemen. The declaration of the court should be sufficient. If the trustees wanted a scheme they could always apply to the Charity Commissioners.

The real issue is whether, in the circumstances, there is jurisdiction to order the settlement of a scheme for the cy-près application of the income. This depends on s13 of the Charities Act 1960 ...

In *In re Lepton's Charity*, Sir John Pennycuick V-C, construed the phrase "spirit of the gift" as meaning the basic intention underlying the gift, such intention being ascertainable from the terms of the relevant instrument read in the light of admissible evidence. I do not think that the absence of any founding document precludes the existence of any 'spirit of the gift'. Accordingly, such spirit must likewise be inferred. For the freemen it was contended that the spirit of the gift was the benefit of the freemen.

I have concluded that the original purposes were and are general charitable purposes for the benefit of the qualifying freemen and their widows. These are presumed to be the purposes laid down in the middle ages. In those days there can be little doubt that the freemen of a borough were a substantial section of the public both numerically and in their social, economic and political importance. As such the class of freemen was then and for several centuries thereafter entirely suitable as a class by reference to which the charitable purposes should be laid down. But I am satisfied that that is no longer so. The effect of the Municipal Corporations Act 1835 was to destroy the political importance of the freemen and thereby to undermine their social and economic importance too. But, of more importance, membership of the class was thereby restricted, in the case of these charities, to those who were the sons of freemen and born in the ancient borough.

The inevitable consequence after over 150 years is that the class has dwindled very considerably. There will come a time, if it has not arrived already, when the class of freemen ceases to be a section of the public at all. It is not necessary to decide whether that time has passed so that a case for a scheme can be made out under s13(1)(e)(ii) of the Act of 1960 because I think it is clear that a sufficient case is made out under paragraph (d).

The original basic intention or spirit of the gift was the benefit of the Borough of Huntingdon. It would, in my judgment, be entirely consistent with that, that in 1993 the class of persons by reference to which the charitable purposes are laid down should be enlarged from the freemen to the inhabitants as a whole. Accordingly, I will direct the settlement of a scheme.'

Comment

Section 13(1)(d) of the Charities Act 1993 provides that the circumstances in which the original purposes of a charitable gift can be altered to allow the property given or part of it to be applied cy-près are:

'(d) Where the original purposes were laid down by reference to an area which has ceased to be a unit, or by reference to a class of persons or to an area which has ceased to be suitable or practicable, regard being had to the spirit of the gift.'

Section 13 of the Charities Act 1993 is a direct re-enactment of the s13 of the Charities Act 1960.

Spence's Will Trusts, Re [1979] Ch 483 Chancery Division (Megarry V-C)

• *Lapse – valid gift subject to limitation*

Facts

A testatrix under the terms of her will left her residuary estate to be divide 'equally between The Blind Home, Scott Street, Keighley and the Old Folk's Home at Hillworth Lodge, Keighley for the benefit of the patients'. The

Keighley and District Association for the Blind was the only charity connected with the blind in the Keighley area. It ran a home in Scott Street which was often called 'The Blind Home', 'The Keighley and District Home for the Blind' and 'Keighley Home for the Blind'. A similar home was also run by the Association at Bingley. At the time the testatrix made her will an old people's home was run by the local authority at Hillworth Lodge, but at the time of the testatrix's death the old people's home had been closed and was being converted into Council offices. The executors of the will sought a declaration as to whether the residuary gift was valid.

Held

1. In making a gift to 'The Blind Home' the testatrix was intending to make provision for the benefit of the patients at the Blind Home, Scott Street, Keighley. However, by the terms of the gift, it was clear that she was not giving the money to augment the endowment of the charity which ran the home. Therefore, the charity could not apply the money for any of its objects but must limit the application of it for the benefit of the patients.
2. The gift to the 'Old Folks Home' failed. It was a gift for a specific purpose behind which there was no general charitable intention. Therefore, as the gift had become impossible before the testatrix died it had lapsed, and there could be no application of the gift of cy-près.

Sir Robert Megarry V-C:

'Counsel's other contention for the Attorney-General was that the will displayed a sufficient general charitable intention for the moiety to be applied cy-près. In doing this he had to contend with *Re Harwood*. This, and cases which apply it, such as *Re Stemson's Will Trusts*, establish that it is very difficult to find a general charitable intention where the testator has selected a particular charity, taking some care to identify it, and the charity then ceases to exist before the testator's death.

This contrasts with cases where the charity described in the will never existed, when it is much easier to find a general charitable intention.

These cases have been concerned with gifts to institutions, rather than gift for purposes. The case before me, on the other hand, is a gift for a purpose, namely the benefit of the patients at a particular old folks home. It therefore seems to me that I ought to consider the question, of which little or nothing was said in argument, whether the principle in *Re Harwood*, or a parallel principle, has any application to such a case. In other words, is a similar distinction to be made between, on the one hand, a case in which the testator has selected a particular charitable purpose, taking some care to identify it, and before the testator dies that purpose has become impracticable or impossible of accomplishment, and on the other hand a case where the charitable purpose has never been possible or practicable?

As at present advised, I would answer "Yes" to that question. I do not think that the reasoning of the *Re Harwood* line of cases is directed to any feature of institutions as distinct from purposes. Instead, I think the essence of the distinction is in the difference between particularity and generality. If a particular institution or purpose is specified, then it is that institution or purpose, and no other, that is to be the object of the benefaction. It is difficult to envisage a testator as being suffused with a general glow of broad charity when he is labouring, and labouring successfully, to identify some particular specified institution or purpose as the object of his bounty. The specific displaces the general. It is otherwise where the testator has been unable to specify any particular charitable institution or practicable purpose, and so, although his intention of charity can be seen, he has failed to provide any way of giving effect to it. There the absence of the specific leaves the general undisturbed. It follows that in my view in the case before me, where the testatrix has clearly specified a particular charitable purpose which before her death becomes impossible to carry out, counsel for the Attorney-General has to face that level of great difficulty in demonstrating the existence of the general charitable purpose which was indicated by *Re Harwood*.

One way in which counsel sought to meet that difficulty was by citing *Re Finger's Will Trusts*. There, Goff J distinguished *Re Harwood* and held that the will before him displayed a general charitable intention. He did this on the footing that the circumstances of the case were "very special". The gift that failed was a gift to an incorporated charity which had ceased to exist before the testatrix died. The "very special" circumstances were, first, that apart from a life interest and two small legacies, the whole estate was devoted to charity, and that this was emphasised by the direction to hold the residue in trust for division "between the following charitable institutions and funds". Second, the charitable donee that had ceased to exist was mainly, if not exclusively, a co-ordinating body, and the judge could not believe that the testatrix meant to benefit that body alone. Third, there was evidence that the testatrix regarded herself as having no relatives.

In the case before me neither of these last two circumstances applies, nor have any substitute special circumstances been suggested. As for the first, the will before me gives seventeen pecuniary legacies to relations and friends, amounting in all to well over one third of the net estate. Further, in *Re Rymer,* which does not appear to have been cited, the will had prefaced the disputed gift by the words "I give the following charitable legacies to the following institutions and persons respectively". These words correspond to the direction which in *Re Finger's Will Trusts* was regarded as providing emphasis, and yet they did not suffice to avoid the conclusion of Chitty J and the Court of Appeal that a gift to an institution which had ceased to exist before the testator's death lapsed and could not be applied cy-près. I am not sure that I have been able to appreciate to the full the cogency of the special circumstances that appealed to Goff J; but however that may be, I can see neither those nor any other special circumstances in the present case which would suffice to distinguish *Re Harwood*.

The other way in which counsel for the Attorney-General sought to meet this difficulty was by relying on *Re Satterthwaite's Will Trusts* (which he said was his best case) and on *Re Knox* which I think may possibly be better. The doctrine may for brevity be described as charity by association. If the will gives the residue among a number of charities with kindred objects, but one of the apparent charities does not in fact exist, the court will be ready to find a general charitable intention and so apply the share of the non-existent charity cy-près. I have not been referred to any explicit statement of the underlying principle, but it seems to me that in such cases the court treats the testator as having shown the general intention of giving his residue to promote charities with that type of kindred objects, and the, when he comes to dividing the residue, as casting round for particular charities with that type of objects to name as donees. If one or more of these are non-existent, then the general intention will suffice for a cy-près application. It will be observed that, as stated, the doctrine depends, at least to some extent, on the detection of "kindred objects" ... in the charities to which the shares of residue are given, in this respect the charities must in some degree by *ejusdem generis*.

Sir Robert Megarry reviewed the previous cases and continued:

'It will be observed that these are all cases of gifts to bodies which do not exist. In such cases, the court is ready to find a general charitable intention ... The court is far less ready to find such an intention where the gift is to a body which existed at the date of the will but ceased to exist before the testator dies, or, as I have already held, where the gift is for a purpose which, though possible and practicable at the date of the will, has ceased to be so before the testator's death. The case before me is, of course, a case in this latter category, so that counsel for the Attorney-General has to overcome this greater difficulty in finding a general charitable intention. Not only does counsel have this greater difficulty: he also has, I think, less material with which to meet it. He has to extract the general charitable intention of the gift which fails from only one other gift: the residue, of course was simply divided into two. In *Re Knox* and *Re Hartley (decd)* the gifts which failed were each among three other gifts, and in *Re Satterthwaite's Will Trusts* there were seven or eight other gifts. I do not say that a general charitable intention or a genus cannot be extracted from a gift of residue equally divided between two; but I do say that larger numbers are likely to assist in conveying to the court a sufficient conviction both of the genus and of the generality of the charitable intention.'

Comment

This is a very thorough exposition by Sir Robert Megarry V-C of the rules applicable to the application of the cy-près doctrine in a case of initial failure of the gift – and of the difficulty in establishing them.

Varsani and Others v *Jesani and Others* [1998] 3 All ER 273 Court of Appeal (Sir Stephen Brown P, Morritt and Chadwick LJJ)

• *Application of s13(1) of the Charities Act 1993 on division of funds on split in charitable organisation*

Facts

In 1967 a charity was established to promote the faith of Swaminarayan, a Hindu sect whose leader was believed to have divine status. On the death of the leader, the sect split into two groups, one of which, the minority, did not recognise the authority of the leader's successor. The majority group brought proceedings seeking a scheme for the administration of the sect's property under s13(1)(e)(iii) of the Charities Act 1993. They were successful at first instance whereupon

the minority group appealed to the Court of Appeal.

Held

Appeal dismissed. The original purpose of the charity had ceased to provide a suitable and effective method of using the available property. The spirit of the gift supported the making of a scheme dividing the property between the two groups.

Morritt LJ:

'Now the jurisdiction to make a cy-près scheme depends on whether the case falls within one or other of the paragraphs of s13(1). The relevant test in this case is whether the original purpose has ceased to provide a suitable and effective method of using the property regard being had to the spirit of the gift.

In my view that test is satisfied in this case. first, there is no doubt what the original purpose of the charity was and is. It was and is the promotion of the faith of Swaminarayan according to the teachings and tenets of Muktajivandasji. Second, until the problems disclosed by the events of 1984 arose those original purposes were both suitable and effective as a method of using the property for both the majority and minority group were agreed on all relevant matters and therefore able to worship together in the temples provided by the charity. Third, the exposure of differing beliefs by the events of 1984 has produced a situation in which neither group is able to worship in the same temple as the other so that the minority group has been excluded from the facilities for the worship the charity was established to provide. Fourth, unless the impasse can be resolved as a matter of faith, so that both groups reunite to embrace the faith the charity was established to promote, the impasse will remain so long as the original purpose remains. Fifth, the impasse cannot be resolved as a matter of faith because the teachings and tenets of Muktajivandasji did not deal with whether a belief in a particular successor to Muktajivandasji or in the divine attributes of a successor were or are essential tenets of the faith. I do not accept that the parts of the 1969 constitution on which counsel for the minority group relied resolve the question. And a decision of the helping committee or this court is not binding as a matter of faith. Thus the impasse and the original purpose of the charity go together. If the original purpose leads in the present circumstances to such an impasse then in my view it is self evident that the original purpose has ceased to be a suitable and effective method of using the available property.

The court is enjoined by s13(1)(e)(iii) to have regard to the spirit of the gift. In my view it does not matter whether the origin of that concept is to be found in *Re Campden Charities* (1881), as suggested by counsel for the Attorney-General in *Re Lepton's Charities* (1972), or in s15 of the Educational Endowments Act 1882 as indicated in the *Report of the Committee on the Law and Practice Relating to Charitable Trusts* ... suggested by counsel for the majority group in this case. Either way the concept is clear enough, namely the basic intention underlying the gift or the substance of the gift rather than the form of the words used to express it or conditions imposed to effect it. It is noteworthy that the phrase is used in s13(1) only in contexts which require the court to make a value judgment. Thus it does not appear in paras (a)(i), (b), (e)(i) or (ii). Moreover, when it is used, in each case except one it appears in the context of suitability. The exception, para (a)(ii), whilst not actually using the word suitable, requires a similar value judgment. The court is not bound to follow the spirit of the gift but it must pay regard to it when making the value judgments required by some of the provisions of s13(1).

For my part I have no hesitation in concluding that the spirit of the gift supports the submission that the court should accept and exercise the jurisdiction conferred by s13(1)(e)(iii) by directing a scheme for the division of the property of the charity between the majority and minority groups. The choice lies between directing such a scheme for the benefit of all those who

down to 1984 shared the belief for the promotion of which the charity was established, and, no doubt, in many cases supported the charity financially as well, even though some of them may no longer do so, and requiring a substantial proportion of the trust property to be spent in litigation which can never finally resolve the problems which divide the two groups. I do not minimise the strength of feeling which arises in connection with disputes such as this. In such cases either or both groups often litigate in preference to permitting a benefit to be conferred on the other. But the spirit of the gift to which the court is to have regard is that which prevailed at the time of the gift when the two groups were in harmony.

Accordingly, I would reject the submissions of both the minority group and the Attorney-General. First, it is not necessary to ascertain the precise limits of the purpose of the charity before deciding whether the case comes within s13(1). The purpose of this charity is clear; it is the promotion of the faith of Swaminarayan according to the teaching and tenets of Muktajivandasji. It is the expression of that purpose in the light of subsequent events which has given rise to the schism with the result that the original purpose has ceased to be a suitable and effective method of using the trust property. Second, it is not a necessary condition for the application of the section that the original purposes have become impossible or impractical, only that the circumstances come within one or other paragraph of s13(1). Thus, even if the inquiries sought were ordered and pursued and ultimately demonstrated that the minority group but not the majority group still embraced the relevant faith, that does not now preclude the application of the section for the outcome of the inquiries would merely demonstrate that the original purpose was not impossible or impractical.

If, as I would hold, there is jurisdiction to make a scheme under s13(1)(e)(iii) that is good reason for not ordering the inquiries suggested by the minority group. Such inquiries would show either that one of the groups no longer professed the relevant faith or both of them still did. For the reasons I have tried to explain the former alternative is irrelevant to the question of jurisdiction to make a cy-près scheme. But if the answer were that both groups still professed the relevant faith then it would be permissible to make an administrative scheme for no alteration of the purpose of the charity would arise. The justification for such a scheme would remain the same, namely to resolve the impasse and avoid the expenditure on costs. Therefore whatever the answers to the proposed inquiries there would be jurisdiction to make the proposed scheme and the same factual justification for doing so ...

In rejecting the submissions for the Attorney-General I do not seek to undermine or belittle in any way the concerns expressed by his counsel to which I have already referred. First, there is his concern that potential donors should not be deterred by a belief that their intentions will be overridden by a too ready use of the cy-près jurisdiction. I agree; but that problem has to be set beside the equal but opposite problem that, in circumstances unforeseen by the donor, his or her bounty may not achieve all that was intended or was reasonably feasible. The balance between those two considerations has to be struck and was struck by Parliament in 1960 when, following the Report of the Committee to which I have referred, it enacted s13 of the Charities Act 1960. Since then it has been the duty of the court fairly to apply the provisions of that section to the circumstances of each case without any predilection either to making or to refusing to make a scheme altering the original purposes of the charity.

The Attorney-General's other concern was that no faith should be treated in relation to the law of charity differently from any other. This is fundamental. The law of charity does not now favour one religion to another. The proposition was authoritatively explained by Lord Reid and applied in *Gilmour* v *Coats*. As I understood it, the concern arose from the belief that if the inquiries sought by the minority group were refused but a scheme as sought by the majority group were ordered that would indicate some difference in the treatment afforded to the two groups in this case when compared with the treatment of comparable groups in *Craigdaillie* v *Aikman* (1813), *A-G* v *Pearson* (1817) or *General Assembly of Free Church of Scotland* v *Overtoun* (1904). It is true that the treatment of the groups would be different but that arises from the fact that since those three cases were determined Parliament has enacted s13 of the Charities Act 1960. The difference in the result is not due at all to the fact that the earlier cases concerned different faiths.'

Comment

Section 13(1) is sufficiently widely drawn to enable a scheme to be devised when the underlying purpose of the charity is no longer possible because of a split in the members of the organisation. Note the concerns of the Attorney-General regarding a too liberal approach to the cy-près doctrine and the court's concern to ensure that all faiths are treated even-handedly.

10 Trustees' Fiduciary Duties

***Abacus Trust (Isle of Man) and
Another v Barr and Others*** [2003] 2
WLR 1362 Chancery Division
(Lightman J)

• *Mistake as to settlor's intentions –
validity of appointment – breach of fiduciary duty – whether appointment void or
voidable*

Facts

A discretionary trust was set up for tax avoidance purposes. When the deed of appointment was drafted, the trustee's representatives made a mistake in the proportions of the settlement, appointing 60 per cent of the fund to the settlor's sons. The settlor was advised that this could not be altered. Nine years later the trustee was advised that the appointment could be challenged on the ground that the trustee would not have made this appointment if when exercising his discretion to do so he had not taken into account irrelevant considerations and failed to take into account relevant considerations. The trustee applied to the court for a determination of the validity of the appointment.

Held

A court would interfere with the exercise of the trustee's discretion if it was clear that he would or might have acted differently had he not failed to take all relevant considerations into account. The appointment was voidable, not because of the mistake but because the trustee had failed to inform himself of the matters which were relevant to the decision and in arriving at his decisions whether and how to exercise his discretionary powers to take into account all relevant but no irrelevant

factors. The question as to whether or not the appointment should be avoided was adjourned.

Lightman J:

'The issue of law raised on this application is the impact on the validity of the appointment of the failure of the trustee to take into account when executing the appointment that the settlor wished that 40 per cent, and not 60 per cent, of the trust fund should be appointed in favour of the sons. The settlor contends that this error renders the appointment totally void. The consequence, if this is correct, is that, notwithstanding the lapse of time and intervening events, the sons are deprived of all entitlement under the appointment, even the 40 per cent share which the settlor intended them to receive, and, subject to a possible defence of change of position, the trustee is entitled to recover from the sons the payments made on the erroneous basis of the validity of the appointment. From an objective viewpoint, and in particular from the viewpoint of the sons, such a "penalty" for the error for which the sons had no responsibility would appear draconian. The sons' primary contention is that on the facts of this case the error does not affect the validity of the appointment. The sons' very much secondary contention is that, even if the error does affect the validity of the appointment, the appointment is not rendered void but merely voidable, and that in deciding whether in its discretion to afford relief and, if so, what relief, the lapse of time, intervening events and considerations of justice for the sons are factors to be weighed by the court. The parties have not addressed evidence or argument to the question of the relief to be afforded if the appointment is held voidable, and they are agreed that, if this issue arises, it should be stood over to be determined, in default of agreement, at a later date.

The existence of the fiduciary duty on the part of trustees governing the exercise of their fiduciary powers requires trustees to inform themselves of the matters which are relevant to the decision (see *Scott* v *National Trust for Places of Historic Interest or Natural Beauty*) and in arriving at their decision whether and how to exercise their discretionary powers to take into account all relevant but no irrelevant factors: see *Edge* v *Pensions Ombudsman*. The fiduciary duty requires trustees to follow a correct procedure in the decision-making process: see Etherton J in *Hearn* v *Younger* citing Staughton LJ in *Stannard* v *Fisons Pension Trust Ltd*. This duty lies at the heart of the rule, which is directed at ensuring for the protection of the beneficiaries under the trust that they are not prejudiced by any breach of such duty.

The rule as stated in *In re Hastings-Bass (deceased)* was expressed in a negative form to the effect that the court should not interfere with the exercise in good faith of a trustee's discretion, notwithstanding that it does not have the full effect which the trustee intended, unless the trustee exceeded the authority given by the trust or it is clear that he would not have acted as he did (a) had he not taken into account considerations which he should not have taken into account or (b) had he not failed to take into account considerations which he ought not to have taken into account.

This rule was restated in a positive form by Warner J in *Mettoy Pension Trustees* v *Evans*, namely that

> "Where a trustee acts under a discretion given to him by the terms of the trust, the court will interfere with his action if it is clear that he would not have acted as he did had he not failed to take into account considerations which he ought to have taken into account."

Warner J went on to state the exercise to be undertaken by the court in deciding whether the trustee has so acted:

> "In a case such as this, where it is claimed that the rule in *Hastings-Bass* applies, three questions must be asked (1) what were the trustees under a duty to consider? (2) Did they fail to consider it? (3) If so, what would they have done if they had considered it?"

A series of subsequent cases, all save one at first instance, have considered and, with only one substantive modification, applied or sought to apply the rule as reformulated by Warner J. It is unnecessary to consider the question raised by Sir Robert Walker, whether the holding in two such cases that the actual or potential adverse tax consequences of the exercise of the power are relevant facts for the purposes of the rule is a step too far. In this regard it may be noted that in *Gibbon* v *Mitchell* Millett J limited the jurisdiction to set aside for mistake to cases where there is a mistake of law or fact as to the effect of the transaction itself as opposed merely to the consequence or advantages to be gained by entering into it. The one substantive modification was made by the Court of Appeal in *Stannard* v *Fisons Pension Trust Ltd*. In that case the trustees of a pension scheme had to make a transfer in respect of transferring employees to a new fund. Sometime ahead of the proposed transfer they decided its quantum in the light of the value of the pension fund as it then stood. Thereafter prior to the date that the transfer was made, there was a recent substantial increase in value of the pension fund, which might have occasioned a change in the trustees' decision. The trustees were not however informed of the increase and accordingly did not have the opportunity to reconsider their previous decision in the light of the new facts. The Court of Appeal held that the failure of the trustees to consider this relevant consideration flawed their decision and that it was sufficient for the court to hold the decision invalid that the trustees only might and not would have taken a different decision if they had done so. It is not apparent from the judgments in that case that the Court of Appeal appreciated that it was departing from the rule in this regard as laid down in *In re Hastings-*

Bass (deceased). The choice between the two criteria remains open: see *Scott* v *National Trust*. Fortunately no such choice is required in this case, for clearly the trustee would not have appointed 60 per cent of the trust fund if it had known of the settlor's true wishes in that regard. I shall need later to refer to a passage in the judgment of Staughton LJ in *Stannard* v *Fisons Pension Trust Ltd* on the issue whether under the rule the exercise of the power is rendered void or voidable.

The first issue before me, raised by Mr Cooper, counsel for the sons, was whether the mistake on the part of the trustee was sufficiently fundamental to bring the rule into play at all. He submitted that there is no scope for application of the rule in this case because there is no sufficient difference between the trustee's understanding of the settlor's wishes regarding the appointment, ie an appointment of 60 per cent of the trust fund, and the settlor's actual wishes, ie an apportionment of 40 per cent of the trust fund. Mr Cooper argued that there is a high threshold for application of the rule, in particular in view of the draconian consequences of its application rendering the appointment void, and that the mistake on the part of the trustee as to the quantum of the appointment is insufficiently fundamental to bring the rule into play. I reject this submission. I am fully sensitive to the draconian consequences of the rule if it does indeed render a decision void and not voidable. I consider that issue later. But it is clear that the rule does not require that the relevant consideration unconsidered by the trustee should make a fundamental difference between the facts as perceived by the trustee and the facts as they should have been perceived. All that is required in this regard is that the unconsidered relevant consideration would or might have made a different appointment or no appointment at all. It is clear on the evidence that the trustee would, if he had known of the settlor's actual wishes for a 40 per cent appointment, have made such an appointment. I accordingly reject the submission.

The second issue, raised by Mr Warren,

counsel for the settlor, was whether it was sufficient to bring the rule into play that there was a mistake on the part of the trustee however it arose. Mr Warren submitted that the erroneous belief of the trustee that the settlor wished to appoint 60 per cent of the trust fund to the sons of itself was sufficient to invalidate the appointment because it meant that the trustee took into account an irrelevant consideration, the erroneous perception of the settlor's wishes, and did not take into account a relevant consideration, the settlor's true wishes, and that this was the position whether or not the responsibility for the mistake on the part of Mr Ward-Thompson was attributable to the settlor or the trustee. I also reject this submission.

In my view, it is not sufficient to bring the rule into play that the trustee made a mistake or by reason of ignorance or a mistake did not take into account a relevant consideration or took into account an irrelevant consideration. What has to be established is that the trustee in making his decision has, in the language of Warner J in *Mettoy Pension Trustees Ltd* v *Evans*, failed to consider what he was under a duty to consider. If the trustee has in accordance with his duty identified the relevant considerations and used all proper care and diligence in obtaining the relevant information and advice relating to those considerations, the trustee can be in no breach of duty and its decision cannot be impugned merely because in fact that information turns out to be partial or incorrect. For example, if the settlor had wished for an appointment of 40 per cent of the trust fund in favour of the sons, but in a letter to the trustee informing the trustee of his wishes by reason of a slip by him or a clerical error by his secretary the settlor had stated that he wanted an appointment of 60 per cent of the trust fund, and if the trustee in accordance with that erroneous expression of wishes had made an appointment of 60 per cent, neither could the trustee be criticised nor could the appointment be challenged under the rule. The trustee took into account the relevant consideration, the wishes of the settlor, and acted reasonably and properly in relying on the letter as the expression of those wishes. The fact that the trustee misapprehended the settlor's true intentions is irrelevant. Likewise a decision by the trustee to appoint quoted shares to a particular value to a beneficiary is not flawed if the shares subsequently turn out at the date of the appointment to have been immensely more valuable or less valuable than their quoted price by reason of a fact not reasonably ascertainable at the time eg an imminent take-over bid or a massive fraud perpetrated on the quoted company.

In summary the rule affords to the beneficiaries the protection of a requirement that the trustee performs its duty in exercising of its discretion and a remedy in case of a default. In the absence of any such breach of duty the rule does not afford the right to the trustee or any beneficiary to have a decision declared invalid because the trustee's decision was in some way mistaken or has unforeseen and unpalatable consequences.

Accordingly turning to the facts of this case, it is not sufficient to invoke the rule that the trustee mistakenly understood that the settlor wished the appointment to extend to 60 per cent of the trust fund when his true intention was 40 per cent. The trustee properly identified the settlor's intention as a relevant consideration. The trustee was informed by Mr Ward-Thompson [of Coopers & Lybrand] that his wish was that the appointment extend to 60 per cent. The fact that Mr Ward-Thompson misunderstood the settlor's true wish and communicated that misunderstanding to the trustee does not of itself establish any breach of duty by the trustee and accordingly scope for application of the rule. To establish the breach of duty and application of the rule, the settlor must go further and show that the trustee was in breach of duty in acting on and relying on what Mr Ward-Thompson told him.

Until some way into the hearing before me, the settlor's case rested on the sufficiency of the existence of a mistake on the part of the trustee as to the true intentions of the settlor to entitle the settlor to invoke the rule. When I intimated that I was minded to determine the second issue as I have done, Mr Warren sought to raise an alternative submission that the trustee was indeed at fault in giving effect to the misunderstanding of the settlor's wishes for which on the evidence Mr Ward-Thompson was responsible and he sought to support this new case with fresh evidence. Mr Cooper did not object to this course. I have accordingly to decide whether indeed the fault in giving effect to Mr Ward-Thompson's transmission of the settlor's wishes is attributable to the trustee. This issue is acutely difficult for a multitude of reasons, including the facts that the issue was raised very much as an afterthought at the end of the day, much of the evidence before the court was not prepared with this issue in mind, Mr Ward-Thompson has declined to give evidence or disclose his files and no party has wished to increase costs by requiring cross-examination to clarify the state of the evidence. Counsel however asked me to do my best on the material before me and I shall do so.

The issue, as it seems to me, very much turns on the role of Mr Ward-Thompson. ... As is common ground the solicitors who drafted the appointment were acting on behalf of the trustee. Mr Ward-Thompson in giving instructions for its preparation in the circumstances can only have done so acting as agent for the trustee. Accordingly in acting as agent for the trustee he misrepresented the settlor's wishes to the solicitors: the appointment accordingly reflected that misrepresentation; and Mr Ward-Thompson, again it can only have been as agent of or adviser to the trustee, required execution of that document by the trustee and protector. In short in the context of the relationships between the parties, it is I think plain that the fault in failing to consider the true wishes of the settlor was that of the trustee, its advisers and agents. The fiduciary duty of the trustee required the trustee to ascertain the wishes of the settlor, in particular since he was the life tenant whose interest in the trust fund was to be overridden and since it was his wishes that the appointment was intended to give effect to. The trustee failed to take adequate measures to ensure that it received a correct rather than a garbled version of the settlor's wishes. Mr Ward-Thompson was under the set-up in operation its appointed vehicle for the eliciting and transmitting of the settlor's wishes to the trustee. The trustee is accordingly responsible for the default in this regard of Mr Ward-Thompson. It is to be noted that Mr Ward-Thompson has declined to give evidence and answer the case made or suggest a different scenario. I should add that my view is reinforced by the consideration that any ambiguity in the structure and arrangements ought to be resolved in favour of the settlor: (1) the "C&L" side were responsible for the structure and arrangements; (2) Mr Ward-Thompson has declined to assist the court; and (3) the trustee perhaps surprisingly failed to seek from the settlor an expression of his wishes in documentary form or provide him with a copy of the proposed appointment before it was executed. In short on the material before me, on the third issue I am satisfied that the trustee failed in its fiduciary duty to ascertain the true wishes of the settlor to which the appointment was intended to give effect and accordingly the rule is brought into play.

The fourth issue raised is whether by reason of application of the rule the appointment is void or voidable. The issue is of critical significance in this case, for the lapse of ten years since the appointment, the signal failure by the settlor, indeed his deliberate decision not, to take any legal advice or any effective action until 2001, his acquiescence until then in the appointment having full legal effect and in particular the payment to the sons as fully entitled thereto of some £400,000 from the settlement must have the greatest significance if the settlement is voidable, but none at all if it is void.

The similarity between the grounds on which a decision by trustees may be attacked and the grounds on which official decision-making is subject to judicial review has been noted: see *Edge* v *Pensions Ombudsman*, and Sir Robert Walker "The Limits of the Principle in *In re Hastings-Bass dec'd*" [2002] PCB 226. But there are three critical differences between public, or administrative, law and private law proceedings. The first is the discretion vested in the court in public law proceedings whether or not to grant relief. The second is a difference in approach to the distinction between what is "void" and what is "voidable". In public law where an act or order is ultra vires, it is a nullity without existence or effect in law, but the terms "nullity" and "void" have no absolute sense: their meaning is relative depending upon the court's willingness to grant relief in any situation. If the court is willing to grant the necessary legal remedies, the act or order is recognised as having no legal effect at all. But the court may hold the act or order invalid, but refuse the applicant relief, eg because he does not deserve a discretionary remedy, because of delay or for some other legal reason. In such a case the void order remains effective and must be accepted as if it is valid. ... The third is the strict time limits insisted upon for commencement of proceedings for judicial review.

By contrast with the position in public law proceedings, in trust proceedings the legal classifications of void and voidable must be respected and there is no such strict time limit, and the court only has a discretion and can only have regard to the lapse of time between the act under challenge and the challenge when the challenged act is voidable and not void. The need in justice for some regard to the lapse of time in cases such as the present when the rule is invoked was underlined by Park J in *Breadner* v *Granville-Grossman*. Such need can only be satisfied if the decision successfully challenged under the rule is voidable and not void.

The authorities leave open the question whether a decision successfully challenged under the rule is voidable or void. The problematic judgment of Farwell LJ in *Cloutte* v *Storey* on the effect of a fraud on a power raises difficulties pointed out by Sir Robert Walker [2002] PCB 226 and cannot be determinative. There are statements in a number of the cases that the decision is void, but it is not clear how far the issue was fully argued, if argued at all, and so far as they do so decide, their weight and otherwise binding effect on me is diluted by the absence of reasoning and accord with principle and by the fact that there appears to have been no reference made to the statement by Staughton LJ in *Stannard* v *Fisons Pension Trust Ltd* ... of the challenge to the decision in that case the court had a discretion whether to declare the trustees' decision invalid. It is necessarily implicit in this statement in the private law context in which it is to be found that he was holding that the court had a discretion whether to avoid the trustees' decision, ie it was voidable only.

What may appear to have been a decision of trustees may on examination prove to have been no decision at all. An example is furnished by *Turner* v *Turner* where the trustees for many years signed every document placed before them by their solicitors, including appointments, without understanding that they had any discretion to exercise. But if the trustees have exercised the discretion conferred upon them, but in doing so have failed to take into account a relevant consideration or have taken into account an irrelevant consideration, it cannot in my view fairly or sensibly be held that they made no decision. It may be held that they made a flawed decision which is open to challenge, but that they made a decision is beyond question. The common law doctrine of non est factum has a very narrow and limited application. The transaction must be essentially different in substance or kind from the transaction intended. ... As Lord Walker suggests, a like requirement as to the essential nature of a transaction is surely called for before the equivalent rule can render a decision in equity no decision at all. The application of the rule ocannot of itself have this effect.

A successful challenge made to a decision under this rule should in principle result in the decision being held voidable and not void. This accords with the ordinary principles of equity that, leaving aside the separate and distinct self-dealing rule, a decision challenged on grounds of breach of fiduciary duty is voidable and not void. That applies to the appointment which, as I have held, falls foul of the rule.

In my view accordingly the appointment in this case is voidable and not void. Whether in the circumstances of this case the appointment should or should not be avoided and, if so, on what terms, is a matter on which I have not been addressed and on which the parties are at liberty to adduce further evidence and make further submissions. I must accordingly adjourn the hearing of this matter until a date when this issue can be argued and determined. There is, however, every reason to believe that to save further expensive contentious litigation the parties can and will seek to settle and agree the outstanding issue and seek any necessary approval by the court.'

Comment
This is a rare example of a case where the exercise of the trustee's discretionary power was open to challenge, not because of the mistake over the settlor's instructions but because of the breach of fiduciary duty in not having ascertained the true wishes of the settlor.

Armitage v *Nurse and Others* [1997] 2 All ER 705 Court of Appeal (Hirst, Millett and Hutchison LJJ)

• *Exclusion of liability clause in trust deed*

Facts
The appellant, Paula, was the principal beneficiary of a 1984 settlement and the respondents were the trustees. Paula alleged that the trustees:

1. had acted contrary to the express provisions of the trust in using the capital to benefit her mother;

2. had failed to obtain proper payment of interest in respect of a loan made to her mother;

3. had failed to give paramount considera-

tion to her best interest but had subordinated them to the interests of her mother.

Clause 15 of the settlement deed provided that no trustee should be liable for any loss or damage to the capital or income of the trust property 'unless such loss or damage shall be caused by his own actual fraud'. The proceedings concerned a preliminary issue as to whether cl 15 operated to absolve the trustees from liability for all or any of the alleged breaches. The judge at first instance held that it did and the Paula appealed to the Court of Appeal.

Held
The words 'actual fraud' in cl 15 simply connoted dishonesty. The clause exempted a trustee from liability for loss or damage unless caused by his own dishonesty, no matter how indolent, impudent, lacking in diligence, negligent or wilful he might have been, and it was not void for repugnancy or lack of public policy. The trustees were absolved from liability and the appeal was dismissed.

Millett LJ:

'It is the duty of a trustee to manage the trust property and deal with it in the interests of the beneficiaries. If he acts in a way which he does not honestly believe is in their interests he is acting dishonestly. It does not matter whether he stands or thinks he stands to gain personally from his actions. A trustee who acts with the intention of benefiting persons who are not the objects of the trust is not the less dishonest because he does not intend to benefit himself.

In my judgment cl 15 exempts the trustee from liability for loss or damage to the trust property no matter how indolent, imprudent, lacking in diligence, negligent or wilful he may have been, so long as he has not acted dishonestly.

The permitted scope of trustee exemption clauses
It is submitted on behalf of Paula that a trustee exemption clause, which purports to exclude all liability except for actual fraud is void, either for repugnancy or as contrary to public policy. There is some academic support for this submission ...'

Millett LJ cited the academic authorities and continued:

'In its consultation paper *Fiduciary Duties and Regulatory Rules, A Summary* (Law Com No 124 (1992)), para 3.3.41, the Law Commission states:

"Beyond this, trustees and fiduciaries cannot exempt themselves from liability for fraud, bad faith and wilful default. It is not, however, clear whether the prohibition on exclusion of liability for 'fraud' in this context only prohibits the exclusion of common law fraud or extends to the much broader doctrine of equitable fraud. It is also not altogether clear whether the prohibition on the exclusion of liability for 'wilful default' also prohibits exclusion of liability for gross negligence although we incline to the view that it does."

This passage calls for two comments. First, the expression "wilful default" is used in the cases in two senses. A trustee is said to be accountable on the footing of wilful default when he is accountable not only for money which he has in fact received but also for money which he could with reasonable diligence have received. It is sufficient that the trustee has been guilty of a want of ordinary prudence ... In the context of a trustee exclusion clause, however, such as s30 of the Trustee Act 1925, it means a deliberate breach of trust (*Re Vickery, Vickery v Stephens*) ... The decision has been criticised, but it is in line with earlier authority ...'

Millett LJ cited the authorities and continued:

'A trustee who is guilty of such conduct either consciously takes a risk that loss will result; or is recklessly indifferent whether it will or not. If the risk eventuates he is personally liable. But if he consciously takes the risk in good faith and with the best intentions, honestly believing that the risk is one which ought to be taken in the interests of the beneficiaries, there is no reason why he should not be protected by an exemption clause which excludes liability for wilful default.

Secondly, the Law Commission was considering the position of fiduciaries as well as trustees, and in such a context it is sensible to consider the exclusion of liability for so-called equitable fraud. But it makes no sense in the present context. The nature of equitable fraud may be collected from the speech of Viscount Haldane in *Nocton* v *Lord Ashburton* and *Snell's Equity*. It covers breach of fiduciary duty, undue influence, abuse of confidence, unconscionable bargains and frauds on powers. With the sole exception of the last, which is a technical doctrine in which the word "fraud" merely connotes excess of vires, it involves some dealing by the fiduciary with his principal and the risk that the fiduciary may have exploited his position to his own advantage. In *Earl of Aylesford* v *Morris* Lord Selborne LC said:

> "Fraud does not here mean deceit or circumvention; it means an unconscientious use of the power arising out of these circumstances and conditions ..."

A trustee exemption clause such as cl 15 of the settlement does not purport to exclude the liability of the fiduciary in such cases. Suppose, for example, that one of the respondents had purchased Paula's land at a proper price from his fellow trustees. The sale would be liable to be set aside. Clause 15 would not prevent this. This is not because the purchasing trustee would have been guilty of equitable fraud, but because by claiming to recover the trust property (or even equitable compensation) Paula would not be suing in respect of an "loss or damage" to the trust. Her right to recover the land would not depend on proof of loss or damage. Her claim would succeed even if the sale was at an overvalue; the purchasing trustee could never obtain more than a defeasible title from such a transaction. But cl 15 would be effective to exempt his fellow trustees from liability for making good any loss which the sale had occasioned to the trust estate so long as they had acted in good faith and in what they honestly believed was Paula's interests. ...

I accept the submission made on behalf of Paula that there is an irreducible core of obligations owed by the trustees to the beneficiaries and enforceable by them which is fundamental to the concept of a trust. If the beneficiaries have no rights enforceable against the trustees there are no trusts. But I do not accept the further submission that these core obligations include the duties of skill and care, prudence and diligence. The duty of the trustees to perform the trusts honestly and in good faith for the benefit of the beneficiaries is the minimum necessary to give substance to the trusts but in my opinion it is sufficient. As Mr Hill pertinently pointed out in his able argument, a trustee who relied on the presence of a trustee exemption clause to justify what he proposed to do would thereby lose its protection: he would be acting recklessly in the proper sense of the term.

It is, of course, far too late to suggest that the exclusion in a contract of liability for ordinary negligence or want of care is contrary to public policy. What is true of a contract must be equally true of a settlement. It would be very surprising if our law drew the line between liability for ordinary negligence and liability for gross negligence. In this respect English law differs from civil law systems, for it has always drawn a sharp distinction between negligence, however, gross, on the one hand and fraud, bad faith and wilful misconduct on the other. The doctrine of the common law is that: "Gross negligence may be evidence of mala fides, but it is not the same thing".'

Comment

The court continues to uphold the standard of liability of trustees laid down in *Re Vickery*, but in its Consultation Paper No 146 the Law Commission canvassed opinion as to what the standard of care imposed on trustees, individual or corporate, should be in relation to the delegation of their powers.

Edge and Others v Pensions Ombudsman and Another [1999] 4 All ER 546 Court of Appeal (Peter Gibson, Ward and Chadwick LJJ)

• *Trustees' duty of impartiality in relation to surplus in a pension fund*

Facts

The trustees of the Industrial Training Boards Pension Fund used a discretionary power of amendment within the pension trust deed to deal with an actuarial surplus by reducing employers' and employees' contributions to the fund. When asked to adjudicate on the amendment, the Pensions Ombudsman found that the trustees were in breach of their duty of impartiality and directed that the scheme should be administered according to its unamended rules. The trustees appealed and at first instance Sir Richard Scott V-C held in their favour that since a court could not have directed the trustees to set aside the deed of amendment nor could the Ombudsman, and further that the Ombudsman could not set aside the decision of the trustees on the ground that it showed undue partiality to the preferred beneficiaries. The Pensions Ombudsman appealed.

Held

Dismissing the appeal, the Court of Appeal held that, provided the trustees had fulfilled their duty to use the discretionary power for its proper purpose, they could not be challenged if they used it so that they appeared to prefer one class of beneficiaries over another. Since it had not been shown that the trustees had misdirected themselves or made an irrational decision, there were no grounds upon which the Ombudsman could have found that they had acted in breach of trust.

Chadwick LJ:

'The trustees' duty

In examining the contention that, in exercising their power to amend the rules, the trustees were subject to a duty to act impar-

tially as between individual or classes of beneficiaries ... it is important to have in mind the circumstances in which the need for amendments arose and the nature of those amendments. A convenient starting point is rule 3:

"The main purpose of the Scheme is the provision of retirement and other benefits for employees of Training Boards and Successor Bodies who are Members of the Scheme. The Trust Fund is to be constituted and maintained by means of periodical and other contributions to be made by the Members and by the Employers in accordance with the Rules."

At the risk of stating the obvious, that "main purpose" rule embodies three concepts which are fundamental to a pension scheme of this nature.

First, the purpose of the scheme is to provide the retirement and other benefits to which the members, pensioners and dependants are entitled under the rules. The scheme is a "defined benefits" scheme: the benefits are fixed by the rules. The scheme is not set up as a unit trust under which the members would be entitled to a proportionate share in the fund.

Second, the fund out of which the benefits are to be provided is constituted and maintained by means of periodic payments. The amount of the payments will depend not only on the rate of contributions but also on the number of members in service from time to time who are contributors and on the number of employers who continue to participate. In that sense, the fund is dynamic. Although it will be possible, at any. given time, to measure the value of the assets then held in the fund, and to measure the liabilities which then have to be met out of those assets (on the basis of termination), that is not a particularly useful exercise unless termination is seen to be imminent What is required is an actuarial valuation of the assets, present and future, taking into account the contributions which are to be made by employers and members over the remaining life of the fund, and an actuarial valuation of the liabilities which will have to be met as employees in service retire and become pensioners (or die and leave dependants).

Third, the task of the trustees is to maintain a balance between assets and liabilities valued on that actuarial basis, so that, so far as the future can be foreseen, they will be in a position to provide pensions and other benefits in accordance with the rules throughout the life of the scheme. That task is to be performed by setting appropriate levels for employers' and members' contributions. If that task could be performed with perfect foresight there would be no surpluses and no deficits. But, because the task has to be performed in the real world, surpluses and deficits are bound to arise from time to time and prudent trustees will aim to ensure that the likelihood of surplus outweighs the risk of deficit Nevertheless, it is no part of the trustees' function, in a fund of this nature, to set levels for contributions which will generate surpluses beyond those properly required as a reserve against contingencies.

The principal tool by which the trustees are enabled to perform the task of maintaining a balance between assets and liabilities valued on an actuarial basis is the "balance of cost" provision in rule 10.1:

> "Each of the Employers shall contribute to the Trust Fund within seven days of the end of each monthly or other accounting period after the Operative Date and whilst it remains one of the Employers *such sum as the Actuary shall certify to be the amount which is required*, in addition to all other contributions of the Employer and the Members in the employment of the Employer, by way of 'Employer's Ordinary Contribution' for such month or other period *in order to make due provision of the benefits secured by the Scheme* in respect of such Members." (our emphasis)

That provision must be read in conjunction with rule 227.2(c) which imposes on the appointed actuary a duty to make periodic valuations of the scheme, and rule 203 which is in these terms:

> "If any periodic valuation by the Actuary shall disclose any surplus, deficiency or anticipated deficiency in the Trust Fund, the Managing Trustees shall ... *with the purpose of maintaining the amount in the Trust Fund in reasonable balance with the liabilities under the Scheme*, request the Actuary to make certification under rule 10 regarding the rate of the Employer's Ordinary Contributions to be payable to the Trust Fund.)." (our emphasis)

... As Sir Richard Scott V-C pointed out ... the ability to maintain the fund in balance ... is limited by the requirement ... that the employers' contributions shall always be greater than or equal to those of the members. But this presents no insuperable difficulty. The rules give the trustees a second tool by which they can maintain the fund in balance. Rules 506.1 and 602.1 require that each member shall, in each contribution year:

> "pay Members' contributions to the Trust Fund *at the rate from time to time prescribed by the Managing Trustees* and in accordance with this Rule." (our emphasis).

If no rate is prescribed under those rules the rate of members' contributions is 6 per cent of pensionable salary) or (under rule 602.1) 5 per cent in the case of a female member who was in service on 31st March 1983. Rules 506.4 and 602.4, which are in the same terms, require:

> "(a) the Managing Trustees shall prescribe the contribution rate or rates for each Contribution Year prior to the commencement thereof; and (b) the Managing Trustees *shall in so prescribing act under the advice of the Actuary* who shall in the absence of special circumstances preserve such a ratio between the contributions to be made by the Members and those to be made by the Employers as will ensure that the Employers' contributions will at all times be equal or greater than the contributions to be made by the Members." (our emphasis)

This second tool is less flexible than the

first, because the power to prescribe can only be exercised in advance of the contribution year. But, if the power to prescribe members' contributions is exercised so as to reduce the rate of contributions below the rate applicable in default, there is additional scope for the actuary in certifying the rate of employers) contributions.

On a true analysis, the trustees did not make use of what we have described as the second tool in the present case. They accepted the actuary's advice that the contribution change should take effect from 1 October 1993. That was a date within the then current contribution year, so that change could not be effected by the "prescribed rate") machinery provided by rules 506 and 602. The change could only be effected by an alteration to the rules. That may be described as the third tool available to the trustees.

Rule 205.1 conferred power on the trustees to alter the rules after notification to the employers, but subject to certain restrictions ... None of those restrictions is in point in the present case. In particular, the rule change did not result in the payment of any part of the fund to the employers. What it did was to facilitate a reduction in the employers' rate of contribution – which is quite a different matter.

The actuary's report, delivered in April 1993, imposed on the trustees: (i) a duty to consider what rate they should prescribe in respect of members' contributions for the next contribution year ... and (ii) a duty to request the actuary to certify the rate at which contributions should be made by employers under rule 10.1. The performance of those duties in circumstances in which there was no related change in benefits would have given little or no scope for the exercise of discretion. In deciding what rate they should prescribe in respect of members' contributions for the next contribution year, the trustees would have been obliged ... to act on the advice of the actuary ...

There was no obligation to make any change to the benefits payable under the rules. But the actuary's report provided an opportunity for the trustees to consider whether the benefits payable under the scheme should be increased. That was an opportunity – which they were obliged to take. They could not ignore the recommendations ... of the actuary's report. They were obliged to consider whether to increase benefits, but, after consideration, they could have decided not to do so. They could have decided to maintain the fund in balance – on the basis of unchanged benefits – by appropriate adjustments to the contribution rates, using the tools which we have described. If they had reached that decision, after proper consideration of the alternatives, they could not have been criticised. The beneficiaries had no right to insist on an increase in benefits: Their right was to have the matter properly considered.

The right to have the matter properly considered gives rise to the requirement that, if there is an actuarial surplus after providing for the estimated liabilities, the trustees must, in deciding whether or not to increase benefits (and, if so, which benefits), act in a way which appears to them fair and equitable in all the circumstances, and so leads to a reasonable expectation amongst beneficiaries that that is what will be done.

The obligation to consider properly the question whether to increase benefits (and, if so, which benefits) will usually require the trustees to consider (amongst other matters) the circumstances in which the surplus has arisen. In deciding what is fair and equitable in all the circumstances, the trustees may be expected to give weight to the claims of those whose contributions are, or will be, the effective source of the surplus. For example, in a pure "balance of costs" scheme, trustees may properly take the view that an actuarial surplus which has arisen through past overfunding ought to be reduced by allowing the employers a future "contributions holiday": see the observations of Millett J in a different context in *Re Courage Group's Pension Schemes, Ryan* v *Imperial Brewing and Leisure Ltd*. In a case where the actuarial surplus arises from prospective overfunding by excessive contributions from members in the futures, the trustees may properly decide that the fair and equitable course is to reduce those contributions, or to increase the benefits of those who will be making those future contributions. If, on the other hand, the surplus has arisen through overfunding which is plainly attributable to members' past contributions, the members who have made those contributions will have a strong claim to an increase in benefits. The circumstances in which it is possible to say, with any degree of confidence, that the surplus is plainly attributable to members' past contributions may be rare in practice – but those circumstances could arise, for example, where the employer has not been called on to contribute at all over the period during which the surplus has accrued.

The need to consider the circumstances in which the surplus has arisen does not lead to the conclusion that the trustees are bound to take any particular course as a result of that consideration. They are not constrained by any rule of law either to increase benefits or to reduce contributions or to adopt any particular combination of those options. Nor does the need to consider the circumstances in which the surplus has arisen lead to the conclusion that the trustees are not required to take – or are prohibited from taking – any other matters into account in deciding what course to adopt. They must, for example, always have in mind the main purpose of the scheme – to provide retirement and other benefits for employees of the participating employers. They must consider the effect that any course which they are minded to take will have on the financial ability of the employers to make the contributions which that course will entail. They must be careful not to impose burdens which imperil the continuity and proper development of the employers' business or the employment of the members who work in that business. The main purpose of the scheme is not served by putting an employer out of business. They must also consider the level of benefits under their scheme relative to the benefits under comparable schemes, or in the pensions market generally. They should ask themselves whether the scheme is attractive to the members whose willingness to continue paying contributions is essential to its future funding. Are the benefits seen by the members to be good value in relation to the contributions; would the members find it more attractive to pay higher contributions for higher benefits or to pay lower contributions and accept lower benefits? The main purpose of the scheme is not served by setting contributions and benefits at levels which deter employees from joining or which causes resentment. And they must ask themselves whether the benefits enjoyed by members in pension have kept up with increases in the cost of living, so that the expectations of those members during their service – that they were making adequate provision for their retirement through contributions to an occupational pensions scheme – are not defeated by inflation.

The matters to which we have referred are not to be taken as an exhaustive or a prescriptive list. It is likely that, in most circumstances, pension trustees who fail to take those matters into account will be open to criticism. But there may well be other matters which are of equal or greater importance in the particular circumstances with which trustees are faced. The essential requirement is that the trustees address themselves to the question what is fair and equitable in all the circumstances. The weight to be given to one factor as against another is for them.

Properly understood, the so-called duty to act impartially – on which the ombudsman placed such reliance – is no more than the ordinary duty which the law imposes on a person who is entrusted with the exercise of a discretionary power: that he exercises the power for the purpose for which it is given, giving proper consideration to the matters which are relevant and excluding from consideration matters which are irrelevant. If pension fund trustees do that, they cannot be criticised if they reach a decision which appears to prefer the claims of one interest – whether that of employers, current employees or pensioners – over others. The preference will be the result of proper exercise of the discretionary power.'

Comment

Chadwick LJ gives a clear analysis of the pension fund trustees' duties. It is interesting to note that in this context the duties include a duty not to impose burdens which imperil the continuity of the employer's business. How can this case be distinguished from *Cowan* v *Scargill* (see Chapter 11, below) where taking into consideration the effect of the trustees' investment policy on the future of the mining industry was held to be a breach of trust?

Guinness plc v *Saunders and Another* [1990] 2 WLR 324 House of Lords (Lords Keith of Kinkel, Brandon of Oakbrook, Templeman, Griffiths and Goff of Chieveley)

• *Trustee's duty to act in the best interests of the beneficiaries – remuneration*

Facts

When Guinness launched its takeover bid for Distillers, a special committee of its directors was set up to implement the takeover bid. The committee appointed a Mr Ward as consultant and he submitted an invoice for £5.2 million in respect of his fees. The committee agreed this remuneration and payment was received in this amount, although the main board of directors did not authorise the payment. While accepting that Mr Ward had performed valuable services, the company contended that the committee's representative would have been in breach of his fiduciary duty to the company in that the payment had not been disclosed to the board of directors as required by s317 of the Companies Act 1985 and by the company's articles of association. The company issued a writ against Mr Ward to recover the £5.2 million and the judge held that Mr Ward held the £5.2 million as constructive trustee for the company. The case eventually went to the House of Lords.

Held

1. The committee of directors had no power

to bind the company as regards the remuneration to be paid to Mr Ward.

2. In the absence of a binding contract Mr Ward was not entitled to claim reasonable remuneration on a quantum meruit basis or under an implied contract. Nor was he entitled to an equitable allowance for his services because, by agreeing to provide his services in return for a substantial fee the size of which was dependent on the value of the takeover bid, he had put himself in a position where his personal interests conflicted irreconcilably with his duty as a director. In such a situation the equitable principle which forbade a trustee making a profit from his trust, unless authorised by the trust instrument, prevented the court from imposing a condition that repayment of the £5.2 million be subject to an equitable allowance for his services.

Lord Templeman:

'Equity forbids a trustee to make a profit out of his trust. The articles of association of Guinness relax the strict rule of equity to extent of enabling a director to make a profit provided that the board of directors contracts on behalf of Guinness for the payment of special remuneration or decides to award special remuneration. Mr Ward did not obtain a contract or a grant from the board of directors. Equity has no power to relax its own strict rule further than and inconsistently with the express relaxation contained in the articles of association. A shareholder is entitled to compliance with the articles. A director accepts office subject to and with the benefit of the provisions of the articles relating to directors. No one is obliged to accept appointment as a director. No director of Guinness who contemplates or accepts service on a committee or has performed outstanding services for the company as a member of a committee may apply to the board of directors to be obtained for a contract or an award of special remuneration. A director who does not read the articles or a director who misconstrues the articles is nevertheless bound by the articles. Article 91 provides clearly enough for the authority of the board of directors to be obtained for the payment of special remuneration and the submissions made on behalf of Mr Ward, based on arts 2, 100(D) and 110, are more ingenious than plausible and more legalistic than convincing. At the board meeting held on 19 January 1986, Mr Ward was present but did not seek then or thereafter to obtain the necessary authority of the board of directors for payment of special remuneration. In these circumstances there are no grounds for equity to relax its rules further than the articles of association provide. Similarly, the law will not imply a contract between Guinness and Mr Ward for remuneration on a quantum meruit basis awarded by the court when the articles of association of Guinness stipulate that special remuneration for a director can only be awarded by the board.'

His Lordship then considered the contractual claim and continued.

'In support of a claim for an equitable allowance, reference was made to the decision of Wilberforce J in *Phipps* v *Boardman*. His decision was upheld by the Court of Appeal and ultimately by this House. In that case, a trust estate included a minority holding in a private company which fell on lean times. The trustees declined to attempt to acquire a controlling interest in the company in order to improve its performance. The solicitor to the trust and one of the beneficiaries, with the knowledge and approval of the trustees, purchased the controlling interest from outside shareholders for themselves with the help of information about the shareholders acquired by the solicitor in the course of acting for the trust. The company's position was improved and the shares bought by the solicitor and the purchasing beneficiary were ultimately sold at a profit. A complaining beneficiary was held to be entitled to a share of the profits on the resale on the ground that the solicitor and the purchasing beneficiary were assisted in the original purchase by the information derived from the trust. The pur-

chase of a controlling interest might have turned out badly and in that case the solicitor and the purchasing beneficiary would have made irrecoverable personal losses. In these circumstances it is not surprising that Wilberforce J decided that in calculating the undeserved profit which accrued to the trust estate there should be deducted a generous allowance for the work and trouble of the solicitor and the purchasing beneficiary in acquiring the controlling shares and restoring the company to prosperity. *Phipps* v *Boardman* decides that in exceptional circumstances a court of equity may award remuneration to the trustee. Therefore, it is argued, a court of equity may award remuneration to a director. As at present advised, I am unable to envisage circumstances in which a court of equity would exercise a power to award remuneration to a director when the relevant articles of association confided that power to the board of directors ...

... There is a fundamental objection to the admission of any claim by Mr Ward whether that claim be based on art 100(D), a quantum meruit, s727 of the 1985 Act or the powers of a court of equity. The objection is that by the agreement with the committee, which is the foundation of Mr Ward's claim to any relief, he voluntarily involved himself in an irreconcilable conflict between his duty as a director and his personal interests. Both before and after 19 January 1986 Mr Ward owed a duty to Guinness to tender to Guinness impartial and independent advice untainted by any possibility of personal gain. Yet by the agreement, which Mr Ward claims to have concluded with the committee and which may have been in contemplation by Mr Ward even before 19 January 1986, Mr Ward became entitled to a negotiating fee payable by Guinness if, and only if, Guinness acquired Distillers and, by the agreement, the amount of the negotiating fee depended on the price which Guinness ultimately offered to the shareholders of Distillers. If such an agreement had been concluded by the board of directors, it would have been binding on Guinness under art 91 but foolish in that the agreement perforce made Mr Ward's advice to Guinness suspect and biased. But at least the conflict would have been revealed to the board. As it was, the agreement was not made by the board and was not binding on Guinness. The agreement was made by the committee and ought not to have been made at all. By the agreement Mr Ward debarred himself from giving impartial and independent advice to Guinness. Mr Ward was a director of Guinness and in that capacity was able to negotiate his own agreement with the committee of which he was a member, and was able to discuss the bid by Guinness for Distillers with the other directors, to advise and participate in decisions on behalf of Guinness relevant to the bid (including a decision to increase the amount of the offer) and to procure the acquisition by Guinness of Distillers and thus to claim £5.2 million from Guinness. I agree with my noble and learned friend Lord Goff that for the purposes of this appeal it must be assumed that Mr Ward acted in good faith, believing that his services were rendered under a contract binding on the company, and that in that mistaken belief Mr Ward may have rendered services to Guinness of great value and contributed substantially to the enrichment of the shareholders of Guinness. Nevertheless, the failure of Mr Ward to realise that he could not properly use his position as director of Guinness to obtain a contingent negotiating fee of £5.2million from Guinness does not excuse him or enable him to defeat the rules of equity which prohibit a trustee from putting himself in a position in which his interests and duty conflict and which insist that a trustee or any other fiduciary shall not make a profit out of his trust.'

Comment

Note that the potential of conflict between the trustee's duty and personal interest is sufficient to defeat the trustee's personal interest in a claim of this nature – it is irrelevant that the trustee was acting in good faith.

Holding and Management Ltd v Property Holding and Investment Trust plc and Others [1989] 1 WLR 1313 Court of Appeal (Lloyd, Nicholls and Farquharson LJJ)

* *Section 30(2) of the Trustee Act 1925*

Facts
Section 30(2) of the Trustee Act 1925 provides:

'A trustee may reimburse himself or pay or discharge out of the trust premises all expenses incurred in or about the execution of the trusts or powers.'

In this case, however, the plaintiff company, as maintenance trustee in respect of a block of flats, had put forward a programme of works which was opposed by the tenants and in respect of which the company applied to the court for directions as to whether the proposed scheme was within its powers. In the course of the hearing a compromise was reached which was advantageous to the tenants.

Held
The trustess were not entitled to an indemnity for costs from the maintenance fund.

Nicholls LJ:

'To be entitled to an indemnity, the costs and expenses in question must have been properly incurred by the trustee. This is axiomatic. In the present case the plaintiff did not bring proceedings to protect the maintenance fund for the benefit of the beneficiaries. The beneficiaries of that fund, as I have sought to indicate, are the tenants plus the landlord. The proceedings were brought against the tenants to establish whether they were obliged to engage the fund to be applied for their benefit beyond what they and the landlord wished. I do not think that costs so incurred were properly incurred.'

Comment

These proceedings were plainly not in the interests of the trust or of anybody else. While the court is at pains to uphold the trustees' right (and duty) to seek guidance from the court when there is a doubt as to the required course of action on their part, it will not encourage vexatious litigation by trustees. Trustees can only recover expenses which are reasonably incurred.

Keech v *Sandford*

See Chapter 6.

Londonderry's Settlement, Re [1965] Ch 918 Court of Appeal (Harman, Danckwerts and Salmon LJJ)

• *No duty to disclose documents relating to trustees' exercise of their discretion*

Facts

The trustees of a settlement created by the seventh Marquess of Londonderry decided to exercise a power under the settlement to bring it to an end and distribute the capital among the beneficiaries. The settlor's daughter was dissatisfied with the amounts the trustees proposed to appoint to her under the powers in bringing the settlement to an end. She asked the trustees to supply her with copies of various documents relating to the settlement. The trustees gave her copies of the appointments and of the accounts but refused to disclose any other documents. The settlor's daughter was not satisfied and she issued a summons asking whether the trustees could be required to disclose: (a) minutes of meetings of the trustees; (b) agendas and other documents for trust meetings; and (c) correspondence relating to the administration of the trust.

Held

The beneficiaries are prima facie entitled to production and inspection of all trust documents in the possession of the trustees – including title deeds and documents relating to the nature and content of their own beneficial interest. But the beneficiaries under a discretionary trust such as this are not entitled to see documents containing confidential information as to the exercise of the discretion where this 'might cause infinite trouble in the family out of all proportion to the benefit which might be received from inspection of the same'.

Harman LJ:

'I have found this a difficult case. It raises what, in my judgment, is a novel question on which there is no authority exactly in point although several cases have been cited to us somewhere near it. The court is really required here to resolve two principles that come into conflict, or at least apparent conflict. The first is that, as the defendant beneficiary admits, trustees exercising a discretionary power are not bound to disclose to their beneficiaries the reasons actuating them in coming to a decision. This is a long-standing principle and rests largely, I think, on the view that nobody could be called upon to accept a trusteeship involving the exercise of a discretion unless, in the absence of bad faith, he was not liable to have his motives or reasons called into question either by the beneficiaries or by the court. To this there is added a rider, namely, that if trustees do give reasons, their soundness can be considered by the court ...

It would seem on the face of it that there is no reason why this principle should be confined to decisions orally arrived at and should not extend to a case like the present, where owing to the complexity of the trust and the large sums involved, the trustees, who act subject to the consent of another body called the appointors, have brought into existence various written documents, including, in particular, agenda for and minutes of their meetings from time to time in order to consider distributions made of the fund and its income ...'

Comment

The court will uphold the confidentiality of the trustees' decision-making process against the beneficiaries' right to information.

Macadam, Re [1946] Ch 73

Chancery Division (Cohen J)

• *Fiduciary must account when has used office to obtain remuneration*

Facts

The trustees of a trust had power under the articles of a company by virtue of their office to appoint two directors to the company. The trustees appointed themselves and received directors' fees. The question arose whether they were entitled to retain these or if they held them for the trust.

Held

They were liable to account for these fees as they had received them by the use of their powers as trustees.

Cohen J:

'I think that the root of the matter really is: Did he acquire the position in respect of which he drew the remuneration by virtue of his position as trustee? In the present case there can be no doubt that the only way in which the plaintiffs became directors was by exercise of the powers vested in the trustees of the will under art 68 of the articles of association of the company. The principle is one which has always been regarded as of the greatest importance in these courts, and I do not think I ought to do anything to weaken it. As I have said, although the remuneration was remuneration for services as director of the company, the opportunity to receive that remuneration was gained as a result of the exercise of a discretion vested in the trustees, and they had put themselves in a position where their interest and duty conflicted. In those circumstances, I do not think this court can allow them to make a profit out of doing so, and I do not think the liability to account for a profit can be con-

fined to cases where the profit is derived directly from the trust estate.'

Comment

This case demonstrates that the trustees' liability to account is strictly enforced.

Norfolk's (Duke of) Settlement Trusts, Re [1981] 3 WLR 455 Court of Appeal (Cumming-Bruce, Brightman and Fox LJJ)

• *Court's inherent jurisdiction to increase or award remuneration*

Facts

The trust was set up in 1958 and comprised large holdings of real estate, stock and shares. There were three trustees of the trust, one of whom was a trust corporation. The trust instrument authorised the trust corporation to charge remuneration for its services at the level of its fees in force at the date of the settlement, ie two shillings (10p) per £100 of capital annually. The acquisition of further real estate redevelopment of properties belonging to the trust in London involved the trust corporation in an exceptional amount of extra work while resulting in substantial increases in the value of the trust. When Capital Transfer Tax was introduced in 1975 the trust corporation rearranged the trust's affairs so as to minimise tax liability. In all these circumstances the trust corporation found that the levels of remuneration fixed were inadequate, mainly because of inflation, and it was therefore operating the trust at a loss to itself. Accordingly, an application was made to the Court under its inherent jurisdiction that the trust corporation: (1) be allowed to raise the general level of remuneration under the trust instrument backdated to 31 March 1977; (2) receive £25,000 for services performed outside the scope of its duties in redeveloping trust property; (3) receive £50,000 for rearranging trust liability so as to reduce Capital Transfer Tax liability; and (4) receive remuneration for services of an exceptional nature performed in the future. Walton J at first instance found, as regards (2) that 'the work of redeveloping trust property was outside the scope of the trustees' duties and was only executed on the basis of an implied promise to pay, thus remuneration would be ordered accordingly. The claims under (1) and (4) would be dismissed as the court had no power to increase the general level of remuneration. The trust company appealed to the Court of Appeal seeking a declaration that the court had power under its inherent jurisdiction to increase the level of remuneration.

Held

The court did have power to increase the level of remuneration where this was beneficial to the trust. The case would be remitted to the Chancery Division to decide if the jurisdiction should be exercised.

Fox LJ:

'If it be the law, as I think it clearly is, that the court has inherent jurisdiction on the appointment of a trustee to authorise payment of remuneration to him, is there any reason why the court should not have jurisdiction to increase the remuneration already allowed by the trust instrument?

Two reasons are suggested. First, it is said that a trustee's right to remuneration under an express provision of the settlement is based on a contract between the settlor and the trustee which the trustee is not entitled to avoid; the benefit of that contract is to be regarded as settled by the trust instrument for the benefit of the beneficiaries. I find that analysis artificial. It may have some appearance of reality in relation to a trustee who, at the request of the settlor, agrees to act before the settlement is executed and approves the terms of the settlement. But very frequently executors and trustees of wills know nothing of the terms of the will until the testator is dead; sometimes in the case of corporate trustees such as banks, they have not even been asked by the testator whether they will act. It is difficult to see with whom, in such cases, the trustees are

to be taken as contracting. The appointment of a trustee by the court also gives rise to problems as to the identity of the contracting party.

The position, it seems to me, is this. Trust property is held by the trustees on the trusts and subject to the power conferred by the trust instrument and by law. One of those powers is the power to the trustee to charge remuneration. That gives the trustee certain rights which equity will enforce in administering the trust. How far those rights can properly be regarded as beneficial interests I will consider later. But it seems to me to be quite unreal to regard them as contractual. So far as they derive from any order of the court they simply arise from the court's jurisdiction and so far as they derive from the trust instrument itself they derive from the settlor's power to direct how this property should be dealt with ...

I conclude that the court has an inherent jurisdiction to authorise the payment of remuneration of trustees and that that jurisdiction extends to increasing the remuneration authorised by the trust instrument. In exercising that jurisdiction the court has to balance two influences which are to some extent in conflict. The first is that the office of trustee is, as such, gratuitous; the court will accordingly be careful to protect the interests of the beneficiaries against claims by the trustees. The second is that it is of great importance to the beneficiaries that the trust should be well administered. If therefore the court concludes, having regard to the nature of the trust, to the experience and skill of a particular trustee and to the amounts which he seeks to charge when compared with what other trustees might require to be paid for their services and to all the other circumstances of the case, that it would be in the interests of the beneficiaries to increase the remuneration, then the court may properly do so.'

Comment

Trustees are entitled, if the trust deed expressly so provides, to charge their reasonable fees. In this case the Court construed this in favour of the trustees when their fees had become unreasonably low and recognised the court's jurisdiction to take action in these circumstances.

Schmidt v *Rosewood Trust Ltd*
[2003] UKPC 26; [2003] 2 WLR 1442 Privy Council (Lords Nicholls of Birkenhead, Hope of Craighead, Hutton, Hobhouse of Woodborough and Walker of Gestingthorpe)

• *Whether beneficiary of a discretionary power or trust has a proprietary right to disclosure of trust documents*

Facts
Vadim Schmidt sought disclosure of documents which related to two discretionary settlements, the Angora Trust and the Everest Trust, in which he had an interest both on his own account and as administrator of his father's estate. At first instance in the Isle of Man, Vadim Schmidt was granted an order for disclosure but the corporate trustee of the settlements, The Rosewood Trust, successfully appealed to the High Court of Justice of the Isle of Man on the ground that Vadim Schmidt was not a beneficiary. Vadim Schmidt then appealed to the Privy Council.

Held
Although a beneficiary's right to disclosure of documents can be classed as a proprietary right, it is best approached as one aspect of the court's inherent jurisdiction to supervise and, where appropriate, intervene in the administration of trusts. The appeal was allowed and the matter remitted to the High Court of the Isle of Man for further consideration.

Lord Walker:

'It has become common for wealthy individuals in many parts of the world (including countries which have no indigenous law of trusts) to place funds at their disposition into trusts (often with a network of underlying companies) regulated by the law of, and managed by trustees resident in, territories with which the settlor (who may be also a beneficiary) has no substantial connection. These territories (sometimes called tax havens) are chosen not for their geographical convenience (indeed face to face meetings between the settlor and his trustees are often very inconvenient) but because they are supposed to offer special advantages in terms of confidentiality and protection from fiscal demands (and sometimes from problems under the insolvency laws, or laws restricting freedom of testamentary disposition, in the country of the settlor's domicile). The trusts and powers contained in a settlement established in such circumstances may give no reliable indication of who will in the event benefit from the settlement. Typically it will contain very wide discretions exercisable by the trustees (sometimes only with the consent of a so-called protector) in favour of a widely-defined class of beneficiaries. The exercise of those discretions may depend on the settlor's wishes as confidentially imparted to the trustees and the protector. As a further cloak against transparency, the identity of the true settlor or settlers may be concealed behind some corporate figurehead.

All these considerations may encourage a settlor to entrust substantial funds to an apparently secure and confidential offshore shelter. But the very same features may, as this case strikingly illustrates, present problems to the close relatives of a settlor who dies unexpectedly as did Mr Vitali Schmidt, (Mr Schmidt), the co-settlor of two Isle of Man settlements called the Angora Trust and the Everest Trust.

The main issue on this appeal is the claim of the petitioner, Mr Schmidt's son, Vadim (the appellant), to obtain trust accounts and other information from the trustees of the two settlements. The sole trustee of each settlement is Rosewood Trust Ltd (Rosewood), an Isle of Man company which is in business as a provider of corporate and trustee services. It is the respondent in this appeal.
...

Counsel have very properly referred the Board to a considerable number of authorities, some of them going back to the early years of the 19th century. It is appropriate to reflect that during the long period covered by these authorities (but especially during the second half of the 20th century) the forms and functions of settlements have changed to a degree which would have astonished Lord Eldon. By the 1930s high rates of personal taxation led some wealthy individuals to make settlements which enabled funds to be accumulated in the hands of overseas trustees. ... This practice increased enormously with the introduction of capital gains tax in 1965. But increasingly stringent anti-avoidance measures encouraged legal advisers to devise forms of settlement under which the true intended beneficiaries were not clearly identified in the settlement. Indeed their interests or expectations were not clearly identified in the settlement. Indeed their interests or expectations were often barely perceptible. Rarely did a beneficiary take an indefeasibly vested interest with an ascertainable market value. Tax avoidance is therefore one element which has strongly influenced the forms of settlements; and once the offshore tax-avoidance industry has acquired standard forms its inclination is to use them, subject perhaps to some more or less skilful adaptation, even for clients whose aim is not to avoid United Kingdom taxation.

There is another element, also linked (though less directly) to taxation, which has encouraged the inclusion in settlements of very widely defined classes of beneficiaries. After the Second World War estate duty was charged in the United Kingdom at very high rates, with much less generous reliefs for agricultural and business property than those now available. A wealthy landowner or businessman might be advised that the safest way to preserve his fortune was to give most of it away, while he was still in the prime of life, to trustees of an irrevocable settlement in discretionary form under which the settlor himself was not a beneficiary. It is not surprising that a settlor in such a position should wish to cover as com-

prehensively as he could all possible current and future claims on his bounty, since he was being asked to make an immediate, irrevocable disposition of much of his wealth, rather than being able to review from time to time the ambulatory dispositions in his will and codicils. But his lawyers might also advise him that the most natural expressions for defining discretionary objects of his bounty (such as "relatives", "old friends", "dependants" or "persons with moral claims") were of doubtful legal efficacy. So there was a tendency to define the class in the widest possible terms. The process can be seen in a long line of cases starting with *In re Gestetner's Settlement*, upholding the validity of an "intermediate" power comparable to that in clause 3.3 of the Everest Trust (that is, a power to add as beneficiaries anyone in the world apart from a very small class of excluded persons).

The Board have to consider what rights or claims to disclosure the appellant has, either personally or as his father's personal representative, under two badly drafted settlements whose terms have been moulded by the sort of influences mentioned above. One possible reaction would be that Mr Schmidt and his colleagues have made their bed and they must lie on it; if they have deliberately entered into a web of camouflage, it is hardly for anyone claiming through them to complain that the position is not transparent. As Lord Greene MR observed, giving the judgment of the court in *Lord Howard de Walden* v *IRC*, if a taxpayer plays with fire it scarcely lies in his mouth to complain of burnt fingers. However, the Board consider that that inclination must be resisted. As already noted, it has not been suggested that the settlements are shams, or tainted with illegality. It is fundamental to the law of trusts that the court has jurisdiction to supervise and if appropriate intervene in the administration of a trust, including a discretionary trust. As Holland LJ said in the Australian case of *Randall* v *Lubrano* cited by Kirby P in *Hartigan Nominees Pty Ltd* v *Rydge*:

"... no matter how wide the trustee's discretion in the administration and application of a discretionary trust fund and even if in all or some respects the discretions are expressed in the deed as equivalent to those of an absolute owner of the trust fund, the trustee is still a trustee."

Several of the numerous authorities referred to by counsel have been concerned with the general characteristics of interests (or rights) under discretionary trusts, on the one hand, and mere powers (of a dispositive character) conferred on trustees in their fiduciary capacity, on the other hand. It is convenient to refer to these before coming to the authorities directly concerned with the disclosure of trust documents or information.

In the important case of *In re Baden's Deed Trusts* the House of Lords finally settled the vexed question of whether the test for validity, in point of certainty of objects, is the same for trusts and powers, or whether the test for trusts is more demanding. It held the test to be the same. That general question arose in the context of a provision (which the Court of Appeal took to be a power, but the House of Lords held to be a trust) for trustees to distribute income "to or for the benefit of any of the officers and employees or ex-officers or ex-employees of [a named company] or to any relatives or dependants of any such persons" (with a power for the trustees to hold up income which did not, as the House of Lords held, prevent the trustees distributing the retentions as income) …'

Lord Walker then quoted at length from Lord Wilberforce's opinion … and continued:

'The passage gives a very clear and eminently realistic account of both the points of difference and the similarities between a discretionary trust and a fiduciary dispositive power. The outstanding point of difference is of course that under a discretionary trust of income, distribution of income (within a reasonable time) is mandatory, the trustees' discretion being limited to the choice of the recipients and the shares in which they are to take. If there is a small, closed class of discretionary objects who are

all sui juris, their collective entitlement gives them a limited power of disposition over the income subject to the discretionary trust. … But the possibility of such a collective disposition will be rare, and on his own the object of a discretionary trust has no more of an assignable or transmissible interest than the object of a mere power.

Apart from the test of certainty being the same and the fact that an individual's interest or right is non-assignable, there are other practical similarities between the positions of the two types of object. Either has the negative power to block a family arrangement or similar transaction proposed to be effected under the rule in *Saunders* v *Vautier* (unless in the case of a power the trustees are specially authorised to release, that is to say extinguish, it). Both have a right to have their claims properly considered by the trustees. But if the discretion is exercisable in favour of a very wide class the trustees need not survey mankind from China to Peru (as Harman J, echoing Dr Johnson, said in *In re Gestetner's Settlement*) if it is clear who are the prime candidates for the exercise of the trustees' discretion.

That thought was developed by Templeman J in *In re Manisty's Settlement*), although he was mainly concerned to contrast the exercise by trustees of an intermediate power (in the sense mentioned above) with the exercise by trustees of a wide special power. He said … that a wide power, whether special or intermediate, does not negative or prohibit a sensible approach by trustees to the consideration and exercise of their powers. …

However, in *Mettoy Pension Trustees Ltd* v *Evans* … took a broader view of the court's power to intervene in the case of a fiduciary dispositive power. …

In *In re Londonderry's Settlement* the Court of Appeal had to consider one of the most important limitations on the right to disclosure of trust documents, that is the need to protect confidentiality in communications between trustees as to the exercise of their dispositive discretions, and in communications made to the trustees by other beneficiaries. That issue can alternatively be seen as an inquiry whether such confidential communications are indeed trust documents. The judgments of the three members of the court (Harman, Dankwerts and Salmon LJJ) are not easy to reconcile. All three referred to *O'Rourke* v *Darbishire* but Harman and Dankwerts LJJ found that Lord Wrenbury's general observations gave little assistance on the issue which concerned them. Only Salmon LJ expressly adopted the proprietary basis of the principle. ...

Their Lordships consider that the more principled and correct approach is to regard the right to seek disclosure of trust documents as one aspect of the court's inherent jurisdiction to supervise, and if necessary to intervene in, the administration of trusts. The right to seek the court's intervention does not depend on entitlement to a fixed and transmissible beneficial interest. The object of a discretion (including a mere power) may also be entitled to protection from a court of equity, although the circumstances in which he may seek protection, and the nature of the protection he may expect to obtain will depend on the court's discretion. ...

Their Lordships are therefore in general agreement with the approach adopted in the judgments of Kirby P and Sheller JA in the Court of Appeal of New South Wales in *Hartigan Nominees Pty Ltd* v *Rydge*. That was a case concerned with disclosure of a memorandum of wishes addressed to the trustees by Sir Norman Rydge (who was in substance, but not nominally, the settlor). Kirby P said:

"I do not consider that it is imperative to determine whether that document is a 'trust document' (as I think it is) or whether the respondent as a beneficiary, has a proprietary interest in it (as I am also inclined to think he does). Much of the law on the subject of access to documents has conventionally been expressed in terms of the 'proprietary interest' in the document of the party seeking access to it. Thus, it has been held that a cestui que trust has a 'proprietary right' to seek all documents relating to the trust ... This

approach is unsatisfactory. Access should not be limited to documents in which a proprietary right may be established. Such rights may be sufficient; but they are not necessary to a right of access which the courts will enforce to uphold the cestui que trust's entitlement to a reasonable assurance of the manifest integrity of the administration of the trust by the trustees. I agree with Professor HAJ Ford's comment, in his book [with Mr W A Lee] *Prinicples of the Law of Trusts*, 2nd edn (1990) Sydney Law Book Co, p425, that the equation of rights of inspection of trust documents with the beneficiaries' equitable rights of property in the trust assets 'gives rise to far more problems than it solves ... the legal title and rights to possession are in the trustees: all the beneficiary has are equitable rights against the trustees ... The beneficiariy's rights to inspect trust documents are founded therefore not upon any equitable proprietary right which he or she may have in respect of those documents but upon the trustee's fiduciary duty to keep the beneficiary informed and to render accounts. It is the extent of that duty that is in issue. The equation of the right to inspect trust documents with the beneficiary's equitable proprietary rights gives rise to unnecessary and undesirable consequences. It results in the drawing of virtually incomprehensible distinctions between documents which are trust documents and those which are not; it casts doubts upon the rights of beneficiaries who cannot claim to have an equitable proprietary interest in the trust assets, such as the beneficiaries of discretionary trusts; and it may give trustees too great a degree of protection in the case of documents, artificially classified as not being trust documents, and beneficiaries too great a right to inspect the activities of trustees in the case of documents which are, equally artificially, classified as trust documents.'" ...

It will be observed that Kirby P said that for an applicant to have a proprietary right might be sufficient, but was not necessary. In the Board's view it is neither sufficient nor necessary. Since *In re Cowin* well over a century ago, the court has made clear that there may be circumstances (especially of confidentiality) in which even a vested and transmissible beneficial interest is not a sufficient basis for requiring disclosure of trust documents; and *In re Londonderry's Settlement* and more recent cases have begun to work out in some detail the way in which the court should exercise its discretion in such cases. There are three such areas in which the court may have to form a discretionary judgment: whether a discretionary object (or some other beneficiary with only a remote or wholly defeasible interest) should be granted relief at all; what classes of documents should be disclosed, either completely or in a redacted form; and what safeguards should be imposed (whether by undertakings to the court, arrangements for professional inspection, or otherwise) to limit the use which may be made of documents or information disclosed under the order of the court.

The proprietary basis of a beneficiary's right to disclosure was fully argued before the Staff of Government Division, which, at paragraph 35, accepted the submission (made on behalf of the appellant) that a proprietary interest, although often found, was not necessary. On this part of the case the Board agrees with the conclusion reached by the Staff of Government Division.'

Lord Walker then reviewed recent case law and concluded:

'Their Lordships have already indicated their view that a beneficiary's right to seek disclosure of trust documents, although sometimes not inappropriately described as a proprietary right, is best approached as one aspect of the court's inherent jurisdiction to supervise, and where appropriate intervene in, the administration of trusts. There is therefore in their Lordships' view no reason to draw any bright dividing line either between transmissible and non-transmissible (that is, discretionary) interests, or between the rights of an object of a discretionary trust and those of the object of a mere power (of a fiduciary character). The differences in this context between trusts

and powers are (as Lord Wilberforce demonstrated in *In re Baden*) a good deal less significant than the similarities. The tide of Commonwealth authority, although not entirely uniform, appears to be flowing in that direction.

However, the recent cases also confirm (as has been stated as long ago as *In re Cowin* ... in 1886) that no beneficiary (and least of all a discretionary object) has any entitlement as of right to disclosure of anything which can plausibly be described as a trust document. Especially when there are issues as to personal or commercial confidentiality, the court may have to balance the competing interests of different beneficiaries, the trustees themselves, and third parties. Disclosure may have to be limited and safeguards may have to be put in place. Evaluation of the claims of a beneficiary (and especially of a discretionary object) may be an important part of the balancing exercise which the court has to perform on the materials placed before it. In many cases the court may have no difficulty in concluding that an applicant with no more than a theoretical possibility of benefit ought not to be granted any relief.

It would be inappropriate for the Board to go much further in attempting to give the High Court of the Isle of Man guidance as to the future conduct of this troublesome matter. But their Lordships can, without trespassing on the High Court's discretion, summarise their views on the different components of the appellant's claims:

1. It seems to be common ground that during Mr Schmidt's lifetime substantial distributions were made for his benefit, all or most by allocation of funds to the two companies ... which were regarded as being (in some sense) Mr Schmidt's. The appellant as Mr Schmidt's personal representative does not accept that these funds have been fully accounted for. His contention is that in respect of allocated funds Mr Schmidt ceased to be a mere discretionary object, and became absolute owner. On the face of it the appellant (as personal representative) seems to have a powerful case for the fullest disclosure in respect of these funds.

2. The appellant as personal representative would also, on the face of it, have a strong claim to disclosure of documents or information relevant to the issue whether, but for the breaches of fiduciary duty (such as for instance overcharging) more funds would have been available for distribution to Mr Schmidt, and would or might have been allocated to him in practice. The Board express no view whatever as to whether the appellant has a case for overcharging or any other breach of fiduciary duty. But claims of that sort have been put forward in the 1998 proceedings, and the possibility must be noted in order to make the position clear.

3. As regards the appellant's personal claims under the Angora Trust since his father's death, his status as a beneficiary of any sort depends on the issue of construction discussed … above.

4. As regards the Everest Trust, the appellant is a possible object of the very wide power in clause 3.3 … but an object who may be regarded … as having exceptionally strong claims to be considered.

Their Lordships will therefore humbly advise Her Majesty that the appeal should be allowed, the order of Deemster Cain restored and the matter remitted to the High Court of the Isle of Man for further consideration in the light of the Board's judgment.'

Comment

Lord Walker stresses that the source of the beneficiary's right to the production of certain trust documents is the trustee's fiduciary duty of disclosure rather than any proprietary right vested in the beneficiary. This widens the application of the rules of access to such documents to include claimants such as Vadim Schmidt applying to the court in his own right and also as his father's personal representative.

Thompson's Settlement, Re [1985] 3 All ER 720 Chancery Division (Vinelott J)

• *Fiduciary self-dealing*

Facts

In 1954 the settlor created a settlement for the benefit of his grandchildren and appointed his two sons, A and B, and his son-in-law as trustees. The settlement comprised substantial agricultural estates including, inter alia, an estate in Scotland, 'the Coupar estate', and an estate in Norfolk, 'the Brancaster estate'. The conveyances of these estates to the trustees provided that a trustee could purchase the estates concerned either at public auction or by private contract provided that in the case of a private contract the sale was conducted by the trustees other than the purchasing trustee. At the date of the settlement the estates were left to a farming company, 'the old company', of which the settlor, his wife and A and B were the directors. When the settlor died in 1964 it was agreed by the settlor's family and the directors that the old company should be wound up. On the dissolution of the old company the lease of the Coupar estate was taken over by a new company belonging to A and his family and the lease of the Brancaster estate was taken over by a partnership between B and his sons. The old company did not assign the leases in either case. In 1969 A and B, as trustees, of the settlement, executed a lease of the Coupar estate in favour of the new company belonging to A and his family. B and his sons had taken possession of the Brancaster estate on the assumption that there had been a valid transfer of the lease to them by the old company. The possibility of appropriating the various trust estates between the three branches of the settlor's family subsequently arose. An issue which emerged from this possibility was whether the Coupar estate and the Brancaster estate should be valued for the purposes of appropriation as being subject to farming tenancies or with vacant possession. In this context the question whether the self-dealing rule had been broken by A and B arose because of their positions as trustees of the settlement and as respective members of the new company and partnership to which leases of the estates had been granted. As trustees of the settlement their concurrence in the assignment of leases in trust property was necessary.

Held

A and B, as trustees, had put themselves in a position when their interest and duty conflicted because they were interested in the company and the partnership which had taken over the leases. Consequently they were precluded from dealing in their capacity as trustees with themselves in their respective capacities as managing director of the company and a member of the partnership.

Vinelott J:

'The first submission of Mr Price was that the self-dealing rule has no application to a sale by trustees to a company, although if any of the trustees has an interest in the company the transaction falls within the fair-dealing rule. He founded this submission on the well-known case of *Farrar* v *Farrars Ltd*. In that case three mortgagees were in possession of the mortgaged property. One of them, J R Farrar, was also solicitor to the mortgagees. The property was sold to a company which was to some extent promoted by J R Farrar and in which he took a small shareholding and for which he also acted as solicitor. He took no part in the negotiation. An action to set aside the transaction failed. Lindley J said:

"A sale by a person to a corporation of which he is a member is not, either in form or in substance, a sale by a person to himself. To hold that it is would be to ignore the principle which lies at the root of the idea of a corporate body, and that idea is that the corporate body is distinct from the persons composing it. A sale by a member of a corporation to the corporation itself is in every sense a sale valid in equity as well as at law. There is no authority for saying that such a sale is not warranted by any ordinary power of sale ... Mr Farrar was not a trustee selling to himself, or to others for him, nor was he buying directly or indirectly for himself, and although a sale by a mortgagee to a company promoted by himself, of which he is the solicitor, and in which he has

shares, is one the company must prove to have been bona fide and at a price at which the mortgagees could properly sell, yet, if such proves to be the fact, there is no rule of law which compels the Court to set aside the sale. *Ex parte Lacey* does not require the Court to hold the sale invalid, however fair and honest it may be, although the judgment in that case does throw upon the company the burden of shewing that the sale was fair and honest."

I do not think that this case assists Mr Price. A was not at the material time simply a shareholder in the new company. He and his wife were directors of the new company and he was its managing director. Their duty as directors was to further the interests of the new company in which, as it happened, they held a majority of the shares at the time of the purported assignment of the lease of the Coupar Grange estate. The position as between the trustees of the grandchildren's settlement and the directors of the new company is the same as it would have been if A had been a trustee of a settlement instead of a director of a company ... B, of course, as a partner is a farming partnership was ...

... In the instant case the concurrence of the trustees of the grandchildren's settlement was required if the leases were to be assigned to or new tenancies created in favour of the new company or partnership. The beneficiaries were entitled to ask that the trustees should give unprejudiced consideration to the question whether they should refuse to concur in the assignments in the expectation that a surrender of the leases might be negotiated from the old company and the estates sold or let on the open market ...

... As I have said, no assignment of the leases was ever executed. In the case of the Brancaster estate the legal title to the lease remained with the old company which has long since been dissolved. Apart from the operation of the self-dealing rule the oral agreement of 5th July 1966 coupled with the subsequent taking of possession of the estate by the partnership would have given rise to a contract enforceable by specific performance. The effect of the application of the rule is that no enforceable contract came into existence. Accordingly there is no valid lease of the estate in favour of the partnership ...'

Comment
Even when there is apparent permission in the trust deed for the trustees to deal in the trust property, the self-dealing rule will be strictly applied by the court strictly in accordance with the terms of the trust deed.

Tito v *Waddell (No 2)* [1977] Ch 106 Chancery Division (Megarry V-C)

• *The self-dealing rule and the fair dealing rule*

Facts
This was a complex case described by Megarry V-C as 'litigation on a grand scale', involving the inhabitants of Banaba Island, known as Ocean Island, a former British Protectorate. Phosphates were mined from the islands and a royalty paid to the islanders, which was considerably less than the islanders believed it should be. In these proceedings they claimed that the Crown, as responsible authority, was subject to a trust for the benefit of the islanders, and was in breach of trust.

Held
If there was a trust it was not a trust in the legal sense, in that it was not one enforceable by the courts. In the course of a wide-ranging judgment, Sir Robert Megarry V-C said on the subject of the self-dealing rule, which he called a disability rather than a duty of the trustee:

'The ... rule is that if a trustee purchases the beneficial interest of any of his beneficiaries, the transaction is not voidable ex debito justitiae, but can be set aside by the beneficiary unless the trustee can show that he has taken no advantage of his position and has made full disclosure to the beneficiary, and that the transaction is fair and honest.'

Comment
This is the case where the self-dealing rule and the fair-dealing rule were formulated by Sir Robert Megarry V-C.

Walker and Others v *Stones and Another* [2000] 4 All ER 412 Court of Appeal (Nourse and Mantell LJJ, Sir Christopher Slade)

• *Breach of trust – whether rule that shareholders cannot recover for company's loss applied to beneficiaries where trust property was majority shareholding in company – liability of partners of solicitor trustees – test for honesty of trustees*

Facts
The defendants were partners in a firm of solicitors and were trustees of a trust (the Bacchus Trust) which was set up for the benefit of his children by George Walker, the chairman of BWG plc. The main trust asset was controlling shares in a holding company which in turn owned a number of companies including Jasaro Ltd. In 1989 Stones, one of the solicitors, in his capacity as trustee, guaranteed a bank loan to Jasaro, the purpose of which was to raise finance through a bond issue for BWG which was in severe financial difficulties. As a result, Jasaro became insolvent and since the trust could not honour its guarantee, the lenders took control of the holding company. The beneficiaries brought an action for breach of trust, claiming that the trustees had exercised their discretionary powers, not for the benefit of the beneficiaries but for the benefit of George Walker and that the transactions were manifestly to their disadvantage since, as a result, the net assets of the Bacchus Trust lost their value. The trustees pleaded the exemption clause in the trust deed which excluded liability as follows:

'In the professed execution of the trusts and powers hereof no Trustee shall be liable
   (i) for any loss to the Trust Fund arising

by reason of any improper investment made in good faith or in consequence of the failure depreciation or loss of any improper investment made in good faith by such Trustee or by any other Trustee or by any delegate or agent appointed in good faith

(ii) for the negligence or fraud of any agent employed by such Trustee although the employment of such agent was not necessary or expedient provided such employment of such agent was in good faith

(iii) by reason of any mistake or omission made in good faith by any Trustee

(iv) by reason of any other matter or thing other than wilful fraud or dishonesty on the part of the Trustee whom it is sought to make liable …'

The trust deed gave the trustees very wide powers of investment.

Held

1. Following *Re Lucking's Will Trusts*, shareholders were not deprived of an action when they could show that the breach of conduct complained of was a breach of another duty owed to the claimant personally rather than as a shareholder.
2. Subject only to the exception for dishonesty, the exemption clause excluded the liability of the trustees for the behaviour complained of.
3. In the case of a solicitor trustee it was not sufficient to ask whether the trustee genuinely believed that they were acting honestly. The test was that, by an objective standard, no reasonable trustee could have believed that what they were doing was for the benefit of the trustees.
4. On this basis, Stones was liable for the breaches complained of but Osborne, the other defendant, was protected by the exemption clause.
5. Breaches of trust committed by a partner in a firm fell outside the ordinary course of the firm's business and the partners were therefore not vicariously liable.

Sir Christopher Slade:

'It is true that the powers of investment and charging trust assets conferred by the trust deed are very wide. However, the mere fact that a trustee is acting within the letter of his powers does not necessarily absolve him from a charge of breach of trust. Subject to the operation of any exemption clause contained in the trust deed, his powers must be exercised reasonably and in good faith and for the purposes for which they were created; he must exercise them in a proper way for the legitimate purposes of the trust …

The normal responsibility of a trustee with a controlling shareholding is set out in the judgment of Brightman J in *Bartlett* v *Barclays Bank Trust Co Ltd* as follows:

"The bank, as trustee, was bound to act in relation to the shares and to the controlling position which they conferred, in the same manner as a prudent man of business. The prudent man of business will act in such manner as is necessary to safeguard his investment. He will do this in two ways. If facts come to his knowledge which tell him that the company's affairs are not being conducted as they should be, or which put him on enquiry, he will take appropriate action. Appropriate action will no doubt consist in the first instance of enquiry of and consultation with the directors, and in the last but most unlikely resort, the convening of a general meeting to replace one or more directors. What the prudent man of business will not do is to content himself with the receipt of such information on the affairs of the company as a shareholder ordinarily receives at annual general meetings. Since he has the power to do so, he will go further and see that he has sufficient information to enable him to make a responsible decision from time to time either to let matters proceed as they are proceeding, or to intervene if he is dissatisfied."

I shall from time to time hereafter refer to the principles thus stated by Brightman J as "the *Bartlett* principles".

The trustees had a controlling interest in JSR Estates, which itself had a controlling interest in Jasaro. By virtue of these interests, they could, if they had chosen, have intervened with the object of preventing the bond issue transactions proceeding. So far from intervening, at least Mr Stones appears to have co-operated in them throughout and indeed on behalf of the trustees executed the guarantee and charge in respect of the shares in JSR Estates. He was present at the meeting at which Jason [one of the directors of Jasaro] signed the three relevant documents required of Jasaro. It appears that, as pleaded, the trustees were acting in reliance on an indemnity from Mr Walker and that even if not, as pleaded, acting at his direction, they may well have been acting on his strong persuasion. It is pleaded – and there is no evidence to suggest the contrary – that they took no steps to satisfy themselves as to any fact or matter which could have enabled them to evaluate the consequences of the bond issue transactions for the Bacchus trust beneficiaries – which in the event turned out to be disastrous.

In the circumstances and on the evidence before us, the appellants have in my judgment established at least a triable issue in their contention that, whether or not they equated the interests of the three children with those of Mr Walker, the trustees entered into or co-operated in the bond issue transactions primarily with the intention of benefiting Mr Walker, Birdcage Walk and BWG and correspondingly did so in breach of trust:

(a) because of clause 20(b) of the Bacchus trust deed which precluded the trustees from exercising any power of discretion themselves in any manner which might benefit an excepted person; and, quite apart from this point;

(b) because they did not exercise their power in a proper way with proper prudence as would a prudent man of business.

This conclusion, however, must be subject to the effect of the two trustee exemption clauses, 14 and 15, contained in the Bacchus trust deed, which assume cardinal importance in this context as will be discussed below. ...

We have been told that it was the judge himself who suggested in the course of argument that in the light of the *Prudential Assurance* case [*Prudential Assurance Co Ltd* v *Newman Industries Ltd*] a beneficiary cannot sue a trustee for allowing damage to be caused to a company in which the trust has a controlling interest when the company itself has a cause of action entitling it to recover for the wrong done to it. In such circumstances, he suggested, no one could sue for a diminution in the value of the shares and only the company concerned could sue for the wrong. This point of law was then adopted and argued on behalf of the trustees and in due course upheld by the judge. He held that (a) the reformulated claims against the trustees in respect of the alleged diversion of funds of Jasaro, Holt and SHL and (b) the allegation of breach of trust contained in the reamended statement of claim, based on their allowing Jasaro to enter into the bond issue transactions must fail because of the *Prudential Assurance* principle. He defined that principle as being:

"in essence that a shareholder in a company cannot sue for damages in respect of the diminution in value of the shares held by him caused by a wrong to the company at least when the company itself has a cause of action entitling it to recover for the wrong to it."

That was, on the facts precisely the situation in the *Prudential Assurance* case itself. In that case, the claimants alleged that:

(a) the defendant directors of Newman Industries Ltd (Newman) had made a fraudulent misrepresentation in a circular to its shareholders concerning the true value of certain assets;

(b) as a result Newman had proceeded to acquire those assets at a loss; and

(c) as a further result the claimants' shares in Newman had diminished in value.

The Court of Appeal held (in effect) that the claimants' claim against the defendant directors was an action to recover damages on the basis that Newman, the company in which the claimants were shareholders, had suffered loss; and that, since the claimants' rights as the holders of shares was merely a right of participation in the company on the terms of its articles of association and any damage done to the company had not affected that right, their claim was misconceived.

The same principle was applied in *Stein* v *Black*, a decision on which the judge also heavily relied. In that case the claimant and the first defendant each held 50 per cent of the issued shares in various companies. The claimant asserted that the first defendant had misappropriated assets of these companies and claimed damages based on the diminution in the value of his shareholdings. He argued that in the unusual circumstances of the case the first defendant owed him personally a fiduciary duty, the breach of which had caused him financial loss. After referring to this submission, Millett LJ said:

> "But that is not the problem. The problem is that the only conduct relied upon as constituting a breach of that duty, however it is described and in whatever detail it is set out, is nevertheless the misappropriation of assets belonging to the old companies, so that the only loss suffered by the plaintiff consists of the diminution in the value of his shareholding by reason of the misappropriation of the assets of the companies in which those shares subsist. Such loss would be fully remedied by the restitution of the value of the misappropriated assets to the companies. It is not alleged that the plaintiff has been induced or compelled to dispose of his shares in the companies at an undervalue by reason of the diminution in value of their assets, he still has them. If the plaintiff were allowed to recover for the diminution in the value of his shares, and the old companies for the misappropriation of their assets, the plaintiff would have double recovery."

An obvious and important distinction between the facts of the present case and those of the *Prudential Assurance* case and *Stein*'s case is that here the claimant beneficiaries were not shareholders of the companies Holt, SHL and Jasaro, whose assets are alleged to have been misappropriated, or of their parent company JSR Estates. Mr Trevor Philipson QC for the appellants has submitted that the *Prudential Assurance* principle does not preclude an action for breach of trust by beneficiaries against trustees who have caused or allowed the value of a trust shareholding to be diminished by causing or allowing the assets of the relevant company, or a subsidiary or sub-subsidiary of such company, to be dissipated by improper diversions or use of its assets.

And indeed a claim of this very nature was allowed by Cross J in *Re Lucking's Will Trusts* (an important authority which was apparently not cited to Rattee J). In that case the defendants were trustees of a will. The trust holdings included a majority holding in a private company. The first defendant's niece had a life interest in one eighth of the estate and an absolute interest in another one eighth. Having acquired knowledge that the managing director was withdrawing substantial sums from the company, the first defendant, who was a director of the company, failed adequately to supervise the managing director's drawings. In an action brought against the trustees by the niece, Cross J held … that the loss with which he was concerned was the decrease in value of the trust shares in consequence of the overdrawings and that the claimant was entitled to recover a proportionate part of this decrease in value.

On the findings of fact in that case, it seems clear that the company itself would have had a cause of action against the first defendant in his capacity as director. But Cross J did not regard this as precluding an action by the beneficiary against him in his capacity as trusts. He said:

> "He cannot say that what he knew or ought to have known about the company's affairs he knew or ought to have known simply as a director with a duty to the company and no-one else. He was in the position he was partly as a representative of the trust and, if and so far as he failed in his duty to the company, he

also failed in his duty to the trust. To hold this is not, as I see it, inconsistent with any principle to be found in *Salomon*'s case."

(The well-known principle of *Salomon* v *Salomon & Co* is that a company is in law an entity quite distinct from its shareholders.)

Re Lucking's Will Trusts was applied by Brightman J in *Bartlett*'s case where he held that the claimants who were beneficiaries under a trust, which (until sale) had formerly had a majority holding in a company, were entitled to compensation by the trustee for loss resulting from its having permitted the company to engage in hazardous speculation in property development.'

Sir Christopher then reviewed the company law authorities and continued:

'From all these authorities … I conclude that the *Prudential Assurance* principle will not operate to deprive a claimant of an otherwise good cause of action in a case where

(a) the claimant can establish that the defendant's conduct has constituted a breach of some legal duty owed to him personally (whether under the law of contract, torts, trusts or any other branch of the law) and

(b) on its assessment of the facts, the court is satisfied that such breach of duty has caused him personal loss, separate and distinct from any loss that may have been occasioned to any corporate body in which he may be financially interested.

… Enough has been said to demonstrate that in concluding that the claim of dishonesty against Mr Stones must fail, the judge was applying a subject test based entirely on Mr Stones' own perception and his own state of mind. In adopting that approach, the judge placed much reliance on his interpretation of the recent decision of this court in *Armitage* v *Nurse*. In that case the court had to consider the construction and effect of a trustees' indemnity clause in the following terms:

"No Trustee shall be liable for any loss or damage which may happen to Paula's fund or any part thereof or the income

thereof at any time or from any cause whatsoever *unless such loss or damage shall be caused by his own actual fraud* …" (Millett LJ's emphasis)

As Millett LJ, in delivering the judgment of the court, said, the clause was "apt to exclude liability for breach of trust in the absence of a dishonest intention on the part of the trustee whose conduct is impugned". I see no material distinction between that clause and clause 15(1)(a)(iv) of the Bacchus trust deed. Millett LJ continued:

"The common law knows no generalised tort of fraud. *Derry* v *Peek* was an action for damages for deceit, that is to say, for fraudulent misrepresentation. In such a case fraud must be proved by showing that the false representation was made knowingly, that is to say, without an honest belief in its truth, or recklessly, that is to say, not caring whether it was true or false. Care needs to be taken when these concepts are applied not to a representation but to a breach of trust. Breaches of trust are of many different kinds. A breach of trust may be deliberate or inadvertent; it may consist of an actual misappropriation or misapplication of the trust property or merely of an investment or other dealing which is outside the trustees' powers; it may consist of a failure to carry out a positive obligation of the trustees or merely of a want of skill and care on their part in the management of the trust property; it may be injurious to the interests of the beneficiaries or be actually to their benefit. By consciously acting beyond their powers (as, for example, by making an investment which they know to be unauthorised) the trustees may deliberately commit a breach of trust; but if they do so in good faith and in the honest belief that they are acting in the interest of the beneficiaries their conduct is not fraudulent. So a deliberate breach of trust is not necessarily fraudulent. Hence the remark famously attributed to Selwyn LJ by Lindley MR in the course of argument in *Perrins* v *Bellamy* 'My old master, the late Lord Justice Selwyn, used to say, "The main duty of a trustee is to commit *judicious* breaches of trust" '… The expression 'actual fraud' in cl 15 is not used to describe the common law tort of deceit. As the judge appreciated it simply means dishonesty. I accept the formulation put forward by Mr Hill on behalf of the respondents which (as I have slightly modified it) is that it 'connotes at the minimum an intention on the part of the trustee to pursue a particular course of action, either knowing that it is contrary to the interests of the beneficiaries or being recklessly indifferent whether it is contrary to their interests or not.' It is the duty of a trustee to manage the trust property and deal with it in the interests of the beneficiaries. If he acts in a way which he does not honestly believe is in their interests then he is acting dishonestly. It does not matter whether he stands or thinks he stands to gain personally from his actions. A trustee who acts with the intention of benefiting persons who are not the objects of the trust is not the less dishonest because he does not intend to benefit himself. In my judgment cl 15 exempts the trustee from liability for loss or damage to the trust property no matter how indolent, imprudent, lacking in diligence, negligent or wilful he may have been, so long as he has not acted dishonestly."

From this passage, Rattee J derived two propositions. First, the deliberate commission of a breach of trust is not necessarily dishonest. Second, it is only dishonest if the trustee committing it does so "either knowing that it is contrary to the interests of the beneficiaries, or being recklessly indifferent whether it is contrary to their interests or not". From this second proposition he derived support for a third proposition which he had stated earlier in his judgment as follows: "It seems to me impossible to call a trustee's conduct dishonest in any ordinary sense of that word, even if he knew he was acting in breach of the terms of the trust, if he so acted in a genuine (even if misguided) belief that what he was doing was for the benefit of the beneficiaries." This third proposition, though not expressly repeated, is reflected by necessary inference ... from which it is clear that the judge took

the view that Mr Stones could not be held to have acted dishonestly in relation to any of his conduct for which he is attacked in these proceedings if he genuinely believed it to have been in the best interests of the Bacchus trust beneficiaries.

This third proposition, which is a crucially important feature of Mr Purle's argument on this appeal, at first sight derives strong support from Millett LJ's dictum that "if they do so in good faith and in the honest belief that they are acting in the interests of the beneficiaries their conduct is not fraudulent".

With respect, however, I find myself unable to agree with the third proposition, if stated without qualification. At least in the case of a solicitor-trustee, a qualification must in my opinion be necessary to take account of the case where the trustee's so-called "honest belief", though actually held, is so unreasonable that, by any objective standard, no reasonable solicitor-trustee could have thought that what he did or agreed to do was for the benefit of the beneficiaries. I limit this proposition to the case of a solicitor-trustee, first because on the facts before us we are concerned only with solicitor-trustees and secondly because I accept that the test of honesty may vary from case to case, depending on, among other things, the role and calling of the trustee: compare *Twinsectra Ltd* v *Yardley* ... In that case the court regarded the standard of honesty applicable to the case of the defendant solicitor, Mr Leach, as being "that to be expected of a reasonably prudent and honest solicitor".

The word "honest" at first sight points exclusively to a state of mind. But, as the *Twinsectra Ltd* case illustrates, its scope cannot be so limited. A person may in some cases act dishonestly, according to the ordinary use of language, even though he genuinely believes that his action is morally justified. The penniless thief, for example, who picks the pocket of a multi-millionaire is dishonest even though he genuinely considers the theft is morally justified as a fair redistribution of wealth and that he is not therefore being dishonest.

... There is no obvious difference of emphasis between the judgments in the *Royal Brunei Airlines* case and *Armitage*'s case so far as they relate to the concept of dishonesty and it has been suggested that they may be irreconcilable. I do not think they are. The decision in the *Royal Brunei Airlines* case was cited to the Court of appeal in *Armitage*'s case. Millett LJ did not purport to distinguish the *Royal Brunei Airlines* case, either on the grounds that it related to the liability of accessories or on any other grounds. As already stated, I can see no grounds for applying a different test of honesty in the context of a trustee exemption clause such as clause 15 of the Bacchus trust deed, from that applicable to the liability of an accessory in a breach of trust. It would be surprising if the court in *Armitage*'s case had regarded itself as differing from the *Royal Brunei Airlines* case without saying so or explaining why. I think that in the relevant passage from his judgment quoted above ... and in particular in saying that if trustees deliberately commit a breach of trust they are not dishonest provided that "they do so in good faith and in the honest belief that they are acting in the interests of the beneficiaries" Millett LJ was directing his mind to the not uncommon case of what Selwyn LJ had once described as "judicious breaches of trust". I think it most unlikely that he would have intended this dictum to apply in a case where a solicitor trustee's perception of the interests of the beneficiaries was so unreasonable that no reasonable solicitor-trustee could have held such belief. Indeed in my opinion such a construction of the clause could well render it inconsistent with the very existence of an effective trust.

Millett LJ analysed the permitted scope of trustee-exemption clauses in *Armitage* v *Nurse*. His analysis in my judgment clearly illustrates the need, as a matter of policy, for the courts to construe clauses of this nature no more widely than their language on a fair reading requires. I cannot believe it would be the intention of the draftsmen of clauses such as clause 15 of the Bacchus trust deed to exempt trustees from liability for a breach of trust in a case such as that postulated at the end of the immediately preceding paragraph.

For all these reasons the judge in my judgment erred in his approach to the construction of the effect of clause 15(1)(a)(iv) of the Bacchus trust deed. That clause in my judgment would not exempt the trustees from liability for breaches of trust, even if committed in the genuine belief that the course taken by them was in the interests of the beneficiaries, if such belief was so unreasonable that no reasonable solicitor-trustee could have held that belief.'

Comment

The Court of Appeal applied a standard of care to solicitor-trustees, pre-empting the statutory standard of care in s1 of the Trustee Act 2000 which enables the particular expertise and circumstances of the trustees to be taken into consideration.

11 Investment of Trust Funds

Bartlett v *Barclays Bank Trust Co (No 1)* [1980] Ch 515 Chancery Division (Brightman J)

• *Trustee's duty of care – special expertise*

Facts

The bank was the trustee of a trust which consisted of 99.8 per cent of the shares in a private company. The trust was created in 1920 and in 1960 the bank needed to raise money to pay death duties on interests in the settlement. It asked the board of the private company to consider the possibility of going public to raise the necessary money. The board said going public would be easier if the company went into property development. The bank did not object to this and subsequently the company engaged in two projects in property development. One project was a disaster while the other was quite profitable, but not sufficiently so to prevent an overall loss on both projects. The beneficiaries brought an action against the bank, claiming it was liable to make good the loss in that it never should have allowed the board of the company to go into property development. In the circumstances, the bank claimed it was entitled to rely on the calibre of the board for investment information and further that, if it could not it ought fairly to be excused under s61 of the Trustee Act 1925.

Held

It was a trustee's duty to conduct trust business with the care of a reasonably prudent man of business. In the case of a professional corporate trustee, such as the bank, the duty of care was higher and the bank was liable for loss caused to a trust by neglect to exercise the special care and skill it professed to have. The bank was under a duty as trustee to ensure it received an adequate flow of information concerning the activities of the board to ensure that it did not embark on hazardous projects and to prevent these from becoming a disaster. In this case, the bank confined itself to such information as it received from the board at annual general meetings. The bank was, therefore, in breach of trust and liable for the loss. Furthermore, the bank was not entitled to rely on s61 of the Trustee Act 1925 as a defence for, although it had acted 'honestly', it had not acted 'reasonably' within s61 and it would in any case be unfair to excuse the bank at the expense of the beneficiaries.

Brightman J considered *Re Lucking*:

'I do not understand Cross J to have been saying that in every case where trustees have a controlling interest in a company, it is their duty to ensure that one of their number is a director or that they have a nominee on the board who will report from time to time on the affairs of the company. He was merely outlining convenient methods by which a prudent man of business (as also a trustee) with a controlling interest in a private company, can place himself in a position to make an informed decision whether any action is appropriate to be taken for the protection of his asset. Other methods may be equally satisfactory and convenient, depending on the circumstances of the individual case ...'

Comment

In this case the court was prepared to recognise that a corporate trustee owed a higher duty of care than a lay trustee.

British Museum (Trustees of the) v *Attorney-General* [1984] 1 All ER 337 Chancery Division (Megarry V-C)

• *Court's power to change powers of investment in changing circumstances*

Facts

In 1960 the Court approved a scheme relating to the investment of funds belonging to the British Museum. By this scheme a number of separate funds were consolidated into three pools, each pool being earmarked for different purposes with special provisions relating to the capital and income thereof. The result of these arrangements was that the fund was until about 1983 able to keep pace with inflation. However, steep rises in the price of museum pieces and the reduction of grants from public funds meant that this could no longer be done and the trustees asked the court to approve a new scheme to enable the balance to be restored to some extent.

Held

A revised version of the scheme would be approved.

Sir Robert Megarry V-C:

'From what I have said it will be seen that much of what I say depends to a greater or lesser extent on the special position of the trustees and the trust funds in the case before me. On the other hand, there is much that is of more general application, and it may be convenient if I attempt to summarise my views.

(1) In my judgment , the principle laid down in the line of cases headed by *Re Kolb's Will Trusts* is one that should no longer be followed, since conditions have changed so greatly in the last 20 years. Though authoritative, those cases were authorities rebus sic stantibus; and in 1983 they bind no longer. However, if Parliament acts on the recommendations of the Law Reform Committee and replaces the 1961 Act with revised powers of investment, the *Kolb* principle may well become applicable

once more. Until then, the court should be ready to grant suitable applications for the extension of trustees' powers of investment, judging each application on its merits, and without being constrained by the provisions of the 1961 Act.

(2) In determining what extended powers of investment should be conferred, there are many matters which will have to be considered. I shall refer to five, without in any way suggesting that this list is exhaustive, or that anything I say is intended to fetter the discretion that the court has to exercise in each case.

(i) The court is likely to give great weight to the width and efficacy of any provisions for advice and control. The wider the powers, the more important these provisions will be. An existing system of proven efficacy, as here, is likely to be especially cogent.

(ii) Where the powers are of great width, as in the present case, there is much to be said for some scheme of fractional division, confining part of the fund to relatively safe investments, and allowing the other part to be used for investments in which the greater risks will be offset by substantial prospects of a greater return. On the other hand, when the powers are appreciably less wide than they are in the present case, I would in general respectfully concur with the views expressed by the Law Reform Committee that no division of the fund into fractions should be required, and that the only division should be into investments which require advice and those which do not. Nevertheless, although a division of the fund into fractions should not be essential, there may well be cases where such a division may be of assistance in obtaining the approval of the court.

(iii) The width of the powers in the present scheme seems to me to be at or near the extreme limit for charitable funds. Without the fractional division of the fund and the assurance of effective control and advice I very much doubt whether such a scheme could have been approved. What the court has to judge is the combined effect of width, division, advice and control, which all interact, together with the standing of the trustees.

(iv) The size of the fund in question is very material. A fund that is very large may well justify a latitude of investment that would be denied to a more modest fund; for the spread of investments possible for a larger fund may justify the greater risks that wider powers will permit to be taken.

(v) The object of the trust may be very material. In the present case, the desirability of having an increase of capital value which will make possible the purchase of desirable acquisitions for the museum despite soaring prices does something to justify the greater risks whereby capital appreciation may be obtained ...'

Comment

While emphasising that his list is not exhaustive, Sir Robert Megarry gives clear guidelines on when it would be appropriate to vary the trustees' investment powers. If the new proposals to vary trustees' investment powers are implemented, *Re Kolb* may well be applied by the court since Parliament will set the criteria and the court will be reluctant to interfere with their recent legislation.

Cowan v Scargill [1984] 3 WLR 501
Chancery Division (Sir Robert Megarry V-C)

• *Trustee's duty to act in the best financial interests of the beneficiaries – ethical investment policies*

Facts

The Mineworkers' Pension Scheme was a trust to provide pensions and lump sums on retirement, injury and certain diseases, and payments for widows and children of those involved in coal mining. The scheme had wide powers of investment and had over £200 million for investment each year. There were ten trustees of the scheme, five appointed by the National Coal Board (the plaintiffs) and five by the National Union of Mineworkers

(the defendants). In 1982 the defendants refused to approve an annual investment plan unless it was amended so that: (a) there was no increase in the percentage of overseas investment; (b) overseas investments already made be withdrawn at the most opportune time; and (c) that there should be no investment in energy industries which were in direct competition with coal. The plaintiffs sought directions as to whether the defendants were in breach of their fiduciary duties.

Held

1. The defendants, as trustees of a pension fund, were governed by the ordinary law of trusts. But as trustees of a pension fund the duty to do the best they could for their beneficiaries had particular relevance because many of those who benefited from the pension scheme had contributed to the pension fund. Further, they could not restrict their range of investments but were under a duty to take advantage of the full range of investment powers granted to them. Accordingly, the defendants, as trustees, could not refuse to concur in making an investment for social or political reasons, as here, when such an investment was in the financial interest of the beneficiaries of the pension fund.

2. The defendants' policy was to further the interests of the mining industry by refusing to concur in investments in energy industries in direct competition with coal. This was not in the best interests of the beneficiaries of the pension fund because most of them had retired from the coal industry or were women and children who had never been engaged in the industry. The defendants were, thus in breach of fiduciary duties.

Sir Robert Megarry V-C:

'I turn to the law. The starting point is the duty of trustees to exercise their powers in the best interests of the present and future beneficiaries of the trust, holding the scales impartially between different classes of beneficiaries. The duty of the trustees towards their beneficiaries is paramount. They must, of course, obey the law; but subject to that, they must put the interests of the beneficiaries first. When the purpose of the trust is to provide financial benefits for the beneficiaries, as is usually the case, the best interests of the beneficiaries are normally their best financial interests. In the case of a power of investment, as in the present case, the power must be exercised so as to yield the best return for the beneficiaries, judged in relation to the risks of the investments in question; and the prospects of the yield of incomes and capital appreciation both have to be considered in judging the return from the investment ...

... This leads me to the second point, which is a corollary of the first. In considering the investments to make trustees must put on one side their own personal interests and views. Trustees may have strongly held social or political views. They may be firmly opposed to any investment in South Africa or other countries, or they may object to any form of investment in companies concerned with alcohol, tobacco, armaments or many other things. In the conduct of their own affairs, of course, they are free to abstain from making any such investments. Yet under a trust, if investments of this type would be more beneficial to the beneficiaries than other investments, the trustees must not refrain from making the investments by reason of the view they hold.

Trustees may even have to act dishonourably (though not illegally) if the interests of the beneficiaries require it. Thus where trustees for sale struck a bargain for the sale of trust property but had not bound themselves by a legally enforceable contract, they were held to be under a duty to consider and explore a better offer that they received and not to carry through the bargain to which they felt in honour bound: see *Buttle* v *Saunders*.

... Third, by way of caveat I should say that I am not asserting that the benefit of the beneficiaries which a trustee must make his paramount concern inevitably and solely means their financial benefit, even if the only object of the trust is to provide finan-

cial benefits. Thus, if the only actual or potential beneficiaries of a trust are all adults with very strict views on moral and social matters, condemning all forms of alcohol, tobacco and popular entertainment, as well as armaments, I can well understand that it might not be for the "benefit" of such beneficiaries to know that they are obtaining rather larger financial returns under the trust by reason of investments in those activities than they would have received if the trustees had invested the trust funds in other investments. The beneficiaries might well consider that it was far better to receive less than to receive more money from what they consider to be evil and tainted sources. "Benefit" is a word with a very wide meaning, and there are circumstances in which arrangements which work to the financial disadvantage of a beneficiary may yet be for his benefit ...'

Comment

At the time when this case was decided, the members of the pension fund working in the coal industry were a minority. Trustees are generally bound to make investment decisions in the best *financial* interests of the beneficiaries. They cannot use investment policy to further their own moral beliefs.

Harries and Others v *Church Commissioners for England and Another* [1992] 1 WLR 1241 Chancery Division (Sir Donald Nicholls V-C)

• *Trustees' investment duties – profitability of investments vis-à-vis ethical, non monetary considerations*

Facts

The Bishop of Oxford and others applied, by originating summons, for a declaration that the Church Commissioners in administering the funds for which, in effect, they were trustees should operate their investment policy by bearing in mind that 'the underlying purpose for which they held their assets was the promotion of the Christian faith through the Church of England'. The plaintiffs thus argued that the Commissioners should not invest 'in a manner which would be incompatible with that purpose even if it involved a risk of incurring significant financial detriment.'

Held

Declaration refused.

Sir Donald Nicholls VC:

'For some time there have been voices in the Church of England expressing disquiet at the investment policy of the commissioners. They do not question either the good faith or the investment expertise of the commissioners. Their concern is not that the commissioners have failed to get the best financial return from their property and investments. Their concern is that, in making investment decisions, the commissioners are guided too rigorously by purely financial considerations, and that the commissioners give insufficient weight to what are now called "ethical" considerations. They contend, moreover, that the commissioners have fallen into legal error. The commissioners attach overriding importance to financial considerations, and that is a misapprehension of the approach they ought properly to adopt when making investment decisions. The commissioners ought to have in mind that the underlying purpose for which they hold their assets is the promotion of the Christian faith through the Church of England. The commissioners should not exercise their investment functions in a manner which would be incompatible with that purpose even if that involves a risk of incurring significant financial detriment. So these proceedings, seeking declaratory relief, were launched by the Bishop of Oxford, who is himself a church commissioner, the Archdeacon of Bedford and the Rev William Whiffen, a parish priest, with the support of the Christian Ethical Investment Group. This is a body set up in 1988 with the object of "promoting a stronger ethical investment policy in the Church of England". I understand that by an ethical investment policy is meant an investment policy which is not guided solely by financial criteria but which takes into account non-financial considerations deduced from Christian morality.

Charity trustees and investment powers

... It is axiomatic that charity trustees, in common with all other trustees, are concerned to further the purposes of the trust of which they have accepted the office of trustee. That is their duty. To enable them the better to discharge that duty, trustees have powers vested in them. Those powers must be exercised for the purpose for which they have been given: to further the purposes of the trust. That is the guiding principle applicable to the issues in these proceedings. Everything which follows is no more than the reasoned application of that principle in particular contexts.

Broadly speaking, property held by charity trustees falls into two categories. First, there is property held by trustees for what may be called functional purposes. The National Trust owns historic houses and open spaces. The Salvation Army owns hostels for the destitute. And many charities need office accommodation in which to carry out essential administrative work. Second, there is property held by trustees for the purpose of generating money, whether from income or capital growth, with which to further the work of the trust. In other words, property held by trustees as an investment. Where property is so held, prima facie the purposes of the trust will be best served by the trustees seeking to obtain therefrom the maximum return, whether by way of income or capital growth, which is consistent with commercial prudence. That is the starting point for all charity trustees when considering the exercise of their investment powers. Most charities need money; and the more of it there is available, the more the trustees can seek to accomplish.

In most cases this prima facie position will govern the trustees' conduct. In most cases the best interests of the charity require that the trustees' choice of investments should be made solely on the basis of well-established investment criteria, having taken expert advice where appropriate and having due regard to such matters as the need to diversify, the need to balance income against capital growth, and the need to balance risk against return.

In a minority of cases the position will not be so straightforward. There will be some cases, I suspect, comparatively rare, when the objects of the charity are such that investments of a particular type would conflict with the aims of the charity. Much-cited examples are those of cancer research charities and tobacco shares, trustees of temperance charities and brewery and distillery shares, and trustees of charities of the Society of Friends and shares in companies engaged in production of armaments. If, as would be likely, in those examples, trustees were satisfied that investing in a company engaged in a particular type of business would conflict with the very objects their charity is seeking to achieve, they should not so invest. Carried to its logical conclusion the trustees should take this course even if it would be likely to result in significant financial detriment to the charity. The logical conclusion, whilst sound as a matter of legal analysis, is unlikely to arise in practice. It is not easy to think of an instance where in practice the exclusion for this reason of one or more companies or sectors from the whole range of investment open to trustees would be likely to leave them without an adequately wide range of investments from which to choose a properly diversified portfolio.

There will also be some cases, again I suspect comparatively rare, when trustees' holdings of particular investments might hamper a charity's work either by making potential recipients of aid unwilling to be helped because of the source of the charity's money, or by alienating some of those who support the charity financially. In these cases the trustees will need to balance the difficulties they would encounter, or likely financial loss they would sustain, if they were to hold the investments against the risk of financial detriment if those investments were excluded from their portfolio. The greater the risk of financial detriment, the more certain the trustees should be of countervailing disadvantages to the charity before they incur that risk.

Another circumstance where trustees would be entitled, or even required, to take into account non-financial criteria would be where the trust deed so provided.

No doubt there will be other cases where trustees are justified in departing from what should always be their starting point. The instances I have given are not comprehensive. But I must emphasise that of their very nature, and by definition, investments are held by trustees to aid the work of the charity in a particular way: by generating money. That is the purpose for which they are held. That is their raison d'etre. Trustees cannot properly use assets held as an investment for other, viz non-investment purposes. To the extent that they do they are not properly exercising their powers of investment. This is not to say that trustees who own land may not act as responsible landlords or those who own shares may not act as responsible shareholders. They may. The law is not so cynical as to require trustees to behave in a fashion which would bring them or their charity into disrepute (although their consciences must not be to tender: see *Buttle* v *Saunders*). On the other hand, trustees must act prudently. They must not use property held by them for investment purposes as a means for making moral statements at the expense of the charity of which they are trustees. Those who wish may do so with their own property, but that is not a proper function of trustees with trust assets held as an investment.

I should mention one other particular situation. There will be instances today when those who support or benefit from a charity take widely different views on a particular type of investment, some saying that on moral grounds it conflicts with the aims of the charity, others saying the opposite. One example is the holding of arms industry shares by a religious charity. There is real difficulty here. To many questions raising moral issues there are not certain answers. On moral questions widely differing views are held by well-meaning responsible people. This is not always so. But frequently, when questions of the morality of conduct are being canvassed, there is no identifiable yardstick which can be applied to a set of facts so as to yield one answer which can be seen to be "right" and the other "wrong". If that situation confronts trustees of a charity, the law does not require them to find an answer to the unanswerable. Trustees may, if they wish, accommodate the view of those who consider that on moral grounds a particular investment would be in conflict with the objects of the charity, so long as the trustees are satisfied that course would not involve a risk of significant investment decisions on the basis of preferring one view of whether on moral grounds an investment conflicts with the objects of the charity over another. This is so even when one view is more widely supported than the other.

I have sought above to consider charity trustees' duties in relation to investment as a matter of basis principle. I was referred to no authority bearing directly on these matters. My attention was drawn to *Cowan v Scargill*, a case concerning a pension fund. I believe the views I have set out accord with those expressed by Megarry V-C in that case, bearing in mind that he was considering trusts for the provision of financial benefits for individuals. In this case I am concerned with charities, whose purposes are multifarious.'

Comment

The Vice-Chancellor places emphasis on the difficulty of applying moral considerations to investment policy – moral judgments are not certain. There may be conflicting view on issues such as armaments and temperance and the trustees must use their own property to advance their own moral views. Although this case concerned a charitable institution, the possibility of carrying out an ethical invest-

ment policy does not seem to be much greater than in the case of a private trust.

Lucking's Will Trusts, Re [1968] 1 WLR 866 Chancery Division (Cross J)

• *Trustees' liabilities*

Facts

Nearly 70 per cent of the shares in a prosperous family company manufacturing show accessories were held by two trustees, Lucking and Block, as part of the estate of the deceased; about 29 per cent belonged to Lucking in his own right, and 1 per cent belonged to Lucking's wife. In 1954 the directors of the company were Lucking, his wife and an old army friend of Lucking's, a Lt Col Dewar whom he had appointed as manager also. In 1956, Block was appointed co-trustee with Lucking. Lt Col Dewar wrongfully drew some £15,000 from the company's bank account in excess of his remuneration, and later he became bankrupt. The money was lost and one of the beneficiaries under the trust sued the trustees for the loss.

Held

In the circumstances, Lucking was liable for the loss; Block would not be held liable as he relied entirely on what Lucking told him.

Cross J:

'The conduct of the defendant trustees is, I think, to be judged by the standard applied in *Speight* v *Gaunt*, namely, that a trustee is only bound to conduct the business of the trust in such a way as an ordinary prudent man would conduct a business of his own.

Now what steps, if any, does a reasonably prudent man who finds himself a majority shareholder in a private company take with regard to the management of the company's affairs? He does not, I think, content himself with such information as to the management of the company's affairs as he is entitled to as shareholder, but ensures that he is represented on the board. He may be prepared to run the business himself as managing director, or, at least, to become a non-executive director while having the business managed by someone else. Alternatively, he may find someone who will act as his nominee on the board and report to him from time to time as to the company's affairs. In the same way, as it seems to me, trustees holding a controlling interest ought ensure so far as they can, that they have such information as to the progress of the company's affairs as directors would have. If they sit back and allow the company to be run by the minority shareholder and receive no more information than shareholders are entitled to, they do so at their risk if things go wrong. In this case, of course, the trust was represented on the board by Mr Lucking. As I see it, however, one ought not to regard him as performing a duty to the trust which it was incumbent on trustees to perform personally, so that Mr Block became automatically responsible for any deficiencies in Mr Lucking, as does a passive trustee who allows his co-trustee to exercise alone discretions which it is their duty of exercise jointly. If these trustees had decided, as they might have done, to be represented on the board by a nominee they would have been entitled to rely on the information given them by that nominee as to the way in which the company's affairs were being managed even though such information was inaccurate or inadequate, unless they had some reason to suspect that it was inaccurate or inadequate. Mr Block, as I see it, cannot have been in a worse position because his co-trustee was the trust's representative on the board than he would have been if the trust's representative had not been a trustee at all. The position of Mr Lucking, on the other hand, as I see it, was quite different. He cannot say that what he knew or ought to have known about the company's affairs he knew or ought to have known simply as a director with a duty to the company and no one else. He was in the position he was partly as a representative of the trust and, in and so far as he failed in his duty to the company, he also failed in his duty to the trust.'

Comment
A distinction was made between the liability of Lucking, who was a major shareholder in the company and who was the trustees' representative on the board, and Block who had no inside knowledge of or control over the company. Block was not treated by the court in these circumstances as a sleeping or passive trustee who would have been liable for the loss.

Nestlé v *National Westminster Bank plc* [1993] 1 WLR 1260 Court of Appeal (Dillon, Staughton and Leggatt LJJ)

• *Duty of trustee towards beneficiary in investment decisions*

Facts
The plaintiff became the sole beneficiary of a trust fund set up by her grandfather of which the bank was the trustee. The beneficiary claimed that the bank had committed a breach of trust by failing to adopt an appropriate investment policy. She claimed that if the trust fund have been properly managed, it would be worth £1 million rather than the £296,000 it was actually worth. Four arguments were put forward in support of this contention:

1. The bank failed to understand the scope of its powers of investment – in particular that it could invest outside the banking and insurance fields which were the areas of the original trust investments. It also failed to appreciate that the proceeds of sale of the family home could be invested in equities.
2. The bank failed to conduct regular reviews of its investments.
3. It had failed to diversify the investments.
4. The bank had favoured the income beneficiaries over the capital beneficiaries in its choice of investments.

Held
The bank was incompetent but nevertheless

not liable. The burden of proof was on the plaintiff to show that she had suffered a loss from the alleged breaches of trust and she had failed to prove that such a loss had been suffered as a result of the bank's investment policy (or lack of one). The standard of care applicable to the bank, as a professional trustee company, was that laid down for all trustees in *Learoyd* v *Whiteley*.

Leggatt LJ:

'No testator, in the light of this example, would choose this bank for the effective management of his investments. But the bank's engagement was as a trustee, and as such, it is to be judged not so much by success as by absence of proven default. The importance of preservation of a trust fund will always outweigh success in its advancement. Inevitably, a trustee in the bank's position wears a complacent air, because the virtue of safety will in practice put a premium on inactivity. Until the 1950s active management of the portfolio might have been seen as speculative, and even in these days such dealing would have to be notably successful before the expense would be justified. The very process of achieving a balance, or (if that be old fashioned) fairness as between the interests of life tenants and those of a remainderman inevitably means that each can complain of being less well served than he or she ought to have been. But by the undemanding standard of prudence the bank is not shown to have committed any breach of trust resulting in loss.

I am therefore constrained to agree that the appeal must be dismissed.'

Comment
This case is interesting for the way in which the court reviewed the bank's investment policy. They were not prepared to judge the conduct of the trustees with hindsight. The inactivity on the part of the trustee could in some instances be seen as caution. For example, 75 per cent of the fund was invested in equities (cf the 50 per cent then permitted by the Trustee Investments Act 1961, the effect of which was expressly varied in the will). The court took the view that it could not be said that a prudent trustee would have invested more of the trust fund in equities. A new statutory standard of care is given in s1 of the Trustee Act 2000.

12 Powers of Trustees

Armitage v *Nurse*

See Chapter 10.

Pilkington v *Inland Revenue Commissioners* [1964] AC 612
House of Lords (Viscount Radcliffe, Lords Reid, Jenkins, Hodson and Devlin)

• *Advancement can include tax avoidance*

Facts

William Norman Pilkington made a will in 1934 by which he left his residuary estate to trustees upon protective trusts for all his nephews and nieces living at his death in equal shares for life. The trust contained a provision that any consent which the nephews and nieces might give during their lifetime to an advancement would not cause a forfeiture of their life interests. There was no provision replacing or excluding s32 of the Trustee Act 1925. When the testator died in 1935 he had one nephew, Richard. Richard had three children, one of whom was the defendant, Penelope Pilkington, in whose favour he wished the trustees to exercise the statutory power of advancement under s32 in order to avoid estate duty. This scheme involved the setting up of a fresh trust to which half of Penelope's presumptive share would be advanced and the income of the same applied for her maintenance until she was 21. The trustees sought a declaration as to whether they could exercise the power of appointment in the manner proposed.

Held

1. Provided the advancement was for the benefit of the person in whose favour it was made, it was no objection that other persons benefited incidentally as a result of the advancement, nor that the money advanced was settled on fresh trusts.
2. There was nothing in s32 which restricted the manner or purpose of an advancement. However, in the circumstances of the case the exercise of the power of advancement would infringe the rule against perpetuities and could not lawfully be made.

Viscount Radcliffe:

'So much for "advancement", which I now use for brevity to cover the combined phrase "advancement or benefit". It means any use of the money which will improve the material situation of the beneficiary. It is important, however, not to confuse the idea of "advancement" with the idea of advancing the money out of the beneficiary's expectant interest. The two things have only a causal connection with each other. The one refers to the operation of finding money by way of anticipation of an interest not yet absolutely vested in possession or, if so vested, belonging to an infant; the other refers to the status of the beneficiary and the improvement of his situation. The power to carry out the operation of anticipating an interest is not conferred by the word "advancement" but by those other words of the section which expressly authorise the payment or application of capital money for the benefit of a person entitled "whether absolutely or contingently on his attaining any specified age or on the occurrence of any other event, or subject to a gift over on his death under any specified age or on the occurrence of any other event, and whether

240

in possession or in remainder or in reversion", etc.

I think, with all respect to the Commissioners, a good deal of their argument is infected with some of this confusion. To say, for instance, that there cannot be a valid exercise of a power of advancement that results in a deferment of the vesting of the beneficiary's absolute title (Miss Penelope, it will be remembered, is to take at 30 under the proposed settlement instead of 20 under the will) is in my opinion to play upon words. The element of anticipation consists in the raising of money for her now before she has any right to receive anything under the existing trusts: the advancement consists in the application of that money to form a trust fund, the provisions of which are thought to be for her benefit. I have not forgotten, of course, the references to powers of advancement which are found in such cases as *Re Joicey, Re May's Settlement* and *Re Mewburn's Settlement* to which our attention is called, or the answer supplied by Cotton LJ in *Re Aldridge* to his own question "What is advancement?"; but I think that it will be apparent from what I have already said that the description that he gives (it cannot be a definition) is confined entirely to the aspect of anticipation or acceleration which renders the money available and not to any description or limitation of the purposes for which it can then be applied.'

Comment

The court considered tax avoidance to be a legitimate reason for advancement. However, the application failed because it breached the perpetuity rules.

Speight v *Gaunt* (1883) 9 App Cas 1 Court of Appeal (Sir George Jessel MR, Lindley and Bowen LJJ)

• *Trustees may delegate and conduct trust affairs as a prudent man of business would his own*

Facts

Gaunt was the trustee of a trust. He employed one Cooke, a stockbroker, to invest £15,000 of the trust funds in stock or shares in companies quoted on the Stock Exchange, on the suggestion of the beneficiaries. Cooke had been in partnership in a firm of stockbrokers of high repute at the time. In accordance with the usual course of business Cooke entered into a contract to buy the shares from a jobber on the Stock Exchange on the next account day. He brought Gaunt a bought note stating that he required the money to pay for the stock and shares on the following day as he was liable to pay for them on the account day. Cheques totalling £15,000 were drawn in favour of and handed to Cooke who left the bought note with Gaunt. In fact Cooke did not complete the transaction to purchase the stock and shares but instead appropriated the cheques to his own use. On being questioned by Gaunt on the matter he made various excuses. Shortly afterwards Cooke was adjudicated bankrupt. The cestuis que trust claimed that Gaunt was liable for breach of trust with respect to the transaction and was personally liable for the loss since he should have paid the £15,000 directly to the bankers of the companies in which the shares had been bought. Gaunt, in defence, argued that he could not be held liable unless it was shown that he had not acted as a prudent man of business would have acted on his own behalf.

Held

Gaunt was not liable; he had acted as a prudent man of business had done and nothing more could have been expected of him as trustee for otherwise no one would become a trustee if a higher standard was imposed on them with regard to trust affairs than they should apply in dealing with their own affairs. This decision was subsequently affirmed by the House of Lords.

Sir George Jessel MR:

'It seems to me that on general principles a trustee ought to conduct the business of the trust in the same manner that an ordinary prudent man of business would conduct his own, and that beyond that there is no liability, or obligation on the trustee. In other words, a trustee is not bound because he is a trustee to conduct business in other than the ordinary and usual way in which similar business is conducted by mankind in transactions of their own. It never could be reasonable to make a trustee adopt further and better precautions than an ordinary prudent man of business would adopt, or to conduct business in any other way. If it were otherwise, no one would be a trustee at all. He is not paid for it. He says, "I take all reasonable precautions, and all the precautions which are deemed reasonable by prudent men of business, and beyond that I am not required to go".'

Comment
This test has been varied by s1 of the Trustee Act 2000.

Vickery, Re [1931 1 Ch 572 Chancery Division (Maugham J)

• *Trustee's powers and liability under s23(1) and s30(1) of the Trustee Act 1925 in employing agents*

Facts
A missionary called Mr Stephens who had no knowledge of business affairs was appointed sole executor of Mrs Vickery's estate by her will. Stephens appointed a solicitor, Mr Jennens, to wind up the estate and also to collect £2141 14s. 5d held in the Post Office Savings Bank and £62 4s in Savings Certificates in May 1927. In September 1927 Stephens was informed by one of the testatrix's sons that Jennens had at one time been suspended from practice. The son asked Stephens to instruct a different solicitor. Stephens did not do so as Jennens repeatedly promised him that matters would be settled quickly. Eventually another solicitor was employed in December 1927 as the estate had not been settled but Jennens absconded without handing over the moneys he had col-

lected and these were lost. The testatrix's sons claimed that Stephens was guilty of a breach of trust and since they were entitled to the moneys under the will they claimed them from Stephens who relied on ss23(1) and 30(1) of the Trustee Act 1925 in defence.

Held
1. Stephens was not liable. Section 23(1) revolutionised the position of a trustee as regards employment of agents and there did not have to be a necessity for the employment as previously required.
2. Under s23(1) a trustee was only liable for loss caused by the misconduct of the agent where such losses occurred because of the trustee's 'default'. Stephens was not guilty of default but only of an error of judgment at the most in appointing Jennens to wind up the estate.
3. Stephens was not liable under s30(1) either, because he had only committed an error of judgment.

Maugham J:

'The question that arises is whether in the circumstances, and in view of my findings as to the facts, the defendant is liable to make good these sums with interest by reason of his negligence either in employing Jennens to receive the sums or in permitting those sums to remain in his hands, in the circumstances of the case for a longer period of time than necessary.

In considering this question, the court has to bear in mind in particular two sections of the Trustee Act 1925. Section 23(1) is as follows: [The judge read the sub-section and continued.] This subsection is new and, in my opinion, authorised the defendant in signing the authorities to Jennens and Jennens to collect the two sums in question; for I do not think it can be doubted that the defendant acted in good faith in employing Jennens for the purpose. It will be observed that the subsection has no proviso or qualification to it such as we find in relation to s23(3). It is hardly too much to say that it revolutionises the position of a trustee or an executor so far as regards the employment of agents. He is no longer required to do any actual work himself, but he may employ a solicitor or other agent to do it, whether there is any real necessity for the employment or not. No doubt he should use his discretion in selecting an agent, and should employ him only to do acts within the scope of the usual business of the agent; but, as will be seen, a question arises whether even in these respects he is personally liable for a loss due to the employment of the agent unless he has been guilty of wilful default.

Section 23(3) is in the following terms: [The judge read the subsection and continued] This subsection is a reproduction with amendments of s17 of the Trustee Act 1893, which replaced s2 of the Trustee Act 1888. It will be observed that para (a) of the subsection related to the production of a deed having endorsed thereon a receipt for money or other property, and that para (i) refers to the receipt of money payable to the trustee under a policy of insurance. In these cases, no doubt, there is no reason why the banker or the solicitor should do anything more than receive the money and pay the same to the trustee or as he shall direct. The proviso must, I think, be limited to these two cases; and, of course, it is not intended to preclude a trustee from keeping trust funds at his bank pending investment or proper use of them; and it has nothing to do, in my opinion, with the case I have to decide, in which the powers given by paras (a) and (c) were not utilised by the defendant. There was no doubt a good reason for not making the proviso extend to subsection 1 of s23, since in many cases where, for example, a banker or other agent is employed by a trustee to receive money, the money cannot at once be conveniently paid to the trustee, but has to be employed by the banker or other agent in a number of ways.

I have now to consider s30(1) of the Trustee Act 1925, a section which replaces s24 of the Trustee Act 1893, which is in its turn re-enacted Lord Cranworth's Act, s31. It is in the following terms: [The judge read the subsection and continued.] Reliance has been placed on the words concluding the subsection "nor for any other loss, unless

the same happens through his own wilful default". To avoid misconception I wish to say that, having regard to the numerous decisions since the enactment of Lord Cranworth's Act in relation to the liability of trustees for innocent breaches of trust, it is impossible now to hold that the words "for any other loss" are quite general, with the result that no trustee is ever liable for breach of trust unless the breach is occasioned by his own wilful default. In my opinion the words are confined to losses for which it is sought to make the trustee liable occasioned by his signing receipts for the sake of conformity or by reason of the wrongful acts or defaults of another trustee or of an agent with whom trust money or securities have been deposited, or for the insufficiency or deficiency of securities of some other analogous loss. It may be noted that if the phrase is not so limited it is difficult to see how there could have been any need for s3 of the Judicial Trustee Act 1896 now re-enacted as s61 of the Trustee Act 1925 or for s29 of the Act, nor would it be possible to explain the numerous cases before 1896 where trustees were made liable for honest mistakes either of construction or fact …

On the other hand, s30(1) expressly refers to the defaults of bankers, brokers, or other persons with whom any trust money or other securities may be deposited, I am unable – dealing here with the more limited case – to escape the conclusion that the trustee cannot be made liable for the default of such a person unless the loss happens through the "wilful default" of the trustee. Before considering the meaning of the words "wilful default" in this connection, I would observe that in the case of *Re Brier* the Court of Appeal, consisting of Lord Selborne LC, and Cotton and Fry LJJ, gave effect to Lord Cranworth's Act s31, and held the trustees and executors not liable inasmuch as it had not been established that the loss occasioned by the agent's insolvency (in a case where, as the law then required, it was shown that the employment of the agent was a proper one) was due to the wilful default of the trustees and executors.

Now the meaning of the phrase "wilful default" has been expounded by the Court of Appeal in the case of *Re Trusts of Leeds City Brewery Ltd's Deed* and in the case of *Re City Equitable Fire Insurance Co*. It should be noted that in both those cases the indemnity given to the trustees in the first case and to the directors and officers of the company in the second case, was worded in a general form so that it could not be contended that they were liable for any matter or thing done or omitted unless it could be shown that the loss so occasioned arose from their own wilful default. This, as I have said, is not true of an ordinary executor or trustee; but the exposition of the phrase "wilful default" is not the less valuable. The Court of Appeal held, following the case of *Re City Equitable Fire Insurance Co*, the decision of Romer J that a person is not guilty of wilful default or default unless he is conscious that, in doing the act which is complained of or in omitting to do the act which it is said he ought to have done, he is committing a breach of his duty, or is recklessly careless whether it is a breach of duty or not, I accept with respect what Warrington LJ said – namely that in the case of trustees there are definite and precise rules of law as to what a trustee may or may not do in the execution of his trust, and that a trustee in general is not excused in relation to a loss occasioned by a breach of trust merely because he honestly believed that he was justified in doing the act in question. But for the reasons which I have given I think that, where an executor employs a solicitor or other agent to receive money belonging to the estate in reliance on s23(1) of the Trustee Act 1925, he will not be liable for a loss of the money occasioned by misconduct of the agent unless the loss happens through the wilful default of the executor, using those words as implying as the Court of Appeal have decided , either a consciousness of negligence or breach of duty, or a recklessness in the performance of a duty ...

Comment

This case has been criticised because the test for 'wilful default' followed that laid down in company law cases.

13 Variation of Trusts

British Museum (Trustees of the) v Attorney-General

See Chapter 11.

Holt's Settlement Trusts, Re [1969] 1 Ch 100 Chancery Division (Megarry J)

- *Variation approved by the court outside the requirements of s53(1)(c) Law of Property Act 1925*

Facts

The settlor executed a settlement in 1959 by which he settled £15,000 on his daughter, Mrs Wilson, for life with remainder to such of her children as attained 21 years. The trust fund increased in value to £320,000 and Mrs Wilson wished to surrender half her life interest in favour of her children but at the same time to vary the trusts so that the children had to attain 30 years before becoming entitled to their shares and to have half the income from each child's share accumulated until they each attained 25 years or for a period of 21 years from the date of the court's order, whichever was the earlier.

Held

The application would be approved.

Megarry J:

'When the arrangement is put into effect there is a disposition of an equitable interest, so that, unless there is some document signed by the adult beneficiaries, or by some agent authorised by them in writing, the requirements of s53(1)(c) are not satisfied. This contention is supported by a reference to the decision by the House of Lords in *Grey* v *Inland Revenue Commissioners* that an oral direction by a beneficiary to his trustees to hold property on certain trusts is a disposition, and that "disposition" must be given its ordinary wide meaning. It is further said that as there is here a transaction under which a moiety of a life interest will pass from Mrs Wilson to her children, this is a fortiori a "disposition". I may add that there is the minor point that the common form of order under the Act does not normally recite that all the adults have consented to the transaction, though where the insertion of such a recital is required by the parties, the registrars insert it.

Let me say at once that there would seem to be no great difficulty in inserting the consequences of this argument for the future. The adults could either execute the arrangement or, perhaps more conveniently, give written authority to their solicitors or counsel to execute it on their behalf. The latter course would usually be the more convenient because not infrequently changes (often minor) have to be made to the arrangement put before the court. It is, however, a fact that many thousands of orders must have been made in the past on the footing of *Re Viscount Hambleden's Will Trusts*. If the argument is right there is the very real difficulty that these orders will, perhaps in most cases, perhaps only in some, have effected no variation of the trusts. This is a consideration which is particularly awkward in that a question of jurisdiction is involved; for if the court has no jurisdiction to make an order which itself varies the trusts, and orders have been made on the footing that the orders do ipso facto vary the trusts, then it seems at least arguable that such orders were made without jurisdiction. It has also been pointed out that the Inland Revenue has for some while acted on the decision, and that orders of the court have been stamped on the footing that they ipso facto vary the terms of the trusts. Yet again, it is plain that the present practice is convenient. It avoids the burden which usually, perhaps, would not be very great, but in individual cases might be substantial, of getting the necessary signatures of the adults either to the document itself or to written authorities. I bear all those considerations in mind: but nevertheless, it seems to me that there is very considerable force in the argument that has been advanced. The decision in *Re Viscount Hambleden's Will Trusts* provides authority to the contrary but no explanation of the grounds for the decision. Accordingly a substantial part of the argument in this case has been directed to the discovery of some basis on which the convenient practice of *Re Viscount Hambleden's Will Trusts* can be rested.

In attempting to summarise Mr Godfrey's argument I am sure I shall fail to do it justice. As I understood it, he submitted that the decision in *Re Viscount Hambleden's Will Trusts* was quite wrong, but that in effect this did not matter. All that the court had to do, he said, was to approve the arrangement (ie the proposal made), and there was no question of the court approving anything which in law amounted to a disposition. The arrangement was not a disposition but merely a bargain or proposal which was not within the ambit of s53(1)(c) of the Law of Property Act 1925. The court, he urged, was not concerned to see that the adults consented and certainly not that they executed any disposition. There might thus be no disposition at all; but the persons specified by s1(1) of the Act of 1958 would be bound by the order of the court approving the arrangement and the other beneficiaries could not in practice go back on what their counsel had assented to, at any rate so far as it has been acted on. The result would be that, although there would be no new equitable interests actually created under the arrangement, all the beneficiaries would by a species of estoppel be treated as if they had those interests. I hope that Mr Godfrey will

forgive me if I say that I find this argument somewhat unattractive. In particular, I find it very hard to believe that Parliament intended the court to approve on behalf of infants arrangements which depended for their efficacy on the uncertainties of estoppel. I bear in mind, too, the wide meaning which *Grey v Inland Revenue Commissioners* gave to the "disposition" in s53(1)(c).

Mr Brookes, for the trustees, boldly asserted that, when correctly read, the Act of 1958 indirectly did what *Re Viscount Hambleden's Will Trusts* said it did. He went back to the words of s1(1) and emphasised that the power of the court was a power exercisable "by order" and that that power was a power to approve an arrangement "varying and revoking" all or any of the trusts. In emphasising those phrases, he said that the right way to read the section was to say that the power of the court was merely a power to make an order approving an arrangement which in fact varied or revoked the trusts, and not an arrangement which failed to do any such thing. When the adults by their counsel assented to the arrangement and the court on behalf of the infants by order approved the arrangement, then there was an arrangement which varied or revoked the trusts. So the order of the court both conferred jurisdiction and exercised it. His escape from s53(1)(c) had a similar dexterity about it: by conferring an express power on the court to do something by order, Parliament in the Act of 1958 had provided by necessary implication an exception from s53(1)(c). He buttressed his contention by a reference to *Re Joseph's Will Trusts*. Vaisey J there accepted that the order which he made directing the trustees to carry the order of the court into effect was neither contemplated by the Act of 1958 nor expressly authorised by it. Rather than read into the Act of 1958 words that are not there, said counsel, one should construe the Act of 1958 as authorising an order which is efficacious to achieve its avowed object. He pointed to the long title of the Act of 1958 which reads:

"An Act to extend the jurisdiction of courts of law to vary trusts in the interests of beneficiaries and sanction dealings with trust property."

I hope that Mr Brookes, too, will pardon me if I say that I did not find his argument compelling. Indeed, at times, I think it tended to circularity. But I find it tempting; and I yield. It is not a construction which I think the most natural. But it is not an impossible construction; it accords with the long title; it accords with the practice which has been relied on for many years in some thousands of cases; and it accords with considerations of convenience. The point is technical, and I do not think that I am doing more than straining a little at the wording in the interests of legislative efficacy.

However, that is not all. Mr Millett, for the tenant for life, provided another means of escape from s53(1)(c) in his helpful reply. Where, as here, the arrangement consists of an agreement made for valuable consideration, and that agreement is specifically enforceable, then the beneficial interests pass to the respective purchasers on the making of the agreement. Those interests pass by virtue of the species of constructive trust made familiarly by contracts for the sale of land, whereunder the vendor becomes a constructive trustee for the purchaser as soon as the contract is made, albeit the constructive trust has special features about it. Section 53, he continued, provides that "This section does not affect the creation or operation of resulting, implied or constructive trusts". Accordingly, because the trust was constructive, s53(1)(c) was excluded. He supported this contention by the decision of the House of Lords in *Oughtred v Inland Revenue Comrs.* He relied in particular on passages in the speeches of Lord Radcliffe and Lord Cohen, albeit that they were dissenting on the main point for decision. He pointed out that, although Lord Jenkins (with whom Lord Keith of Avonholm concurred) had not decided the point, he had assumed for the purposes of his speech that it was correct, and that the rejection of the contention by Lord Denning was in a very brief passage. Mr Millett accepts that if there were to be

some subsequent deed of family arrangement which would carry out the bargain then this deed might well be caught by s53(1)(c); but that, he said, cannot affect the "arrangement", and the parties might well be willing to let matters rest on that. It seems to me that there is considerable force in this argument in cases where the agreement is specifically enforceable, and in its essentials I accept it. At all events it supports the conclusions that in such cases the practice established by *Re Viscount Hambleden's Will Trusts* is right. For this and the other reasons that I have given, though with some hesitation, I accordingly hold this to be the case.

Finally, before turning to the second main point, I should mention that in this case the arrangement carries out its purpose by revoking all the existing trusts and establishing a new set of trusts. That being so, it is said that some difficulty arises on the wording of s1(1) of the Act of 1958. This merely empowers the court to approve an arrangement "varying or revoking all or any of the trusts", and so, it is said, the court cannot approve an arrangement which, instead of merely "revoking" or merely "varying", proceeds to revoke and then to set up new trusts, thereby producing an effect equivalent to the process of settlement and resettlement. The section, it is argued, says nothing of establishing new trusts for old. As a matter of principle, however, I do not really think that there is anything in this point, at all events in this case. Here the new trusts are in many respects similar to the old. In my judgment, the old trusts may fairly be said to have been varied by the arrangement whether the variation is effected directly by leaving some of the old words standing and altering others, or indirectly, by revoking all the old words and then setting up new trusts partly, though not wholly, in the likeness of the old. One must not confuse machinery with substances and it is the substance that matters. Comparing the position before and after the arrangement takes effect, I am satisfied that the result is a variation of the old trusts, even though effected by the machinery of revocation and resettlement.

Mr Brookes for the trustees pressed me with the decision in *Re Towler's Settlement Trusts*. He accepts that the point is not a mere matter of form, that is, whether in form there is a mere series of variations of the existing trusts, or whether in form there is a revocation and declaration of new trusts, but he says that the form gives some indications as to whether there is a mere variation or not. For myself, I cannot see much force in this; for so much depends on the individual draftsman who prepares the arrangement. One draftsman may choose to effect the arrangement by a series of variations of the existing trusts. Another may prefer to effect precisely the same variations by the formally more radical process of revocation and new declaration. In any event *Re Towler's Settlement Trusts* seems to me to be an entirely different case. There the infant was within eighteen days of attaining her majority and obtaining an absolute interest in the trust property. The existing trusts were at their very end, and what in substance was proposed was to make a new settlement of what was on the point of becoming an absolute unfettered interest. Further, although Wilberforce J rejected the wider proposal put before him, he did in fact make some variation in the trusts; and I cannot read the case as going so far as I think that counsel would take it. It is not, of course, for the court to draw the line in any particular place between what is a variation and what on the other hand is a completely new settlement. A line may, perhaps, one day emerge from a sufficiently ample series of reported decisions, but for the present all that is necessary for me to say is whether the particular case before me is on the right side or the wrong side of any reasonable line that could be drawn. In this case I am satisfied that the arrangement proposed falls on the side of the line which bears the device "variation".'

Comment

The court applied a wide definition of 'variation'. The judgment moves towards the application of s53(2) in *Neville v Wilson* (Chapter 2 above).

Pettifor's Will Trusts, Re [1966] Ch 257 Chancery Division (Pennycuick J)

• *Section 1(1)(c) Variation of Trusts Act 1958 – persons unborn*

Facts

By his will a testator left half his residuary estate on trust for his daughter, Sarah, for life with remainder to three beneficiaries and any children that might be born to Sarah who attained 21 years, in equal shares absolutely. Thus, the shares in remainder could only be reduced by the birth of further children to Sarah. It was desired to distribute the property under this residuary trust among the beneficiaries subject to a small insurance premium being paid to insure against the contingency of further children being born to Sarah. At the time of the testator's death Sarah was 78. The question arose whether an application under s1(1) VTA 1958 was appropriate in the circumstances.

Held

This was not a case where the VTA 1958 was appropriate since the contingency in issue could not possible happen, viz childbirth by a woman of 78. The Act was only concerned with possible contingencies.

Pennicuick J:

'It seems to me that an application under the Variation of Trusts Act 1958, to cover that contingency, namely, in the event of the birth of a child to a woman of seventy-eight, is misconceived and is not a proper application to make under the Act. It was, of course, well established prior to the enactment of the Perpetuities and Accumulations Act 1964, that for the purpose of the rule against perpetuities a woman was never to be presumed to be past childbearing. On the other hand, it is equally well established that in the middle or late fifties, a woman has become incapable of childbearing. In the case of a woman in the seventies not only would trustees be authorised to distribute a fund on that footing without any doubt or question, but the court would, I think, normally consider it an unnecessary waste of money for the trustees to come to the court and ask for leave so to distribute. Trustees can with complete safety and propriety deal with their funds on the basis that a woman of seventy will not have a further child. It does not seem to me that protection against this impossible contingency is a matter which can properly be dealt with by way of variation of existing trusts. The proper way to deal with it, if the intervention of the court were to be sought at all, would be an application to the court in its administrative jurisdiction for leave to carry out the existing trusts without variation, on the footing that the contingency will not happen ...'

Comment

This case falls outside the scope of the VTA altogether because the eventuality is impossible, there is no need for a variation.

Steed's Will Trusts, Re [1960] Ch 407 Court of Appeal (Lord Evershed MR, Willmer and Upjohn LJJ)

• *The court will take the settlor's intention into account in considering proposed variations.*

Facts

Property was devised to a woman on protective trusts for her life, then it devolved after her death to any person she should appoint. She exercised this general power of appointment in her own favour and wished to eliminate the protective trust to give herself an absolute interest. The only other persons potentially entitled were a possible future husband (or husbands) of the woman (she was still unmarried) and their issue who would only become entitled if she committed some act, such as becoming bankrupt, which terminated her life interest and gave rise to a discretionary trust in favour of those persons. These contingencies were remote and an unlikely possibility for even if she married she was beyond the normal age of childbearing.

Held

The woman had not been given an absolute interest initially by the testator because he feared that she would give it away to a prodigal brother and leave herself without financial support, thus the variation would not be approved. The Court decided the issue on this point, but also stated that they had to consider the claims of any future husband under the discretionary trusts.

Lord Evershed MR:

'This is in more ways than one, including matters of procedure, a somewhat unusual case, as counsel for the plaintiff observed. It is also in many respects an unhappy case, and I cannot refrain from expressing my own sympathy for the plaintiff on the one side and for the three defendant trustees on the other.

I propose in this judgment to forbear from entering, except where absolutely necessary, into matters of fact which might only serve to rub salt into existing wounds. Suffice it say that the plaintiff was one who served loyally and most skilfully for a long period of time the testator and the testator's wife. In consideration for those services the testator included in his will provisions for her benefit, contained in cl 9 and cl 10. It is quite plain on the evidence that the testator, while anxious to show his gratitude to the plaintiff was no less anxious that she should be well provided for and not exposed to the temptation, which he thought was real, of being, to use a common phrase, sponged on by one of her brothers. I fully accept that the plaintiff's natural affection for that brother is not a matter which one can in any sense condemn. Blood is, after all, thicker than water, and the happiness of the plaintiff, according to her own view at any rate, is very much linked up with the association with that brother and the brother's daughter and wife. On the other side, however, are these trustees on whom has been placed an obligation, a duty to give effect to the intentions of the man who provided the money ...

... In the present case, the proposed variation (ie the "arrangement") which the plaintiff puts forward may be most briefly and accurately stated as involving this: in cl 9 of the will the words "upon protective trusts as defined by s33 of the Trustee Act 1925" should be omitted, and similarly in the next clause the word "protective" should be omitted. If those words were omitted, the result would be that the plaintiff would become absolutely entitled to the property, because she would then be the life tenant, having appointed by irrevocable deed to herself the reversion: and that is what she seeks.

The trustees have taken the view that it is not an arrangement which, having regard to their conception of their duties and the wishes of their testator, they should approve. For my part, I do not think that approval on behalf of the trustees is the court's function in this case, though the court in exercising its general discretion will certainly pay regard to what the trustees say and the grounds for their saying it. Nor can I see, if this was the learned judge's view, that the court is called on by the language of this section to approve the arrangement or proposal on behalf of the proposer; that is to say, whether they think she was wise or unwise to put her idea forward. The duty of the court, as I read the section, on the facts of this case is, that they must approve it on behalf of the only person or persons who might have an interest under the discretionary trusts and whose presence under the trusts now prevents the plaintiff saying that she can put an end to the settlement.

Having regard to the plaintiff's age, no doubt it is true to say that she will not and cannot now have children, but she might marry, and marry more than once. She says, with some reason, that having lived for fifty-three years unmarried she does not feel in the least likely to marry now. Well, that may well be right, though many have said that before and subsequent events have proved them wrong. That, however, is neither here nor there. There does exist a discretionary trust, and a future husband of the plaintiff is a person interested under those trusts, on whose behalf the court must now approve the proposal. Having regard to what has

happened between the plaintiff and her brother, it is possible that strictly speaking there has been a forfeiture and if so, the future husband or husbands would be within para (b) of the subsection, but if not he or they would be within para (d). Again, I think that does not, for present purposes, matter.

I repeat that the duty of the court is now to consider whether in the exercise of its discretion, which is framed in the widest possible language, it should approve the arrangement on behalf of what has been described in argument as the spectral spouse of the plaintiff. In doing that, what must the court consider? Not, I conceive, merely the material benefit or detriment of such spouse. Certainly not if he is to be regarded as being a person under para (d) though if he is to be regarded as falling under para (b) it is expressly enjoined that the court shall not approve the arrangement unless it is for his benefit. As I have said, I do not read this Act as to mean that the court's duty in the exercise of this very wide and, indeed, revolutionary discretion is confined to saying; "Would it really much harm this spectral spouse if we approve the proposal?" Bearing in mind, of course, the admitted possibility that the spouse might cease to be spectral and become a reality, I think what the court is bound to do is to see whether, looked at on behalf of the persons indicated, it approves the arrangement. It is the arrangement which has to be approved, not just the limited interest of the person on whose behalf the court's duty is to consider it. If that is right, it then follows that the court must regard the proposal as a whole, and, so regarding it, then ask itself whether in the exercise of its jurisdiction it should approve that proposal on behalf of the person who cannot give a consent, because he is not in a position to do so. If that is a right premise, then it follows that the court is bound to look at the scheme as a whole, and when it does so, to consider, as surely it must, what really was the intention of the benefactor. That such is a proper approach is at least supported by the provisions of RSC Order 55 r14A(3A) (Annual Practice 1960, p1525), which provides that in the case of an application under this Act, where there is a living settlor the living settlor is to be a party before the court. That rule seems to me to reinforce what I conceive to underlay this provision, viz that the court must, albeit that it is performing its duty on behalf of some person who cannot consent on his or her own part, regard the proposal in the light of the purpose of the trust as shown by the evidence of the will or settlement itself, and of any other relevant evidence available.

Having so formulated the duty, I have, for my part, come to the conclusion that it would not be right for the court in the exercise of its discretion to approve this variation or arrangement. I am not uninfluenced in coming to that conclusion by any means by the circumstance that the learned judge obviously did not think it was a proposal which should be approved, though it is quite true that, for reasons which I have indicated, it may be said that he was looking at it and basing his jurisdiction on an interpretation of the section which I have not been altogether able to share, ie that it was his duty to approve it on behalf of the proposer, the plaintiff, and also that the scheme must be regarded as intended to be in some sense inter partes and, therefore, that he had to approve it on behalf of the trustees. Disagreeing, if that is a fair view of his judgment, with that premise, nevertheless it is quite clear, I think, that the judge was by no means unsympathetic to the feelings and views of the plaintiff, but on the other hand was no less clear in his mind that the arrangement was one which so cut at the root of the testator's wishes and intentions that it was not one the court should approve. After all, if one is asked to approve this proposal on behalf of a spectral spouse (if I may revert to that phrase), one must ask why is the spectral spouse there at all under the trust? If one asks that question, nearly everything else, as it seems to me, follows. There is no doubt why the spectral spouse is there. It was part of the testator's scheme, made as I think manifest by the language which I have read from the will, that it was the intention and the desire of the testator that this trust should be available for the plaintiff so that she would have proper provision made for her throughout her life, and would not be exposed to the risk that she might, if she had been handed the money, part with it in favour of another individual about whom the testator felt apprehension, which apprehension is plainly shared by the trustees.

For those reasons, therefore, I also conclude adversely to the plaintiff that we should not exercise jurisdiction under the Act of 1958 to approve the arrangement which has been put forward, and which I have tried to define. That is the end of the case. I only repeat the sympathy I have felt in a distressing matter of this kind, both with the plaintiff and with the trustees, whose difficulties in discharging their duty are obvious. I should like to express the hope that perhaps time, the healer, will do much to put an end to these troubles.

Where, under the proviso to s1(1) of the VTA 1958 the court is required to take into account the "benefit" of an arrangement to any person on whose behalf its approval is sought, this will include social and moral benefit as well as fiscal benefit and the former may well outweigh the latter.'

Comment

In this case, it was clearly not in the best interests of the beneficiary for the court to remove the restrictions imposed by the testator for her own protection, and the court was bound to implement the intention of the testator.

14 Breach of Trust I: Personal Remedies

Diplock, Re [1948] Ch 465 Court of Appeal (Lord Greene MR, Wrottesley and Evershed LJJ)

• *Remedies in rem and in personam for breach of trust*

Facts

Caleb Diplock, who died in March 1936, left a will by the terms of which the executors were directed to apply his residuary estate 'for such charitable institution or institutions or other charitable or benevolent object or objects in England' as they should in their absolute discretion think fit. The residuary estate amounted to approximately £263,000 and the executors proceeded to distribute it among 139 charities of their choice without obtaining any directions from the court. However, the next of kin challenged the validity of the bequest on the grounds of uncertainty and in *Chichester Diocesan Fund and Board of Finance Ltd* v *Simpson* the House of Lords upheld their challenge.

The next of kin then proceeded to recover the funds which had been wrongfully distributed by the executors. First, they made claims in personam against the executors or their estates and these were compromised with the approval of the court. Then they brought actions against a number of the institutions who had benefited under the distribution. In most cases the institutions had been sent cheques which they had paid into their accounts. Some had put the money to one side in a special account and had earmarked it for a particular purpose. Others had used the money to alter and enlarge buildings and land owned by them. The next of kin made two claims against the institutions: (1) a claim in personam based on an alleged equity in an unpaid creditor, legatee or next of kin to recover from an overpaid beneficiary or, as stranger to the estate who was not entitled to any payment; and (2) a claim in rem to trace identifiable assets, whether mixed or unmixed, into the hands of a volunteer who had wrongly received them.

Held

1. As to the claim in personam:
    This was available to the next of kin in the circumstances alleged. There was established the existence of an equity to recover from an overpaid or wrongly recipient and this equity might be available equally to an unpaid or underpaid creditor, legatee or next of kin.
    a) This claim was not defeated by the fact that the payment to the recipient had been made under a mistake of law as opposed to a mistake of fact.
    b) The next of kin should claim first against the personal representatives and the claim against the institutions should give credit for the amount recovered from the personal representatives.
    c) The claim lay only for the principal; interest was not recoverable.
    d) The period of limitation applicable to the claim was 12 years under s20 of the Limitation Act 1939. This ran from the date when the right to receive the share or interest accrued (normally one year from death).
2. As to the claim in rem:
    a) Where money in the hands of a trustee or other fiduciary agent had been mixed with that of another, the person with an equitable interest in that money could trace this money into the

mixed fund, or any assets purchased out of the mixed fund. It did not matter whether the fund had been mixed by an innocent volunteer or the trustee or fiduciary agent or whether the money had been passed on mixed by the trustee or fiduciary agent to the volunteer. For this remedy to apply, three conditions must be satisfied:

i)   There must be a fiduciary relationship between the claimant and the original holder of the money, ie the next of kin and the personal representative in this case. This gave the claimant an equitable interest in the money.

ii)   The money or any asset purchased out of it must still be in existence either separately or as part of a mixed fund.

iii) The imposition of a charge in favour of the claimant must not cause an injustice to the volunteer.

b)   Where the money had been passed to the innocent volunteer unmixed and he had kept it apart from his own funds then the innocent volunteer held the money on behalf of the claimant, ie the next of kin.

c)   If the money had been passed to the innocent volunteer and he had mixed it with his own money, then the claimant and the innocent volunteer ranked pari passu as regards the mixed fund. If the mixing had taken place in an active banking account then the rule in *Clayton's Case* applied. If the mixing had taken place through the innocent volunteer applying the money he had received to alter, improve or extend his own property, no tracing would be allowed as a charge in favour of the claimant would work an injustice to the innocent volunteer. Similarly, if the money had been used by the innocent volunteer to clear a blot on his title to certain property, tracing would not be allowed as this would also work an injustice to the volunteer.

Lord Greene MR:

'The claim in personam
What then is the conclusion to be drawn on this part of the appellants' claim from what we fear has been a long citation of the authorities? It is not, we think, necessary or desirable that we should attempt any exhaustive formulation of the nature of the equity invoked which will be applicable to every class of case. But it seems to us, first, to be established and that the equity may be available equally to an unpaid or underpaid creditor, legatee, or next of kin. Second, it seems to us that a claim by a next of kin will not be liable to be defeated merely (a) in the absence of administration by the court; or (b) because the mistake under which the original payment was made was one of law rather than fact; or (c) because the original recipient, as things turn out, had no title at all and was a stranger to the estate; though the effect of the refund in the last case will be to dispossess the original recipient altogether rather than to produce equality between him and the claimant and other persons having a like title to that of the recipient. In our judgment there is no authority either in logic or in the decided cases for such limitations to the equitable right of action. In our judgment also there is no justification for such limitations to be found in the circumstances which gave rise to the equity. And as regards the conscience of the defendant upon which, in this as in other jurisdictions equity is said to act, it is prima facie at least a sufficient circumstance that the defendant, as events have proved, has received some share of the estate to which he was not entitled. "A party", said Sir John Leach in *David* v *Frowd* "claiming under such circumstances has no great reason to complain that he is called upon to replace what he has received against his right."

On the other hand, to such a claim by an unpaid beneficiary, there is, in our judgment, at least in circumstances such as the present, one important qualification. Since the original wrong payment was attributable to the blunder of the personal representatives, the right of the unpaid beneficiary is in the first instance against the wrongdoing executor or administrator, and the beneficiary's direct claim in equity against those overpaid or wrongly paid should be limited to the amount which he cannot recover from the party responsible. In some cases the amount will be the whole amount of the payment wrongly made, eg where the executor or administrator is shown to be wholly without assets or is protected from attack by having acted under an order of the court.

Authority for this qualification is to be found in the judgment of Sir J Strange in the case of *Orr* v *Kaines*, where he observed that, if the executor is insolvent, an unpaid legatee is admitted to claim direct from the wrongly paid recipient because "the principal case went upon the insolvency of the executor." It is true that no direct authority for the qualification is to be found in any of the other decided cases; but in none of those cases where the direct claim was allowed, did it appear in fact that there was an executor or administrator against whom a claim might have been made or successfully made. Roper in the passage which we have cited from his text book treats the qualification as established by the authority of *Orr* v *Kaines*: where the unpaid legatee "can have no redress against" the personal representative the direct claim is justified since otherwise he would be without a remedy.

The distinction between tracing at common law and tracing in equity

[At pp518–521 the distinctions between the claim in rem at common law and at equity were explained:]

Before passing to a consideration of the case of *Sinclair* v *Brougham* we may usefully make some observations of our own as to the distinction between the attitude of the common law and that of equity to these questions.

The common law approached them in a strictly materialistic way. It could only appreciate what might almost be called "physical" identity of one thing with another. It could treat a person's money as

identifiable so long as it had not been mixed with other money. It could treat as identifiable as the money, other kinds of property acquired by means of it, provided that there was no admixture of other money. But it is noticeable that in this latter case the common law did not base itself on any known theory of tracing such as that used in equity. It proceeded on the basis that the unauthorised act of purchasing was one capable of ratification by the owner of the money (per Lord Parker in *Sinclair* v *Brougham*). Certain words of Lord Haldane in *Sinclair* v *Brougham* may appear to suggest a further limitation, that "money" as we have used that word was not regarded at common law as identifiable once it had been paid into a bank account. We do not, however, think it necessary to discuss this point at length.

We agree with the comments of Wynn-Parry J upon it and those of Atkin LJ (as he then was) in *Banque Belge* v *Hambrouk*. If it is possible to identify a principal's money with an asset purchased exclusively by means of it we see no reason for drawing a distinction between a chose in action such as a banker's debt to his customer and any other asset. If the principal can ratify the acquisition of the one, we see no reason for supposing that he cannot ratify the acquisition of the other.

We may mention three matters which we think are helpful in understanding the limitation of the common law doctrine and the reasons why equity was able to take a more liberal view. They are as follows:

(1) The common law did not recognise equitable claims to property, whether money or any other form of property. Sovereigns in A's pocket either belonged in law to A or they belonged to B. The idea that they could belong in law to A and that they should nevertheless be treated as belonging to B was entirely foreign to the common law. This is the reason why the common law doctrine finds its typical exemplification in cases of principal and agent. If B, a principal, hands cash to A, his agent, in order that it may be applied in a particular manner, the cash in the eyes of the common

law, remains the property of B. If, therefore, A instead of applying it in the authorised manner, buries it in a sack in his garden and uses it for an unauthorised purchase, B can, in the former case, recover the cash as being still his own property and in the latter case, affirm the purchase of something bought with his money by his agent. If, however, the relationship of A and B was not one which left the property in the cash in B but merely constituted a relationship of debtor and creditor between them, there could, of course, have been no remedy at law under this head since the property in the cash would have passed out of B into A.

(2) The narrowness of the limits within which the common law operated may be linked with the limited nature of the remedies available to it. Specific relief as distinct from damages (the normal remedy at common law) was confined to a very limited range of claims as compared with the extensive uses of specific relief developed by equity. In particular, the device of a declaration of charge was unknown to the common law and it was the availability of that device which enabled equity to give effect to its wider conception of equitable rights.

(3) It was the materialistic approach of the common law coupled with and encouraged by the limited range of remedies available to it that prevented the common law from identifying money in a mixed fund. Once the money of B became mixed with the money of A its identification in a physical sense became impossible; owing to the fact of mixture there could be no question of ratification of an unauthorised act; and the only remedy of B, if any, lay in a claim for damages.

Equity adopts a more metaphysical approach. It found no difficulty in regarding a composite fund as an amalgam constituted by the mixture of two or more funds each of which could be regarded as having, for certain purposes, a continued separate existence. Putting it another way, equity regarded the amalgam as capable, in proper circumstances, of being resolved into its component parts.

Adapting, for the sake of contrast, the phraseology which we have used in relation to the common law, it was the metaphysical approach of equity coupled with and encouraged by the far-reaching remedy of a declaration of charge that enabled equity to identify money in a mixed fund. Equity, so to speak, is able to draw up a balance sheet on the right-hand side of which appears the composite fund and on its left-hand side the two or more funds of which it is to be deemed to be made up.

Regarded as a pure piece of machinery for the purpose of tracing money into a mixed fund or into property acquired by means of a mixed fund, a declaration of charge might be thought to be a suitable means of dealing with any case where one person has, without legal title, acquired some benefit by the use of the money of another – in other words, any case of what it often called 'unjust enrichment'. The opinion of Lord Dunedin in *Sinclair* v *Brougham* appears to us to come very nearly to this, for he appears to treat the equitable remedy as applicable in any case where a superfluity, expressed or capable of being expressed in terms of money, is found to exist. Such a view would dispense with the necessity of establishing as a starting point the existence of a fiduciary or quasi-fiduciary relationship or of a continuing right of property recognised in equity. We may say at once that, apart from the possible case of Lord Dunedin's speech, we cannot find that any principle so wide in its operation is to be found enunciated in English law. The conditions which must exist before the equitable form of relief becomes available will be considered later in this judgment. But one truism may be stated here in order to get it out of the way. The equitable form of relief whether it takes the form of an order to restore an unmixed sum of money (or property acquired by means of such a sum) or a declaration of charge upon a mixed fund (or upon property acquired by means of such a fund) is, of course, personal in the sense that its efficacy is founded upon the jurisdiction of equity to enforce its rules by acting upon the individual. But it is not personal in the sense that the person against whom an order of this nature is sought can be made personally liable to repay the amount claimed to have belonged to the claimant. The equitable remedies pre-suppose the continued existence of the money either as a separate fund or as part of a mixed fund or as latent in property acquired by means of such a fund. If, on the facts of any individual case, such continued existence is not established, equity is as helpless as the common law itself. If the fund, mixed or unmixed, is spent upon a dinner, equity, which dealt only in specific relief and not in damages, could do nothing. If the case was one which at common law involved breach of contract the common law could, of course, award damages but specific relief would be out of the question. It is, therefore, a necessary matter for consideration in each case where it is sought to trace money in equity, whether it has such a continued existence, actual or notional, as will enable equity to grant specific relief.

Innocent volunteers
[At p523 the judgment dealt with the question of whether tracing was permitted by equity into a mixed fund where the fund had been given already mixed to the innocent volunteer or where the mixing had been carried out by the innocent volunteer. At first instance, Wynn-Parry J held that such a claim must fail in limine. The Court of Appeal disagreed with him and set out the principles applicable in such a case at pp524:]

Where an innocent volunteer (as opposed to a purchaser for value without notice) mixes "money" of his own with "money" which in equity belongs to another person, or is found in possession of such a mixture, although that other person cannot claim a charge on the mass superior to the claim of the volunteer, he is entitled nevertheless to a charge ranking pari passu with the claim of the volunteer. And Lord Parker's reasons for taking this view appear to have been on the following lines: Equity regards the rights of the equitable owner as being "in effect rights of property" though not recognised as such by the common law, just as a vol-

unteer is not allowed by equity in the case, eg of a conveyance of the legal estate in land, to set up his legal title adversely to the claim of a person having an equitable interest in the land, so in the case of a mixed fund of money the volunteer must give such recognition as equity considers him in conscience (as a volunteer) bound to give to the interest of the equitable owner of the money which has been mixed with the volunteer's own. But this burden on the conscience of the volunteer is not such as to compel him to treat the claim of the equitable owner as paramount. That would be to treat the volunteer as strictly as if he himself stood in a fiduciary relationship to the equitable owner which ex hypothesi he does not. The volunteer is under no greater duty of conscience to recognise the interest of the equitable owner than that which lies upon a person having an equitable interest on one of two trust funds of "money" which have become mixed towards the equitable owner of the other. Such a person is not in conscience bound to give precedence to the equitable owner of the other of the two funds.

We may enlarge upon the implications which appear to us to be contained in Lord Parker's reasoning. First of all, it appears to us to be wrong to treat the principle which underlies *Hallett*'s case as coming into operation only where the person who does the mixing is not only in a fiduciary position but is also a party to the tracing action. If he is a party to the action he is, of course, precluded from setting up a case inconsistent with the obligations of his fiduciary position. But supposing that he is not a party? The result cannot surely depend on what equity would or would not have allowed him to say if he had been a party. Suppose that the sole trustee of (say) five separate trusts draws £100 out of each of the trust banking accounts, pays the resulting £500 into an account which he opens in his own name, draws a cheque for £500 on that account and gives it as a present to his son. A claim by the five sets of beneficiaries to follow the money of their respective trusts would be a claim against the son. He would stand in no fiduciary relationship to any of them. We recoil from the conclusion that all five beneficiaries would be dismissed empty handed by a court of equity and the son left to enjoy what in equity was originally their money. Yet that is the conclusion to which the reasoning of the learned judge would lead us. Lord Parker's reasoning, on the other hand, seems to us to lead to the conclusion that each set of beneficiaries could set up its equitable interest which would prevail against the bare legal title of the son as a volunteer and that they would be entitled to share pari passu in so much of the fund or its proceeds as remained identifiable.

An even more striking example was admitted by Mr Pennycuick QC to be the result of his argument, and he vigorously maintained that it followed inevitably from the principles of equity involved. If a fiduciary agent takes cash belonging to his principal and gives it to his son, who takes it innocently, then so long as the son keeps it unmixed with other cash in one trouser pocket, the principal can follow it and claim it back. Once, however, the son, being under no fiduciary duty to the principal, transfers it to his other trouser pocket in which there are reposing a coin or two of his own of the same denomination, the son, by a sort of process of accretion, acquires an indefeasible title to what the moment before the transfer he could not have claimed as his own. This result appears to us to stultify the beneficent powers of equity to protect and enforce what it recognises as equitable rights of property which subsist until they are destroyed by the operation of a purchase for value without notice.

The error into which, we respectfully suggest, the learned judge has fallen is in thinking that what, in *Hallett*'s case was only the method (there appropriate) of bringing a much wider-based principle of equity into operation – viz the method by which a fiduciary agent, who has himself wrongfully mixed the funds, is prohibited from asserting a breach of his duty – is an element which must necessarily be present before equity can afford protection to the equitable rights which it has brought into

existence. We are not prepared to see the arm of equity thus shortened.

Innocent volunteers using money to improve their assets
[At pp546–54 the judgment deals with the situation where the volunteer has used the money in the alteration or improvement of assets and whether tracing would be permitted in such circumstances:]

In the present cases, however, the charities have used the Diplock money, not in combination with money of their own to acquire new assets, but in the alteration and improvement of assets which they already owned. The altered and improved asset owes its existence, therefore, to a combination of land belonging to the charity and money belonging to the Diplock estate. The question whether tracing is possible and if so to what extent, and also the question whether an effective remedy by way of declaration of charge can be granted consistently with an equitable treatment of the charity as an innocent volunteer, present quite different problems from those arising in the simple case above stated. In the case of the purchase of an asset out of a mixed fund, both categories of money are, as we have said, necessarily present throughout the existence of the asset in an identifiable form. In the case of adaption of property of the volunteer by means of trust money, it by no means necessarily follows that the money can be said to be present in the adapted property. The beneficial owner of the trust money seeks to follow and recover that money and claims to use the machinery of a charge on the adapted property in order to enable him to do so. But in the first place the money may not be capable of being followed. In every true sense, the money may have disappeared. A simple example suggests itself. The owner of a house who, as an innocent volunteer, has trust money in his hands given to him by a trustee uses that money in making an alteration to his house so as to fit it better to his own personal needs. The result may add not one penny to the value of the house. Indeed, the alteration may well lower its value; for the alteration, though convenient to the owner, may be highly inconvenient in the eyes of a purchaser. Can it be said in such cases that the trust money can be traced and extracted from the altered asset? Clearly not, for the money will have disappeared leaving no monetary trace behind: the asset will not have increased (or may even have depreciated) in value through its use.

But the matter does not end here. What, for the purposes of the inquiry, is to be treated as "the charity property"? Is it to be the whole of the land belonging to the charity? or is it to be only that part of it which was altered or reconstructed or on which a building has been erected by means of Diplock money? If the latter, the result may well be that the property, both in its original state and as altered or improved, will, when taken in isolation, have little or no value. What would be the value of a building in the middle of Guy's Hospital without any means of access through other parts of the hospital property? If, on the other hand, the charge is to be on the whole of the charity land, it might well be thought an extravagant result if the Diplock estate, because Diplock money had been used in reconstructing a corner of it, were to be entitled to a charge on the entirety.

But it is not merely a question of locating and identifying the Diplock money. The result of a declaration of charge is to disentangle trust money and enable it to be withdrawn in the shape of money from the complex in which it has become involved. This can only be done by sale under the charge. But the equitable owner of the trust money must in this process submit to equality of treatment with the innocent volunteer. The latter too, is entitled to disentangle his money and to withdraw it from the complex. Where the complex originates in money on both sides there is no difficulty and no inequity. Each is entitled to a charge. But if what the volunteer had contributed is not money but other property of his own such as land, what then? You cannot have a charge for land. You can, it is true, have a charge for the value of land, an entirely different thing. Is it equitable to compel the innocent

volunteer to take a charge merely for the value of the land when what he has contributed is the land itself? In other words, can equity, by the machinery of a charge give to the innocent volunteer that which he has contributed so as to place him in a position comparable with that of the owner of the trust fund? In our opinion it cannot.

In the absence of authority to the contrary our conclusion is that as regards the Diplock money used in these cases it cannot be traced in any true sense; and further that even if this were not so, the only remedy available to equity, viz, that of a declaration of charge, would not produce an equitable result and is inapplicable accordingly.'

Comment
This is the most significant judgment on the remedies available to recover trust property. It explains very clearly the rights to trace into trust property and their limitations.

Swindle and Others v *Harrison and Another* [1997] 4 All ER 705 Court of Appeal (Evans, Hobhouse and Mummery LJJ)

• *Breach of fiduciary duty – causal link between breach and loss*

Facts
Mrs Harrison put up her house as security for a mortgage to buy a hotel which was to be run as a family restaurant business. She did so on the understanding that the balance of the purchase price would be funded by a second mortgage to a brewery and on this basis contracts were exchanged for the purchase of the hotel. The brewery refused to grant the mortgage, whereupon a member of the firm of solicitors acting on the purchase stepped in and gave the family a bridging loan of £75,000 secured by a first charge on the hotel. The solicitor did not disclose to Mrs Harrison that the firm knew the brewery did not intend to make the loan, nor that the firm was making a hidden profit on the mortgage. When the busi-

ness failed and Mrs Harrison could not keep up the mortgage payments her house was possessed by the mortgage company and she transferred title to the hotel to her son, subject to the legal charge in favour of the solicitors. The solicitors issued proceeding seeking possession of the hotel. Mrs Harrison counterclaimed, inter alia, breach of fiduciary duty and sought damages or equitable compensation for the loss of her equity in her house. The recorder dismissed this counterclaim because the breach of fiduciary duty had not caused her loss. Mrs Harrison appealed to the Court of Appeal claiming that it was not necessary to prove a causal link between the breach of fiduciary duty and the loss suffered and that the solicitors were liable to restore her to the position she was in when their breach of duty occurred.

Held

The appeal was dismissed. In order to recover compensation for breach of fiduciary duty, a plaintiff had to show that the loss he had suffered had been caused by the defendant's breach of duty. Further, unless the breach could properly be regarded as the equivalent of fraud, Mrs Harrison was not entitled to be placed in the same position as she was before the breach occurred but only in the same position as she would have been if the breach of duty had not occurred.

Evans LJ:

'It is now well established that a solicitor owes his client a general duty of skill and care, though its scope is always subject to the terms of his retainer in the particular case.

Equity has also recognised duties going beyond the common law duties of skill and care which may be undertaken by individuals, depending on "the circumstances in which they were acting". These are the duties of fidelity and loyalty which are described as "fiduciary" and which exist independently of, though often in conjunction with, a duty of care. There is no doubt that a solicitor owes his client these duties also:

"The principal is entitled to the single-minded loyalty of his fiduciary. This core liability has several facets. A fiduciary must act in good faith: he must not make a profit out of his trust; he must not place himself in a position where his duty and interest may conflict; he may not act for his own benefit or the benefit of a third person without the informed consent of his principal. This is not an exhaustive list ... (*Bristol & West Building Society* v *Mothew*)."

In the present case, Mr Bannister submits that *because* the plaintiffs were in breach of duty, *therefore,* applying *Brickenden* v *London Loan and Savings Co*, they are liable to restore the second defendant financially to the position she was in when their breach of duty occurred. It is not relevant, he says, to inquire whether or not she would have completed the purchase in any event. It is enough that she did in fact do so, and was enabled to do so by the plaintiffs' loan.

I would reject this argument, because the authorities also show, in my judgment, that what I have called the stringent rule of causation or measure of damages does not apply as regards breaches of equitable duties unless the breach can properly be regarded as the equivalent of fraud. In other cases, the plaintiff is entitled to be placed in the same position financially as he would have been in if the breach of duty had not occurred – not necessarily the same as he was in before it occurred.

These propositions seem to me to be established by *Bristol & West Building Society* v *Mothew*. The defendant had not breached his duties of loyalty and fidelity to his principal and so he could not be held to be liable for losses suffered as the result of entering into the transaction, as distinct from the consequences of the particular breach. Those were likely to be minimal (because, in short, the principal would have made the mortgage loan in any event) and they did not include the intervening market loss. The consequent need to identify the scope of the particular duty which has been breached is entirely consistent, in my view, with the approach to common law damages set out in Lord Hoffmann's *South Australia* speech.

It is also consistent, in my judgment, with the House of Lords decision in *Target Holdings Ltd* v *Redferns*. The defendants have committed a breach of trust, but the default was remedied and therefore they were not liable to "reconstitute the fund". They remained liable to pay compensation, but the amount had to be assessed at the date of judgment rather than the date of breach. The plaintiffs had obtained precisely what they would have acquired had no breach occurred, and therefore, they appeared to have suffered no compensatable loss.

Evans LJ quoted extensively from Lord Browne-Wilkinson's judgment in *Target Holdings*, which he called "the stringent test of causation" and continued:

'I return therefore to Mr Bannister's submission in the present case. There is no finding and no allegation of fraud or of any breach of fiduciary duty which might be regarded as the equitable equivalent of fraud. Nor was the plaintiffs' loan itself inconsistent with the duties which they owed her. Their breach of duty consisted in failing to disclose material facts to the second defendant, as the judge held, and it can be assumed that she would be entitled to claim rescission of the loan agreement, if rescission was possible, and that she is now entitled to recover damages, or compensation, for the consequences of the breach. But the prima facie measure of such loss is the amount by which she is worse off now than she would have been if those breaches had not occurred. The failure to disclose cannot be said to have led to the making of the loan, even on a "but for" basis, precisely because disclosure of the true facts would not have affected her decision to accept it. Since she would have accepted the loan and completed the purchase, even if full disclosure had been made to her, she would have lost the value of the equity in her home in any event. She cannot recover damages or compensation for that loss, in my judgment, except on proof *either* that the plaintiffs acted fraudulently or in a manner equiva-

lent to fraud *or* that she would not have completed the purchase if full disclosure had been made, ie if the breach of duty had not occurred. She can do neither, and in my judgment her claim for damages must fail.'

Comment
The three recent cases of *Nestlé* (see Chapter 11), *Target Holdings* and *Swindle* v *Harrison* firmly establish that it is not enough to prove a breach of fiduciary duty – even a very serious one, as happened in all three cases. It is essential to establish a causal link between the financial loss suffered and the breach. Does this lower the standard expected of trustees and other fiduciaries?

Target Holdings v *Redferns (A Firm) and Another* [1995] 3 All ER 785 House of Lords (Lord Browne-Wilkinson, Lords Keith, Ackner, Jauncey and Lloyd)

• *Duties of a solicitor acting for mortgagees – breach of trust – remedy – restitution*

Facts
Target advanced £1,525,000 by way of a mortgage to P, with Redferns acting as solicitor for both Target and P. The loan was to be used to finance the purchase of a property declared to Target to have a value of £2 million and a purchase price also of £2 million. However, unknown to Target but know to Redferns, the purchase price was in fact only £775,000. P therefore created a string of companies to purchase the land which resulted in P ultimately appearing to buy it for £2 million. P subsequently defaulted on the mortgage. Target took possession, sold the property for £500,000 and, after discovery of the full facts, sought to claim against Redferns for breach of trust. In defence, Redferns argued that Target had lost nothing through their conduct as Target had always been prepared to advance the loan amount of £2 million.

Target applied for summary judgment against Redferns. At first instance this was refused, with Redferns being granted leave to defend, conditional upon an interim payment of £1 million to Target. On appeal by both Target (in respect of the refusal of summary judgment) and Redferns (in respect of the conditional leave to defend), the Court of Appeal held Redferns to be in breach of trust and liable to Target by way of restitution of the full loan as if it had never been advanced, less any credit by Target from having repossessed and sold the property.

Held

The House of Lords by a unanimous decision allowed Redferns' appeal. Redferns' breach of trust could only be said to have caused the actual loss ultimately suffered by Target (ie the shortfall between the money advanced and the amount recovered on sale of the property) if it could be shown that, but for the breach of trust, the transactions would not have gone ahead. This was not a matter for O.14 proceedings and pending a full trial it was appropriate to assume that the transaction would have gone ahead: Redferns would be given unconditional leave to defend. As to the merits, Lord Browne-Wilkinson (who gave the only judgment) thought it highly likely that the money had been essential to enable the transaction to go ahead and but for Redferns' breach of trust, Target would probably not have advanced any money and, therefore, not have suffered any loss.

Lord Browne-Wilkinson:

'The argument both before the Court of Appeal and your Lordships concentrated on the equitable rules establishing the extent and quantification of the compensation payable by a trustee who is in breach of trust. In my judgment this approach is liable to lead to the wrong conclusions in the present case because it ignores an earlier and crucial question, viz is the trustee who has committed a breach under any liability at all to the beneficiary complaining of the breach? There can be cases where, although

there is an undoubted breach of trust, the trustee is under no liability at all to a beneficiary. For example, if a trustee commits a breach of trust with the acquiescence of one beneficiary, that beneficiary has no right to complain and an action for breach of trust brought by him would fail completely. Again, there may be cases where the breach gives rise to no right to compensation. Say, as often occurs, a trustee commits a judicious breach of trust by investing in an unauthorised investment which proves to be very profitable to the trust. A carping beneficiary could insist that the unauthorised investment be sold and the proceeds invested in authorised investments: but the trustee would be under no liability to pay compensation either to the trust fund or to the beneficiary because the breach has caused no loss to the trust fund. Therefore, in each case the first question is to ask what are the rights of the beneficiary: only if some relevant right has been infringed so as to give rise to a loss is it necessary to consider the extent of the trustee's liability to compensate for such loss.

The basic right of a beneficiary is to have the trust duly administered in accordance with the provisions of the trust instrument, if any, and the general law. Thus, in relation to a traditional trust where the fund is held in trust for a number of beneficiaries having different, usually successive, equitable interests, (eg A for life with remainder to B), the right of each beneficiary is to have the whole fund vested in the trustees so as to be available to satisfy his equitable interests when, and if, it falls into possession. Accordingly, in the case of a breach of such a trust, involving the wrongful paying away of trust assets, the liability of the trustee is to restore to the trust fund, often called 'the trust estate', what ought to have been there.

The equitable rules of compensation for breach of trust have been largely developed in relation to such traditional trusts, where the only way in which all the beneficiaries' rights can be protected is to restore to the trust fund what ought to be there. In such a case the basic rule is that a trustee in breach of trust must restore or pay to the trust estate either the assets which have been lost to the estate by reason of the breach or compensation for such loss. Courts of Equity did not award damages but, acting in personam, ordered the defaulting trustee to restore the trust estate … If specific restitution of the trust property is not possible, then the liability of the trustee is to pay sufficient compensation to the trust estate to put it back to what it would have been had the breach not been committed … Even if the immediate cause of the loss is the dishonesty or failure of a third party, the trustee is liable to make good that loss to the trust estate if, but for the breach, such loss would not have occurred … Thus the common law rules of remoteness of damage and causation do not apply. However, there does have to be some causal connection between the breach of trust and the loss to the trust estate for which compensation is recoverable, viz. the fact that the loss would not have occurred but for the breach …

Hitherto, I have been considering the rights of beneficiaries under traditional trusts where the trusts are still subsisting and therefore the right of each beneficiary, and his only right, is to have the trust fund reconstituted as it should be. But what if at the time of the action claiming compensation for breach of trust those trusts have come to an end? Take as an example again the trust for A for life with remainder to B. During A's lifetime B's only right is to have the trust duly administered and, in the event of a breach, to have the trust fund restored. After A's death, B becomes absolutely entitled. He of course has the right to have the trust assets retained by the trustees until they have fully accounted for them to him. But if the trustees commit a breach of trust, there is no reason for compensating the breach of trust by way of an order for restitution and compensation *to the trust fund* as opposed to the beneficiary himself. The beneficiary's right is no longer simply to have the trust duly administered: he is, in equity, the sole owner of the trust estate. Nor, for the same reason, is restitution to the trust fund necessary to protect other beneficiaries. Therefore, although I do not wholly rule out the possibility that even in those circumstances an order to reconstitute the fund may be appropriate, in the ordinary case where a beneficiary becomes absolutely entitled to the trust fund the court orders, not restitution to the trust estate, but the payment of compensation directly to the beneficiary. The measure of such compensation is the same, ie the difference between what the beneficiary has in fact received and the amount he would have received but for the breach of trust.

Thus, in *Bartlett* v *Barclays Bank Trust Co Ltd (No 2)* by the date of the judgment some of the shares settled by the trust deed had become absolutely vested in possession … The compensation for breach of trust, though quantified by reference to what the fund would have been but for the breach of trust, was payable directly to the persons who were absolutely entitled to their shares of the trust fund … Accordingly, in traditional trusts for persons by way of succession, in my judgment once those trusts have been exhausted and the fund has become absolutely vested in possession, the beneficiary is not normally entitled to have the exhausted trust reconstituted. His right is to be compensated for the loss he has suffered by reason of the breach.'

Comment
Following *Nestlé* v *National Westminster Bank plc* (above Chapter 11), there must be a causal link between the loss suffered and the breach of trust.

Westdeutsche Landesbank Girozentrale v *Islington London Borough Council* [1996] 2 All ER 961 House of Lords (Lords Goff of Chieveley, Browne-Wilkinson, Slynn of Hadley, Woolf and Lloyd of Berwick)

• *Interest rate swap agreement – restitution – whether compound interest recoverable from date sum paid*

Facts

The bank entered into an interest rate swap agreement with the council. In proceedings brought against another local authority, such arrangements were declared to be beyond the scope of authority of the council concerned. This rendered the agreement between Westdeutsche and Islington London Borough Council void ab initio. The bank therefore brought proceedings for the recovery of monies advanced to the council and the material point to be decided by the House of Lords was whether the council was liable to pay simple or compound interest.

Held

By a 3:2 majority the House of Lords held that the council was not liable to pay compound interest. This was a common law action for money had and received on which only simple interest was payable. In the absence of fraud, courts of equity had never awarded compound interest except against a trustee or other person owing fiduciary duties in lieu of an account of profits improperly made by a trustee. The bank held the money under a contract rendered void because it was subsequently declared ultra vires. It did not hold the money under a resulting trust and there were no other circumstances under which the council could be said to hold the money under a fiduciary duty to the bank.

Lord Browne-Wilkinson:

> '*Was there a trust? The argument for the bank in outline*
> The bank submitted that, since the contract was void, title did not pass at the date of payment either at law or in equity. The legal title of the bank was extinguished as soon as the money was paid into the mixed account, whereupon the legal title became vested in the local authority. But, it was argued, this did not affect the *equitable interest*, which remained vested in the bank (the retention of title point). It was submitted that whenever the legal interest in property is vested in one person and the equitable interest in another, the owner of the

legal interest holds it on trust for the owner of the equitable title: "the separation of the legal from the equitable interest necessarily imports a trust." For this latter proposition (the separation of title point) the bank, of course, relies on *Sinclair* v *Brougham* and *Chase Manhattan Bank NA* v *Israel-British Bank (London) Ltd.*

> The generality of these submissions was narrowed by submitting that the trust which arose in this case was a resulting trust "not of an active character" ... This submission was reinforced, after completion of the oral argument by sending your Lordships Professor Peter Birks' paper "Restitution and Resulting Trusts" in *Equity and Contemporary Legal Developments, Papers presented at the First International Conference on Equity* (ed Goldstein, 1992) p335. Unfortunately, your Lordships have not had the advantage of any submission from the local authority on this paper, but an article by William Swadling "A New Role for Resulting Trusts?" (1996) 16 LS 110 puts forward counter-arguments which I have found persuasive.

> It is notable that the bank did not found any argument on the basis that the local authority was liable to repay either as a constructive trustee or under the in personam liability of the wrongful recipient of the estate of a deceased person established in *Re Diplock.*

> *The breadth of the submission*
> Although the actual question in issue on the appeal is a narrow one, on the arguments presented it is necessary to consider fundamental principles of trust law. Does the recipient of money under a contract subsequently found to be void for mistake or as being *ultra vires* hold the moneys received on trust even where he had no knowledge at any relevant time that the contract was void? If he does hold on trust, such trust must arise at the date of receipt or, at the latest, at the date the legal title of the payer is extinguished by mixing moneys in a bank account: in the present case, it does not matter at which of those dates the legal title was extinguished. If there is a trust two con-

sequences follow: <u>(a)</u> the recipient will be personally liable, regardless of fault, for any subsequent payment away of the moneys to third parties even though, at the date of such payment, the "trustee" was still ignorant of the existence of any trust … . <u>(b)</u> as from the date of the establishment of the trust (ie receipt or mixing of the moneys by the "trustee") <u>the original payer will have an equitable proprietary interest in the moneys so long as they are traceable into whomsoever's hands they come other than a purchaser for value of the legal interest without notice</u>. Therefore, although in the present case the only question directly in issue is the personal liability of the local authority as a trustee, <u>it is not possible to hold the local authority liable without imposing a trust</u>, which, in other cases, will create property rights affecting third parties because moneys received under a void contract are "trust property".

The relevant principles of trust law

(1) Equity operates on the conscience of the owner of the legal interest. In the case of a trust, the conscience of the legal owner requires him to carry out the purposes for which the property was vested in him (express or implied trust) or which the law imposes on him by reason of his unconscionable conduct (constructive trust).

(2) Since the equitable jurisdiction to enforce trusts depends upon the conscience of the holder of the legal interest being affected, he cannot be a trustee of the property if and so long as he is ignorant of the facts alleged to affect his conscience, ie until he is aware that he is intended to hold the property for the benefit of others in the case of an express or implied trust, or, in the case of a constructive trust, of the factors which are alleged to affect his conscience.

(3) In order to establish a trust there must be identifiable trust property. The only apparent exception to this rule is a constructive trust imposed on a person who dishonestly assists in a breach of trust who may come under fiduciary duties even if he does not receive identifiable trust property.

(4) Once a trust is established, as from the date of its establishment the beneficiary has,

in equity, a proprietary interest in the trust property, which proprietary interest will be enforceable in equity against any subsequent holder of the property (whether the original property or substituted property into which it can be traced) other than a purchaser for value of the legal interest without notice.

These propositions are fundamental to the law of trusts and I would have thought uncontroversial. However, proposition (2) may call for some expansion. There are cases where property has been put into the name of X without X's knowledge but in circumstances where no gift to X was intended. It has been held that such property is recoverable under a resulting trust (see *Birch* v *Blagrave, Childers* v *Childers, Re Vinogradoff, Allen* v *Jackson, Re Muller, Cassin* v *Mutual Cash Order Co Ltd*). These cases are explicable on the ground that, by the time action was brought, X or his successors in title have become aware of the facts which gave rise to a resulting trust; his conscience was affected as from the time of such discovery and *thereafter* he held on a resulting trust under which the property was recovered from him. There is, so far as I am aware, no authority which decides that X was a trustee, and therefore accountable for his deeds, at any time before he was aware of the circumstances which gave rise to a resulting trust.

Those basic principles are inconsistent with the case being advanced by the bank. <u>The latest time at which there was any possibility of identifying the "trust property" was the date on which the moneys in the mixed bank account of the local authority ceased to be traceable when the local authority's account went into overdraft in June 1987.</u> At that date, the local authority had no knowledge of the invalidity of the contract but regarded the moneys as its own to spend as it thought fit. <u>There was therefore never a time at which both (a) there was defined trust property and (b) the conscience of the local authority in relation to such defined trust property was affected. The basic requirements of a trust were never satisfied.</u>'

Lord Browne-Wilkinson then considered the bank's argument in detail on the retention of title point and the separation of title point and continued:

'*Resulting trust*
This is not a case where the bank had an equitable interest which predated receipt by the local authority of the upfront payment. Therefore, in order to show that the local authority became a trustee, the bank must demonstrate circumstances which raised a trust for the first time either at the date on which the local authority received the money or at the date on which payment into the mixed account was made. Counsel for the bank specifically disavowed any claim based on a constructive trust. This was plainly right because the local authority had no relevant knowledge sufficient to raise a constructive trust at any time before the moneys, upon the bank account going into overdraft, became untraceable. Once there ceased to be an identifiable trust fund, the local authority could not become a trustee (*Re Goldcorp Exchange Ltd*). Therefore, as the argument for the bank recognised, the only possible trust which could be established was a resulting trust arising from the circumstances in which the local authority received the upfront payment.

Under existing law a resulting trust arises in two sets of circumstances: (a) where A makes a voluntary payment to B or pays (wholly or in part) for the purchase of property which is vested either in B alone or in the joint names of A and B, there is a presumption that A did not intend to make a gift to B: the money or property is held on trust for A (if he is the sole provider of the money) or in the case of a joint purchase by A and B in shares proportionate to their contributions. It is important to stress that this is only a *presumption*, which presumption is easily rebutted either by the counter-presumption of advancement or by direct evidence of A's intention to make an outright transfer. ... (b) where A transfers property to B *on express trusts*, but the trusts declared do not exhaust the whole beneficial interest ... Both types of resulting trust are tradi-

tionally regarded as examples of trusts giving effect to the common intention of the parties. A resulting trust is not imposed by law against the intentions of the trustee (as is a constructive trust) but gives effect to his presumed intention. Megarry J in *Re Vandervell's Trusts (No 2)* suggests that a resulting trust of type (b) does not depend on intention but operates automatically. I am not convinced that this is right. If the settlor has expressly, or by necessary implication, abandoned any beneficial interest in the trust property, there is in my view no resulting trust: the undisposed of equitable interest vests in the Crown as bona vacantia: see *Re West Sussex Constabulary's Widows, Children and Benevolent (1930) Fund Trusts*.

Applying these conventional principles of resulting trust to the present case, the bank's claim must fail. There was no transfer of money to the local authority on express trusts: therefore a resulting trust of type (b) above could not arise. As to type (a) above, any presumption of resulting trust is rebutted since it is demonstrated that the bank paid, and the local authority received, the upfront payment with the intention that the moneys so paid should become the absolute property of the local authority. It is true that the parties were under a misapprehension that the payment was made in pursuance of a valid contract. But that does not alter the actual intentions of the parties at the date the payment was made in pursuance or the moneys were mixed in the bank account. As the article by William Swadling, "A New Role for Resulting Trusts?" demonstrates, the presumption of resulting trust is rebutted by evidence of any intention inconsistent with such a trust, not only by evidence of an intention to make a gift.

Professor Birks "Restitution and Resulting Trusts" in *Equity and Contemporary Legal Developments*, while accepting that the principles I have stated represent "a very conservative form" of definition of a resulting trust, argues from restitutionary principles that the definition should be extended so as to cover a perceived gap in the law of "subtractive unjust enrichment" so as to give a plaintiff a proprietary remedy when he has transferred value under a mistake or under a contract the consideration for which wholly fails. He suggests that a resulting trust should arise wherever the money is paid under a mistake (because such mistake vitiates the actual intention) or when money is paid on a condition which is not subsequently satisfied.

As one would expect, the argument is tightly reasoned but I am not persuaded. The search for a perceived need to strengthen the remedies of a plaintiff claiming in restitution involves, to my mind a distortion of trust principles. First, the argument elides rights in property (which is the only proper subject matter of a trust) into rights in "the value transferred". A trust can only arise where there is defined trust property: it is therefore not consistent with trust principles to say that a person is a trustee of property which cannot be defined. Second, Professor Birks' approach appears to assume (eg in the case of a transfer of value made under a contract the consideration for which subsequently fails) that the recipient will be deemed to have been a trustee from the date of the original receipt of money, ie the trust arises at a time when the "trustee" does not, and cannot, know that there is going to be a total failure of consideration. This result is incompatible with the basic premise on which all trust law is built, viz that the conscience of the trustee is affected. Unless and until the trustee is aware of the factors which give rise to the supposed trust, there is nothing which can affect his conscience. Thus neither in the case of a subsequent failure of consideration or in the case of a payment under a contract subsequently found to be void for mistake or failure of condition will there be circumstances, at the date of receipt, which can impinge on the conscience of the recipient, thereby making him a trustee. Thirdly, Professor Birks has to impose on his wider view an arbitrary and admittedly unprincipled modification so as to ensure that a resulting trust does not arise when there has only been a failure to perform a contract, as opposed to total failure of consideration. Such arbitrary

exclusion is designed to preserve the rights of creditors in the insolvency of the recipient. The fact that it is necessary to exclude artificially one type of case which would logically fall within the wider concept casts doubt on the validity of the concept.

If adopted, Professor Birks' wider concepts would give rise to all the practical consequences and injustices to which I have referred. I do not think it right to make an unprincipled alteration to the law of property (ie the law of trusts) so as to produce in the law of unjust enrichment the injustices to third parties which I have mentioned and the consequential commercial uncertainty which any extension of proprietary interests in personal property is bound to produce.'

Lord Browne-Wilkinson then reviewed the authorities principally relied upon that a resulting trust arises in the circumstances of this case and continued:

'The stolen bag of coins

The argument for a resulting trust was said to be supported by the case of a thief who steals a bag of coins. At law those coins remain traceable only so long as they are kept separate: as soon as they are mixed with other coins or paid into a mixed bank account they cease to be traceable at law. Can it really be the case, it is asked, that in such circumstances the thief cannot be required to disgorge the property which, in equity, represents the stolen coins? Money can only be traced in equity if there has been at some stage a breach of fiduciary duty, ie if either before the theft there was an equitable proprietary interest (eg the coins were stolen trust money) or such interest arises under a resulting trust at the time of the theft or the mixing of the moneys. Therefore, it is said, a resulting trust must arise either at the time of the theft or when the moneys are subsequently mixed. Unless this is the law, there will be no right to recover the assets representing the stolen moneys once the moneys have become mixed.

I agree that the stolen moneys are traceable in equity. But the proprietary interest which equity is enforcing in such circumstances arises under a constructive not a resulting trust. Although it is difficult to find clear authority for the proposition, when property is obtained by fraud equity imposes a constructive trust on the fraudulent recipient: the property is recoverable and traceable in equity. Thus, an infant who has obtained property by fraud is bound in equity to restore it …

Restitution and equitable rights
Those concerned with developing the law of restitution are anxious to ensure that, in certain circumstances, the plaintiff should have the right to recover property which he has unjustly lost. For that purpose they have sought to develop the law of resulting trusts so as to give the plaintiff a proprietary interest. For the reasons that I have given in my view such development is not based on sound principle and·in the name of unjust enrichment is capable of producing most unjust results. The law of resulting trusts would confer on the plaintiff a right to recover property from, or at the expense of, those who have not been unjustly enriched at his expense at all, for example the lender whose debt is secured by a floating charge and all other third parties who have purchased an equitable interest only, albeit in all innocence and for value.

Although the resulting trust is an unsuitable basis for developing proprietary restitutionary remedies, the remedial constructive trust, if introduced into English law, may provide a more satisfactory road forward. The court by way of remedy might impose a constructive trust on a defendant who knowingly retains property of which the plaintiff has been unjustly deprived. Since the remedy can be tailored to the circumstances of the individual case, innocent third parties would not be prejudiced and restitutionary defences, such as change of position, are capable of being given effect. However, whether English law should follow the United States and Canada by adopting the remedial constructive trust will have to be decided in some future case when the point is directly in issue.

The date from which interest is payable
The Court of Appeal held that compound interest was payable by the local authority on the balance for the time being outstanding, such interest to start from the date of the receipt by the local authority of the upfront payment of £2.5 million in June 1987. Although, for the reasons I have given, I do not think the court should award compound interest in this case, I can see no reason why interest should not start to run from the date of the upfront payment. I agree with the judgment of Leggatt LJ in the Court of Appeal that there is no good ground for departing from the general rule that interest is payable as from the date of the accrual of the cause of action.'

Comment
Although the point of law which came to the House of Lords was the relatively minor point on whether compound interest was payable, this is a landmark case for the whole of the law of trusts. Lord Browne-Wilkinson assesses and redefines the law of resulting trusts, tentatively suggests that English law should be thinking of adopting the concept of the remedial constructive trusts (subsequently declined in *Re Polly Peck International plc* – Chapter 6 above) and gives a useful analysis on the doctrine of tracing.

15 Breach of Trust II: Tracing

Agip (Africa) Ltd v *Jackson*

See Chapter 6.

Barlow Clowes International Ltd (In Liquidation) and Others v *Vaughan and Others* [1992] 4 All ER 22 Court of Appeal (Dillon, Woolf and Leggatt LJJ)

• *Tracing – mixing of investment funds –* Clayton's Case

Facts

The appellant was appealing against a decision holding that certain assets remaining after the Barlow Clowes International liquidation be distributed in accordance with the rule in *Clayton's Case*, ie that money deposited in an account and mixed be distributed on the assumption that withdrawals were in the same order as deposits – the 'first in, first out' rule.

Held

The appeal was allowed. The express wording of the investment application forms indicated all monies would form part of a common fund. It would be inappropriate to apply the rule in *Clayton's Case* as this would conflict with the investor's express or implied expectations as to how the fund would be distributed.

Woolf LJ:

> 'The approach, in summary which I would adopt to resolving the issues raised by this appeal [is] as follows:
> (1) While the rule in *Clayton's Case* is prima facie available to determine the interests of investors in a fund into which their investments have been paid, the use of the rule is a matter of convenience and if its application in particular circumstances would be impracticable or result in injustice between the investors it will not be applied if there is a preferable alternative.
> (2) Here the rule will not be applied because this would be contrary to either the express or inferred or presumed intention of the investors. If the investments were required by the terms of the investment contract to be paid into a common pool this indicates that the investors did not intend to apply the rule. If the investments were intended to be separately invested, as a result of the investments being collectively misapplied by BCI a common pool of the investments was created. Because of their shared misfortune, the investors will be presumed to have intended the rule to apply.
> (3) As the rule is inapplicable the approach which should be adopted by the court depends on which of the possible alternative solutions is the most satisfactory in the circumstances. If the North American solution is practical this would probably have advantages over the pari passu solution. However, the complications of applying the American solution in this case make the third solution the most satisfactory.
> (4) It must however be remembered that any solution depends on the ability to trace and if the fund had been exhausted will not be able to claim against moneys which were subsequently paid into the fund.'

Comment

Woolf LJ describes the 'North American solution' referred to above as follows:

> 'This solution involves treating credits to a bank account made at different times and from different sources as a blend or cocktail with the result that when a withdrawal is made from the account it is treated as a

withdrawal in the same proportions as the different interests in the account (here of the investors) bear to each other at the moment before the withdrawal is made. This solution should produce the most just result, but in this case, as counsel accept, it is not a live contender, since while it might just be possible to perform the exercise the costs involved would be out of all proportion even to the sizeable sums which are here involved.'

Boscawen and Others v *Bajwa and Others* [1996] 1 WLR 328 Court of Appeal (Stuart Smith, Waite and Millett LJJ)

• *Tracing and subrogation*

Facts

Mr Bajwa exchanged contracts for the sale of his property for £165,000. The purchasers were purchasing with the aid of a mortgage of £140,000 from the Abbey National Building Society which the Abbey National sent to the purchasers' solicitors by telegraphic transfer. The purchasers were instructed to use the mortgage monies only for the purposes of the purchase and, if this did not take place for any reasons to return the monies to Abbey National. Following conversations with Mr Bajwa's solicitors on 16 August 1990, the funds were telegraphed on to them and on 23 August Mr Bajwa's solicitors telegraphed them on to the Halifax plc to pay off the mortgage on Mr Bajwa's property. In October 1990, the purchaser's solicitors ceased to practice and the sole practitioner who ran the firm was the subject of a bankruptcy order. The sale fell through and the purchasers failed to acquire legal title to the property. They were declared judgment creditors of Mr Bajwa and were granted a charging order on the property. They brought proceedings against Mr Bajwa and Abbey National for enforcement of the charging order. An order for the sale of the property was made. Abbey National brought a counterclaim for an interest in the proceeds

of sale. At first instance it was held that £137,405 of Abbey National's advance could be traced into the funds of the Halifax and that they were entitled to a charge on the property by way of subrogation to the rights of the Halifax. The plaintiffs appealed on the grounds that Abbey National's money had been used to discharge a debt and no right to trace arose.

Held

Appeal dismissed. Abbey National had the right to trace because they were the principals in a fiduciary relationship with the purchaser's solicitors and had never intended to be an unsecured creditor. They intended to retain a beneficial interest in the money unless and until the purchase and the mortgage were completed. This gave rise to a right of subrogation.

Millett LJ:

'Equity lawyers habitually use the expressions "the tracing claim" and "the tracing remedy" to describe the proprietary claim and the proprietary remedy which equity makes available to the beneficial owner who seeks to recover his property *in specie* from those into whose hands it has come. Tracing properly so called, however, is neither a claim nor a remedy but a process. Moreover it is not confined to the case where the plaintiff seeks a proprietary remedy; it is equally necessary where he seeks a personal remedy against the knowing recipient or knowing assistant. It is the process by which the plaintiff traces what has happened to his property, identifies the persons who have handled or received it, and justifies his claim that the money which they handled or received (and, if necessary, which they still retain) can properly be regarded as representing his property. He needs to do this because his claim is based on the retention by him of a beneficial interest in the property which the defendant handled or received. Unless he can prove this he cannot (in the traditional language of equity) raise an equity against the defendant or (in the modern language of restitution) show that the defendant's unjust enrichment was at his expense.

If the plaintiff succeeds in tracing his property, whether in its original or in some changed form, into the hands of the defendant, and overcomes any defences which are put forward on the defendant's behalf, he is entitled to a remedy. The remedy will be fashioned to the circumstances. The plaintiff will generally be entitled to a personal remedy; if he seeks a proprietary remedy he must usually prove that the property to which he lays claim is still in the ownership of the defendant. If he succeeds in doing this, the court will treat the defendant as holding the property on a constructive trust for the plaintiff and will order the defendant to transfer it, *in specie,* to the plaintiff. But this is only one of the proprietary remedies which are available to a court of equity. If the plaintiff's money has been applied by the defendant, for example, not in the acquisition of a landed property, but in its improvement, then the court may treat the land as charged with the payment to the plaintiff of a sum representing the amount by which the value of the defendant's land has been enhanced by the use of the plaintiff's money. And if the plaintiff's money has been used to discharge a mortgage on the defendant's land, then the court may achieve a similar result by treating the land as subject to a charge by way of subrogation in favour of the plaintiff.

Subrogation therefore is a remedy, not a cause of action … It is available in a wide variety of different factual situations in which it is required in order to reverse the defendant's unjust enrichment. Equity lawyers speak of a right of subrogation, or of an equity of subrogation, but this merely reflects the fact that it is not a remedy which the court has a general discretion to impose whenever it thinks it just to do so. The equity arises from the conduct of the parties on well settled principles and in defined circumstances, which make it unconscionable for the defendant to deny the proprietary interest claimed by the plaintiff. A constructive trust arises in the same way. Once the equity is established, the court satisfies it by declaring the property in question subject to a charge, by way of subrogation in the one case, or a constructive trust in the other.

It is still a prerequisite of the right to trace in equity that there must be a fiduciary relationship which calls the equitable jurisdiction into being … That requirement is satisfied in the present case by the fact that, from the first moment of its receipt by Dave and Co in their general client account, the £140,000 was trust money held in trust for the Abbey National.'

Comment

This case gives a clear account of the role of the right to trace in trusts law.

Diplock, Re

See Chapter 14.

Foskett v *McKeown and Others*
[2000] 3 All ER 97 House of Lords (Lords Browne-Wilkinson, Steyn, Hoffmann, Hope of Craighead and Millett)

• *Whether beneficiaries can trace into the proceeds of a life policy where their fund has been mixed with other money to pay premiums*

Facts

Mr Murphy was a property developer who received funds from purchasers for properties which he agreed to build for them in Portugal. He held these moneys on an express trust for their benefit. In his personal capacity, he took out a life insurance policy and paid the first two annual premiums of £10,200 each out of his own funds. He paid at least the third and fourth premiums by taking money out of the purchasers' trust fund and mixing it with his own money in and out of various bank accounts. Murphy committed suicide. The insurers paid out £1 million to Mr Murphy's children who were the named beneficiaries of the policy. The purchasers claimed entitlement to at least 40 per cent of the money paid to the children. The majority of the Court of Appeal held that the purchasers could trace into the premiums but not into the policy. They appealed to the House of Lords.

Held (Lords Steyn and Hope dissenting)
Entitlement under the policy represented the traceable proceeds of the premiums paid out of the purchasers' trust fund and it followed that the purchasers were entitled to the insurance money paid on Murphy's death in the same shares and proportions as was represented by premiums paid with money taken from their fund. The policy moneys would be divided in proportion to the contributions which the parties had made to the premiums.

Lord Millett:

'My Lords, this is a textbook example of tracing through mixed substitutions. At the beginning of the story the purchasers were beneficially entitled under an express trust to a sum standing in the name of Mr Murphy in a bank account. From there the money moved into and out of various bank accounts where in breach of trust it was inextricably mixed by Mr Murphy with his own money. After each transaction was completed the purchasers' money formed an indistinguishable part of the balance standing to Mr Murphy's credit in a bank account. From there the money moved into and out of various bank accounts where in breach of trust it was inextricably mixed by Mr Murphy with his own money. After each transaction was completed the purchasers' money formed an indistinguishable part of the balance standing to Mr Murphy's credit in his bank account. The amount of that balance represented a debt due from the bank to Murphy, that is to say a chose in action. At the penultimate stage the purchasers' money was represented by an indistinguishable part of a different chose in action, viz the debt prospectively and contingently due from an insurance company to its policyholders, being the trustees of a settlement made by Mr Murphy for the benefit of his children. At the present and final stage it forms an indistinguishable part of the balance standing to the credit of the respondent trustees in their bank account.

Tracing and following
The process of ascertaining what happened to the purchasers' money involves both tracing and following. These are both exercises in locating assets which are or may be taken to represent an asset belonging to the purchasers and to which they assert ownership. The processes of following and tracing are, however, distinct. Following is the process of following the same asset as it moves from hand to hand. Tracing is the process of identifying a new asset as the substitute for the old. Where one asset is exchanged for another, a claimant can elect whether to follow the original asset into the hands of the new owner or to trace its value into the new asset in the hands of the same owner. In practice his choice is often dictated by the circumstances. In the present case the purchasers do not seek to follow the money any further once it reached the bank or insurance company, since its identity was lost in the hands of the recipient (which in any case obtained an unassailable title as a bona fide purchaser for value without notice of the purchasers' beneficial interest). Instead the purchasers have chosen at each stage to trace the money into its proceeds, viz the debt presently due from the bank to the account holder or the debt prospectively and contingently due from the insurance company to the policy holders.

Having completed this exercise, the purchasers claim a continuing beneficial interest in the insurance money. Since this represents the product of Mr Murphy's own money as well as theirs, which Mr Murphy mingled indistinguishably in a single chose in action, they claim a beneficial interest in a proportionate part of the money only. The transmission of a claimant's property rights from one asset to its traceable proceeds is part of our law of property, not of the law of unjust enrichment. There is no "unjust factor" to justify restitution (unless "want of title" be one, which makes the point). The claimant succeeds if at all by virtue of his own title, not to reverse unjust enrichment. Property rights are determined by fixed rules and settled principles. They are not discretionary. They do not depend upon ideas of what is "fair, just and reasonable". Such concepts, which in reality mask decisions of legal policy, have no place in the law of property.

A beneficiary of a trust is entitled to a continuing beneficial interest not merely in the trust property but in its traceable proceeds also, and his interest binds every one who takes the property or its traceable proceeds except a bona fide purchaser for value without notice. In the present case the purchasers' beneficial interest plainly bound Mr Murphy, a trustee who wrongfully mixed the trust money with his own and whose every dealing with the money (including the payment of the premiums) was in breach of trust. It similarly binds his successors, the trustees of the children's settlement, who claim no beneficial interest of their own, and Mr Murphy's children, who are volunteers. They gave no value for what they received and derive their interest from Mr Murphy by way of gift.

Tracing

We speak of money at the bank and of money passing into and out of a bank account. But of course the account holder has no money at the bank. Money paid into a bank account belongs legally and beneficially to the bank and not to the account holder. The bank gives value for it, and it is accordingly not usually possible to make the money itself the subject of an adverse claim. Instead a claimant normally sues the account holder rather than the bank and lays claim to the proceeds of the money in his hands. These consist of the debt or part of the debt due to him from the bank. We speak of tracing money into and out of the account, but there is no money in the account. There is merely a single debt of an amount equal to the final balance standing to the credit of the account holder. No money passes from paying bank to receiving bank or through the clearing system (where

the money flows may be in the opposite direction). There is simply a series of debits and credits which are causally and transactionally linked. We also speak of tracing one asset into another, but this too is inaccurate. The original asset still exists in the hands of the new owner, or it may have become untraceable. The claimant claims the new asset because it was acquired in whole or in part with the original asset. What he traces, therefore, is not the physical asset itself but the value inherent in it.

Tracing is thus neither a claim nor a remedy. It is merely the process by which a claimant demonstrates what has happened to his property, identifies its proceeds and the persons who have handled or received them, and justifies his claim that the proceeds can properly be regarded as representing his property. Tracing is also distinct from claiming. It identifies the traceable proceeds of the claimant's property. It enables the claimant to substitute the traceable proceeds for the original asset as the subject matter of his claim. But it does not affect or establish his claim. That will depend on a number of factors including the nature of his interest in the original asset. He will normally be able to maintain the same claim to the substituted asset as he could have maintained to the original asset. If he held only a security interest in the original asset, he cannot claim more than a security interest in its proceeds. But his claim may also be exposed to potential defences as a result of intervening transactions. Even if the purchasers could demonstrate what the bank had done with their money, for example, and could thus identify its traceable proceeds in the hands of the bank, any claim by them to assert ownership of those proceeds would be defeated by the bona fide purchaser defence. The successful completion of a tracing exercise may be preliminary to a personal claim (as in *El Ajou* v *Dollar Land Holdings plc*) or a proprietary one, to the enforcement of a legal right (as in *Trustees of the Property of FC Jones & Sons (A Firm)* v *Jones*), or an equitable one.

Given its nature, there is nothing inherently legal or equitable about the tracing exercise. There is thus no sense in maintaining different rules for tracing at law and in equity. One set of tracing rules is enough. The existence of two has never formed part of the law in the United States: see Scott *The Law of Trusts* (4th edn, 1989) pp605–609. There is certainly no logical justification for allowing any distinction between them to produce capricious results in cases of mixed substitutions by insisting on the existence of a fiduciary relationship as a precondition for applying equity's tracing rules. The existence of such a relationship may be relevant to the nature of the claim which the plaintiff can maintain, whether personal or proprietary, but that is a different matter. I agree with the passages which my noble and learned friend Lord Steyn has cited from Professor Birks' essay "The necessity of a unitary law of tracing" in *Making Commercial Law: Essays in Honour of Roy Goode* (1997) and with Dr Lionel Smith's exposition in his comprehensive monograph *The Law of Tracing* (1997), see particularly pp120–130, 277–279 and 342–347.

This is not, however, the occasion to explore these matters further, for the present is a straightforward case of a trustee who wrongfully misappropriated trust money, mixed it with his own, and used it to pay premiums on an equity linked policy of life assurance on his own life. The nature of the policy should make no difference in principle, though it may complicate the accounting. The second is that he had previously settled the policy for the benefit of his children. This should also make no difference. The claimant's rights cannot depend on whether the wrongdoer gave the policy to them by his will, or if during his lifetime whether he did so before or after he had recourse to the claimant's money to pay the premiums. The order of events does not affect the fact that the children are not contributors but volunteers who have received the gift of an asset paid for in part with misappropriated trust moneys.'

Comment

The matter was complicated by the fact that the sums paid out under the life assurance policy would have been the same whether or not the additional contributions had been paid from the purchasers' fund. Rejecting an unjust enrichment analysis, Lord Hope agreed with the majority in the Court of Appeal that the purchasers were not entitled 'to participate in the amount of the death benefit except to the extent necessary for them to recover the premiums, with interest, which were paid from their money which had been misappropriated.'

Goldcorp Exchange Ltd, Re [1994] 3 WLR 199 Privy Council (Lords Templeman, Mustill, Lloyd of Berwick and Sir Thomas Echelbaum)

• *Equitable lien*

Facts

Goldcorp were bullion dealers who held stocks of bullion for customers until future delivery. They were put into receivership by the Bank of New Zealand and the bank claimed that the bullion was an asset of Goldcorp and property had never passed to the customers because the bullion had never been separated from the company's trading stock despite assurances in Goldcorp's advertising material. There were three classes of customers: non-allocated customers whose bullion had never been ascertained; a Mr Liggett who bought gold coins from Goldcorp which were never ascertained; and clients of a company, Walker & Hall Limited, which had subsequently been taken over by Goldcorp who had contracts with Walker & Hall Ltd.

Held

The assurances in the brochures did not constitute a declaration of trust in favour of the first two categories of customers and no fiduciary relationship arose. Property did not pass in law or in equity in the unascertained goods.

However, at first instance the judge found in favour of the Walker & Hall claimants but this was overturned by the Court of Appeal and then restored by the House of Lords.

Lord Mustill:

'On the facts found by the judge, the company as bailee held bullion belonging to the individual Walker & Hall claimants, intermingled the bullion of all such claimants, mixed that bullion with bullion belonging to the company, withdrew bullion from the mixed fund and then purchased more bullion, which was added to the mixed fund, without the intention of replacing the bullion of the Walker & Hall claimants. In these circumstances, the bullion belonging to the Walker & Hall claimants which became held by the company's receivers consisted of bullion equal to the lowest balance of metal held by the company at any time.

The Walker & Hall claimants now seek to go further and ask the court to impose an equitable lien on all the property of the company at the date of the receivership to recover the value of their bullion unlawfully misappropriated by the company.'

Lord Mustill considered the authorities and continued:

'The law relating to the creation and tracing of equitable proprietary interests is still in a state of development. In *Attorney-General for Hong Kong* v *Reid,* the Board decided that money received by an agent as a bribe was held in trust for the principal who is entitled to trace and recover property representing the bribe. In *Lord Napier and Ettrick* v *Hunter*, the House of Lords held that payment of damages in respect of an insured loss created an equitable charge in favour of the subrogated insurers so long only as the damages were traceable as an identifiable fund. When the scope and ambit of these decisions and the observations of the Board in the *Space Investments* case fall to be considered, it will be necessary for the history and foundations in principle of the creation and tracing of equitable proprietary interests to be the subject of close examination …

In the present case, it is not necessary or appropriate to consider the scope and ambit of the observations in the *Space Investments* case or their application because all members of the Board are agreed that it would be inequitable to impose a lien in favour of the Walker & Hall claimants. Those claimants received the same certificates and trusted the company in a manner no different from other bullion customers. There is no evidence that the debenture holders and the unsecured creditors at the date of the receivership benefited directly or indirectly from the breaches of trust committed by the company or that Walker & Hall bullion continued to exist as a fund latent in property vested in the receivers.

In these circumstances, the Walker & Hall claimants must be restored to the remedies granted to them by the trial judge.'

Comment

The claimants were seeking to trace into an unascertained mass of bullion and the court applied the same principles as those which apply when claimants are seeking to trace into a mixed fund of money.

Note: The Board referred to is the Board of the Privy Council.

Hallett's Estate, Re (1880) 13 Ch D 696 Court of Appeal (Jessel MR, Baggallay and Thesiger LJJ)

- *Priorities in tracing where trustee/fiduciary has mixed different funds*

Facts

Hallett, a solicitor was one of the trustees of a marriage settlement made for the benefit of himself, his wife and children. He also acted as solicitor to a trust of which a Mrs Cotterill was a beneficiary, but he was not a trustee of the Cotterill trust. Hallett mixed money belonging to the marriage settlement and money he had received on behalf of the Cotterill trust together with his own money in his private bank account. He drew on this account for his own purposes and paid in sums to the account subsequently. At his death his estate was insolvent so there was not enough to meet his personal debts and the claims of the two funds. Two matters were put before the court: (1) could Mrs Cotterill trace the funds belonging to the trust under which she was a beneficiary even though Hallett had not been a trustee of that trust; and (2) if she was entitled to trace, how payments from the fund should be allocated as between the creditors of Hallett's estate, the Cotterill trust and the marriage settlement.

Held

1. There was a fiduciary relationship between Hallett and Mrs Cotterill. He had received trust property with knowledge that it was trust property and mixed it with his own money improperly. Mrs Cotterill was therefore entitled to trace.

2. Where a trustee had mixed beneficiary's money with his own in one fund the beneficiary had a first charge on the whole fund for the trust money.

3. Where a trustee mixes trust monies with his own monies, as between the trustee and the beneficiary, the rule in Clayton's case does not apply. Instead, it is presumed that the trustee acted with an honest intention and therefore exhausted his own money in the account first. Therefore, if any monies remained in the account after all the trustee's money had been withdrawn this belonged to the beneficiary.

4. As there were sufficient monies in the estate to satisfy the claims of Mrs Cotterill and the marriage settlement it was unnecessary to consider the position in tracing as between the claimants themselves.

Sir George Jessel MR:

'The modern doctrine of Equity as regards property disposed of by persons in a fiduciary position is a very clear and well-established doctrine. You can, if the sale was rightful, take the proceeds of the sale, if you can identify them. If the sale was wrongful, you can still take the proceeds of the sale., in a sense adopting the sale for the purpose of taking the proceeds, if you can identify them. There is no distinction, therefore, between a rightful and a wrongful disposition of the property, so far as regards the right of the beneficial owner to follow the proceeds. But it very often happens that you cannot identify the proceeds. The proceeds may have been invested together with money belonging to the person in a fiduciary position in a purchase. He may have bought land with it, for instance, or he may have bought chattels with it. Now, what is the position of the beneficial owner as regards such purchases? I will, first of all, take his position when the purchase is clearly made with what I will call, for shortness, the trust money, although it is not confined, as I will shew presently, to express trusts. In that case, according to the now well-established doctrine of Equity, the beneficial owner has a right to elect either to take the property purchased, or to hold it as a security for the amount of the trust money laid out in the purchase; or, as we generally express it, he is entitled at his election, either to take the property, or to have a charge on the property for the amount of the trust money. But in the second case where a trustee has mixed the money with his own, there is this distinction, that the cestui que trust, or beneficial owner, can no longer elect to take the property, because it is no longer bought with the trust money simply and purely, but with a mixed fund. He is, however, still entitled to a charge on the property purchased, for the amount of the trust money laid out in the purchase; and the charge is quite independent of the fact of the amount laid out by the trustee. The moment you get a substantial portion of it furnished by the trustee, using the word 'trustee' in the sense I have mentioned, as including a person in a fiduciary relation, the right to the charge follows. That is the modern doctrine of equity.'

Comment

This case gave us the doctrine subsequently applied in, among other cases, *Foskett* v *McKeown* above.

Ministry of Health v Simpson [1951] AC 251 House of Lords (Lords Simonds, Normand, Oaksey, Morton and MacDermott)

• *Personal remedy against a recipient of funds under a breach of trust*

Facts
This was an appeal from the judgment of the Court of Appeal in *Re Diplock* where the facts are set out in full. The relevant point, and decision, of the appeal is set out in Lord Simonds' judgment.

Held
Lord Simonds:

'The problem for determination can be simply stated and it is perhaps surprising that the sure answer to it is only to be found by examination of authorities which go back nearly three hundred years. Acting under a mistake the personal representatives of a testator whose residuary disposition is invalid distribute his residuary estate upon the footing that it is valid. Have the next of kin a direct claim in equity against the person to whom it has been wrongfully distributed? I think that the authorities clearly establish that, subject to certain qualifications … they have such a claim.

I think it is important in a discussion of this question to remember that the particular branch of the jurisdiction of the Court of Chancery with which we are concerned relates to the administration of the assets of a deceased person. While in the development of this jurisdiction certain principles were established which were common to it and to the comparable jurisdiction in the execution of trusts, I prefer to look solely at the authorities which are strictly germane to the present question: it is from them alone that the nature and extent of the equity are to be ascertained.

Before I turn back to the seventeenth century when the Court of Chancery was gradually wresting from the spiritual courts the jurisdiction in administering the assets

of deceased persons and framing apt rules to that end, I will refer first to a statement made by Lord Davey early in this century which, as I think, illuminated the position. In *Harrison* v *Kirk* Lord Davey says this:

"But the Court of Chancery, in order to do justice and to avoid the evil of allowing one man to retain what is really and legally applicable to the payment of another man, devised a remedy by which, where the estate had been distributed either out of court or in court without regard to the rights of a creditor, it has allowed the creditor to recover back what has been paid to the beneficiaries or the next of kin who derive from the deceased testator or intestate."

The importance of this statement is manifold. It explains the basis of the jurisdiction, the evil to be avoided and its remedy: its clear implication is that no such remedy existed at common law: it does not suggest that it is relevant whether the wrong payment was made under error of law or of fact: it is immaterial whether those who have been wrongly paid are beneficiaries under a will or next of kin, it is sufficient that they derive title from the deceased. It is true that Lord Davey expressly dealt with a claimant creditor, not a beneficiary or next of kin. I shall show your Lordships that what he said of the one might equally be said of the other. It would seem strange if a Court of equity, whose self-sought duty it was to see that the assets of a deceased person were duly administered and came into the right hands and not into the wrong hands, devised a remedy for the protection of the unpaid creditor but left the unpaid legatee or next of kin unprotected …

Finally, my Lords, I must say some words on an argument of a more general character put forward on behalf of the appellant. The Court of Chancery, it was said, acted upon the conscience, and, unless the defendant had behaved in an unconscientious manner, would make no decree against him. The appellant or those through whom he claimed, having received a legacy in good faith and having spent it without knowledge of any flaw in their title, ought not in conscience to be ordered to refund ... Upon the propriety of a legatee refusing to repay to the true owner the money that he has wrongly received I do not think it necessary to express any judgment ... The broad fact remains that the Court of Chancery, in order to mitigate the rigour of the common law or to supply its deficiencies, established the rule of equity which I have described and this rule did not excuse the wrongly paid legatee from repayment because he had spent what he had been wrongly paid. No doubt the plaintiff might by his conduct and particularly by laches have raised some equity against himself; but if he had not done so, he was entitled to be repaid. In the present case the respondents have done nothing to bar them in equity from asserting their rights.'

Comment

The court upheld the right of the next of kin to recover against the innocent recipients of the Diplock moneys. One of the trustees of the fund committed suicide because of the breach of trust – further evidence of the onerous nature of trusteeship.

National Westminster Bank plc v Somer International (UK) Ltd
[2003] 3 WLR 64 Court of Appeal (Peter Gibson, Potter and Clarke LJJ)

• *Money paid under a mistake – estoppel by representation – change of position*

Facts

The bank paid $US76,708.57 into Somer International's account with them by mistake. Somer International were expecting a payment from one of their customers of between US70,000 and 78,000. Believing the mistaken payment to be the one they were expecting, they dispatched further orders to the value of £13,000 to the same customer. By the time the bank notified Somer International of the mistake, they had lost the opportunity to recover the sums owing from the customer who, in the meantime, had gone into liquidation. The bank brought proceedings to recover the mistaken payment. At first instance the judge held that the bank was estopped from recovering the payment to the extent to which Somer International had placed detrimental reliance on it. It was further held that Somer International could not claim the sums they might have recovered from their customer had they not been misled by the mistaken payment. The company appealed.

Held

The appeal was dismissed. The doctrine of estoppel by representation was governed by considerations of justice and equity. Although the doctrine would give the transferee the right to keep the whole of the mistaken payment, in the present case the payment by the bank bore no relation to the size of the detriment and it would therefore be unconscionable for Somer International to keep the balance of the payment left over after reimbursement for the shipments subsequently made to the customer.

Potter LJ:

'In *Scottish Equitable plc* v *Derby*, the claimant insurance company had overstated the amount of a pension fund available to the defendant, as a result of which he received a substantial overpayment, the company having overlooked the fact that he had previously exercised an option to take an early retirement benefit. The result of the benefits accruing to the defendant were, in broad terms, that he received an overpayment of some £172,000, while incurring expenditure of some £9,600 in making modest improvements to his lifestyle in reliance on the overstatement received. At first instance, Harrison J, in referring to the *Avon CC* case [*Avon CC* v *Howlett*], cited the reservations contained in the individual judgments which we have quoted and said as follows:

"On the face of it, therefore, *Avon CC* v *Howlett* provides strong support for the defendant's submission that, some detriment having been shown, estoppel should operate as a complete defence. However, it is important to bear in mind two matters. Firstly, the reservations expressed by the Court of Appeal as to the ambit of the decision in that case, and, secondly, the fact that that case was decided before the House of Lords recognised the defence of change of position in the *Lipkin Gorman* case (*Lipkin Gorman (A Firm)* v *Karpnale Ltd*."

He went on to say:

"In my judgment, it would be unconscionable, or clearly inequitable, to allow the defendant to keep the whole of the overpayment of £172,451 when his detriment was limited to £9,662 of that amount. In those circumstances and having regard to the dicta of the Court of Appeal, which I have just quoted, I do not consider that I am bound by *Avon CC* v *Howlett* to hold, in the circumstances of this case, that estoppel must operate as a complete defence. Secondly, there is the fact, as I have mentioned, that the case was decided before the House of Lords recognised the defence of change of position in the *Lipkin Gorman* case. In the latter case, Lord Goff remarked that previously these kind [sic] of cases have been dealt with on the basis of estoppel."

Before turning to the decision on appeal in the *Scottish Equitable* case, I pause to make reference to the decision of Jonathan Parker J in *Philip Collins Ltd* v *Davis*, in which he was concerned with a change of position defence in a situation where he did not regard the making of the payments sought to be repaid as amounting to a representation for the purposes of estoppel by representation. In so holding, he made the following observation:

"In any event, as I read the relevant authorities, the law has now developed to the point where a defence of estoppel by representation is no longer apt in restitutionary claims where the most flexible defence of change of position is in principal available ..."

He then went on to find that the ingredients of the defence of change of position had

been established in respect of half the overpayment claimed.

In his leading judgment in the Court of Appeal, affirming the decision of Harrison J, in the *Scottish Equitable* case, Robert Walker LJ asked three questions, the second and third of which were how far the defence of change of position assisted the payee in the circumstances of the case and what part (if any) had estoppel to play now that the defence of change of position has been recognised. So far as change of position was concerned, he referred to the view of Andrew Burrows, *The Law of Restitution* (1993), pp424-428, that there is a narrow and wide version of the defence.'

Potter LJ then quoted at length from Robert Walker LJ's judgment in the *Scottish Equitable* case and continued:

'It seems to me that the facts of this case are such that, assuming the judge was correct in holding that a representation had been made by NatWest upon which Somer acted to its detriment in consigning further goods to Mentor to the value of some £13,000 but in no further respect, it involves this court in facing directly the questions raised by Robert Walker LJ. In the *Scottish Eqitable* case the actual detriment found by the court, and which Scottish Equitable conceded it would not seek to recover, was some £9,600 out of a total overpayment of £172,451, a ratio of 1:17, giving rise to an overpayment of £162,790. While it could not be said that the detriment to Mr Derby was de minimis, it could readily be held that it was unconscionable and inequitable to allow him to retain the vast bulk of the overpayment, when his real detriment was limited to such a small proportion, and hence within the exception to the "all or nothing" rule recognised in the *Avon CC* case. The instant case is, by reason of the sums involved, a somewhat less glaring illustration of an unjustifiable windfall to the defendant. That said, however, in cases of payments made under a mistake of fact, it is difficult to see why principles of equity and unconscionability should not apply to cover any case in which it appears a substantial windfall would otherwise be incurred by the transferee at the expense of the mistaken transferor. ...

It is unattractive that, in a case of moneys paid over under a mistake of fact and sought to be recovered on the basis of unjust enrichment, the extent of the recovery should depend on whether or not, at the time of the transfer of the moneys, the transferor represented by words or conduct that the transferee was entitled to such payment. When the mistake occurs, particularly in the context of a banker/customer relationship, whether or not an actual representation as to entitlement was made or can be spelt out is largely fortuitous and ex hypothesi the result of accident rather than deliberate conduct. It also seems clear that, where there has been such a representation, the only substantial hurdle standing in the way of recovery, subject to an appropriate equitable adjustment in relation to the actual "detriment" suffered, is the view that the historical origin and technical status of estoppel by representation as a rule of evidence dictates an "'all or nothing" solution, the effect of which is that, once the representation has been acted on to the detriment of the transferee, the contrary may not be asserted. This differs from the position in the case of so-called "equitable" or "promissory" estoppel in respect of which a specific promise to waive or refrain from enforcing rights may be withdrawn on reasonable notice and, in "proprietary" estoppel, where when giving effect to the interest or right in property which the party raising the estoppel asserts, the court assumes discretion as to the terms on which such relief is granted. In this respect estoppel by representation also differs in nature from the defence of "change of position" which is only permitted to prevail to the extent that it would be inequitable to require the transferee to return the money.'

Comment

This case establishes the point that estoppel by representation no longer entails the right to retain the whole of the mistaken payment but only that part which but for the mistake would not have been spent by the defendant.

Philip Collins Ltd v Davis and Another [2000] 3 All ER 808
Chancery Division (Jonathan Parker J)

• *Restitution – change of position*

Facts

Following a world tour by the singer, Phil Collins, a 15-track recording of the live performances was released. Under the terms of their contract for the tour, members of the backing group were entitled to royalties for any performances which were used for the recording. The defendants played on five of the tracks used on the recording but under a mistake were paid as if they had contributed to all 15 tracks. In 1997 the company informed Davis, one of the backing artists affected, that a mistake had been made and informed him that they would take steps to recover the overpayments. In the proceedings, Davis and his co-defendant pleaded, inter alia, change of position and estoppel by representation, contending that each payment received was a representation upon which they had relied to their detriment.

Held

Under the terms of the contract, the royalties to be paid to the defendants were in respect of the five tracks on which they had performed only. The mere tendering of a payment did not amount to a representation without more. The overpayments which were paid periodically over a long period, had caused a change of position because the defendants had increased their level of outgoings, but the change of position did not provide a defence to the whole claim as there was no evidence that the level of outgoings would have been reduced if the sums to which they were entitled had been paid.

Jonathan Parker J:

'If the recovery of the overpayments is to be denied in the instant case, it must be denied not as a matter of discretion but of legal principle. What, then, are the relevant legal principles, in the context of the instant case?

For obvious reasons, it would not be appropriate for me to attempt to set out an exhaustive list of the legal principles applicable to the defence of change of position, but four principles in particular seem to me to be called into play in the instant case.

In the first place, the evidential burden is on the defendant to make good the defence of change of position. However, in applying this principle it seems to me that the court should beware of applying too strict a standard. Depending on the circumstances, it may well be unrealistic to expect a defendant to poroduce conclusive evidence of change of position, given that when he changed his position he can have had no expectation that he might thereafter have to prove that he did so, and the reason why he did so, in a court of law ... In the second place, as Lord Goff stressed in the passage from his speech in the *Lipkin Gorman* case quoted above, to amount to a change of position there must be something more than mere expenditure of the money sought to be recovered "because the expenditure might in any event have been incurred ... in the ordinary course of things". In the third place, there must be a causal link between the change of position and the overpayment. In *South Tyneside Metropolitan BC* v *Svenska International plc*, Clarke J, following Hobhouse J in *Kleinwort Benson Ltd* v *South Tyneside Metropolitan BC*, held that, as a general principle, the change of position must have occurred after receipt of the overpayment, although in Goff & Jones the correctness of this decision is doubted (see pp 822–3). But whether or not a change of position may be anticipatory, it must (as I see it) have been made as a consequence of the receipt of, or (it may be) the prospect of receiving, the money sought to be recovered: in other words it must, on the evidence, be referable in some way to the payment of that money. In the fourth place, as Lord Goff also made clear in his speech in the *Lipkin Gorman* case, in contrast to the defence of estoppel the defence of change of position is not an "all or nothing" defence: it is available only to the extent that the change of position renders recovery unjust.'

Comment

These are the dicta approved by Robert Walker LJ in *Scottish Equitable plc* v *Derby* (below). While it is not necessary to prove every item of expenditure, the expenditure must be referable in some way to the overpayment – again, there must be a causal link.

Russell-Cooke Trust Co v *Prentis and Others* [2003] 2 All ER 478
Chancery Division (Lindsay J)

• *Rule in* Clayton's Case – *application of the 'first in, first out' rule – whether 'North American' solution appropriate – whether fund to be distributed in proportion to the amount of investments*

Facts

A sole practitioner solicitor sent up an investment fund (SPIP)which offered a fixed return of 15 per cent on investments which were held in the solicitor's client account. The Law Society intervened in the running of his practice and substantial shortfalls in income and capital were discovered. The court was asked to rule on the correct method of distribution of the assets between three possible options:

1. according to the 'first in, first out' rule in *Clayton's Case*;
2. on the basis of a rolling charge – the 'North American' method; or
3. in accordance with the proportions in which the investors had contributed to the fund – the 'pari passu' method.

Held

The rule in *Clayton's Case* had not been chal-

lenged in recent cases but had been distinguished on the facts of individual cases. The
rule was not applied when a contrary intention arose from the facts of the case and the
facts of the present case rebutted the presumption of an intention to implement a 'first in,
first out' scheme. In accordance with the
Solicitors' Accounts Rules, a pari passu
scheme should be applied.

Lindsay J quoted at length from *Barlow
Clowes International Ltd (In Liquidation)* v
Vaughan and continued:

'In the *Barlow Clowes* case Woolf LJ
referred to common misfortune. He had
earlier referred to Morritt J's comment in
*Re Eastern Capital Futures Ltd (In
Liquidation)* ... where that judge had
referred to there being no suggestion in that
case that any client or class of client was
more or less innocent than any other and
that the equities between them were thus
equal. Woolf LJ referred ... to shared misfortune again. Leggatt LJ returned to the
subject of common misfortune. However,
such references cannot be enlarged into
support for a proposition that, wherever
there is a shared common misfortune,
clearly discernible separate property rights
are to be surrendered or overridden.
Investors may, so to speak, be in the same
boat but that, of itself, does not require
anyone to give up the life jacket which he
is already plainly wearing.

As I shall come to when examining for the
separate trusts solution, there were undoubtedly some cases of the specific allocation
of some assets – legal charges – to specific
and identified investors in proportions inter
se that were ascertained or ascertainable.
Miss Tipples' argument, based on common
misfortune, would require that even those
specific allocations were to be overridden
by reference to such a misfortune having
befallen all investors. As I have said, her
argument as Mr Wonnacott urges, would
require some form of divesting of those specific property interests in favour of the pool.
Indeed, even to suppose that the misfortune
was common to all may be unjustified in

some cases, where the charged property
specifically allocated might prove sufficient
to meet the specific debt for which it was
given as security. There is, in my judgment,
no way in which the invocation of a
"common misfortune" can lead to a pool
solution such as to require all charged properties to be SPIP assets from which all SPIP
liabilities are to be met.

There is no other or further argument in
favour of the pool solution and accordingly
I reject it. ...

In jurisdictions unbound by *Clayton's
Case* and by subsequent English authorities
on the subject, *Clayton's Case* has very
often been roundly criticised ... The modern
approach in England has generally not been
to challenge the binding nature of the rule
but rather to permit it to be distinguished by
reference to the facts of the particular case.
Thus in *Barlow Clowes International Ltd
(In Liquidation)* v *Vaughan* ... Woolf LJ,
after a full citation of the authorities, held ...
that the rule did not apply where circumstances from which a counter intention
might be presumed were found. Such relevant circumstances could include acts and
omissions after the investor had made his
investment and also the injustice between
investors if a rule so arbitrary in its effects
were to be imposed ... Leggatt LJ also saw
the rule as capable of being displaced by a
presumed intention. He regarded it as capricious, arbitrary and inapposite. It is plain
from all three of the judgments in the
Barlow Clowes case, the third being that of
Dillon LJ, that the rule can be displaced by
even a slight counterweight. Indeed, in
terms of its actual application between beneficiaries who have in any sense met a
shared misfortune, it might be more accurate
to refer to the exception that is, rather than
the rule in, *Clayton's Case*.

Here, in *Prentis*' case, there is, in my
view, an available counterweight; it is quite
plain that payments out of the No 2 account
over the period of its operation showed a
pattern of allocation or appropriation such
than one could not say that payments in led
to allocations by way of payments out in the
same sequence. On the contrary, allocation

was on occasion completely out of step with the sequence in which payments in had been made. That, as it seems to me, was only to be expected and could reasonably have been foreseen by investors from the publicity material I have described. If, say, a given loan of £100,000 was intended to be made by the SPIP but that investments of only, say, £95,000 were currently available, then if two further investments were expected of, say, £15,000 and £5,000 respectively, they being expected shortly, it would surely have been foreseen to make more sense to await that of £5,000, even if it came in second, rather than dividing the £15,000 first received over two or more loans. Whilst the brochures made it plain that investments might be combined, nothing indicated combinations would be made up in a strict temporal sequence and a moment's reflection by an investor or, indeed, an inquiry into what, in practice, was done, would have been likely to lead to a conclusion that there would be no such strict sequence. It is, as I see it, one thing to apply a "first in, first out" rule where it might have been expected or intended by the investors to be applied and where nothing is known inconsistent with its being so expected or intended but quite another to presume it as an intention where both a reasonable contemplation of what was intended and the known facts can be seen to be inconsistent with it. On that ground, I shall not apply *Clayton's Case* to payments in and unallocated payments made out of the No 2 account.

As for the "North American" method, this is described by Dillon LJ in the *Barlow Clowes* case ... as a system used to avoid a loss falling first on the depositor who happened to have made the first deposit in point of time. If that reason does not exist where, as here, *Clayton's Case* is not being applied in any event, that prime reason to adopt the method falls away. The method is, in any event, complicated and may be expensive to apply.

Accordingly I prefer a pari passu system as was the solution adopted in the *Barlow Clowes* case. It is, to my mind, the system

least unfairly distributing loss of an account that should have been dealt with in accordance with the Solicitors' Accounts Rules 1991.'

Comment
Lindsay J favours the pari passu method of distribution as the fairest in the circumstances of this case and the least complicated by compariston with the 'North American' of distribution.

Scottish Equitable plc v *Derby*
[2001] 3 All ER 818 Court of Appeal (Simon Brown, Robert Walker and Keene LJ)

• *Restitution – defence of change of position*

Facts
Derby held a single-premium pensions policy with Equitable Life on which he had taken an early retirement option. This was not recorded on the company's records and subsequently in 1995 he received a computer printout showing that his fund with Equitable Life stood at £201,938, rather than the £29,486 which was due to him after exercise of the early retirement option. Derby received a lump sum of £51,333 and a further £150,604 was reinvested for him with another pension provider. Thus he received an overpayment of £172,451. Before Equitable Life became aware of the overpayment, Derby used £41,671 to pay off some of the mortgage on the matrimonial home and spent a further £9,600 on modest improvements to his lifestyle. Equitable Life brought an action to recover the overpayment. The second pension company repaid the sum invested with them but Derby raised the defence of change of position in relation to the sums overpaid to him. The judge at first instance held that the defence could be raised in respect of the sum of £9,600 but not in respect of the mortgage repayment. Derby appealed.

Held

The appeal was dismissed. There must be a causal link between the sum paid and the change of position pleaded. The repayment of the mortgage was not a detriment – the repayment would have to be made in any event.

Robert Walker LJ:

'Change of position
The facts of the *Lipkin Gorman* case [*Lipkin Gorman* v *Karpnale Ltd* ... in which the House of Lords recognised the defence of change of position, are well known. The gaming club had received large sums of money misappropriated by a solicitor who was addicted to gambling, but it had changed its position by paying out on his winning bets. Lord Goff ... noted that in the past, where change of position had been relied on by the defendant, it had been usual to treat the problem as one of estoppel ...

There were two main objections to that sort of approach. First, estoppel required there to have been a representation made by one party on which the other had placed reliance and had acted to his detriment: but in many cases involving a dishonest third party (such as the *Lipkin Gorman* case itself) the true owner had done nothing that could possibly be regarded as the making of a representation ... Second, estoppel was ... an inflexible, all or nothing, defence. Lord Goff observed ... "Considerations such as these provide a strong indication that, in many cases, estoppel is not an appropriate concept to deal with the problem."

Lord Goff went on:

"In these circumstances, it is right that we should ask ourselves: why do we feel that it would be unjust to allow restitution in cases such as these? The answer must be that, where an innocent defendant's position is so changed that he will suffer an injustice if called upon to repay or to repay in full, the injustice of requiring him so to repay outweighs the injustice of denying the plaintiff restitution. If the plaintiff pays money to the defendant under a mistake of fact, and the defendant then, acting in good faith, pays the money or part of it to charity, it is unjust to require the defendant to make restitution to the extent that he has so changed his position."

He noted the general acceptance of the defence in other common law jurisdictions ... Lord Goff said:

"I am most anxious that, in recognising this defence to actions of restitution, nothing should be said at this stage to inhibit the development of the defence on a case by case basis, in the usual way ... At present I do not wish to state the principle any less broadly than this: that the defence is available to a person whose position has so changed that it would be inequitable in all the circumstances to require him to make restitution or, alternatively to make restitution in full. I wish to stress, however, that the mere fact that the defendant has spent the money, in whole or in part, does not of itself render it inequitable that he should be called upon to repay, because the expenditure might in any event have been incurred by him in the ordinary course of things. I fear that the mistaken assumption that mere expenditure of money may be regarded as amounting to a change of position for present purposes has led in the past to opposition by some to recognition of a defence which in fact is likely to be available only on comparatively rare occasions In this connection I have particularly in mind the speech of Lord Simonds in *Ministry of Health* v *Simpson*."

The judge noted the view, put forward by Andrew Burrows (*The Law of Restitution* (1993) pp425–428) that there is a narrow and a wide version of the defence of change of position, and that the wide view is to be preferred. The narrow view treats the defence as "the same as estoppel minus the representation" (so that detrimental reliance is still a necessary ingredient). The wide view looks to a change of position, causally linked to the mistaken receipt, which makes it inequitable for the recipient to be required to make restitution. In many cases either test produces the same result but the wide view extends protection to (for instance) an innocent recipient of a payment which is later stolen from him ...

In this court, Mr Stephen Moriarty QC (appearing with Mr Richard Handyside for Scottish Equitable) did not argue against the correctness of the wide view, provided that the need for a sufficient causal link is clearly recognised. The fact that the recipient may have suffered some misfortune (such as a breakdown in his health, or the loss of his job) is not a defence unless the misfortune is causally linked (at least on a "but for" test) with the mistaken receipt. In my view Mr Moriarty was right to make that concession. Taking a wide view of the scope of the defence facilitates "a more generous approach … to the recognition of the right to restitution" (Lord Goff in the *Lipkin Gorman* case); and compare Lord Goff's observations in *Kleinwort Benson Ltd* v *Lincoln City Council*.

The criticisms of the judgment made by Mr Bernard Weatherill QC (appearing with Mr Paul Emerson for Mr Derby) were directed, not so much to the principles of law enunciated by the judge, as to the way in which he applied those principles to the facts as he found them. Before considering those criticisms in detail I think it may be useful to note that when a person receives a mistaken overpayment there are, even on the narrow view as to the scope of the defence, a variety of conscious decisions which may be made by the recipient in reliance on the overpayment. Some are simply decisions about expenditure of the receipt: the payee may decide to spend it on an asset which maintains its value, or on luxury goods with little second-hand value, or on a world cruise. He may use it to pay off debts. He may give it away. Or he may make some decision which involves no immediate expenditure, but is nevertheless causally linked to the receipt. Voluntarily giving up his job, at an age when it would not be easy to get new employment, is the most obvious example. Entering into a long-term financial commitment (such as taking a flat at a high rent on a ten-year lease which would not be easy to dispose of) would be another example. The wide view adds further possibilities which do not depend on deliberate choices by the recipient.

Mr Weatherill criticised the judge for looking simply at particular items of expenditure (the £9,662 which was conceded, the sum used to pay off the mortgage and the sum paid to the Norwich Union) and for paying insufficient attention to Mr Derby's decision to slow down his work, and his omission to take alternative steps to provide for the future of himself and his family. I would readily accept that the defence is not limited (as it is, apparently, in Canada and some states of the United States) … to specific identifiable items of expenditure. I would also accept that it may be right for the court not to apply too demanding a standard of proof when an honest defendant says that he has spent an overpayment by improving his lifestyle, but cannot produce any detailed accounting: see the observations of Jonathan Parker J in *Philip Collins Ltd* v *Davis*, with which I respectfully agree. The defendants in that case were professional musicians with a propensity to overspend their income, and Jonathan Parker J took a broad approach …

In the present case, however, the judge made some clear findings of fact … to the effect that the improvements which Mr Derby was able to make in his family's lifestyle, between June 1995 and October 1996, were very modest and not irreversible, and that there was nothing that he could usefully have done to make provision for the future. Mr Weatherill has submitted that that seriously understates the devastating effect which the demand for repayment has had on Mr Derby, with his annual income after tax being reduced at a stroke from a sum of the order of £20,000 to the sum of the order of £12,000 (these figures do not include Mrs Derby's earned income). It is easy to accept that Scottish Equitable's demand for repayment must have come as a bitter disappointment to Mr Derby, and it is impossible not to feel sympathy for him, beset as he now is by financial problems, matrimonial problems and health problems. But the court must proceed on the basis of principle, not sympathy, in order that the defence of change of position should not, as Burrows puts it a p426, "disintegrate into a case by case discretionary analysis of the justice of individual facts, far removed from principle". Mr Weatherill took the court to various passages in the transcript of Mr Derby's oral evidence, but I am not persuaded that the judge erred in his findings of fact or that he failed to take advantage of seeing and hearing the witnesses.

Mr Weatherill submitted that the payment-off of the mortgage was a change of position, but I cannot accept that submission. In general it is not a detriment to pay off a debt which will have to be paid off sooner or later … It might be if there were a long-term loan on advantageous terms, but it was not suggested that that was the case here; and as the judge said … the evidence was that the house was to be sold in the near future.

In relation to the Norwich Union policy it was argued below that Mrs Derby had certain rights or claims because of the impending divorce … I found this argument rather surprising since it appears from the terms of the policy that Mrs Derby is named as a payee in respect of a reversionary annuity of £6,760 a year but that her right to the annuity ceases on divorce (although Mrs Derby may be able to take advantage of the new pension-sharing arrangements introduced by the Welfare Reform and Pensions Act 1999). However, it was only by reference to the impending divorce that Mr Weatherill attacked the judge's conclusion … that Mrs Derby's rights were no impediment to the unwinding of the policy to which Norwich Union is prepared to agree. Her potential rights on divorce do not depend on her having a power to veto the unwinding of the policy, nor do they have the effect of conferring such a power on her. They do not in my view assist Mr Derby's argument on change of position.

For these reasons the judge was in my view correct to accept the defence of change of position only in relation to the sum of £9,662.'

Comment
Robert Walker LJ explained the doctrine of change of position through the concept of a wide view and a narrow view, followed by clear examples of how this would be applied, presupposing that a causal link can be established between the mistaken payment and the subsequent expenditure.

16 Equitable Remedies

American Cyanamid Co v Ethicon Ltd [1975] AC 396 House of Lords (Lords Diplock, Dilhorne, Cross, Edmund-Davies and Salmon)

• *Conditions for issue of an interlocutory injunction*

Facts

The plaintiffs were suing for a patent infringement but the case was expected to take some time to prepare and come to full hearing. They applied for an interlocutory injunction to prevent the defendants from marketing the product in the meantime, arguing that this was necessary because if the product were introduced and practitioners and patients became accustomed to its use, it might be impossible for the plaintiff company to cease or cause to cease the use without losing its own good name, and thus it would be irrevocably prejudiced.

Held

The interlocutory injunction would be granted, and Lord Diplock took the opportunity to restate and modify the principles on which an interlocutory injunction might be granted. In particular, the old view that the plaintiff needed to establish a prima facie case meant that in order to get an interlocutory injunction the plaintiff had to present his case as if it were to the full hearing.

Lord Diplock:

'When an application for an interlocutory injunction to restrain a defendant from doing acts alleged to be in violation of the plaintiff's legal right is made on contested facts, the decision whether or not to grant an interlocutory injunction has to be taken at a time when ex hypothesi the existence of the right or the violation of it, or both, is uncertain and will remain uncertain until final judgment is given in the action. It was to mitigate the risk of injustice to the plaintiff during the period before that uncertainty could be resolved that the practice arose of granting him relief by way of interlocutory injunction ... The object of the interlocutory injunction is to protect the plaintiff against injury by violation of his right for which he could not be adequately compensated in damages recoverable in the action if the uncertainty were resolved in his favour at trial.

... The governing principle is that the court should first consider whether if the plaintiff were to succeed at the trial in establishing his right to a permanent injunction he would be adequately compensated by an award of damages for the loss he had sustained as a result of the defendant's continuing to do what was sought to be enjoined between the time of the application and the time of the trial. If damages in the measure recoverable at common law would be an adequate remedy and the defendant would be in a financial position to pay them, no interlocutory injunction should normally be granted, however strong the plaintiff's claim appeared to be at that stage.

... If damages would not provide an adequate remedy for the plaintiff in the event of his succeeding at the trial, the court should then consider whether, on the contrary hypothesis that the defendant were to succeed at trial in establishing his right to do what was sought to be enjoined, he would be adequately compensated under the plaintiff's undertaking as to damages for the loss he would have sustained by being prevented from doing so between the time of the application and the time of the trial. If damages in the measure recoverable under such an undertaking would be an adequate remedy and the plaintiff would be in a financial position to pay them, there would be no reason on this ground to refuse an interlocutory injunction.

... It is where there is doubt as to the adequacy of the respective remedies in damages available to either party or both, that the question of balance of convenience arises.

... Where other factors appear to be evenly balanced it is a counsel of prudence to take such measures as are calculated to preserve the status quo ...

... The extent to which the disadvantages to either party would be incapable of being compensated in damages in the event of his succeeding at the trial is always a significant factor in assessing where the balance of convenience lies.

... If the extent of uncompensatable disadvantage to each party would not differ widely, it may not be improper to take into account in tipping the balance the relative strength of each party's case as revealed by the affidavit evidence adduced on the hearing of the application. This, however, should be done only where it is apparent on the facts disclosed by evidence as to which there is no credible dispute that the strength of one party's case is disproportionate to that of the other party.

... In addition ... there may be many other special factors to be taken into consideration in the particular circumstances of individual cases.'

Comment

Lord Diplock emphasises here that the purpose of an interlocutory injunction is to preserve the status quo of the parties pending full trial. All equitable remedies are discretionary and he sets out in the judgment the factors which the court will take into consideration when deciding whether or not to grant the injunction.

Derby & Co Ltd and Others v *Weldon and Others (No 2)* [1989] 1 All ER 1002 Court of Appeal (Lord Donaldson of Lymington MR, Neill and Butler-Sloss LJJ)

• *Mareva injunctions (now freezing orders)*

Facts

The plaintiffs were seven associated companies which were part of a US banking group. The first and second defendants were directors of a London commodity dealing company, CML which was owned by the third defendant, a Panamanian company and the fourth a Luxembourg company. Both defendant companies were under the control of the first and second defendant. In 1981 CML was acquired by the plaintiff group but continued to be managed by the first and second defendant. While under their management, CML offered very extensive credit to a Far Eastern commodity dealer which became insolvent owing CML £35 million, of which only £1.5 million was recovered by the plaintiffs. They brought an action against the defendants, alleging breach of contract, conspiracy and fraudulent breach of fiduciary duty. The plaintiffs were granted a Mareva injunction restricting the first and second defendants from dealing with their assets worldwide until judgment in the action. The judge granted a similar order against the fourth defendant but refused to do so against the third defendant because of the difficulty of enforcing the order in Panama. The fourth defendant appealed on the grounds that the court had no jurisdiction to grant a Mareva injunction against them because it was a precondition for the granting of a Mareva injunction that the defendant had some assets within the jurisdiction of the court and the fourth defendant had no such assets. The plaintiffs cross-appealed against the refusal of an order against the third defendant.

Held

The appeal was dismissed and the cross appeal

was allowed. The court had jurisdiction to grant a pre-judgment Mareva injunction over a defendant's foreign assets, notwithstanding that he had no assets within the jurisdiction, if such an order was necessary to prevent the defendant from taking action to frustrate subsequent orders of the court. However, where there were sufficient assets within the jurisdiction the injunction should be confined to those assets. The court had jurisdiction to grant a Mareva injunction against both the third and fourth defendants.

Lord Donaldson MR:

'The complexity of the issues involved in this action is only matched by the size of the sums in dispute, not less than £25 million and probably more. However, the issues in the appeal and cross-appeal which concern protective interlocutory measures, Mareva injunctions, the appointment of receivers and disclosure of the nature, amount and whereabouts of assets, are much more confined. So far as the action as a whole is concerned, it is sufficient to say that the plaintiffs complain that they have been defrauded by the defendants by or in connection with dealings in the cocoa market …

The Mareva injunction generally
The fundamental principle underlying this jurisdiction is that, within the limits of its powers, no court should permit a defendant to take action designed to ensure that subsequent orders of the court are rendered less effective than would otherwise be the case. On the other hand, it is not its purpose to prevent a defendant carrying on business in the ordinary way or, if an individual, living his life normally pending the determination of the dispute, nor to impede him in any way in defending himself against the claim. Nor is its purpose to place the plaintiff in the position of a secured creditor. In a word, whilst one of the hazards facing a plaintiff in litigation is that, come the day of judgment it may not be possible for him to obtain satisfaction of that judgment fully or at all, the court should not permit the defendant artificially to create such a situation.'

Comment
The grant of a Mareva injunction is subject to rules very similar to those which apply to the grant of Anton Piller orders. The two orders are often applied for and granted together, the one to secure the evidence and the other to secure the means of settlement. Note, however, that Lord Donaldson says that a Mareva injunction does not make the plaintiff a secured creditor of the defendant.

Douglas and Others v *Hello! Ltd*
[2001] 2 All ER 289 Court of Appeal (Brooke, Sedley and Keene LJJ)

• *Injunction – breach of confidence – s12 and Schedule 1 (Part I, arts 8 and 10) Human Rights Act 1998*

Facts
Michael Douglas and Catherine Zeta-Jones entered into an agreement with the publishers of *OK* magazine for the exclusive publication of their wedding photographs. They went to considerable lengths to ensure that no one present at the wedding other than the publishers' photographer took pictures or video films. Two days after the wedding Catherine Zeta-Jones heard that Hello! was intending to publish unauthorised pictures and the claimants were granted an injunction to prevent their publication. Hello! appealed to the Court of Appeal, claiming that, when the injunction was granted and subsequently continued by the court at first instance, the court had failed to consider whether s12(3) of the Human Rights Act 1998 gave the rights granted under art 10(1) of the European Convention on Human Rights (rights to freedom of expression) priority over those granted under art 8 (rights to a family life).

Held
The appeal was allowed because the balance of convenience favoured Hello!'s case. Section 12(3) of the Human Rights Act 1998 concerned the approach of the courts at the

interlocutory stage of proceedings, before the balance was struck between the rights of the parties at full trial. It did not give priority of any one human right over another.

Brooke LJ:

'I now turn to the question we had to decide in the exercise of our own discretion (given that we do not know how the judge decided to exercise the discretion vested in him ...). If this matter goes forward and the claimants' case succeeds at trial, the bill which Hello! will have to pay is likely to be enormous, but this is a risk it decided to take, with its eyes open, after we discharged the injunction. We had to decide a very different matter, that is to say whether the court should continue the injunction which would prevent over half a million copies of issue 639 from reaching its readers at all. It goes without saying that this is a case concerned with freedom of expression. Although the right to freedom of expression is not in every case the ace of trumps, it is a powerful card to which the courts of this country must always pay appropriate respect.

What, then, are the principles which should govern the exercise of our discretion? The House of Lords has laid down a general rule which governs most cases in which a court is invited to grant an interim injunction restraining the defendant until the trial of the action from doing the things of which the claimant makes complaint. (See *American Cyanamid Co v Ethicon Ltd*). Once a judge has decided that there is a serious issue to be tried, he is required to weigh the respective risks that injustice may result from his deciding one way or the other on necessarily incomplete and untested evidence. On the one hand there is the risk that if the injunction is refused but the claimant succeeds in establishing at the trial his legal right, for the protection of which the injunction had been sought, he may in the meantime have suffered harm and inconvenience which is similarly irrecompensable. This is what is sometimes described as the balance of convenience.

There has always been a category of case in which amore stringent threshold is

required. In *NWL Ltd* v *Woods* Lord Diplock identified that type of case in these terms:

"Where ... the grant or refusal of the interlocutory injunction will have the practical effect of putting an end to the action because the harm that will have been already caused to the losing party by its grant or its refusal is complete and of a kind for which money cannot constitute any worthwhile recompense, the degree of likelihood that the plaintiff would have succeeded in establishing his right to an injunction if the action had gone to trial is a factor to be brought into the balance by the judge in weighing the risks that injustice may result from his deciding the application one way rather than the other."

Occasionally Parliament intervenes to make clear its wishes in particular contexts. For instance, in the context of trade disputes, s17(2) of the Trade Union and Labour Relations Act 1974 provided that if a defendant claimed that he acted in contemplation of furtherance of a trade dispute –

"the court shall, in exercising its discretion whether or not to grant the injunction, have regard to the likelihood of that party's succeeding at the trial of the action in establishing the matter or matters which would ... afford a defence to the action."

In the *NWL* case, Lord Diplock and Lord Fraser of Tullybelton, who formed the majority of the three judge Appellate Committee of the House of Lords, rejected a contention that this meant that the court had to have regard to this matter to the exclusion of other matters, or that it was to be treated as of overriding or paramount importance, or given any other special legal status. The likelihood (and the degree of likelihood) of the defendant succeeding in setting up his defence was a factor to which the court had to have regard when determining where the balance of convenience lay. Lord Fraser observed ... that if the court considered that the defendant was virtually certain to establish the defence it would naturally give more weight to this factor than if it considered that the prospect of successfully establishing the defence was doubtful.

Parliament resorted to a different drafting technique in s12(3) of the Human Rights Act 1998. This subsection reads:

> "No [relief which, if granted, might affect the exercise of the convention right to freedom of expression] is to be granted so as to restrain publication before trial unless the court is satisfied that the applicant is likely to establish that publication should not be allowed."

I agree with what Keene LJ says about the effect of this statutory provision ... [see below], to which I have nothing to add. ...

On the facts of the present case, using the *American Cyanamid* test, there is clearly a serious issue to be tried in relation to the claims made by all three claimants. Although the evidence they adduced is often rather impersonal, and one might reasonably be sceptical about the efficiency of some of the security measures, given that no less than six different cameras were later found in the possession of people who had passed through the security checks, it appears that a real effort was made to inform everyone who entered the relevant parts of the hotel that the occasion had characteristics of confidentiality. In other words, people were being trusted to participate in this private occasion, in whatever role, on the strict understanding that they might not take photographic images of what they saw. There was also evidence to the effect that the images could not have been taken by someone from outside who was not bound by these obligations of confidence.

In those circumstances it would certainly be arguable, if the appropriate facts were established at trial, that "unauthorised" images were taken on this private occasion by someone in breach of his or her duty of confidence, and that they therefore constituted "confidential information" as to what was going on at the wedding and the wedding reception. In so far as Mr Douglas and Ms Zeta-Jones have not vested in OK! the right to bring this action to protect the subject matter of their agreement, they have retained the relevant rights themselves. The claimants have also adduced evidence to the effect that Hello! was on notice that this "information" was confidential, in the sense that the principle of notice was explained by Lord Goff of Chieveley in *A-G* v *Guardian Newspapers Ltd (No 2)*.

I cannot, however, exclude the possibility that the trial judge might find, as Sedley LJ has suggested ... that the photographer was an intruder with whom no relationship of trust or confidence had been established. In that event the court would have to explore the law relating to privacy when it is not bolstered by considerations of confidence.

In this context art 10(2) of the Convention provides a potential justification for denying the right to freedom of expression not only by restrictions that are necessary "for preventing the disclosure of information received in confidence" but also "for the protection of the reputation or rights of others". On the hypothesis I have suggested ... above, the question would arise whether Mr Douglas and Ms Zeta-Jones had a right to privacy which English law would recognise.

It is well known that this court in *Kaye* v *Robertson* said in uncompromising terms that there was no tort of privacy known to English law. In contrast, both academic commentary and extra-judicial commentary by judges over the last ten years have suggested from time to time that a development of the present frontiers of a breach of confidence action could fill the gap in English law which is filled by privacy law in other developed countries. This commentary was given a boost recently by the decision of the European Commission of Human Rights in *Earl Spencer* v *UK*, and by the coming into force of the Human Rights Act 1998. ...

English law, as is well known, has been historically based on freedoms, not rights. The difference between freedom-based law and rights-based law was memorably expressed by Lord Goff of Chieveley in the course of his speech in the *Guardian Newspapers* case when he said he could see no inconsistency between English law on freedom of speech and art 10 of the Convention. He said:

> "The only difference is that, whereas art 10 of the Convention, in accordance with its avowed purpose, proceeds to state a fundamental right and then to qualify it, we in this country (where everybody is free to do anything, subject only to the provisions of the law) proceed rather upon an assumption of freedom of speech, and turn to our law to discover the established exceptions to it."

It is against this background of freedom-based law that the law of confidentiality has been developed. For a very long time the judges of the Court of Chancery exercised an equitable jurisdiction to retrain freedom of speech in circumstances in which it would be unconscionable to publish private material. If information is accepted on the basis that it will be kept secret, the recipient's conscience is bound by that confidence, and it will be unconscionable for him to break his duty of confidence by publishing information to others (see *Stephens* v *Avery*). Of course, "there is no confidence as to the disclosure of inequity", and the cases show how, on occasion, the courts were willing to permit publication on that, or other grounds, even though the information to be published was originally given in confidence ...'

Brooke LJ then reviewed the case law and continued:

> 'When it is read more closely, however, the convention ... seems to be primarily concerned with giving individuals rights against the state (to be equated with public authorities in the language of art 8(2). Thus art 8(2) is concerned only with the circumstances in which a public authority may legitimately interfere with the exercise by an individual of his right to private and family life and s8 of the Human Rights Act is concerned only with the power of a court to award compensation against acts of public authorities for unlawful acts which are incompatible with a Convention right. The Human Rights Act gives the court no such statutory power to order one private entity to pay compensation

to another in respect of a breach of Convention rights.

An English judge interpreting the Human Rights Act and the Convention is therefore confronted with something of a dilemma. On the one hand, art 8(1) of the Convention appears to create a right, exercisable against all the world, to respect for private and family life. On the other hand, art 8(2) of the Convention, s8 of the Human Rights Act, and the general philosophy of both the Convention and the Act (namely that these rights are enforceable only against public authorities), all appear to water down the value of the right created by art 8(1). ...

In *A* v *UK* it was the deficiencies of the common law in relation to the physical chastisement of children which led the court to conclude that the United Kingdom had violated the Convention. This country narrowly escaped a similar finding by the European Commission of Human Rights in *Earl Spencer*'s case. A photograph of Lady Spencer had been taken with a telephoto lens while she was walking in the grounds of a private clinic at which she was receiving treatment. This photograph was published under the caption: "SO THIN": Victoria walks in the clinic grounds this week". Relying on the decision of this court in *Kaye* v *Robertson*, she did not pursue a claim in the English courts, but the Commission held that she should have pursued her remedies in these courts first. It appears that the eloquence of the advocate for the United Kingdom government persuaded the Commission that English law provided her with a potentially satisfactory remedy in an action for breach of confidence.

In this respect the Commission relied heavily on the strong and detailed case of the applicants in the domestic proceedings which pointed to their former friends as the direct source of the essential confidential information that had been published. Its determination ended in these terms:

> "Accordingly, the Commission considers that the parties' submissions indicate that the remedy of breach of confidence

(against the newspapers and their sources) was available to the applicants and that the applicants have not demonstrated that it was insufficient or ineffective in the circumstances of their cases. It considers that, in so far as relevant doubts remain concerning the financial awards to be made following a finding of a breach of confidence, they are not such as to warrant a conclusion that the breach of confidence action is ineffective or insufficient but rather a conclusion that the matter should be put to the domestic courts for consideration in order to allow those courts, through the common law system in the United Kingdom, the opportunity to develop existing rights by way of interpretation."

The Commission appears to be saying that since the authorities in this country have been content to leave it to the judges to develop the law in this sensitive field, it is the judges who must develop the law so that it gives appropriate recognition to art 8(1) rights ...

So far as Hello!'s case is concerned, it appears to me on the evidence that there is a substantial risk that if an injunction killing this weekly edition of Hello! were to turn out to have been wrongly granted, Hello! would suffer damages which it would be extremely difficult to quantify in money terms. Although I take into account Mr Myerson's emollient evidence in answer, there appears on first impression to be a good deal of force in Ms Cartwright's evidence to the effect that Hello! would be likely to suffer losses over and above the financial loss associated with killing this edition which it would be very difficult to compute in money terms.

So far as OK! is concerned, if it wins at the trial, it will be able to have recourse to the very powerful weapon, fashioned by equity, of requiring Hello! to account to it for all the profits it has made from the publication of issue 639. Even if it prefers to pursue its remedy in damages, I cannot see anything in its evidence which would make it particularly difficult for experienced accountants to compute its financial losses.

Before deciding to pay Mr Douglas and Ms Zeta-Jones sums of the magnitude set out in its agreement with them, OK! must have had a pretty good idea of the income stream it hoped to generate from the exploitation of the rights it was acquiring. Since Hello! did not publish issue 639 until after it had seen OK!'s evidence in this court, it could not realistically maintain that the losses claimed by OK! were too remote or were otherwise unforeseeable. I have not overlooked Mr Ashford's evidence about the possible adverse effect of this incident on the success, or otherwise, of next year's planned float on the stock market, but Mr Ashford did nto spell out in any way the possible impact this might have on OK! itself, as opposed to its owners.

It therefore appears to me that the balance of convenience, as between OK! and Hello! therefore favours Hello! because it might be very difficult for Hello! to compute its losses in money terms if issue 639 was killed, whereas OK! did not appear to face the same difficulties if publication was allowed. There was no suggestion in the evidence that Hello! might be unable to pay the huge sums it might be held liable to pay (whether as damages or by way of an account of profits) if this action succeeded at trial.

As between these two parties, therefore, the balance of convenience appeared to favour leaving OK! to assert it legal rights at the trial of what is essentially a commercial dispute between two magazine enterprises which are not averse to exercising spoiling tactics against each other. I am not sorry to reach this conclusion because although it would have been wrong to withhold relief on equitable grounds alone, features of OK!'s past conduct, even making allowance for the fact that it did not have much time to defend itself against Hello!'s charges, appear to have made it an unattractive suitor for the bounty of a court of equity. The case of *Express Newspapers plc v News (UK) Ltd*, which Mr Carr showed to us, is not directly applicable, because Browne-Wilkinson V-C was concerned in that case with "tit for tat" behaviour by competing newspapers within the context of a single legal action, but it is illustrative of the reasons why courts are not likely to lean over backwards to grant equitable relief to magazines which behave in the manner attributed to OK! ...

The matter which gave me greater cause for hesitation was whether having decided that the balance of convenience favoured the withholding of injunctive relief so far as OK! was concerned, Mr Douglas and Ms Zeta-Jones were nevertheless entitled to the protection of an injunction. In the end, I came to agree with the views expressed on this issue by Sedley LJ, to which I have nothing to add.

I would add that I have read the judgment of Keene LJ and agree, for the reasons he gives, that if we are not willing to continue the injunction on confidence grounds, there is certainly no reason to continue it on the basis of the complaint of malicious false-hood or unlawful interfrerence with contractual relations ...'

Keene LJ:

'For my part, I do not accept that there is any need for conflict between the normal meaning to be attached to the words in s12(3) and the Convention. The subsection does not seek to give a priority to one Convention right over another. It is simply dealing with the interlocutory stage of proceedings and with how the court is to approach matters at that stage in advance of any ultimate balance being struck between rights which may be in potential conflict. It requires the court to look at the merits of the case and not merely to apply the *American Cyanamid* test. Thus the court has to look ahead to the ultimate stage and to be satisfied that the scales are likely to come down in the applicant's favour. That does not conflict with the convention, since it is merely requiring the court to apply its mind to how one right is to be balanced, on the merits against another's right without building in additional weight on one side. In a situation such as the one postulated by Mr Tugendhat, where the non-art 10 right is of fundamental importance to the individual,

such as the art 2 right to life, the merits will include not merely the evidence about how great is the risk of that right being breached, but also a consideration of the gravity of the consequences for an applicant if the risk materialises. The nature of the risk is part of the merits, just as it would be at trial when the balance had to be struck. That is as relevant at the interlocutory stage as it would be at trial. But that does not require any strained interpretation of s12(3).

Certainly s12(3) is making prior restraint (ie before trial) more difficult in cases where the right to freedom of expression is engaged than where it is not. That is not a novel concept in English law. As was said by Laws J in *R* v *Advertising Standards Authority Ltd, ex parte Vernons Organisation Ltd*:

"... there is a general principle in our law that the expression of opinion and the conveyance of information will not be restrained by the courts save on pressing grounds. Freedom of expression is as much a sinew of the common law as it is of the European Convention on Human Rights ..."

Perhaps more to the point, the jurisprudence of the European Court of Human Rights is generally hostile to prior restraint by the courts. Prior restraints on publication are not prohibited by the Convention, as the European Court of Human Rights made clear in *Observer* v *UK*, the "Spycatcher" case, but in that same case it went on to say:

"On the other hand, the dangers inherent in prior restraints are such that they call for the most careful scrutiny on the part of the Court. This is especially so as far as the press is concerned, for news is a perishable commodity and to delay its publication, even for a short period, may well deprive it of all its value and interest."

It is impossible to accept that a statutory provision requiring a court to consider the merits of the case and to be satisfied that the balance is likely to be struck in favour of the applicant before prior restraint is to be granted is incompatible with the Convention. It follows that no strained reading of the language of s12(3) is needed to render it compatible with Convention rights. The wording can be given its normal meaning. Consequently the test to be applied at this stage is whether this court is satisfied that the applicant is likely to establish at trial that publication should not be allowed. Even then, there remains a discretion in the court.'

Comment
Having established that OK!, if successful, could recover damages or an account of profit in compensation for publication by Hello!, on a balance of convenience analysis it would do more to preserve the status quo between the parties to discontinue the injunction. Keene LJ also made the point that Michael Douglas and Catherine Zeta-Jones had voluntarily waived their rights under art 8 by permitting publication of the wedding photographs by OK! and in these circumstances could not then assert them over Hello!'s art 10 rights to freedom of expression.

In *Douglas and Others* v *Hello! Ltd and Others (No 3)* Lindsay J explained that equitable jurisdiction of confidence is based on the duty of good faith and the moral duty of fair dealing:

'(i) Breach of confidence is an established cause of action but its scope now needs to be evaluated in the light of obligations falling upon the court under s6(1) of the Human Rights Act 1998. ... That can be achieved by regarding the often opposed rights conferred respectively by arts 8 and 10 of the European Convention for the Protection of Human Rights and fundamental Freedoms 1950 (as set out in Sch 1 to the Human Rights Act 1998) as absorbed into the action for breach of confidence and as thereby to some extent giving it new strength and breadth ... The Convention thus comes into play even in private law cases ... It will be necessary for the courts to identify, on a case by case basis, the principles by which the law of confidentiality must accommodate arts 8 and 10 ... The weaker the claim for privacy, the more likely it will be out-

weighed by a claim based on freedom of expression ... A balance between the conflicting interests has to be struck. ...

(ii) The right to freedom of expression described in art 10(1) of the Convention is, by art 10(2) "subject to such ... conditions as are prescribed by law and are necessary in a democratic society ... for the protection of the ... rights of others [and] for preventing the disclosure of information received in confidence ...". The art 10(1) right to freedom of expression is thus expressly made subject not only to the art 8 right for respect to private and family life but also in rights recognised by the law as to confidence, even where those latter rights are not themselves Convention rights. In consequence, privacy rights under art 8 may not, as such, require to be considered in a particular case but none the less there can be an internal conflict within art 10 between the art 10(1) freedom and the art 10(2) rights under the law of confidence to which art 10(1) is made subject.

(iii) The Council of Europe Resolution 1165 of 1998 gives some guidance which includes a recognition that information about some people's lives has become a highly lucrative commodity for certain sections of the media and that protection is to be given against interference by the media ... Thus even a public figure, which includes those in the arts, is entitled to a private life although he or she may expect and accept that his or her circumstances will be more carefully scrutinised by the media ... That is not to say, though, that the fact that an individual has achieved prominence on the public state means that his private life can be laid bare by the media. ...

(iv) If public attention has been courted by a claimant then that may lead that claimant to have less ground upon which to object to intrusion. ...

(v) Freedom of expression on the media's part, as a counter-force to, for example, privacy is not invariably the ace of trumps but it is a powerful card to which the court must always pay appropriate respect. ... Put another way, there is no "presumptive priority" given to such freedom of expression when it is in conflict with another convention right ... Nor, as it seems to me, is there any such presumptive priority where the conflict is with rights under the law of confidence; it would be pointless of art 10(2) to make freedom of expression subject to such rights if it invariably overrode them.

(vi) Where the court is considering whether to grant any relief which, if granted, might affect the exercise of the Convention right to freedom of expression, then the court, where the proceedings relate to material which is claimed or appears to be journalistic, must have particular regard, inter alia, to any relevant privacy code. ...

(vii) There is such a code in place, that of the Press Complaints Commission (the PCC code), the relevant edition of which is that last modified in December 1999 ...

(viii) The regard which the PCC code requires to be had to whether the material is about to become available to the public is an echo of s12(4)(a)(ii) of the Human Rights Act 1998, where that is a feature to which the court, in a journalistic matter, is to pay particular regard. However, that someone else – for example a complainant – is about to publish is not to be taken as necessarily justifying publication by the defendant; that authorised publication is due in a moment may, on the contrary, make it harder for the unauthorised publisher to justify his breach – see eg *Times Newspapers Ltd* v *MGN Ltd* (where authorised publication of the full Thatcher memoirs was due in ten days' time).

(ix) If there is an intrusion in a situation in which a person can reasonably expect his privacy to be respected then that intrusion will be capable of giving rise to liablility in an action for breach of confidence unless the intrusion can be justified ...

(x) It is still the case that a duty of confidence arises whenever the party subject to the duty is in a situation where he either knows or ought to know that the other person can reasonably expect his privacy to be protected ...

(xi) The existence of a relation such as may create a duty of confidence may, and

in personal confidence cases commonly will, have to be inferred from the facts ...

(xii) The fact that the information at issue is obtained by unlawful activity does not mean that its publication will necessarily be restrained but that unlawful means have been used to obtain the information may be a compelling factor when a discretion comes to be exercised ...

(xiii) It can be right to regard unauthorised photographs as "information" for the purposes of the law of confidence. In the case before me the unauthorised photographs have been said to convey the information "This is what the wedding and the happy couple looked like" ... The law of confidence can well encompass photographs of such an event and no less so because the event could have been described in words or by drawings ...

(xiv) It is a familiar course for Chancery judges to grant injunctions to restrain the publication of photographs taken surreptitiously in circumstances such that the photographer is to be taken to have known that the occasion was a private one and that the taking of photographs by outsiders was not permitted ...

(xv) It is well settled that equity may intervene to prevent a publication of photographic images taken in breach of confidence. If, on some private occasion, the prospective claimant makes it clear, expressly or impliedly, that no photographic images are to be taken of them, then all those present will be bound by the obligation of confidence created by their knowledge (or imputed knowledge) of that restriction ...

It does not follow from the fact that an item has passed into the public domain that it must be taken to have remained there in such a way that its confidentiality has been irretrievably lost. The fact that the unauthorised or authorised photographs were published in November 2000 does not, of itself, therefore deny the claimants a perpetual injunction. Whilst these proceedings have brought back into the public eye the fact that there were unauthorised photographs, I think it likely, given that the far better authorised pictures were also, of course, put into the public domain, that the look of the unauthorised photographs has passed out of the public mind. I thus see the claimants as in a position to ask for an injunction restraining the defendants such as is sought by the claimants in para 1 of the prayer to their re-re-amended particulars of claim. I indicate immediately, though, that I shall be willing to accept an undertaking of the Hello! defendants in lieu. Such an injunction or undertaking will, in practical terms, make delivery-up unnecessary.

For the reasons I have given, I hold the Hello! defendants to be liable to all three claimants under the law as to confidence. It will have been noted that an important step in my coming to that conclusion has been that, on balancing rights to confidence against freedom of expression for the purpose of granting or withholding relief, I have been required by statute to pay, and have paid, regard to the PCC code. The Hello! defendants broke their own industry's code.'

Imutran Ltd v *Uncaged Campaigns Ltd and Another* [2001] 2 All ER 385 Chancery Division (Sir Andrew Morritt V-C)

• *Interlocutory injunction – freedom of expression – s12 and Schedule 1 (Part I, art 10) Human Rights Act 1998*

Facts

Imutran was researching into the replacement of human organs with animal organs. Uncaged Campaigns (UCL) received documents belonging to Imutran from an anonymous source which they knew to be confidential but nevertheless they used information which the documents contained. Imutran were granted interim injunctions to prevent infringement of their copyright in the information and they applied to have this injunction continued.

Held

The application to continue the injunction was

granted. In reaching this decision, under s12(3) of the Human Rights Act 1998, the court had to consider whether Imutran was 'likely to establish' at full trial that publication should not be allowed. Sir Andrew Morritt rejected the defendants' contention that s12(3) imposed a higher standard than the common law test for the grant of an interim injunction.

Sir Andrew Morritt V-C:

'As I have indicated the causes of action on which Imutran relies are
(1) breach of confidence and
(2) infringement of copyright.
Relevant to both issues is
(3) what is the proper approach of the court to an application for interim injunction such as this in which the right to freedom of expression guaranteed by art 10 of the European Convention for the Protection of Human Rights and Fundamental Freedoms (Rome, 4 November 1950) (as set out in Sch 1 to the Human Rights Act 1998) (the Convention) is material? This depends on the proper construction and application of s12 of the 1998 Act. It is convenient to deal with this issue first.

Until the decision of the House of Lords in *American Cyanamid* v *Ethicon Ltd*, it was generally considered that an applicant for interlocutory relief had to show a strong prima facie case ... In the *American Cyanamid* case the House of Lords substituted for the strong prima facie case the concept of "a serious question to be tried" or "a real prospect of succeeding in his claim to a permanent injunction at the trial". That threshold test is amplified in cases in which the grant or refusal of an interim injunction would have the practical effect of putting an end to the action. In such a case the strength or otherwise of the claimant's case (in excess of the threshold of a serious question to be tried) must be brought into the balance in weighing the risk of injustice to either party by the grant or refusal of the injunction sought (see *NWL Ltd* v *Woods*). It is against that background that s12 of the 1998 Act must be considered.

So far as material s12 of the 1998 Act provides:

"(1) This section applies if a court is considering whether to grant any relief which, if granted, might affect the exercise of the Convention rights to freedom of expression. ...

(3) No such relief is to be granted so as to restrain publication before trial unless the court is satisfied that the applicant is likely to establish that publication should not be allowed.

(4) The court must have particular regard to the importance of the Convention right to freedom of expression ..."

Two issues were raised before me. The first is whether the requirement in subsection (3) of s12 that the applicant "is likely to establish" at the trial that publication should not be allowed alters the threshold test established by the *American Cyanamid* case in relation to cases to which s12 applies. The second is whether the provisions of subsection (4) of s12 require the court to place special and extra weight on the Convention right to freedom of expression. I will deal with them in turn.

Counsel for the defendants submitted that the requirement of likelihood imposed a higher standard than that formulated in the *American Cyanamid* case. I did not understand this to be disputed by counsel for Imutran. He submitted that whatever the standard was his case satisfied it. Theoretically and as a matter of language likelihood is slightly higher in the scale of probability than a real prospect of success. But the difference between the two is so small that I cannot believe that there will be many (if any) cases which would have succeeded under the *American Cyanamid* test but will now fail under the terms of s12(3) of the 1998 Act. Accordingly I propose to apply the test of likelihood without any further consideration of how much more probable that now has to be. See *Douglas* v *Hello!*.

In the case of subsection (4), it must be borne in mind that the courts emphasised the importance of freedom of expression or speech long before the enactment of the 1998 Act. See 8(2) *Halsbury's Laws* (4th edn reissue) para 107 and cases there cited. But neither those cases nor the provisions of s12(4) of the 1998 Act require the court to treat freedom of speech as paramount. There are many reported cases in which the court has had to balance freedom of expression or speech with other aspects of the public interest. See also *Snell's Equity* (30th edn 2000) paras 45–75.

In those circumstances I do not consider that the subsection is intended to direct the court to place even greater weight on the importance of freedom of expression than it already does. As I said in *Ashdown* v *Telegraph Group Ltd* ... the requirement "to pay particular regard" contemplates specific and separate consideration being given to this factor.'

Comment
This is a clear analysis of the application of arts 10 and s12 of the Human Rights Act to the existing tests for the grant of an interim injunction.

Universal Thermosensors Ltd v *Hibben* [1992] 3 All ER 257 Chancery Division (Sir Donald Nicholls V-C)

• *Anton Piller orders (now search orders)*

Facts
The defendants were former employees of the plaintiff who had set up a rival company. The plaintiff obtained an order from the court for the recovery of documents and equipment and an injunction prohibiting them from using confidential information obtained during their employment. The defendants sued, claiming damages, including exemplary damages, for loss suffered because the terms of the order were too wide and for defects in the execution of the order.

Held
The effect of the injunction restraining the defendants from dealing with customers it had

already approached was to put them out of business and the plaintiff in a better position for the future than if there had been no misuse of information and in those circumstances the protection given to the plaintiff by the injunction went beyond that required for the proper protection of its legitimate rights. Accordingly, the defendants were entitled to damages under the plaintiff's undertaking.

Sir Donald Nicholls V-C:

'*Anton Piller orders*
This case furnishes an illustration of both the virtues and vices of Anton Piller orders. The virtue was that the plaintiff was enabled to recover the item 3 list and the item 4 list and other documents, which, I strongly suspect, would never have seen the light of day if less Draconian steps, such as an order for delivery up of all documents containing confidential information regarding the plaintiff's customer contacts, had been the limit of the relief granted to the plaintiff. In all probability, incriminating evidence of that nature would simply have been destroyed.

But this result was achieved at a very high price. As I have said, the defendants' claims arising out of the faulty execution of the Anton Piller order were disposed of by an agreement reached between the parties during the course of the trial. It would, therefore, be quite wrong for me to say anything which might be understood as criticism of the conduct of those, and in particular the solicitors, who were responsible for the execution of the Anton Piller order in this action. Nevertheless, from the undisputed facts which emerged before me certain lessons are to be learned. I draw attention to these points, in the hope that thereby these problems will not arise again. The Anton Piller procedure lends itself all too readily to abuse. This has been highlighted more than once: see the powerful judgments of Scott J in *Columbia Pictures Industries* v *Robinson* and Hoffmann J in *Lock International* v *Beswick*. My impression is that these warning signals have been heeded, and that Anton Piller orders are, rightly, made much more sparingly than previously. But arising out of the history of what occurred in the present case, the following points may be noted.

(1) Anton Piller orders normally contain a term that before complying with the order the defendant may obtain legal advice, provided this is done forthwith. This is an important safeguard for defendants, not least because Anton Piller orders tend to be long and complicated, and many defendants cannot be expected to understand much of what they are told by the solicitor serving the order. But such a term, if it is to be of use, requires that in general Anton Piller orders should be permitted to be executed only on working days, in office hours, when a solicitor can be expected to be available. In the present case Mrs Hibben was alone in her house, with her children in bed. She was brought to the door in her night attire at 7.15 am and told by a stranger knocking at her door that he had a court order requiring her to permit him to enter, that she could take legal advice forthwith, but otherwise she was not permitted to speak to anyone else at all. But how could she get legal advice at that time in the morning? She rang her solicitor's office but predictably there was no response.

(2) There is a further feature of the situation to which I have just alluded which must never be allowed to occur again. If the order is to be executed at a private house, and it is at all likely that a woman may be in the house alone, the solicitor serving the order must be, or must be accompanied by, a woman. A woman should not be subjected to the alarm of being confronted without warning by a solitary strange man, with no recognisable means of identification, waving some unfamiliar papers and claiming an entitlement to enter her house and, what is more, telling her she is not allowed to get in touch with anyone (except a lawyer) about what is happening.

(3) In the present case a dispute arose about which documents were taken away, and from which of the premises visited. Understandably, those who execute these orders are concerned to search and seize and

then get away as quickly as possible so as to minimise the risk of confrontation and physical violence. Nevertheless, in general Anton Piller orders should expressly provide that, unless this is seriously impracticable, a detailed list of the items being removed should be prepared at the premises before they are removed, and that the defendant should be given an opportunity to check the list at the time.

(4) Anton Piller orders frequently contain an injunction restraining those on whom they are served from informing others of the existence of the order for a limited period. This is to prevent one defendant from alerting others to what is happening. There is an exception for communication with a lawyer for the purpose of seeking legal advice. In the present case that injunction was expressed to last for a whole week. That is far too long. I suspect something went awry with the drafting of the order in this case.

(5) In the present case, there was no officer or employee of TPL or Emoco present when their offices and workshops were searched and documents and components taken away. This is intolerable. Orders should provide that, unless there is good reason for doing otherwise, the order should not be executed at business premises save in the presence of a responsible officer or representative of the company or trader in question.

(6) The making of an Anton Piller order in this case can be seen to be justified by what was discovered. But it is important not to lose sight of the fact that one thing which happened was that Mr James carried out a thorough search of all the documents of a competitor company. This is most unsatisfactory. When Anton Piller orders are made in this type of case consideration should be given to devising some means, appropriate to the facts of the case, by which this situation can be avoided.

(7) Anton Piller orders invariably provide for service to be effected by a solicitor. The court relies heavily on the solicitor, as an officer of the court, to see that the order is properly executed. Unhappily, the history in the present case, and what has happened in other cases, show that this safeguard is inadequate. The solicitor may be young and have little or no experience of Anton Piller orders. Frequently he is the solicitor acting for the plaintiff in the action, and however diligent and fair minded he may be, he is not the right person to be given a task which to some extent involves protecting the interests of the defendant. I think there is force in some of the criticisms set out in the invaluable article by Professor Dockray and Mr Hugh Laddie QC (1990) 106 LQR 601. It seems to me that the way ahead here, pursuing one of the suggestions made in that article, is that when making Anton Piller orders judges should give serious consideration to the desirability of providing, by suitable undertakings and otherwise,

(a) that the order should be served, and its execution should be supervised, by a solicitor other than a member of the firm of solicitors acting for the plaintiff in the action,

(b) that he or she should be an experienced solicitor having some familiarity with the workings of Anton Piller orders, and with judicial observations on this subject (eg as summarised in *The Supreme Court Practice*,

(c) that the solicitor should prepare a written report on what occurred when the order was executed,

(d) that a copy of the report should be served on the defendants, and

(e) that in any event and within the next few days the plaintiff must return to the court and present that report at an inter partes hearing, preferably to the judge who made the order.

As to (b), I can see advantages in the plaintiff being required to include in his evidence, put to the judge in support of his application for an Anton Piller order, details of the name of the solicitor and of his experience.

Of course, this procedure would add considerably to the cost of executing an Anton Piller order. The plaintiff would have to be responsible for paying the fees of the solicitor in question, without prejudice to a decision by the court on whether ultimately those costs should be borne in whole or in part by the defendant. But it must be appreciated, and certainly it is my view, that *in suitable and strictly limited cases,* Anton Piller orders furnish courts with a valuable aid in their efforts to do justice between the two parties. Especially is this so in blatant cases of fraud. It is important therefore that these orders should not be allowed to fall into disrepute. If further steps are necessary to prevent this happening, they should be taken. If plaintiffs wish to take advantage of this truly Draconian type of order, they must be prepared to pay for the safeguards which experience has shown are necessary if the interests of defendants are fairly to be protected.'

Comment

Sir Donald Nicholls' recommendations were subsequently incorporated into a *Practice Direction* of July 1994 with the additional requirements that the items removed should be insured where appropriate and that applications should be heard in open court.

Verrall v *Great Yarmouth Borough Council* [1981] QB 202 Court of Appeal (Lord Denning MR, Roskill and Cumming-Bruce LJJ)

• *Specific performance of a contractual licence*

Facts

On 4 April 1979 the Borough Council contracted to allow the National Front to hold their annual conference in a council hall in October 1979. The political control of the council changed and the new council resolved to rescind approval of the use of the hall by the National Front and to refund their money. The National Front sought specific performance.

Held

The court could protect any interest in land, including a licence of short duration, by specific performance or injunction and even where the licensee's licence was wrongfully

repudiated before he entered. The new council was bound by what the old council did, and the old council had taken into account the dangers of trouble as well as the principles of freedom of speech and freedom of assembly. An order for specific performance would be made.

Lord Denning MR:

'Counsel on behalf of the council submitted that the council could determine the licence effectively despite the contract. He relied on *Thompson* v *Park*. In that case two school masters amalgamated their schools. The one who was in the school gave a licence to the other to come on to the premises. Later on he revoked the licence. The other then forced his way in. The court granted an injunction to stop the other from entering the premises. Goddard LJ said as to a licence:

"Whether it has been rightly withdrawn or wrongly withdrawn matters nothing for this purpose. The licensee, once his licence is withdrawn, has no right to re-enter on the land ... If he does, he is a common trespasser."

Basing himself on that dictum and on a passage in *Salmond on Torts*, counsel for the council said that a licensor has a power effectively to determine the licence. He may not have a right to do so lawfully, but he has a power to do so effectively; so that the licensee could not get specific performance of the licence but only damages.

That is not good law. The decision of the House of Lords in *Winter Gardens Theatre (London) Ltd* v *Millenium Productions Ltd* has made all the difference. Viscount Simon said:

"... a third variant of a licence for value ... occurs, as in the sale of a ticket to enter premises and witness a particular event, such as a ticket for a seat at a particular performance at a theatre or for entering private ground to witness a day's sport. In this last class of case, the implication of the arrangement however it may be classified in law, plainly is that the ticket entitled the purchaser to enter and, if he behaves himself, to remain on the premises until the end of the event which he has paid his money to witness."

Since the *Winter Gardens* case, it is clear that once a man has entered under his contract of licence, he cannot be turned out. An injunction can be obtained against the licensor to prevent his being turned out. On principle it is the same if it happens before he enters. If he has a contractual right to enter, and the licensor refuses to let him come in, then he can come to the court and in a proper case get an order for specific performance to allow him to come in. An illustration was taken in the course of the argument. Supposing one of the great political parties, say the Conservative Party, had booked its hall at Brighton for its conference in September of this year; it had made all its arrangements accordingly; it had all its delegates coming; it had booked its hotels, and so on. Would it be open to the Brighton corporation to repudiate that agreement, and say that the Conservative Party could not go there? Would the only remedy be damages? Clearly not. The court would order the corporation in such a case to perform its contract. It would be the same in the case of the Labour Party, or whoever it may be. When arrangements are made for a licence of this kind of such importance and magnitude affecting many people, the licensors cannot be allowed to repudiate it and simply pay damages. It must be open to the court to grant specific performance in such cases.'

Comment
The disruption to the party concerned, regardless of the views it promotes, is the paramount consideration here – damages would not be an adequate remedy for repudiation of the contract.

Old Bailey Press

The Old Bailey Press Integrated Student Law Library is tailor-made to help you at every stage of your studies, from the preliminaries of each subject through to the final examination. The series of Textbooks, Revision WorkBooks, 150 Leading Cases and Cracknell's Statutes are interrelated to provide you with a comprehensive set of study materials.

You can buy Old Bailey Press books from your University Bookshop, your local Bookshop, directly using this form, or you can order a free catalogue of our titles from the address shown overleaf.

The following subjects each have a Textbook, 150 Leading Cases, Revision WorkBook and Cracknell's Statutes unless otherwise stated.

Administrative Law
Commercial Law
Company Law
Conflict of Laws
Constitutional Law
Conveyancing (Textbook and 150 Leading Cases)
Criminal Law
Criminology (Textbook and Sourcebook)
Employment Law (Textbook and Cracknell's Statutes)
English and European Legal Systems
Equity and Trusts
Evidence
Family Law
Jurisprudence: The Philosophy of Law (Textbook, Sourcebook and
    Revision WorkBook)
Land: The Law of Real Property
Law of International Trade
Law of the European Union
Legal Skills and System
    (Textbook)
Obligations: Contract Law
Obligations: The Law of Tort
Public International Law
Revenue Law (Textbook,
    Revision WorkBook and
    Cracknell's Statutes)
Succession (Textbook, Revision
    WorkBook and Cracknell's
    Statutes)

Mail order prices:	
Textbook	£15.95
150 Leading Cases	£12.95
Revision WorkBook	£10.95
Cracknell's Statutes	£11.95
Suggested Solutions 1999–2000	£6.95
Suggested Solutions 2000–2001	£6.95
Suggested Solutions 2001–2002	£6.95
101 Questions and Answers	£7.95
Law Update 2004	£10.95

Please note details and prices are subject to alteration.

To complete your order, please fill in the form below:

Module	Books required	Quantity	Price	Cost
		Postage		
		TOTAL		

For the UK and Europe, add £4.95 for the first book ordered, then add £1.00 for each subsequent book ordered for postage and packing.
For the rest of the world, add 50% for airmail.

ORDERING

By telephone to Mail Order at 020 8317 6039, with your credit card to hand.

By fax to 020 8317 6004 (giving your credit card details).

Website: www.oldbaileypress.co.uk
E-Mail: mailorder@oldbaileypress.co.uk

By post to: Mail Order, Old Bailey Press at Holborn College, Woolwich Road, Charlton, London, SE7 8LN.

When ordering by post, please enclose full payment by cheque or banker's draft, or complete the credit card details below. You may also order a free catalogue of our complete range of titles from this address.

We aim to despatch your books within 3 working days of receiving your order. All parts of the form must be completed.

Name

Address

Postcode   E-Mail   Telephone

Total value of order, including postage: £

I enclose a cheque/banker's draft for the above sum, or

charge my   ☐ Access/Mastercard   ☐ Visa   ☐ American Express

Cardholder: ....

Card number

☐☐☐☐ ☐☐☐☐ ☐☐☐☐ ☐☐☐☐

Expiry date   ☐☐☐☐

Signature: ....Date: ....